The Sacco-Vanzetti Affair

The Sacco-Vanzetti Affair
AMERICA ON TRIAL

MOSHIK TEMKIN

Yale University Press   New Haven & London

Designed by James J. Johnson and set in Stemple Garamond type by Keystone Typesetting, Inc.
Printed in the United States of America.

Library of Congress Cataloging-in-Publication Data

Temkin, Moshik, 1971–
The Sacco-Vanzetti Affair : America on trial / Moshik Temkin.
p. cm.
Includes bibliographical references and index.
ISBN 978-0-300-12484-2 (alk. paper)

1. Sacco-Vanzetti Trial, Dedham, Mass., 1921.
2. Trials (Murder)—Massachusetts—Dedham. I. Title.
KF224.S2T46 2009
345.73′0252309744—dc22
2008045606

A catalogue record for this book is available from the British Library.

This paper meets the requirements of ANSI/NISO Z39.48-1992 (Permanence of Paper).
It contains 30 percent postconsumer waste (PCW) and is certified
by the Forest Stewardship Council (FSC).

10 9 8 7 6 5 4 3 2 1

For my family

Woe betide anyone who winds his way through the labyrinth of the theory of happiness in search of some possible advantage to be gained by releasing the criminal from his punishment or from any part of it, or who acts in the spirit of the pharisaical saying: "it is better that one man should die than that the whole people should go to ruin." For if justice perishes, there is no further point in men living on this earth.

—IMMANUEL KANT, *The Metaphysics of Morals*

He who goes voluntarily to America, cannot complain of losing what he leaves in Europe.

—SAMUEL JOHNSON, *Taxation No Tyranny*

The trouble with the world is that there is no responsibility. In the court the DA says that it is not his fault that we are there. He is paid to prosecute men and he can't help himself. The judge says he has nothing to do with the case except to charge the jury on the law. He says the jury brings in the verdict. The jury says it looks to the judge for guidance so they are not responsible. Then you ask the Governor and he says it is up to the advisory committee. But the committee says it is the witnesses who make the case. The witnesses say they couldn't help being where they are. They didn't ask to be called. And then there are guards before our cells. They say they are sorry for us but they can't do anything about it. Then, when they come to strap us in the chair they will say they had nothing to do with it as that is how they earn their living. Well, I guess only Nick and I are responsible.

—BARTOLOMEO VANZETTI, 1927

Contents

Acknowledgments

In the course of working on this book, I incurred many debts, most of them of the good kind, and while I may never be able to repay them, I will try to reciprocate somehow, starting by offering my profound gratitude to all who share in the responsibility for this book seeing the light of day.

Professionally, my biggest thanks go to Alan Brinkley, who as the supervisor of the unruly dissertation upon which this book is based and in the face of the most daunting schedule in academia, always found the time to read my work, point me in the right direction, and find ways to keep me afloat. Ira Katznelson helped me untangle many analytical knots, and from the time this project was in its inception he has been its most scrupulous critic and consistent champion. I was the beneficiary of Victoria de Grazia's acumen, enthusiasm, generosity, and uncanny ability to *strenuously* suggest the book I hadn't heard of or the idea I hadn't thought of. I was also fortunate to have in my corner two model young historians: Sam Moyn read more drafts than anyone should ever have to suffer through and invariably made brilliant, helpful comments; Bev Gage offered advice and feedback, kindly shared her own work with me, and saved me from several infelicities.

While working on this project, I benefited from the generosity of scholars, colleagues, and friends on both sides of the Atlantic. In this regard, two mentors stand out: Robert O. Paxton, who inspired me by his own exemplary work to become a professional historian in the first place, and Tony Judt, whom I have long admired as a public intellectual and historian and who provided me with opportunities both professional and extracurricular. For their help and guidance at different stages, I owe thanks to Volker Berghahn, Istvan Deak, Jim Loeffler,

Michael Stanislawski, Lisa Tiersten, and Isser Woloch. I also owe deep debts of gratitude to Rachel Cowan, for hosting me so often in her beautiful riverside home, and to Deborah Rubin, without whose help I could not have finished this project.

This work would not have been possible without the assistance of diligent archivists and librarians on two continents. I am grateful to the staffs of the Rare Books and Manuscripts Department at the Boston Public Library, the Special Collections Department at the Harvard University Law School Library, the Houghton Library at Harvard University, the University Archives and Special Collections Department at the Brandeis University Library, the Département des manuscrits occidentaux at the Bibliothèque Nationale de France (Richelieu) in Paris, the Bibliothèque de Documentation Internationale Contemporaine in Nanterre, the Archives d'histoire contemporaine at the Fondation Nationale des Sciences Politiques in Paris, the Centre d'Histoire du Syndicalisme in Paris, the Archives de la Préfecture de Police in Paris, the Rare Books and Manuscripts Department at the Columbia University Libraries, the Tamiment Library at New York University, the International Institute of Social History in Amsterdam, the Centre International de Recherches sur l'Anarchisme in Lausanne, the Rare Book and Manuscript Department at the University of Illinois at Urbana-Champaign Library, the Bertrand Russell Research Center at McMasters University Library, the Beinecke Rare Book and Manuscript Library at Yale University, the Nation Institute in New York, and Butler Library at Columbia University.

Much of this book was written in France, a haven of productive writing. At Sciences Po, where I spent the 2004–2005 academic year, Pascal Delisle and his staff at the Centre Américain created a convivial work setting. Denis Lacorne and Daniel Sabbagh kindly invited me to present my work at the Centre d'Etudes et Recherches Internationales. I am also indebted to Alain Corbin for his imaginative comments on an early version of this project, and to Ronald Creagh for his research advice. In 2006–2007, I was the lucky guest of the Institute for Scholars at Reid Hall, where Danielle Haase-Dubosc and her colleagues Naby Avcioglu and Brune Biebuyck were lavishly supportive. François Weil welcomed me to the Centre d'Etudes Nord-Américaines at the Ecole des Hautes Etudes en Sciences Sociales, whose members also provided lively discussion and comments on a version of what became Chapter 2, and where I later spent the 2007–

2008 academic year, teaching and working on the final revisions to the manuscript.

I tested some of my ideas on unsuspecting audiences at the Lehman Center for American History at Columbia University, the Western Society for French History's 2006 meeting in Long Beach, California, the department of history at the University of Southern California, the department of American studies at the Hebrew University in Jerusalem, the Center for International Studies at the University of Cambridge, and the European Humanities University (in exile from Minsk, Belarus) in Vilnius, Lithuania. I especially thank Duncan Bell, Menahem Blondheim, Richard Wightman Fox, Joel Isaac, Michael Miller, Almira Ousmanova, Ramzi Rouighi and Vanessa Schwartz. Thanks are also due to David Levering Lewis, for sharing with me some of his matchless expertise on W. E. B. Du Bois and Alfred Dreyfus; Raef Zreik, for putting me up during trips to Cambridge, Massachusetts; Jude Browne, for doing the same in Cambridge, England; and Evelyn Ledyard and Sophie Grandsire, for cheerful administrative support.

The transition from messy dissertation to completed book was smoother than I feared, and for this I owe thanks first and foremost to my agents, Sarah Chalfant and Edward Orloff, who not only believed that this nerdy project could become a publishable book but while dealing with my constant doubts led me to my editor Jonathan Brent. At Yale University Press, Susan Laity is an outstanding, sensitive manuscript editor. For their support and help at the editing stage, I thank Sarah Miller and Annelise Finnegan. For their sharp comments and helpful feedback, I thank the three anonymous readers for the press. Toward the end of the process, Michelle Lussier proved indispensable in helping obtain the images that appear in this book.

I finished revising this book while beginning a new job at Harvard University, where colleagues at the Kennedy School of Government, including Mary Jo Bane, Ashton Carter, Pepper Culpepper, Alex Keyssar, Tarek Masoud, Ernest May and Monica Toft, have warmly welcomed me to a wonderful intellectual community.

Finally, those closest to me deserve a different order of thanks. This work has its origins, I think, in heated discussions of justice, politics, and everything else under the sun with my parents and sister in living rooms and at dinner tables in Israel, Mexico, and America. My family set me on this path and saw me through it; I hope they can be proud of the result.

I would never have been in a position to acknowledge anyone, however, were it not for Muriel Rouyer, who created a home for me in a faraway land, filled it with the kind of love that allowed me to finally finish, and then gave me the greatest gift I could ever receive, our son Noam Félix. *Merci, mignonne.*

Introduction

Sacco, Vanzetti, and the Historian

In 1920, Nicola Sacco and Bartolomeo Vanzetti, two young Italian immigrants and revolutionary anarchists living and working in Massachusetts, the former as a heel trimmer and the latter as a fish peddler, were arrested for the robbery and murder of a factory paymaster and security guard in South Braintree, an industrial suburb of Boston. They were convicted in 1921, and later sentenced to death. They were not executed, however, until 1927, by which time their previously obscure criminal case, one of many to occur in the United States in the immediate aftermath of World War I, had become the premier cause célèbre of its day, and even of the twentieth century, an unprecedented legal and political battle that put American justice—indeed, America itself—on trial and involved political leaders, public intellectuals, religious figures, legal experts, business elites, artists, diplomats, government officials, and countless ordinary men and women, American and non-American. But the execution of Sacco and Vanzetti was not the end of the Sacco-Vanzetti affair; in some ways, it was just the beginning.

Today, Sacco and Vanzetti are still fairly well-known names in the United States, Europe, Latin America, and elsewhere. But the wider meanings of their history are not. There have been numerous volumes published on the Sacco-Vanzetti case, and even on Sacco and Vanzetti themselves, focusing in particular on the crime and the trial. But most writers have been interested primarily in two things: first, trying to show whether Sacco and/or Vanzetti were guilty of robbery and murder and second, in a related way, trying to show whether their trial was fair. These authors have thus spent many years and boundless energy trying to answer an essentially unanswerable question—"Did they do it?"—and despite the massive study of evidence, ballistics, and other paraphernalia, as well as of the legal and criminal record, we are no closer to a resolution now than we were in the 1920s.[1]

But whether they have thought Sacco and Vanzetti innocent or guilty, the many chroniclers of the case have largely neglected its powerful repercussions in the United States and, especially, abroad. Because they have treated the case primarily as an episode in the history of the state of Massachusetts, they have failed to grapple with its impressive national and global reach—dutifully noting that the men and their cause stirred enormous excitement and controversy but usually failing to explain why or even how. And because they have not generally distinguished between the very different situations in 1921 (when Sacco and Vanzetti were convicted) and 1927 (when they were put to death), historians have so far missed one of the most important elements of the Sacco and Vanzetti story: its dramatic transformation from criminal *case* to public *affair*. The crime and legal process (the case) began to fascinate historians, and even the general public, because of the controversy (the affair) that followed, but ironically, scholars have not explored the origins of their own interest in the case. And so while it is certainly important to study the criminal and legal aspects of the case, as well as Sacco and Vanzetti's biographies (as many have), this book largely avoids those well-beaten paths. Rather, its first task is to trace and explain the evolution from an unremarkable local criminal and legal case to a national and international cause célèbre—an evolution that was never predetermined or obvious.[2]

The shift did not happen right away, but when it did it was dramatic. Starting in 1926, and even more in 1927 (and, indeed, ever since), Sacco and Vanzetti and their cause ceased to be a matter of interest primarily to anarchists and other left-wing radicals. As the two men's execution neared, their case attracted widespread mainstream public attention across the United States and around the world and involved people and groups who had no previous connection to the defendants, to anarchism, or to the legal process itself. It became an urgent law-and-order concern when the turmoil and violence around the case grew to critical levels that drew a serious response from local and state authorities worldwide. It became a major diplomatic concern as the U.S. government and its representatives abroad found themselves dealing with what they had long preferred to see as strictly a local legal issue. And, perhaps most tellingly, at its height the case became a touchstone issue that any group of political or social consequence in

both the Americas and Europe was obligated to respond to if it wanted
to stay publicly relevant. In the United States, influential voices in
the political, legal, and intellectual spheres took the lead in protesting
or supporting Sacco and Vanzetti's punishment, creating entirely new,
passionate divisions. Abroad, particularly in Europe and Latin America, outrage and controversy over the case added fuel to the fire of
anxiety over the changing place of the United States in the world in the
aftermath of World War I. Perhaps no other event until the Vietnam
War evoked as much anti-American sentiment among non-Americans
who were otherwise prone to hold a favorable view of the United
States.

In its international heyday, in the late 1920s, the Sacco-Vanzetti
affair was frequently compared to, and derived much of its symbolic
power from, the Dreyfus affair. That notorious 1890s episode—in
which a Jewish officer in the French army, the victim of a conspiracy
within the military central staff and of anti-Semitism in fin-de-siècle
French society, was found guilty of high treason, publicly stripped of
his rank, and sentenced to permanent prison exile on Devil's Island,
but eventually freed and vindicated—heavily influenced the public
perception of the Sacco-Vanzetti case, obviously and especially (but
not exclusively) in France, where it became widely known as "America's Dreyfus affair."[3]

The parallels between the two affairs are indeed striking. In both
instances men convicted by the state of serious crimes protested their
sentences and professed their innocence, were championed by an increasingly large public (including, crucially, groups and individuals
with considerable power and influence), and eventually stood at the
center of major, divisive national and international controversies that
have echoed for decades. Both cases attained totemic status as examples of grave injustices inflicted by the powerful against the powerless,
by state or national authorities against isolated individuals—injustices
that were later exposed by brave souls in the open space of public
opinion. Both cases, in the eyes of many, were the result of the per-
sistence and pervasiveness of racism and prejudice, and of widespread
fears of radicalism, foreigners, and change. Both cases raised an enduring question of principle: Who comes first, the individual or the state?
And both affairs occurred after the advent of what the historian Carl
Schorske called "politics in a new key."[4] The Dreyfus affair thus casts a

formidable shadow over the Sacco-Vanzetti affair and therefore over much of this book.

There are, however, crucial distinctions to make at the outset between the two affairs. Aside from the most obvious of these—Dreyfus was sent to lifelong prison exile on a desolate tropical island while Sacco and Vanzetti were sentenced to death; Dreyfus was released and rehabilitated, Sacco and Vanzetti were executed—the origins, nature, and details of the two cases also differed significantly. Dreyfus was a wholly apolitical man accused of a political crime. Sacco and Vanzetti were thoroughly political men accused of a nonpolitical crime. The Dreyfus case involved a conspiracy and a scandal: after their exposure, it became clear that the officer was innocent, and the national debate at the height of the affair transformed primarily into an argument over principle. Should the military be held accountable and accept the public consequences for punishing the wrong man? By the same token, should Dreyfus, as a loyal soldier, have challenged—and ultimately destroyed—the authority of his superiors, upon which was based, so his opponents insisted, the entire fabric of the French nation? In Sacco and Vanzetti's case, the defendants' guilt and innocence of the original crime were, and continue to be, in question. They were never vindicated in the same way that Dreyfus was; had they been pardoned, it would have been not over the clarity of their innocence but over the unfairness of their trial. This last distinction, a particularly important one, would have an enormous effect on the differences between the subsequent long-term legacies of the two affairs.

Captain Alfred Dreyfus was an Alsatian Jew (albeit from a well-off family), thus presumably an "outsider" of sorts in late-nineteenth-century France. But he was also a rising military officer in the Central Staff, and because of his position, the high-profile nature of his alleged crime, and his personal background, he drew considerable public attention from the start. His case had its origins in the heart of the French elite, and it had a national component by definition. Sacco and Vanzetti, working-class Italian immigrants and anarchists, were "outsiders" by any American yardstick, and their trial was held in a particularly provincial corner of one state shortly after the United States as a whole had experienced one of the most socially and politically turbulent periods in its history. Because Sacco and Vanzetti were proletarian, their case had a clear class element that had not entered the

Dreyfus case: indeed, while the radical left, in the United States and elsewhere, was the first group to support the two men, French radicals of the 1890s had not at first taken much of an interest in Dreyfus—since the man was both an army officer and a bourgeois Jew, they saw his case as an internal dispute within the ruling class.

In contrast to Third Republic France, with its highly centralized political life (based in Paris) and the prestige traditionally accorded to its intellectual elite, the United States in Sacco and Vanzetti's era was far more politically and socially heterogeneous and decentralized, and American independent intellectuals played a more marginal political role than did their more glamorous French counterparts. When the novelist Emile Zola published his open letter to the president of the republic, "J'Accuse," in 1898, charging the French government with anti-Semitism and wrongfully imprisoning Dreyfus, it generated an explosive response—both positive and negative—that no American writer of the 1920s, however famous, could have hoped for.[5] Unlike Dreyfus, Sacco and Vanzetti did not draw much national attention at first. Their alleged crime was banditry, a common occurrence in the United States in that period. Their case began in obscurity; its origins were at the margins, not the center, of American life.

More broadly, the Dreyfus affair was the culmination of more than a century of French struggles. It exploded the way it did because it represented a climactic clash between the two principal political forces fighting for mastery of postrevolutionary France: supporters of republican values on the one hand, their traditionalist opponents on the other—hence the stark and long-lasting divide between Dreyfusards and anti-Dreyfusards in French political and intellectual life. Dreyfus himself was a personally and politically uninspiring figure (another distinction, if one wishes, between his case and Sacco and Vanzetti's), but his case held enormous importance because through it long-standing tensions in France came to a head. The United States in the 1920s was *not*, to put it somewhat simplistically, this kind of society: the decade has been described by historians as politically anticlimactic, conformist, business-oriented, and nonideological, and although these descriptions are misleading, the Sacco-Vanzetti case did not immediately represent an obvious and clearly defined confrontation within American society. In time, though, this case too would acquire profound symbolic, and nationally divisive, power.

There were also significant differences in the social, cultural, and political impacts and effects of the two affairs. The Dreyfus affair brought about the fundamental transformation of French politics and society, including the separation of Church and State in 1905–1906, the advancement of individual rights at the expense of the traditionalist centers of power, and the subsequent rise of the socialist movement and political Zionism.[6] Sacco and Vanzetti left no such lasting and obvious traces on U.S. or international institutions; in this sense, their legacy is far less established. But this is not to say that they were ultimately less significant than Dreyfus. Whereas the Dreyfus case was at first important primarily to the French, from the start the Sacco-Vanzetti case was an international, not just an American or a Massachusetts, concern, and it was accompanied by worldwide political violence, which had not been part of the Dreyfus affair. Judging merely by the sheer volume, variety, and even venom of the responses to their case, Sacco and Vanzetti mattered enormously, in the 1920s and beyond, in the United States and around the world, to disparate and deeply engaged constituencies. But whereas Captain Dreyfus has found a clear place in the French historical narrative, the equivalent cannot be said for Sacco and Vanzetti, whose place in American history—and in European or international history, for that matter—remains unclear, despite the lasting ubiquity of their names.[7]

And yet just as the Dreyfus affair continued to loom large in France and elsewhere long after the captain himself drifted out of the spotlight, so the Sacco-Vanzetti affair refused to die with the execution of the two men. On the contrary: it continued to reverberate in the United States and abroad, in powerful but as yet unexplained ways. And so the second aim of this book is to describe and analyze the diverse and contradictory ways in which different people and groups shaped the meanings of the Sacco-Vanzetti case over space and time and thus to help clarify Sacco and Vanzetti's place in twentieth-century history and beyond.[8] More broadly, the book seeks to illuminate the American and international political cultures in which the Sacco-Vanzetti affair took root. While historians of the United States have focused mostly on the case's criminal and legal aspects, historians of Europe, with few exceptions, have largely—and oddly—ignored it altogether or treated it as strictly an American story, despite the fact that in several European nations it was as explosive a public concern as it was in the United States, and a defining generational moment for people and groups of virtually all political stripes. This book endeavors to explain how that came to be.

During the seven years in which I researched and wrote this book, the always complicated relationship between the United States and the rest of the world has taken a sudden and alarming turn for the worse. If historians are to make sense of this relationship, they need to look closely at how it developed over time.[9] The Sacco-Vanzetti affair emerged as a major international concern at the height of one of the most sensitive and tumultuous periods in the history of America's interaction with the world, and particularly Europe, a period that, in a number of ways, resembles our own. The affair was generated not only by the widespread notion that Sacco and Vanzetti were punished purely for their politics and ethnicity but also by the potent reaction to the post–World War I rise of American global supremacy and, concomitantly, American isolationism. The result of this protest, both national and foreign, was complex and paradoxical. It turned Sacco and Vanzetti into famous men, put tremendous pressure on American authorities, created a raucous controversy in the United States over the intervention of foreigners in American matters, and led to a backlash that sealed Sacco and Vanzetti's fate: the two men were executed not *despite* the international campaign on their behalf but rather *because* of it.

Beyond telling the story of Sacco and Vanzetti's ordeal, the book aims, then, to recount and explain a larger and longer history. For the late historian Arthur Schlesinger, Jr., whose own father had been involved in the campaign on behalf of Sacco and Vanzetti, the Sacco-Vanzetti case was unique in that the historian "could fix upon it as a way of penetrating the deepest conflicts in American life."[10] As was true in the Dreyfus affair, in the Sacco-Vanzetti affair events and reactions that appeared to be about one thing—the murder trial of two immigrants in Massachusetts—turned out to reflect much broader concerns. In its use of the Sacco-Vanzetti affair as a prism through which to refract light on wider issues in American and international history, this book is also, ultimately, about the ways that politics came to function in the twentieth century.

The controversy over Sacco and Vanzetti is still ongoing, not only because the truth about the 1920 crime in South Braintree is not known (and never will be) nor because for many their story represents what one author called "The Never-Ending Wrong."[11] The Sacco-

Vanzetti affair presents us with many eerie and sobering correlations to the present. Global political action, terrorism, justice and injustice, jingoism, xenophobia, radicalism, and the treatment of immigrants and minorities in both the United States and Europe are topics as central in our day as they were in Sacco and Vanzetti's. Ultimately, the executions revealed how fractured the relationship between America and the rest of the world had become—and in many ways it remains so. In these senses, the affair is very much alive, and shows no signs of dying out.

CHAPTER 1

"The Two Most Famous Prisoners in the World"

From Case to Affair

Before the Sacco-Vanzetti affair, there was the Sacco-Vanzetti case. Initially, there seemed to be little remarkable about it. It began when Nicola Sacco and Bartolomeo Vanzetti, two Italian resident aliens who had been living and working in the United States since 1908, were arrested on May 5, 1920, for taking part in the robbery and murder of a shoe factory paymaster, Frederick Parmenter, and his security guard, Alessandro Berardelli, in South Braintree, Massachusetts, on April 15. Although every aspect of the case would later become the subject of endless heated debate, the details of the crime, at least, were clear enough. The victims had been carrying the factory payroll (about $15,770) through the main street of the industrial suburb of Boston when two men who had been standing next to a fence pulled out their guns and fired, instantly killing one of the men and fatally wounding the other. The gunmen ran with the dropped cash boxes to a getaway car, in which two or three accomplices were waiting, and the entire gang sped away from the scene, leaving behind several witnesses. It was a professional job, and Sacco and Vanzetti, neither of whom had a criminal record, were not suspects at first. But they were soon caught in a dragnet set up by local police to trap an Italian friend of theirs. Because both men were carrying guns at the time of their arrest and lied to the police (neither apparently had any idea that he was being questioned in connection with a robbery and murder), they were held for further questioning and soon charged for the South Braintree crime.

From the start the state treated Sacco and Vanzetti as inseparable and did not attempt to make distinctions between them. If one stood trial, so would the other. The prosecution could make some plausible

connections between Sacco and the scene of the crime in South Braintree, but it had no compelling physical evidence against Vanzetti. And
so it prefaced Sacco and Vanzetti's joint murder trial by first trying Vanzetti alone for a failed holdup attempt on December 24, 1919, in nearby
Bridgewater (in which nothing was stolen and no one was hurt). Vanzetti's alibi—at the time of the holdup, he insisted, he was selling eels to
Italian Christmas shoppers on the streets of Plymouth—was confirmed
by more than a dozen witnesses, none of whom spoke English. Fearful
of revealing his radical background, Vanzetti did not take the stand in
his defense. His own lawyer performed poorly. He was found guilty
and given the maximum sentence, twelve to fifteen years. Thus, conveniently for the prosecution, Vanzetti arrived at his and Sacco's murder
trial at Dedham with a prior conviction for a similar crime.[1]

Banditry of this sort was hardly rare in that economically harsh
period, and the Sacco-Vanzetti murder trial, though it was a big deal
locally and held in an extremely tense atmosphere, did not make major
national headlines at first; as one New York reporter dismissively described the case to his editor, "There's no story in it . . . just a couple of
wops in a jam."[2] During their trial, Sacco and Vanzetti were seated in a
barred metal cage in the center of the court, a constant reminder of
the supposed menace they presented to respectable American society. The evidence against the two men, who pleaded not guilty, was
mostly circumstantial, save for the prosecution's disputed attempt to
tie Sacco's cap to the scene of the crime and his revolver to the shooting. The prosecution could not even show that the two men possessed
any of the money from the robbery. Instead, it based much of its case
on Vanzetti's earlier conviction for the failed Bridgewater holdup and
on what it called consciousness of guilt, reminding the all-white local
jury that the Italian defendants had lied to the police at every opportunity and behaved "suspiciously" before their arrest.

But what most made this trial case starkly different from the start
from the many other banditry trials of the day, was the defendants'
background. These were not the habitual criminals who dominated the
rap sheets. At the time of his arrest, Nicola Sacco, originally from
Toremaggiore, a small town near Foggia, in southern Italy, was a
twenty-nine-year-old family man who spent much of his little free
time cultivating a vegetable garden at the back of his house and made a
decent living as a skilled worker trimming heels in a shoe factory in
Stoughton. Bartolomeo Vanzetti, who came to the United States from

Villafalletto, a village near Cuneo in northwestern Italy, was an unmarried thirty-two-year-old unskilled laborer who barely made ends meet selling fish in the streets, an occupation he chose after a long succession of brutish, menial jobs mainly because it allowed him to spend the day outdoors. But their occupations and their personal lives were only part of their American story. Both men had been radicalized after their arrival in the United States by the poverty, injustice, and brutal exploitation of workers that they saw in the world's most advanced capitalist society. "The nightmare of the lower classes," Sacco would write from prison to his six-year-old daughter in 1927, "saddened very badly your father's soul."[3]

They became committed revolutionaries, joining Luigi Galleani's circle of militant "direct action" anarchists who during those years operated mostly in the United States and were later suspected of carrying out both the June 1919 bombing of the home of Attorney General A. Mitchell Palmer and the notorious September 1920 Wall Street bombing in New York. The jury at Sacco and Vanzetti's trial learned in fascinating (and legally irrelevant) detail how the pair had gone to Mexico during the war to avoid having to register for the draft (as resident aliens, they would not have been sent to the army anyway). What was not exactly known at the time was that they had traveled there to join about sixty of the Galleanisti in Monterrey, in northern Mexico, and prepare for a triumphant return to Italy, where they planned to join a revolution at the end of the war. They spent a scorching summer—as anyone who has spent time in Monterrey in July or August can imagine—living on next to nothing. When their European plan fell through, both men returned to Massachusetts, resumed work, and continued their political activity.[4]

Although they had been in the United States for twelve years, neither Sacco nor Vanzetti knew much English when they were arrested. They were part of an internationalist movement, but their social circles and personal lives existed mostly in Italian, anarchist, and working-class isolation. They knew no lawyers. Indeed, the only somewhat powerful people they knew were those higher up in the revolutionary chain. In mounting their legal defense, they depended at first on other radicals, primarily the Italian anarchist leader Carlo Tresca and the IWW (International Workers of the World) activist Elizabeth Gurley Flynn. Tresca and Flynn together recruited Sacco and Vanzetti's first primary defense attorney, Fred Moore, a veteran

IWW lawyer from California who had previously defended or helped defend a number of radicals, including, most notably, the Italian syndicalists Joseph Ettor and Arturo Giovannitti, dubiously put on trial for murder in the aftermath of the 1912 "Bread and Roses" strike in Lawrence, Massachusetts. Ettor and Giovannitti had won their freedom, as had a number of Moore's clients elsewhere. But in other cases Moore had been less successful. Brash and irreverent, later rumored by his own friends to be a regular user of cocaine, Moore infuriated the judge by wearing his hair long, California-style, and occasionally taking off his shoes while in court.[5]

The judge, Webster Thayer, turned out to be Sacco and Vanzetti's real curse over the long term. An elderly, conformist, vain, none-too-bright Dartmouth man who had presided over Vanzetti's first trial and had doled out the harshest possible sentence, he did not bother to hide from anyone willing to listen his obsession with "arnuchists," as he continually pronounced it, and his instinctive loathing of the defendants, their lawyers, and their supporters. Thayer—who, it was much later revealed, had lobbied his superior to be appointed judge in the Sacco-Vanzetti case by promising that he was a "stern and righteous" judge who would make sure the defendants "got what they deserved" —began and ended the trial with crude patriotic exhortations that had nothing to do with the case at hand. He let friends and strangers alike know that Moore's legal tactics, which had been successful elsewhere, would not get far in *his* court. He allowed the prosecution to coach its own witnesses on the stand and to question Sacco and Vanzetti about their radical background; at one point, prosecutor Fred Katzmann tricked Sacco into making an impassioned, irrelevant, and extremely self-damaging speech espousing revolutionary anarchism and attacking American capitalism. A score of alibi witnesses for the defense, almost all Italians, were disbelieved. Character witnesses for the defense were disallowed. It did not help matters that Moore, despite his undeniable energy and resourcefulness in the face of a hostile court and an atmosphere extremely unfriendly to his clients, ran a scattershot defense and made an uneven closing argument. To no one's great surprise, Sacco and Vanzetti were convicted in July 1921. It had taken the jury all of three hours to reach its verdict.[6]

Sacco and Vanzetti were not the first radicals put on trial in the United States whose cases would be seen by adherents of the left as representative of a profound American hostility toward radicals or immigrants, especially radical immigrants—indeed, toward anyone who dared defy the inexorable national forward march of capitalism. To many of their supporters, at least at first, Sacco and Vanzetti were simply two more names on a depressingly long list of radicals, including Tom Mooney, Albert Parsons, and Joe Hill, who were railroaded for crimes they probably did not commit in times of extreme political intolerance.

On the surface, Sacco and Vanzetti shared much with some of these earlier defendants, though their differences would soon become apparent. Their arrest and trial took place in the aftermath of the postwar Red Scare, during which the U.S. government had made the repression of political dissent one of its top priorities. As successive generations of historians have observed, as a result of these policies and of the serious economic recession of 1919, much of American society descended in the wake of World War I into collective political paranoia and violence, willingly directed and stoked by the authorities, and primarily aimed against labor groups, immigrants, and the left. To some of their sympathizers in 1920, Sacco and Vanzetti seemed to be merely two more random victims of this harsh social and political climate and of the American tradition of harassing and persecuting outspoken left-wing activists. The year before, U.S. Attorney General Palmer had ordered government raids in which thousands of people were rounded up and held in appalling conditions. Some of those arrested were genuine revolutionaries, but most were unfortunates whose real crime was being immigrants from southern and eastern Europe. Hundreds of these immigrants were eventually deported. The Red Scare was particularly acute in conservative and declining Massachusetts, where the predominantly white Protestant citizenry, already suspicious and resentful of the growing Catholic population (both Italian and Irish), lived in constant fear of radical "subversives" and foreigners.[7]

The fear swung both ways. Some of the federal government's harshest measures were enacted against Sacco and Vanzetti's comrades, the Galleanisti, especially the editors of the journal *Cronaca sovversiva*, which not only had objected to the war, thus bringing about its immediate closure by the postmaster general in 1917, but consistently called for revolution by violent means. At the end of the war, the editors (including Galleani himself) were deported to Italy and elsewhere, but other Galleanisti remained in the United States, determined to continue the revolutionary struggle and rebuild the movement. On the night before their arrest, as Palmer's agents were cracking down on radical and labor groups throughout the country, Sacco and Vanzetti learned that their friend and fellow Galleanista Andrea Salsedo had fallen to his death from a federal government building in New York, where he was being interrogated by agents of the Bureau of Investigation (a precursor of the FBI). The authorities later claimed that Salsedo had killed himself; but the Galleanisti were convinced that he was thrown to his death and that the federal government was prepared not just to deport but to kill them. Sacco and Vanzetti's legal defenders would later argue that based on these well-founded fears, the two men had good reason, in their minds, both to carry arms and to lie to the police when they were arrested.

In broader perspective, Sacco and Vanzetti's trial took place in a period during which the revolutionary left, in Europe as well as the United States, was mired in severe crisis, both external and internal. The heady days of strong, organized militant labor were over. World War I had already done much to destroy international working-class solidarity: in 1914, most of the Marxist political parties of Europe had put their national identities ahead of their internationalist ideals, pitting workers of opposing nationalities against each other on the battlefield during the four-year bloodbath; the socialist left was never able to recover from the splits and infighting that ensued. The October 1917 Bolshevik Revolution in Russia, the first occasion that a Marxist revolutionary party was able to come to national power, brought about the creation of Communist parties worldwide in 1919 and 1920 and, as a result, a permanent split in the international socialist movement. It also had a terrifying effect in Western nations, including the United States, as a previously obscure revolutionary movement suddenly transformed into a sovereign government with global ideological ambitions, ruling over a vast territory. In the aftermath of the war, revolutionaries elsewhere, hoping to reprise the Bolsheviks' stunning success, found themselves on the losing side of a series of brutal civil wars, after which they suffered violent retribution, most notoriously in Germany and Italy. And the international anarchist movement, of which Sacco and Vanzetti were loyal soldiers, was past its heyday and now entering its final decline.[8]

In the United States, the crisis of the socialist and radical left was

exacerbated by social and political unrest and violence that reached
new heights immediately following World War I. In 1919 the severe
economic recession and a wave of labor strikes (all brutally repressed),
as well as a series of violent so-called race riots in several major cities,
made a war between labor and capital seem imminent to many Americans.[9] In reality the federal government, as part of a long-term political
program, had set out to systematically destroy militant labor groups
and to do so it whipped up popular terror of radicals and foreigners to
a fever pitch. To be sure, this "radical menace," while exaggerated for
political purposes, was not purely imagined. A series of bombings in
1919, including the one at the attorney general's home, shocked the
general public, as did the bombing of Wall Street in 1920 (carried out,
in all likelihood, by the Galleanista revolutionary Mario Buda) that
killed thirty-nine people and injured hundreds more. Although the
culprits were neither identified nor arrested, the federal authorities
attributed the bombings to revolutionaries, and scholars have since
pointed to Galleanisti activists (and close friends of Sacco and Vanzetti's) as having probably carried them out. These acts also led Congress to increase federal funding for the fight against radicals, bol-
stering the Bureau of Investigation in the Department of Justice and
kick-starting the storied career of J. Edgar Hoover.[10]

These militant acts, however, were committed less out of confidence than out of desperation. Whatever the federal government's
rhetoric and the widespread public fears, the revolutionary left in the
postwar years was fighting not for power but for its life. In this climate, liberals and other moderates, who often shared the general public's fear and hatred of communism and anarchism, rarely spoke out in
defense of beleaguered radicals and immigrants, some because they
agreed with government policy, some out of fear for their own position and status.[11] In sum, in the early post–World War I years the
international revolutionary left, of which Sacco and Vanzetti were a
part, was on the defensive, persecuted by national authorities in the
Americas and Europe, and its adherents were bickering among themselves. The revolutionary left could do little for two hapless Italians on
trial in Massachusetts.

It is highly doubtful whether Sacco and Vanzetti would have been
judged differently at their trial had they been represented by other
counsel. But Moore, their lawyer, sensing—probably correctly, given
Vanzetti's conviction and harsh sentencing at the Bridgewater trial—

that his clients stood little chance in Judge Thayer's court, adopted a strategy that had often worked effectively in the past but was now out of step with the changing times: a "Class Defense against a Class Prosecution." By moving the Sacco-Vanzetti trial, in effect, from the court in provincial Dedham to what he considered the "court of world opinion," Moore hoped to generate international protest—to what purpose was not entirely clear. Judging by his own correspondence, Moore was equal parts propagandist and attorney, working as hard at mobilizing radicals as he did at handling his clients' legal defense. To this end he asked such radical journalists as Eugene Lyons, John Beffel, and Art Shields to try to galvanize public opinion, especially in Europe. Hoping for the best in the United States as well, he sent letters about the case to such public figures as Senator William Borah, Clarence Darrow, Emma Goldman, labor leader Samuel Gompers, labor lawyer Morris Hillquit, Fiorello La Guardia, journalist Freda Kirchwey, Walter Lippmann, Henry Cabot Lodge, Rabbi Judah Magnes, and union activist Grace Scribner.[12]

Too much of the literature on Sacco and Vanzetti, by both proponents and opponents of their cause, has described Moore as a public relations wizard who almost single-handedly turned the obscure Sacco-Vanzetti case into a national and international cause célèbre. This is one of the most glaring misconceptions about the entire history of the affair.[13] In reality, little about Moore's handling of the case was novel: rather, he brought to it methods that had sometimes worked for him and other radical lawyers in previous, prewar cases. Moore had little influence at home or abroad, and he was apparently not even tracked by the Bureau of Investigation. He also continually squabbled with Sacco and Vanzetti's Italian anarchist comrades, who never trusted him (and could be extremely difficult themselves), and the Italian anarchist newspaper *L'adunata* often attacked him, with increasing vehemence.[14] Sending out letters willy-nilly, as Moore did, did not and could not amount to an effectively orchestrated campaign, and the Sacco-Vanzetti case did not become a source of widespread national and international attention until well after Moore had disappeared from the scene.

In 1921 those who responded to his calls for worldwide agitation were usually like-minded radicals and workers, especially anarchists in solidarity with their two imprisoned comrades. These activists were largely mobilized by the radical press, especially among Italian communities. They were capable of rallies and even occasional serious violence—especially in South America, where the anarchist movement was still stronger than anywhere else in the world, and Italian immigrants made up a high percentage of the labor movement.[15] October 1921, for example, was a particularly violent month: bombs exploded in U.S. consulates in Portugal and Brazil, and an anarchist set off another in Paris in a failed attempt to assassinate Myron T. Herrick, the American ambassador to France. In Italy, Sweden, Holland, Belgium, Switzerland, Norway, Britain, Mexico, Cuba, Argentina, and elsewhere, American diplomats received threatening letters and encountered noisy protests outside their buildings.[16]

Latin Americans, who had witnessed or experienced some of the most unpleasant sides of the new U.S. imperial power in the preceding decades, probably had the strongest reasons for resenting the United States generally and the treatment of Sacco and Vanzetti specifically. Some of the angriest Latin American radical protest over the case could also be quite colorful. A letter from a Cuban anarchist group to the U.S. consul in Havana promised: "If Sacco and Vanzetti are killed you will pay us with your life. . . . There are anarchists and dynamite in Cuba. . . . If they are executed, you will fall sooner or later. Who laughs last laughs best." A Communist group in Chile wrote to the U.S. consul in Santiago: "I have pleasure in informing you that your life will be in danger if our communist comrades . . . are condemned to death." In Veracruz, Mexico, an anarchist pamphlet assured the U.S. government that "the proletariat of the world spits on you . . . YOU DISGUST US, MISERABLES! Woe to you, if you are deaf! Where is your culture? Why did you place that dummy which you call liberty at the entrance to New York City? Give freedom to Sacco and Vanzetti, or the proletariat will disembowel you."[17]

Still, the Latin American radicals had almost no influence on the legal and political authorities in the United States and Massachusetts who determined Sacco and Vanzetti's fate. Demonstrations, threats, and even bombings may have been good for militant morale, and the Sacco-Vanzetti cause temporarily lit a fire under a crisis-stricken and declining anarchist movement in various parts of the world. But in 1921 there was no real political or diplomatic pressure on anyone in the United States to help Sacco or Vanzetti. The lack of official protest from any European or Latin American government led the Department of Justice to conclude (optimistically, from its point of view) that "the [case] has aroused considerable feeling in many of the foreign countries, but this feeling, as well as all activities and demonstrations growing out of same, is confined to a restricted class of citizens in all of the countries. Those who have concerned themselves with the case are all . . . agitators who have been preaching radicalism and communism in their countries prior to the conviction of Sacco and Vanzetti."[18]

These "agitators" were in no real position to help the defendants; indeed, in the short run, their impact in the United States was probably harmful to Sacco and Vanzetti. The Bureau of Investigation kept meticulous files on Sacco-Vanzetti demonstrations and activities abroad and on support for Sacco and Vanzetti at home. On October 28, 1921, William J. Burns, director of the Bureau, instructed his agents to begin documenting any and all activity on their behalf. Some sent in alarming reports: one agent in Oakland, for example, reported in November 1921 that "if Sacco and Vanzetti are electrocuted, on that day [their supporters] will start a reign of terror all over the United States. There are a lot of quarry workers and miners among the bunch who will furnish the powder." The cool-headed agent added that "the Oakland Wobblies [IWW members] were strongly represented at this meeting and promised to aid the Dagoes."[19]

Much of the American press covered the protest in favor of Sacco and Vanzetti, if at all, in a spirit of fear— of the Red Menace, of revolution, of the threat to the American way. Since the end of the war, the mass media were rife with lurid stories about "Reds" and their plans to take over the country and, for that matter, the world. When Wall Street was bombed—after Sacco and Vanzetti were arrested but before their trial began—authorities were quick to call the attack an act of revenge for their arrests. (The Department of Justice, apparently convinced of this, planted an undercover agent in the Dedham prison in a clumsy attempt to obtain information from Sacco or his visitors. The experiment quickly went awry: the distrustful Sacco immediately suspected the new prisoner, who was placed in an adjacent cell, of being an informant and refused to talk to him.)[20] The usually dry *New York Times* reported that "Reds" in France were planning violent revenge on American officials if Sacco and Vanzetti were executed.[21] Yellow newspapers in Boston and New York reported that the Department of Justice had thwarted a supposed international plot by Sacco-Vanzetti supporters to begin a "reign of terror" in which American government buildings would be bombed over three consecutive days.[22]

With some notable exceptions such militant groups obviously specialized more in making threats than in carrying them out, but it is clear that given the way the popular press treated the issue such alarming reports, whether or not they were true, did not help Sacco and Vanzetti's chances for justice at a time when many Americans were convinced (or *being* convinced) that a Red uprising was around the corner. Indeed, it is safe to surmise that the real or imagined violence perpetrated by radicals in 1920 and 1921 over the case disturbed more people in the United States and abroad than did the trial itself.

Sacco and Vanzetti did enjoy some American support in this early period; it came chiefly from a number of marginalized, small, occasionally overlapping groups. One was the Italian immigrant radical left, for obvious and natural reasons the first group to stand in solidarity with the accused men.[23] Also rallying to them were American members of the international anarchist and Communist movements—two tiny groups that despised each other but shared an enmity toward capitalism and the bourgeoisie, which they felt had done in the two men. Sacco and Vanzetti could also count on the support of the IWW and its offshoots. Perhaps the most important group in their camp consisted of a few people within Boston's closely knit high society. These progressive Brahmins were attracted to the Sacco-Vanzetti case because of their geographical proximity to it and their interest in social reform and the rehabilitation of prisoners. Many of these sympathetic New Englanders were wealthy middle-aged society women, such as Elizabeth Glendower Evans, Gertrude Winslow, and Jessica Henderson, who saw Sacco and Vanzetti as misguided but gentle immigrants, the victims of poverty, lack of education, and the Red Scare. Evans, known to friends as "Auntie Bee," became a mother figure to the two men. She attended their trial and appeals, visited them in prison (something their more radical friends could not readily do), wrote letters to the authorities, published articles, organized petitions, and formed the first public committees to raise money for their legal defense. Although this group would later be eclipsed in the Sacco-Vanzetti campaign, it provided a consistent core of support for the two imprisoned men.[24]

Other groups joined these efforts. Chief among them was the recently created American Civil Liberties Union (ACLU), which would score some public successes in the 1920s, most notably in helping embarrass William Jennings Bryan and the fundamentalists at the Scopes "Monkey Trial" in Dayton, Tennessee, in 1925.[25] All together, however, this early support for Sacco and Vanzetti did not amount to more than the sum of its parts. The different groups had little to do with one another; the Communists, in particular, came to resent the involvement of Brahmins and liberal groups like the ACLU in what they saw as a proletarian and revolutionary concern. The anarchists increasingly resented the involvement of their revolutionary rivals and usurpers, the Communists, in what they saw as primarily an anarchist concern. Both of these movements were anathema to the general public. And what all these groups had in common was, first, an inability to attract the interest of a broader public to the injustice that, they claimed, had been done to Sacco and Vanzetti, and second, a lack of influence in either the legal or the political process in Massachusetts. Outside the radical press (little of which was published in English anyway) there was relatively little American newspaper coverage of the Sacco-Vanzetti case in its early stages. The exceptions were such progressive venues as the *Nation* and the *New Republic,* and even those journals became consumed by the Sacco-Vanzetti story only after 1926. In 1921 the *New Republic,* still stunned by the Palmer raids and the domestic effects of the war (the editors had warmly supported American entry in 1917 and then come to regret it), framed its concerns about the case in terms of the potential violence that it would stir up among immigrant workers.[26] But they need not have worried: American workers, on the whole, going through some truly hard times, were not much stirred by the case in 1921. According to an intrepid government informant in attendance, Elizabeth Gurley Flynn even complained in a Sacco-Vanzetti sympathy meeting hosted by Jewish socialists in New York that whereas European workers were doing the best they could for Sacco and Vanzetti, "the working class [in the United States] is currently asleep and will never be able to wash away the negligence it has shown toward the two victims of class warfare."[27]

But Flynn's comparison may have been exaggerated. In Europe, as in the United States, the case was at first a source of outrage mostly to left-wing radicals, who saw Sacco and Vanzetti as two more names in a long list of the victims of capitalism's war against the proletariat. Like their American counterparts, Sacco and Vanzetti's early supporters in Europe were reminded of what they saw as the case's precedents: the Haymarket episode, the Mooney case, the execution of Joe Hill (a Swedish immigrant), and the wartime jailings of the radical labor leaders "Big Bill" Haywood and Eugene Debs. In 1920 and 1921, Sacco and Vanzetti were almost strictly the concern of militants. Most Europeans, recovering from the devastation of foreign and civil wars, had more pressing matters to worry about than the plight of two Italians in far-away Massachusetts.

In France, though, intellectuals disturbed by the Sacco-Vanzetti case could make an impact because of their high public profile and relative propinquity to power. In 1921 thus came the first stirrings of the elite involvement that would become a staple of "l'affaire Sacco et Vanzetti" in France some years later. The seventy-seven-year-old Anatole France, recipient of that year's Nobel Prize for literature, published a prescient piece addressed "To the People of America" in the *Nation,* calling for the release of "two innocent men."[28] As he saw it, the Sacco-Vanzetti case was produced by the same chauvinism that on a greater scale had led to the horrific, pointless carnage of the Great War. The case also reminded him of the Dreyfus affair, a cataclysmic episode that was still fresh in French political memory. The comparison with the Dreyfus case would become a major theme of the French (and worldwide) Sacco-Vanzetti campaign in the late 1920s. But no American of comparable stature would make such a public intervention until at least five years later. As late as 1924, even as other European intellectuals were making their voices heard on the issue, the only well-known American writer on record as supporting Sacco and Vanzetti was H. L. Mencken, the irreverent editor of the *American Mercury.*[29]

And so between 1922 and late 1926, while Sacco and Vanzetti's lawyers appealed the convictions (under one of the many peculiar laws of Massachusetts, at each new appeal the defendants had to appear before the same judge who had presided over their original trial) and the legal process moved at a glacial pace, Sacco and Vanzetti slipped out of the public eye. Even the Italian-language press in the United States paid the case relatively scarce attention; in these interim years, the flame of their cause was kept alive by radical friends and supporters around the world, as well as by their Brahmin patrons on the defense committee and the ACLU.[30] European and Latin American radicals published pamphlets and even held occasional demonstrations, but without making much of a dent on broad public opinion, let alone on the Massachusetts authorities responsible for the case. And in 1924 the long-standing and increasingly powerful nativist and isolationist sentiment in the United States finally culminated in the passage of the National Origins Act, which set strict quotas for immigration and was designed to keep unwanted foreigners, especially from Japan and eastern and southern Europe, out of the country.[31]

In the United States those most interested in the case during this period might have been officials at the Bureau of Investigation, who under rising star Hoover (appointed to head the Bureau in 1924) clung, at least officially, to the conviction that the Galleanisti planned to take revolutionary action against the U.S. government. While the mainstream press neglected the Sacco-Vanzetti case in these years, the future FBI paid it detailed attention. Meanwhile, Sacco and Vanzetti themselves remained in prison; consistently and forcefully protesting their innocence, apprehensive about the death sentence that would certainly be imposed on them if their legal appeals eventually failed, both men periodically went on lengthy hunger strikes, suffered nervous breakdowns, and were treated in mental facilities.[32]

In late 1926, however, after five long years in the shadows, the Sacco-Vanzetti case returned in dramatic fashion to the public sphere, and by 1927 it had captured national and worldwide attention far beyond the previous scope of the militant left and intelligence agents. Both European and American observers were taken aback by the transformation; as a skeptical writer for the conservative British journal *Outlook* put it, commenting on the new European fascination with Sacco and Vanzetti, "Thousands of men have been convicted and sentenced on evidence very much weaker than appeared in this case, and there has not been the hullabaloo which for some unaccountable reason has been created in this case."[33] Why did so many people devote so much attention to this particular instance of American justice? What was the "unaccountable reason," as the *Outlook* put it, for the "hullabaloo"?

It can be useful to mark the formal beginning of the Sacco-Vanzetti affair, at least in the United States, as October 23, 1926, when Judge Thayer denied Sacco and Vanzetti's final motion for a new trial. The motion had been filed on the basis of a sensational confession in 1925 by a Portuguese-born career criminal, Celestino Madeiros—a former cellmate of Sacco's—that he was a part of the gang that committed the South Braintree robbery and murder, and that neither Sacco nor Vanzetti was involved. It was the seventh time that Thayer had rejected their appeals, and in doing so he disregarded the mounting evidence that they might be innocent, or at least had established reasonable doubt as to their guilt. Thayer had also dismissed appeals that were based on his own clearly prejudicial behavior, including, in one case, asking a member of one of his social clubs whether he had seen "what I did to those anarchistic bastards the other day." Sacco and Vanzetti were clearly at the mercy of a small-time judge who seemed to delight in his mastery over the fate of two men whose politics he both completely misunderstood and profoundly hated. Thrust into the international public limelight, Thayer (who for a while seemed to enjoy the attention he was getting in his old age) became almost as much of a household name as Sacco and Vanzetti themselves—a villain to Sacco-Vanzetti supporters worldwide, a hero to their opponents at home.[34]

Sacco and Vanzetti's lawyers turned twice to the Massachusetts supreme court, but in April 1927 their second appeal was rejected on the grounds that the court (under another antiquated and absurd state law) could intervene only in matters of "the law," not in questions involving either "the evidence" or the "interests of justice," and was thus not in a position to consider Madeiros's confession or any new evidence introduced since the original trial in 1921. Thus the court could not (or would not) overturn Thayer's verdict. It was a serious blow to the defense, which had staked everything on the logic and fairness of the state legal system. Sacco and Vanzetti returned that month to Thayer's court, where the judge promptly sentenced the two men to death by electrocution.

But before their sentencing the two made stirring courtroom speeches that were transcribed and disseminated throughout the world, especially via the radical press. The powerful symbolism that many people across a broad ideological spectrum carried away from the celebrated courthouse scene of April 5, 1927, was that of a recalcitrant and cynical judge, representing a reactionary and frightened establishment, coldly pronouncing death upon two humane victims, representing the oppressed and poor of the world. Sacco, barely containing himself, spoke first. "I never knew, never heard, even read in history anything so cruel as this court," he began. "I know the sentence will be between two classes, the oppressed class and the rich class, and there will always be collision between one and the other. We fraternize the people with the books, with the literature. You persecute the people, tyrannize them and kill them. We try the education of the people

always. You try to put a path between us and some other nationality. . . .
That is why I am here today on this bench, for having been of the oppressed class. Well, you are the oppressor. You know it, Judge Thayer—
you know all my life, you know why I have been here, and after seven
years that you have been persecuting me and my poor wife, and you still
today sentence us to death. I would like to tell all my life, but what is the
use?" Vanzetti, looking straight at Thayer (who reportedly stared off
into space), followed with perhaps his most famous words, in a speech
that lasted nearly an hour:

> I am innocent. . . . In all my life I have never stolen and I have never
> killed and I have never spilled blood. . . . I have struggled all my life,
> since I began to reason, to eliminate crime from the earth. . . . Every man
> of understanding in the world, not only in this country but also in other
> countries . . . the flower of mankind of Europe, the better writers,
> the greatest thinkers of Europe, have pleaded in our favor. The great-
> est scientists, the greatest statesmen of Europe have pleaded in our
> favor. . . . The whole world has said that it is wrong and I know that it is
> wrong. . . . It is seven years that we are in jail. What we have suffered
> during these seven years no human tongue can say, and yet you see me
> before you, not trembling, you see me looking in your eyes straight, not
> blushing, not changing color, not ashamed or in fear. . . . We have proved
> that there could not have been another judge on the face of the earth
> more prejudiced, more cruel, and more hostile than you have been
> against us. . . . I would not wish to a dog or to a snake, to the most low
> and misfortunate creature of the earth—I would not wish to any of
> them what I have had to suffer for things that I am not guilty of. I am
> suffering because I am a radical and indeed I am a radical. I have suf-
> fered because I was an Italian and indeed I was an Italian. I have suffered
> more for my family and for my beloved than for myself. But I am so
> convinced to be right that you can only kill me once but if you could
> execute me two times, and if I could be reborn two other times, I would
> live again to do what I have done already.[35]

The case was quickly moving from the margins to the mainstream
of American life. After Thayer's October 1926 ruling, the *Boston Herald*, a mild-mannered daily that previously had shown little sympathy
with Sacco and Vanzetti, had published an eye-opening editorial entitled "We Submit." The author, F. Lauriston Bullard—who, in another sign of the changing times, won a Pulitzer Prize for the piece—
criticized Thayer's decision and called for a reexamination of the case.

"We do not know," wrote Bullard, "whether these men are guilty or not. We have no sympathy with the half-baked views which they profess. But as months have merged into years and the great debate over this case has continued, our doubts have solidified slowly into convictions, and reluctantly we have found ourselves compelled to reverse our original judgment. We hope the supreme [state] judicial court will grant a new trial on the basis of the new evidence not yet examined in open court. . . . We hope that our Governor will call to his aid a commission of disinterested men of the highest intelligence and character to make an independent investigation in his behalf." Such a response to the case from such a newspaper would have been inconceivable five years earlier, possibly even just a year earlier.[36]

Why did the ruling—and the sentencing the following April—elicit startlingly different reactions from those aroused in 1921 or 1924? What were the new circumstances that allowed the Sacco-Vanzetti case to finally emerge as an affair? The entire context of the case had changed, in the United States as elsewhere. By 1926 and 1927, the Galleanisti, their threats and their dynamite, were no longer the political issue they once had been. The labor wars had calmed, thanks mainly to the federal government's repression of militant labor groups, and among the general public a working-class uprising was not the frightening specter it had been just a few years earlier. Owing to the National Origins Act, immigration (especially from Italy) had slowed to a mere trickle and was no longer the divisive issue it had once been. And the U.S. involvement in the world war had come to be seen in many quarters, both isolationist and internationalist, as a huge mistake, with the Sacco-Vanzetti case—indeed, the entire Red Scare—one of its most unfortunate byproducts. Liberals, in particular, began to regain some of their verve, and the Sacco-Vanzetti camp benefited to a large degree from this backlash.

The historian William Leuchtenberg, in his influential study *The Perils of Prosperity* (1958), tried to put his finger on the pulse of the period. "By the end of 1920," he argued, "the Red Scare was over [and] the nation, as it felt secure once more from external threats, came to realize that the internal danger had been vastly exaggerated too. The Red Scare appeared, together with the War and League of Nations issues, to be another instance of the political intensity of the [Woodrow] Wilson regime." To Leuchtenberg, the election in 1920 of Warren G. Harding based on his vague promise of a "return to normalcy" meant the rapid decline of all things political in American life. Harding, after all, had himself contributed to this cooling-down process by stating that "too much has been said about Bolshevism in America."[37]

Leuchtenberg's interpretation, which still represents a standard view of the 1920s as a not-especially-political decade in the United States, demands and has since received serious qualification. To begin with, it would be hard in principle for anyone, even an eminent historian, to assess what "the nation" as a whole felt or thought (this was a kind of thinking common to the liberal historiography of the 1950s). More to the point, other historians have recently shown that Red Scare policies continued in key ways to function well into the late 1920s and long beyond. And the controversy that raged over Sacco and Vanzetti was one of many examples (including, among others, the rise of the "second" Ku Klux Klan and Marcus Garvey's Back to Africa movement) that show that political tension and conflict were very much alive in the United States in the 1920s.[38]

Sacco-Vanzetti's flamboyant transition from case to affair in the United States was thus *not* the product of the end of the Red Scare or the demise of ideological politics. Rather, it was born, at least partially, of an overlapping of political sensibilities, a transition period. It is true that the purely Wilsonian phase of the Red Scare, of which the case itself (in its criminal and legal senses) *had* been a product, was probably over by 1926. In the late 1920s, legal, political, and intellectual criticism of what had taken place in the Red Scare had become more sustained and prominent, voiced by people who had either come to their senses, or regained their confidence, or finally found an audience. On the other hand, many of those who had executed the policies that had made the Red Scare so efficient (and, in that context, had helped trap Sacco and Vanzetti in Massachusetts) were not gone from the legal or political scene. Just eight years earlier, they had not encountered or even expected much resistance to their policies. In other words, in the United States the Sacco-Vanzetti affair can be seen in part as a late-1920s showdown between a Red Scare establishment and its increasingly confident critics. The first group was on the decline and the second on the rise, and their political trajectories crossed at about equal strength in the summer of 1927, as the legal case came to its conclusion.

It is true that even in 1920 and 1921, at the time that Sacco and Vanzetti's legal ordeal began, some progressive jurists, such as Louis

Brandeis, Felix Frankfurter, and Zechariah Chafee, along with the ACLU, had battled Palmer and Wilson's repressive policies.[39] But Sacco and Vanzetti could not fully benefit from this kind of progressive or liberal championing until a broader public—especially elites in the political and intellectual establishment—changed the way they thought about the war and its effects on American life, and even more so the way they thought about Sacco and Vanzetti themselves. Since the two men had been tried for a nonpolitical crime, influential elites became involved with their story only once the full political meanings of the case came into focus and could be tied to their own concerns. For Sacco and Vanzetti's radical supporters the political meanings of the case had been clear from the start, but for establishment figures like Brandeis or Frankfurter they appeared only later. A defense of the two anarchists, beginning in 1926 and strengthening in 1927, became intertwined for these liberals with a phase of breast-beating over the U.S. involvement in the war and the ensuing political repression—including the persecution and upcoming execution of Sacco and Vanzetti.[40]

The new, broader receptiveness to the idea that Sacco and Vanzetti were victims of a massive injustice was also brought about by changes at the individual level. Fred Moore, the controversial attorney from California, was fired from the case in 1924 by a furious Sacco, who signed his final letter to Moore "your implacable enemy now and forever"; his replacement was William Thompson, a conservative Boston attorney with ties to legal and political power in Massachusetts.[41] Sacco and Vanzetti themselves had gone from being rather obscure immigrant radicals to folk heroes for many, particularly—but no longer only—among workers worldwide, for whom the imprisoned Italians had become increasingly powerful symbols of the continuing oppression, and potential solidarity, of the proletariat in the postwar industrial world. And even some strict "law and order" types in the United States, as we shall see, had a hard time reconciling the personas of the two defendants with the crime for which they had been convicted.

Vanzetti, in particular, had endeared himself to intellectuals and activists from Mexico to France to China.[42] From the point of view of the Massachusetts authorities seeking good publicity, he could not have been a worse prisoner: in no way did he fit the profile of a bandit. A voracious reader, his English constantly improving, he became known as something of an intellectual himself, famous for his

eloquent, witty prison letters and courtroom pathos. As opposed to
the relentlessly cheerless Sacco, Vanzetti managed occasionally to view
his ordeal with a kind of wry, charming humor. He also took it as an
opportunity to meet people, make friends, learn, teach, grandstand,
and proselytize. He wrote a number of raw manuscripts, including
two autobiographical pamphlets and a brief history of Italian syndicalist thought.[43] His voluminous correspondence includes thoughtful
ruminations (in English) on history, philosophy, and current affairs,
including the connections between the Bolshevik Revolution, the rise
of Mussolini, the influence of the publisher William Randolph Hearst,
and the state of the labor movement, as well as on complex works such
as William James's *Principles of Psychology* (1893) and Charles and
Mary Beard's *The Rise of American Civilization* (1927).[44]

As imagery came to play an increasing role in the affair, thanks to
the global spread of pamphlets and illustrated propaganda, Vanzetti's
appeal became visual as well as verbal. With his full, drooping mustache, dark eyes, and penetrating gaze, he even looked the part of the
charismatic philosopher-saint in the pictures and drawings cherished
by his supporters everywhere. (The climax of the case in 1927 coin-
cided with the advent of camera flashbulbs, ushering in the so-called
golden age of photojournalism, a fact that probably contributed to
Sacco and Vanzetti's iconic posterity.) A seemingly endless parade of
poets and artists compared him to Jesus Christ, an image that would
become even more loaded, and common, after he was executed.[45] To
others, Vanzetti looked and sounded like a dreamy, gentle man, utterly
incapable of violence. People who met him in prison often recounted
their visits with awe.[46] He befriended a variety of unlikely people
whom he never would have dreamt of knowing before 1920 when he
was peddling fish in Plymouth or toiling in some dingy factory. Most
important, genuinely impressed by the help he received from nonanarchists, including New England Brahmins like his new friend "Auntie
Bee," he underwent a subtle political transformation, outwardly abandoning his purely revolutionary stance, and although he continued to
define and think of himself as an anarchist and Galleanista, this change
probably made him more palatable, even attractive, to a larger public.
Vanzetti's reputation as a sensitive utopian dreamer (as opposed to
militant revolutionary anarchist) was the origin of the latter-day liberal
myth of "the humble fish peddler and the good shoemaker," a description that obscured his and Sacco's real political background and aims.

Despite his frequent apocalyptic statements, Vanzetti seems never to have completely lost hope that perhaps the executions would eventually be stopped, and his relatively sunny outlook, bolstered by the global outpouring of support he and Sacco received, affected the thinking of many in the growing Sacco-Vanzetti camp. Nothing in his actions suggested that he wanted to die. Sacco, on the other hand, remained both pessimistic and an unblinking revolutionary to the end. He was more reclusive than Vanzetti and distrustful of all nonanarchists. He did not share Vanzetti's intellectual curiosity and did not take as much comfort in the public and international support for their cause. Only a successful proletarian uprising, he believed, could save them, and since he was grounded enough in reality to know that this was not likely to happen in time, the belief did nothing to lighten his understandably gloomy mood. More than anything else, he missed his wife and children, and his house and garden, terribly. And whereas Vanzetti, who had already been sentenced for the 1919 Bridgewater crime, was allowed to work in the dismal Charlestown prison among the general population, Sacco (who evidently suffered from deep, untreated depression) remained confined to his solitary cell in the Norfolk County prison, until he was finally transferred to death row (to a cell adjacent to Vanzetti's) at Charlestown.[47] His English, though it improved, remained poor. In the end, he also turned out to be wiser than Vanzetti about their prospects.

In May 1927, shortly after Judge Thayer had sentenced his clients to death, attorney William Thompson resigned in frustration from the case. He would continue his involvement in the legal proceedings until August, but officially he handed over the defense to his colleague Arthur Hill (another Brahmin). In earlier months, the defense committee had toyed with the idea of bringing the liberal attorney Clarence Darrow to the legal team instead of, or in addition to, Thompson. Darrow, then perhaps the most celebrated trial lawyer in the nation, was fresh from several sensational courtroom performances, most notably in the 1924 Leopold-Loeb case in Chicago (in which he saved two young thrill killers of German-Jewish origin from certain execution), the 1925 Sweet trial in Detroit (in which his black client was acquitted of killing a white man), and, also in 1925, the Scopes trial in Dayton, Tennessee (where he embarrassed the star witness for the prosecution, the populist legend William Jennings Bryan). Vanzetti, however, rejected the idea in a message to the defense committee: "To me it seems positive that if Mr. Thompson cannot obtain a new trial from the Massachusetts courts, still less could Darrow obtain it, for, just think the resentment and hostility that his personality and his coming from Chicago would arise in the black-gowned hangers. It also seems that the actual place of the case would allow him a very small opportunity to display his capacities. . . . We have so many reasons to a new trial, that if it will be denied, as I expect, it will be solely because they want to kill us at any cost, and if so, which lawyer could help? None!"[48]

Among most of Sacco and Vanzetti's supporters, Thompson's departure was met with more understanding than anger. The entire process, especially Thayer's intransigence and hostility, had clearly shaken this deeply conservative lawyer and man of the establishment, who for the first time in his professional life had experienced the unpleasant, unfair, and absurd side of American justice. Thompson conveyed his feelings in an interview with the *New York World:* "I went into this case as a Harvard man, a man of old American tradition, to help two poor aliens who had, I thought, been unjustly treated. I have arrived at a humbler attitude. Not since the martyrdoms of the sixteenth century has such steadfastness to a faith, such self-abnegation as that of these two poor Italians, been seen on this earth. The Harvard graduate, the man of old American tradition, the established lawyer, is now quite ready to say that nowhere in his soul is there to be found the strength, the faith, the splendid gentility, which make the man, Bartolomeo Vanzetti."[49]

These striking words exemplify the way many people outside the far left had come to think of the case, and of the defendants, by 1927. Moreover, Thompson's long involvement in the case, his conviction that his clients were innocent, and his unabashed admiration for Vanzetti, drew the engagement of the elite legal network centered in the Harvard Law School—particularly that of Frankfurter, protégé of the progressive Supreme Court justices Louis Brandeis and Oliver Wendell Holmes. Initially made aware of the case in 1921 by his wife, Marion Frankfurter, a friend of Elizabeth Glendower Evans's, Frankfurter eventually made a close study of the Dedham trial. In March 1927 he published an article in the well-disseminated and respectably conservative *Atlantic Monthly;* it was soon expanded and published as a book, *The Case of Sacco and Vanzetti.*[50]

The case was already becoming a hot topic when Frankfurter's

article and book appeared, but their publication was a hugely significant moment in the public history of the affair and a boon for
the Sacco-Vanzetti camp. Frankfurter argued that the trial had been
deeply flawed and unfair. He vehemently criticized Thayer's biased
conduct. He showed the close connection between the trial and the
lingering hysteria of the war years; Sacco and Vanzetti were convicted,
Frankfurter dryly contended, because of the "deliberate effort [on the
part of the judge and the prosecution] to excite the emotions of jurors
still in the grip of war fever."[51] It was the first study of the case by an
established legal expert, and, particularly because the author stressed
the legal process and eschewed political argument, it had an enormous
and immediate public impact, convincing previously hesitant or uninformed liberals and conservatives on both sides of the Atlantic that
executing Sacco and Vanzetti would constitute a grave miscarriage of
justice.

Frankfurter's article was first slotted for publication in the *New
Republic,* whose progressive editor Herbert Croly had (cautiously)
adopted the Sacco-Vanzetti cause. But Frankfurter was asked by El-
lery Sedgwick, editor of the *Atlantic Monthly,* to publish the article
in his magazine instead, and with Croly's permission, Frankfurter
agreed.[52] This signified a crucial difference in reception: the *Atlantic*
had a much broader, and more conservative, readership. The venue of
publication also helped the essay stand out among the many other
commentaries, especially in the liberal press, that had begun to denounce the Sacco-Vanzetti trial. The main strength of Frankfurter's
article, however, was its detailed analysis of the original trial, which no
one of his standing had undertaken before.

Frankfurter's entry into the Sacco-Vanzetti fray sparked a growing focus on the peculiarities and absurdities of the trial, now seen by
journals and newspapers such as the *Nation* and the *New York World*
as something of a kangaroo court, typical of the Red Scare in a particularly provincial corner of the country. In his wake, dozens of law
professors sent new petitions to the Massachusetts governor.[53] More
important, it helped crystallize the new shape of the Sacco-Vanzetti
controversy in the United States. No longer could the case be portrayed strictly as a struggle between the haves and the have-nots.
Frankfurter and other social, legal, and intellectual elites now stood at
the forefront of the campaign, and these new supporters became perhaps the most hated targets of Sacco and Vanzetti's many opponents.

If previously the case could be seen as a symbolic battle between the Harvard establishment and the slum dwellers of the world—a battle that was much easier for the establishment to win—the new battle lines were drawn within Harvard itself, as it were. As if to press home that point, in April 1927, 205 members of the graduating class at the Harvard Law School, led by the dean, Roscoe Pound, signed a petition asking Massachusetts governor Alvan T. Fuller to grant clemency to Sacco and Vanzetti.[54] The philosophy professor William Hocking made a speech in front of about a thousand people at the university in which he described the impending executions as "the incredible, the essentially disgraceful situation."[55] And in the wake of faculty activity, there was even some student protest—a precursor to the radicalism of the 1930s—at the heart of the most pampered class. The *Harvard Crimson* explicitly compared the Sacco-Vanzetti case to the Dreyfus affair: as with the French-Jewish officer, against whom "the charge of treason served but as a thin screen behind which was fought another race and religious battle," Sacco and Vanzetti, as the young editors saw it, were "nominally" tried for murder, while "economic doctrines played an important part in the evidence submitted to [the] jury."[56]

To those who demanded that the Sacco and Vanzetti executions go through, a single article by Frankfurter in the *Atlantic* was potentially more dangerous than all earlier radical demonstrations and petitions combined, and nothing showed this fear more than the Massachusetts Department of Safety's wiretap of Frankfurter's telephone in 1927.[57] But Frankfurter went beyond writing a book: he became the unofficial legal adviser to the Sacco-Vanzetti defense committee in Boston, which, to the chagrin of many Sacco and Vanzetti supporters, assumed the leadership of the entire campaign as the executions drew nearer.

In 1927 the defense committee also radically changed its makeup. Aldo (Aldino) Felicani, fellow Galleanista and friend of the defendants, and the driving force in the committee since 1921, was joined by Gardner "Pat" Jackson, a well-to-do socialite, Harvard dropout, former *Boston Globe* reporter, and part-time stockbroker, who was originally from Colorado.[58] This unlikely duo—secretive Italian anarchist and freewheeling liberal westerner—somehow embodied the nature of the Sacco-Vanzetti campaign in the heated days of 1927. It was a fairly eclectic collaboration across political and cultural lines that attempted, a decade before the advent of the Popular Front, to fuse the far left with the liberal left in a common goal. Felicani commanded the attention of the militant rank and file while Jackson's role was to mobilize the social and political elements needed for effective political action: business leaders, political figures, journalists, legal experts.[59] It was not an equal collaboration, though: at the height of the affair radicals were ordered, or expected, to remain in the background, leaving the big names to take center stage. And it was a partnership that belied the powerful tensions and conflicts among Sacco-Vanzetti supporters in the United States and elsewhere.

These supporters in 1927 can be divided into roughly two main groups: the first, those who chose a legalist-pragmatic approach, stressing proper procedure and confidence in the existing judicial and political system; the second, those who opted for politicized, extralegal protest and radical action. In France and elsewhere in Europe, where the radical left was considerably stronger than in the United States, one expression of this divide, as we shall see, was the fight between revolutionaries and nonrevolutionaries in the Sacco-Vanzetti camp. Another distinction was between supporters who saw the case in terms of class and those who saw it in terms of law. Yet a third division was between those who focused solely on saving Sacco and Vanzetti's lives (even if this meant having their sentences commuted to life in prison) and those who insisted on their innocence, demanded their freedom, and connected their cause to a broader political and social struggle.

These interrelated and occasionally overlapping divisions can be loosely traced to the personalities of Sacco and Vanzetti themselves, with the latter frequently calling for cooperation across political lines and expressing occasional optimism that the bourgeois system could do the right thing in the end, and the former convinced that "the history of all the government it were always and every time the martyrdom of the proletariat."[60] But in the primary internal struggle, between working within the system or without it, the defense committee in Boston, under Frankfurter's strong behind-the-scenes influence, pursued the first option. Their most significant decision, much maligned by more radical supporters, was to attempt to save the two men after Thayer sentenced them to death by appealing to the executive office of the state of Massachusetts—the governor. Counting on the growing support of establishment figures in the United States, as well as on pressure from political figures and intellectuals in Europe, they gambled that Governor Fuller—a former bicycle repairman and auto dealer—would be forced to pardon the defendants, or at least to grant them a new trial. Vanzetti himself petitioned the governor, on May 3, 1927, for his and Sacco's freedom. (Sacco agreed in principle with the petition's content but refused to sign it on the grounds that he could not put his name on any official document not addressed to "the people.") In the petition, Vanzetti proudly called himself an anarchist, and as "precedents" and "authorities" for his position he cited Thomas Jefferson, Tom Paine, Ralph Waldo Emerson, and Lev Tolstoy, among others. The petition expressed Vanzetti's ecumenical, even Americanized, conception of what anarchism meant—and revealed the amount of prison reading he had been doing.[61]

Under the direction of Frankfurter and the defense committee, the Sacco-Vanzetti campaign in 1927 was aimed at what can only be called a mainstream American and international audience. Gone were the allusions to the class struggle and the oppression of labor that had figured prominently in 1921. Instead the defense committee's 1927 pamphlets and bulletins stressed the injustices of the trial and the mountain of evidence in favor of the defendants. It focused on individuals, primarily Thayer and prosecutor Katzmann, rather than on the system or class justice. It stressed the need to protect the integrity of the American justice system rather than a desire to do away with that system. Though constantly under attack from radicals who worried that the Sacco-Vanzetti movement had become too bourgeois and perilously close to the powers that be, the Felicani-Jackson committee focused on recruiting big names to the fold. Similar defense committees were formed around the world, with perhaps the most successful group based in France; though founded and led by anarchists, it too eventually emphasized collaboration with nonrevolutionaries, especially intellectuals of the democratic left.

Frankfurter, to be sure, was not individually responsible for the frenzy that enveloped the Sacco-Vanzetti case in 1927. But his intervention did eventually push a hesitant and complacent media, obsessed as they may have been with the social frivolities and celebrity scandals of the day, to pay more attention to what had actually happened in Massachusetts. Even newspapers and journals that had been uniformly hostile toward radicalism in general, and Sacco and Vanzetti in particular (if they had paid them any attention at all), began to express concern about the case. The *New York Times,* for example, no friend of anarchists, published a hard-hitting article on the case by the British writer H. G. Wells. Liberal venues such as the *Nation,* the *New Republic,* and the *New York World,* which had practically ignored the case for the preceding five or six years, now began to see Sacco and Vanzetti as the victims of the postwar xenophobic frenzy. The most prominent American political commentators of the 1920s, including Croly and his former protégé Walter Lippmann (editor of the *World*), took up the Sacco-Vanzetti case as one of their primary concerns. They focused on what they saw as the absurdities of Massachusetts law, and New York critics like Lippmann portrayed the state, and Boston especially, as an embarrassing bastion of reaction and intolerance, stuck somewhere between the Gilded Age and the world of Sinclair Lewis's *Main Street.*

This liberal protest had clear limits, however, and especially after the executions it would be held up to harsh mockery by more radical critics. In general liberals held dearly to the belief that the system, as it were, would simply not allow Sacco and Vanzetti to be killed. To the growing anger and consternation of radicals, the *World* and the *New Republic* called for a retrial or a reexamination of the case rather than for Sacco and Vanzetti's freedom. To Frankfurter and other establishment figures, demonstrations and protest of the radical stripe were anathema, and they refused to connect the case to any general problem with American justice or society, let alone with capitalism or liberal democracy.

Indeed, the political and legal campaign on behalf of Sacco and Vanzetti became so fearful of radical influence that even the well-meaning ACLU became an unwanted factor. "I hope very deeply you will do nothing until after the Sacco-Vanzetti case is out of the way completely," Frankfurter wrote at one point to the organization's leadership. "If the Civil Liberties Union and other like-minded organizations now come in, it is bound to be entangled with the efforts on behalf of Sacco and Vanzetti, and all such entanglements would hurt the cause of those men. I speak from a great deal of attention to the situation and a detailed familiarity, I believe, with the governing forces of the community."[62]

The thorniest issue for elite liberals like Frankfurter was Thayer, whom they saw as an unfortunate and dated aberration in an otherwise workable justice system. Indeed, their explanation of the case often amounted to little more than a conspiracy concocted by self-serving prosecutors and secretive law enforcement officials, or as Frankfurter

formally put it, "part of a collusive effort between the District Attorney and agents of the Department of Justice to rid the country of
these two Italians because of their Red activities."[63] It did not readily
occur to them that the trial was a symptom of larger, structural social,
legal, and political ills. This outlook would change after the executions.
But the insistence of many liberals on the aberrational rather than
representative quality of the case was partly responsible for the later
scholarly and public obsession with the question of Sacco and Vanzetti's guilt or innocence, at the expense of more important questions
about the broader context in which the case occurred.[64]

Harvard professors, liberal editors, and Brahmin activists probably came closer than the militant left ever could to actually rescuing
Sacco and Vanzetti in 1927. But when their efforts ultimately failed,
and the two anarchists were put to death despite all the liberal expectations to the contrary, the political and intellectual fallout was enormous. "No single act," wrote Leuchtenberg in 1958, "did more to turn
liberal intellectuals to radicalism."[65] On the American left the main
beneficiary was ultimately the Communist movement, which, ironically, did (or could do) little for the two anarchists when they were
alive but predicted the outcome of the case quite accurately. But all this
was to come later.

As for the European side of the affair, the shift from the relative
quiet of 1922–1925 to the storm of 1926–1927 cannot be explained by
a mere change of personnel or propaganda tactics in Boston or New
York. The international, especially European, aspects of the Sacco-
Vanzetti affair have been misunderstood, or even outright ignored, by
historians and pundits alike. Too many writers, for example, have
attributed the impact of the case in Europe to the low-handed machinations of clever radical masterminds, spreading misleading but effective propaganda from smoke-filled rooms in Boston or Berlin. This
is a facile explanation that does not take into account (or chooses to
overlook) the good reasons Europeans had to criticize American justice in the 1920s.

Many of the same European intellectuals who were disturbed by
the Sacco-Vanzetti case in 1926 or 1927 had already been shocked by
the 1925 Scopes trial, in which a Tennessee schoolteacher who had
dared to teach evolutionary theory was convicted of violating a state

law by a jury of his peers. (The French social scientist André Siegfried, for example, devoted a large portion of his 1926 study *Les Etats-unis d'aujourd'hui,* to the significance of that case.)[66] Looking at the issue from another, more sympathetic angle, ethnic Italian or working-class solidarities were also not the only reasons for the remarkable degree of European interest in Sacco and Vanzetti in 1927. In Europe, as in the United States, the case would not have become an affair without the growing involvement and attention of people and groups outside the working class, the Italian communities, and the radical left. This is true even of Latin American nations, such as Argentina, where support for Sacco and Vanzetti ultimately became joined, as in France, with a more inclusive human-rights agenda.[67]

The simplest, most immediate reason for the heightened European agitation over the case beginning in 1926 was the fact that Sacco and Vanzetti were actually facing a death sentence. Up to that point, many Europeans paying attention to goings-on in America were aware that an injustice had taken place in Massachusetts (or, as Anatole France had put it in his 1921 piece in the *Nation,* "in one of your states"). When it became clear that the executions were imminent, a general sense of outrage gave way to a much more focused sense of fear and urgency. On a humanitarian level, for many European observers the six-year wait that Sacco and Vanzetti were having to endure between their trial and their executions was horrifyingly cruel. "What fills us with horror," an editorialist for the British journal *New Statesman and Nation* explained, "is the long drawn-out agony which these men, guilty or innocent, must have suffered through six years, during which they must in imagination have died many times. It is hardly possible to imagine any moral torture so terrible as this . . . horrible! Inhuman!" (ellipsis in original). The Viennese daily *Neues Wiener Tagblatt* angrily agreed: "If Sacco and Vanzetti are executed they will not only pay the penalty imposed on them by dying in the electric chair, but they will pay an additional penalty of six years' exquisite torture. That additional penalty is not authorized by law. . . . What kind of government is it which permits such things?"[68] This excruciatingly long wait between convictions and executions—and not necessarily a principled opposition to the death penalty per se—was one aspect of the Sacco-Vanzetti case that rallied to the two men's cause even those who usually wanted nothing to do with revolution or radicals,

including Captain Alfred Dreyfus, who in the 1890s had himself lan-
guished for more than four years in desolate prison exile on Devil's
Island while hoping for legal redress.

Indeed, the transformation from case to affair began somewhat
earlier in Europe than in the United States. In the spring and summer
of 1926, before most Americans outside the radical left had shown
much interest in Sacco and Vanzetti's fate or even realized the significance of their case, a number of prominent and moderate European
public figures sent petitions on their behalf to both Fuller and President Calvin Coolidge. In July, Paul Loebe, Social Democratic president of the German Reichstag, sent an official telegram to the White
House with the rather polite words, "I request a pardon for Sacco and
Vanzetti." That month, a number of German public figures, among
them Albert Einstein (physics luminary and pacifist), Count Berns-
dorff (former ambassador to the United States), Fritz Kreisler (vio-
linist extraordinaire), Maximilian Harden (high-profile journalist),
Thomas Mann (admired author) and Princess Lichnowski (socially
conscious aristocrat), jointly cabled Fuller and Coolidge requesting a
retrial for Sacco and Vanzetti.[69]

American officials were alerted to the fact that things in Europe
were rapidly changing when Fuller, on a visit to Paris in November
1926, was greeted by dozens of protesters who angrily accosted the
governor and demanded that he remove Judge Thayer from the proceedings. "It appears that [Fuller] does not have the protection of any
body guard at any time on his trip to France," a worried Department
of Justice agent wrote to J. Edgar Hoover, newly appointed director of
the Bureau of Investigation. The U.S attorney general's office then
decreed that all American officials traveling to Europe or Latin America would require security from that point on.[70]

In Europe, as in the United States, 1927 was the pivotal year in the
full transformation from case to affair, and the dissemination of Frankfurter's study had much to do with this.[71] Prominent politicians and
intellectuals joined the radical left in protesting the upcoming executions. European intellectual critics, it should be noted, did not necessarily share the concerns of their American liberal counterparts. To
them, the bizarre specificities of Massachusetts law were not the point,
nor was any particular individual involved in the case. The problem,
rather, lay with 1920s America writ large. From Frankfurter's study
they drew conclusions that the law professor had not himself dared

make. In France, Britain, Germany, and elsewhere in Europe and beyond, there was a growing perception that the Sacco-Vanzetti case was the symptom of an America gone completely wild after the war, drunk on its own economic and global power, crushing the weak, persecuting the alien, flouting international opinion, isolated from the rest of the world, ignoring reasonable appeals from even the heads of friendly democratic states.

Many European intellectuals, particularly in France, had already long been describing the United States as a mechanical, amoral, conformist, hyper-materialistic society that condemned solidarity and free expression and did not care about basic notions of fairness; the Sacco-Vanzetti case confirmed these Europeans' worst suspicions about the "soullessness" of modern American civilization.[72] To H. G. Wells, for example, Thayer himself was far less important than "Thayerism," a "mental attitude" closely linked with the rise of fascism in many parts of Europe. This mentality, Wells argued, had virtually taken over American society: "Thayerism . . . is a widely diffused and dangerous force in the modern world. . . . What is the matter with Judge Thayer is not that he is anti-moral, but that he is—to put it mildly— extremely obtuse mentally and morally. This mental and moral obtuseness seems to have extended . . . to a considerable body of opinion in the United States which sustained him in the crushing of these two unfortunates."[73]

European reactions to the case were powerful enough to have a considerable effect on Americans who came into contact with the protest on that side of the Atlantic. No one should have been surprised that American radicals would have taken heed of European criticisms of the case; they had been doing so since 1921. But the new voices in the chorus of controversy were far more conservative and unexpected. Early in 1927, the *Monthly Bulletin* of the Sacco-Vanzetti defense committee published an appeal by E. A. Filene, the American department-store magnate and a philanthropist with wide European business connections.[74] Even Richard W. Child, who was the U.S. ambassador to Italy at the time of Sacco and Vanzetti's 1921 trial and was threatened at the time by anarchists in Rome (or so he claimed), was one of many American establishment figures to express unease at the nearing executions. In the *Bulletin,* Child explained that while he had "good reason to resent the campaign" on behalf of Sacco and Vanzetti, "those of us who are striving to make punishment for crime swift and certain realize to what extent we would be set back by an internationally advertised tragedy of error, based upon slow and inflexible uncertainty."[75]

As the executions approached, the transatlantic climate heated up markedly. In *L'oeuvre quotidien,* a group of "French intellectuals" published an "open letter to American intellectuals," arguing that if Sacco and Vanzetti were killed, U.S. citizens would find themselves "unwelcome" in Europe.[76] This warning was borne out by various incidents in 1927. Numerous European cities endured angry protests that resulted in casualties and destruction of property. There were also increasing reports of the harassment of American tourists. This was part of a larger general pattern of international violence in response to the Sacco-Vanzetti case; this was also the somewhat darker side of the globalization of protest of which the Sacco-Vanzetti campaign was perhaps the first premier modern example (the Dreyfus affair, by contrast, had not been accompanied by international violence, though in France there were widespread riots against Jews).

What the violent aspects of the Sacco-Vanzetti protest had in common, at least on the surface, was the symbolic choice of U.S. targets. In both Europe and Latin America there were numerous acts of violence that drew the attention not only of local authorities but also of the U.S. government. These were more widespread and severe than those of 1920 or 1921. On March 24, 1927, two bombs exploded in Buenos Aires, one at the Boston Bank and another at the New York City Bank, killing two people and destroying parts of the buildings. On July 22, 1927, two more bombs went off in the Argentinean capital, one at the George Washington monument and another in front of the Ford Motor Agency. On August 6, 1927, bombs exploded outside the U.S. consulate in Sofia and in front of the Ford Motor Agency in Rosario, Argentina. In response to these developments, the U.S. government took new diplomatic and propagandistic steps: in an effort to assuage some of the Latin Americans' rage (and, perhaps more important, in the hope of containing the lingering popularity of Latin American revolutionary movements), the embassies in Mexico City, Buenos Aires, and Montevideo dispatched a complete account of the Sacco-Vanzetti case to local newspapers, presenting the official position of the Massachusetts authorities.[77] Throughout the world, however, U.S. diplomats failed to convince angry protesters (and nervous governments) that the government of the United States, and even the president himself, had no influence whatsoever over goings-on in the state of Massachusetts. To many this seemed no more than a pitiful excuse; certainly the president could intervene if he so wished. Otherwise what was the point, many wondered, of having a national government at all?

Much of the violence against Americans abroad, at least the incidents widely reported in the United States, took place in Italy. In early August, the *Boston Herald* reported that Americans traveling in the north of the country, especially in Turin and Milan, were forced to flee across the Swiss border for fear of attacks after they were warned at their hotels and by local police that they were in danger. In Como, a group of American tourists was reportedly assaulted and injured by locals. Americans arriving at Swiss-Italian frontier railway stations were "strongly advised" by the border authorities not to enter Italy.[78] Even in the Ticino—the Italian part of Switzerland—they were not safe: in Lugano, Americans complained that they were insulted and harassed by crowds in the streets while policemen looked on and jeered.[79]

These reports created a highly awkward situation for the Italian dictator Benito Mussolini. The duce was struggling to simultaneously consolidate his relatively new regime, maintain good relations with the United States, advocate for clemency for his two countrymen, crush the remaining left-wing opposition to his rule, and win the allegiance of Italian diasporas everywhere. The Sacco-Vanzetti episode, in these regards, made for complicated politics. Mussolini denied the reports about the attacks on Americans in his country, calling them "false and exaggerated," but the negative public impression, in both the United States and Italy, had already been made.[80]

If one of the most important elements in the transition from case to affair was the overt involvement of world leaders and thus the elevation of the case from mere local crime to major diplomatic concern, Mussolini's role was crucial. The situation in Italy vis-à-vis the Sacco-Vanzetti case was made particularly complex by the fledgling nature of fascist rule during this period. Since Italy was the two defendants' home country, it was to be expected that nationalist emotions over the case there (and among Italian communities elsewhere) would run high. Ironically, the problem Mussolini now faced was partly of his own making: there was an obvious connection between his ceaseless stoking of nationalist sentiment and the powerful Italian ethnic solidarity with Sacco and Vanzetti.

In 1921 Italian left-wing radicals had been as active as their counterparts elsewhere in Europe in protesting the Sacco-Vanzetti trial. But
after Mussolini's seizure of power in 1922, political expression in Italy
was severely and increasingly limited, and the left was effectively muzzled and suppressed. By 1927 any popular protest essentially had to be
channeled through the national leadership. Italians outraged over the
Sacco-Vanzetti case were thus not in the same position as, say, the
French or the British to make their feelings known directly (except
through petitions to U.S. consuls and similar actions). There was no
longer a free press, and they could not demonstrate publicly unless
authorized to do so (and they were not). Instead, Italians who wished
to express their anger had to appeal to the duce, who would make an
official protest on their behalf. This is one way of explaining the high
degree of localized violence against Americans: there were few other
outlets for anger. It was left to Mussolini to fill the ironic role of trying
to save two left-wing Italian revolutionaries—in principle, mortal enemies of his own movement—from execution in a democratic nation
with which he was trying to maintain a good relationship. The Italian
press dutifully followed suit, repeatedly pleading for Sacco and Vanzetti's lives in the weeks before they were scheduled for execution.[81]

Tension over the case in Italy grew stronger the closer Sacco and
Vanzetti came to the electric chair. On August 5, 1927, after Fuller
authorized the executions, the United Press reported: "All Italy has
been thrown into the deepest grief by [Fuller's] decision." The report
added that the Italian people "looked hopefully . . . toward Premier
Mussolini to make some dramatic gesture toward the President of the
United States or the Governor of Massachusetts." The fascist press,
the report concluded, "has been vehement in [its] condemnation."[82]

But Mussolini, his usual bluster notwithstanding, was reduced to
groveling in front of the Americans, in secret. He wrote a letter to
Henry P. Fletcher, Child's successor as U.S. ambassador to Italy, "in
absolutely confident nature," as he put it, urging him to persuade
Fuller to commute the death sentence. In his attempt to influence
American leaders, Mussolini argued that mercy for Sacco and Vanzetti
would "reveal the difference between Bolshevik and American methods and would avoid creating two martyrs." He also sent a telegram on
July 23 with a message that he wished to convey directly to Fuller: he
spoke of "terrible circumstances" for Sacco and Vanzetti, asked the

governor to commute their sentence, and added, "I do not believe that clemency would mean a victory for subversives, it is certain that the execution of Sacco and Vanzetti would provide a pretext for a vast and continuous subversive agitation throughout the world."[83]

Shortly before the executions, Mussolini again pleaded with Fletcher, and was under the impression, perhaps because he had had such a close relationship with Child, that his message would be sent on to Coolidge. But not even the fawning dictator could crack the president's official indifference to the case, and Mussolini's communications were sent, like all others that arrived at the White House, directly to Fuller's office in Boston. And there are signs that Mussolini took the case as personally as any ordinary Italian protester: he had a letter that was sent to him by Sacco's father, Michele, published in the fascist official newspaper—which also published Mussolini's sympathetic answer to the letter, in which he claimed that he was doing all he could to save Michele's son.[84]

Mussolini's attitude toward the case, as the historian Philip Cannistraro has shown, had evolved over time. Between 1920 and 1922, Mussolini, perhaps surprisingly, adopted the Sacco-Vanzetti cause in the process of his rise to power because he still grudgingly respected anarchists and believed that they shared his fight with the socialists and Communists—who were, to him, the primary moral enemies of the fascisti. With Mussolini's seizure of power in 1922 came an additional incentive to support Sacco and Vanzetti: the desire to draw the allegiance of Italians in the United States (as well as that of all other Italian diasporas) to his regime.[85] After 1924 the duce adopted a more diplomatic approach to the case, thanks to his good relationship with the Coolidge administration and his apparent belief (shared by many others) that Fuller would someday become U.S. president.

Ultimately, though, in trying to save Sacco and Vanzetti Mussolini was primarily driven by a sense of kinship with the imprisoned radicals, whom the duce saw as distant versions of himself. Aside from his largely irrelevant belief that the two men were innocent, Mussolini also retained a certain pride in his own past as a syndicalist revolutionary; in his earlier years on the militant left, he had criticized the United States for its treatment of the Haymarket anarchists and persecution of Ettor, Giovannitti and other Italian radicals of the IWW in the 1900s and 1910s. Later in life Mussolini would bemoan the fact that "the fascists in America did not lift a finger . . . to save Sacco and Vanzetti. The socialist ranks among the emigrants, anarchist and maximalist [*sic*], did much more."[86]

But despite his supposed affinity with Sacco and Vanzetti, and probably because of his fear of the United States—or perhaps simply out of indecision—Mussolini never made his appeals on the matter public.[87] Instead, as the historian Emilio Gentile has shown, he made a point of complimenting Americans whenever he got the chance, in line with the fascisti's generally positive view of the United States in this period. (Mussolini, according to his ambassador to Washington, always enjoyed meeting U.S. officials.)[88] In his first "Message to the American People" in 1926, Mussolini called himself "a sincere admirer of America's civilization." The United States, he explained, had "made a sizeable contribution to the spiritual activity of the world," and in it were to be found, "despite its European origins, a new form which was rich in powerful and entirely original elements." At other times, Mussolini sang the praises of "American sociableness" (as he put it), the "splendid collective sense that always wins over individual selfishness." Individual Americans, the dictator claimed, "have given themselves a school, a language, a magnificent collective morality, so that their mass feeling is awareness and power." In the United States, he believed, "every American always owes something to his countrymen, to his city, to the state, to the nation, in both a civic and a social sense," not because he was forced to do so by law, "but as solidarity, as an obvious fact, as a moral duty": " I love that wholly American sense," the duce gushed, "of the majority which decides and which everyone, with no exception, must follow." Mussolini favorably contrasted this collectivist American spirit to that pervading in Europe, which suffered, in his view, from an "individualist and decadent particularism."[89]

All this was obviously more an expression of Mussolini's own fantasies about the fascist state under his rule and his contempt for the entrenched European bourgeoisie than a realistic assessment of life in the United States, about which the duce knew next to nothing. And he had a clear interest in making pronouncements that would sound agreeable, at least in his own imagination, to an American audience. It is ironic, in any case, that consciously or not, Mussolini turned a common European interwar criticism of America inside out: the Europeans were selfish and decadent, the Americans moral and civilized.[90]

In writing about the Sacco-Vanzetti case, the Italian press promoted the duce's self-glorifying image of the new Italy. Newspaper editorialists complimented the Italian public on their "restraint," which *Il Tevere,* in typically self-congratulatory fashion, attributed to the "remarkable discipline and correctness" of life under fascism. At the same time, the writer added that "this course has been followed at a great price, since 'nameless agony agitates the hearts of millions.'" Other venues were not as polite. *Il messagero* insisted, for instance, that "justice which strikes coldly in the face of a question of judicial error and after arousing hopes in the breasts of the condemned is atrocious."[91]

Despite their deference to their dictator, then, some Italian newspapers did not hesitate to criticize the Americans' treatment of Sacco and Vanzetti, and at the height of the affair their editorials were often similar to what one could read in France or Germany. But there were also strange and telling instances of censorship. The editorial of *Il tribuna* the day after the executions argued, "[Thus] concludes shamefully one of the blackest judicial events that man can recall"; this sentence was removed from the later edition of that day's paper. The rest of the piece, however, was left untouched: "This tragedy has happened in a country which calls itself democratic and free, but this is in theory.... In practice, America wished to show that she admits no law but her own—not even the laws of humanity." Other Italian editorials used generic contemporary anti-American terms such as "America's mechanical civilization." And, ironically for a piece penned under a fascist dictatorship which had recently seized power through violence, an editorial in *Giornale d'Italia* stated that "the execution shows that the free democratic republic of America punished political crime with death." More straightforwardly, *Lavore d'Italia* argued that "in the overbearing and stupid cruelty of the American magistrates there was the intention of challenging Europe and European civilization." At the same time, there were attempts to understand the American establishment point of view, though even in this case the sympathy was often mixed with sarcasm and resentment: according to *Il Tevere,* "The United States reacted against a colossal attempt at intimidation.... America was afraid of being the victim of a trick. She was afraid of falling into a sentimental trap and of losing the shining prestige which renders that nation the arbiter of the law of the whole world. America feared that Sacco-Vanzetti were a Trojan horse sent by ancient and envious Europe."[92]

Mussolini was not the only rising world leader, or European dictator, with a vested interest in Sacco and Vanzetti's destiny. In the Soviet Union, Joseph Stalin used the Sacco-Vanzetti case in a calculating way that had little, if anything, to do with a sense of justice or identification with the defendants. Mussolini probably had more at stake in the case than did Stalin, and historians might credit the duce with a genuine concern for the two imprisoned Italians, even though his motives were first and foremost political. Stalin, on the other hand, really cannot be suspected of losing sleep over the individual fate of the two anarchists. But the Soviet dimension of the Sacco-Vanzetti affair, which has been oddly neglected, demonstrates first the ways in which the Massachusetts criminal case attained truly international import and second how the affair became enmeshed with broader international politics. In this regard we can see the case's significance for both Soviet internal political life and the worldwide left. Although Stalin's approach to the case reflected internal interests more than a genuine adoption of the defendants' cause, he helped shape the ways in which that cause took shape around the world, especially after the executions.

In the Soviet Union, as elsewhere, many people expressed their support for Sacco and Vanzetti in diverse ways. But the Soviet reaction to the case gave a strong top-down impression; the interest emanated from the highest political echelon, Stalin himself. Why would the Soviet leader show any interest in two Italian anarchist prisoners in the United States? A brief detour into the minutiae of interwar Soviet politics is required here. Having risen to the top of the Soviet Communist Party in the 1920s, Stalin became embroiled in a bitter and evershifting power struggle with his internal Bolshevik rivals, principally Nikolai Bukharin and Leon Trotsky. In 1927, the year that the Sacco-Vanzetti affair was at its height, Stalin was maneuvering ideologically at the same time that he was consolidating his power within the party. As numerous scholars have shown, the two processes were inextricably linked. After he succeeded in having Trotsky expelled from the party in 1927, Stalin appropriated major portions of his rival's ideology of "permanent revolution" in order to turn against Bukharin, his remaining competitor for power and the originator of the "socialism in one country" doctrine.[93] At Stalin's behest, the Communist International (Comintern) decided in 1927 to move the entire movement "leftward," abandoning the previously official ideology of socialism in one country and adopting the new goal of "world revolution," thus immediately abolishing collective political action with all other groups on the left, including anarchists. In effect, because of the Soviet Communist Party's control over Communist Party leaderships worldwide, this meant an immediate end to unified radical protest over the Sacco-Vanzetti case.[94]

Since the 1960s, several revisionist writers have posited that liberal intellectuals worldwide (including in the United States) who supported the Sacco-Vanzetti cause believed that they were upholding universal principles of justice, when all they were really doing was the bidding of the Communist International, which supposedly wished to discredit and shame the United States. This notion is false for a number of reasons. First, the main goal of the Comintern in 1927 was not to shame the United States but to gain control of the political left internationally and promote the interests of the regime in Moscow. Second, and more important, rather than trying to fool liberals around the world into supporting a covert Communist cause, Stalin and the Comintern actually wanted to fool the world into thinking that Sacco-Vanzetti *was* a Communist cause. In other words, they needed to reconcile the growing international solidarity with the two Italian anarchists with Stalin's own new policy, which estranged Communists from the rest of the left, including the anarchist movement itself, which in the Soviet Union was outlawed. Sacco and Vanzetti had become such a popular international cause by 1927 that Stalin sought to exploit it in his struggle for mastery of the worldwide left, as well as of his own party and country.

The Soviet leader regularly granted scripted interviews to foreign delegations of sympathetic Communist journalists, and the historian can glean insights even from these tightly controlled events. In November 1927, two months after their execution, Stalin discussed Sacco and Vanzetti in front of approximately eighty international delegates. In response to the prepared question "How do you estimate the situation in Western Europe? Are revolutionary events to be expected within the next few years?" he replied: "There is 'unrest' in the centers of European capitalism. . . . The conditions for new revolutionary activities are maturing. . . . The clearest indication of the growing crisis of capitalism, and the clearest manifestation of the mounting discontent and anger of the working class, are the events connected with the murder of Sacco and Vanzetti. What is the murder of two working men for the capitalist mincing machine? Have not scores and hundreds of workers been killed up till now every week, every day? But the murder of two workers, Sacco and Vanzetti, was enough to set the working class all over the world in motion. . . . This shows that things are getting hotter and hotter for capitalism."[95]

This was a bald attempt on Stalin's part to connect the violent aftermath of the Sacco and Vanzetti executions with the direction he had pushed the international Communist movement in 1927; in December of that year he further elaborated on this theme in his speech at the Fifteenth Congress of the Soviet Communist Party in Moscow. Contrary to what one prominent historian of the case has written, Stalin did not say on this occasion that the Sacco-Vanzetti case was "the most important world event since the October 1917 revolution."[96] He had no need to. Rather, promoting the new Comintern line of world revolution that he had himself initiated, Stalin linked what he called "the revolutionary demonstrations in France and Germany in connection with the murder of Sacco and Vanzetti" with the British general strike of 1926, the workers' "revolution action" in Vienna, and the (relative) electoral successes of the Communist Parties in both Poland and Germany. "All these facts undoubtedly indicate," he concluded, "that Europe is entering a new period of revolutionary upsurge. If a fact like the murder of Sacco and Vanzetti could give rise to working-class demonstrations, it undoubtedly indicates that revolutionary energy has accumulated in the depths of the working class and is seeking . . . a cause, an occasion . . . to break to the surface and hurl itself upon the capitalist regime."[97]

Earlier, in the summer of 1927, as the uproar over Sacco and Vanzetti reached its peak, and the international Communist movement championed the cause as its own, the Soviet press had heralded Stalin's statements, with *Izvestia* calling the imminent executions "one of the most hideous crimes of class justice" and *Pravda* promising that "[Fuller's] decision [to execute Sacco and Vanzetti] will make a lasting impression on the minds of the world's working masses."[98] Yet at the same time that Stalin and the cowed Soviet press were bemoaning Sacco and Vanzetti's plight, and workers throughout the Soviet Union were instructed to attend sympathy meetings for them, the authorities had intensified their ongoing campaign—especially following the logic of the "leftward" turn of the Communist International—to eradicate the last vestiges of anarchism in the Soviet Union.

This repression of anarchists was dutifully reported by anti-Soviet activists in the West, including the exiled Russian anarchist intellectual Alexander Berkman (who was deported from the United States in 1919 along with his colleague and lover Emma Goldman), who wrote a grim report called "The Sacco-Vanzetti Case in Russia." The newsletter in which Berkman published his piece followed the ramifications of the case in the Soviet Union as part of its fight against "Bolshevik terrorism." Elsewhere, the newsletter angrily reported on an invitation extended by the Soviets to Sacco's wife to visit Russia, calling it "an act of disgusting hypocrisy, in view of the fact that numerous Russian Saccos and Vanzettis are filling the Bolshevik prisons." It also described a leaflet distributed by Russian anarchists in August 1927 that read, "Fellow workers, while protesting against the murder of Sacco and Vanzetti, do not forget their comrades imprisoned in Russia. Demand the right to propagate in our country the ideas for which anarchists in every land are sacrificing their lives." The appeal concluded with a reference to "the *Bolsheviki* keeping in prison and exile the Russian comrades of Sacco and Vanzetti while at the same time the communist government pleads for the friendship and favor of the American financial and commercial plutocracy."[99]

Berkman reported that the Soviet authorities had arrested an anarchist in Odessa merely for having this leaflet in his possession. That arrest prompted an open letter to the authorities from Olga Taratuta, a Ukrainian anarchist originally imprisoned by the tsarist government in the 1900s for an attempt on the life of a government official, then freed during the Revolution. Taratuta defied the Bolshevik government to arrest her as well, since she had in her possession not one but *two* copies of the Sacco-Vanzetti leaflet, but she mockingly predicted that it would not dare do so because she was too popular in Russia and too familiar to too many people outside the Soviet Union. Taratuta charged the Bolsheviks with arresting anarchists simply because they were less prominent than she was. At that point, Berkman concluded, anyone who supported Sacco and Vanzetti anywhere in the Soviet Union was in danger of arrest, exile, or worse. At the same time that the remaining anarchists were harassed and imprisoned, Stalin ordered the construction of the famous Sacco-Vanzetti Pencil Factory, outside Moscow—an establishment that would forever associate, among the Soviet citizenry, the names of the two men with the pencils and crayons that their children used—and had many streets and squares throughout the Soviet Union renamed in honor of Sacco and Vanzetti.[100]

The ramifications of Stalin's policies quickly became evident outside the Soviet Union. But they had an effect very different from what many anti-Communists later claimed. The Communists did not "take over" the Sacco-Vanzetti camp; rather, they joined it, then helped splinter it. Communist Party leaders everywhere immediately dropped out of any cross-ideological Sacco-Vanzetti protests and proceeded to denounce other left-wing protesters as traitors to the revolutionary cause. In France, for example, where the left-wing agitation over the case had been more intense than perhaps anywhere else in Europe, this translated into a war of words between anarchists and Communists, and the Sacco-Vanzetti camp there split just at the moment the case reached its conclusion (and the affair reached its peak). The violent riots in Paris on August 23, 1927, for instance, which broke out in direct response to Sacco and Vanzetti's executions, were dominated by Communist activists, who at the same time refused to participate in Sacco-Vanzetti rallies organized by anarchists. In the United States, the Communists took to denouncing the Boston defense committee (which, to be sure, did everything in its power to dissociate itself from all radical political expression, including and especially Communist), and all other non-Communist Sacco-Vanzetti activists, as stooges of the bourgeoisie.

Mussolini and Stalin were just two of numerous international political figures who helped transform the Sacco-Vanzetti case into an affair and shape the course it took. In the weeks before the execution, as the case began to consume the time and energy of governments outside the United States and turned into a real diplomatic crisis, leaders of U.S. allies in Europe made direct appeals to Fuller and Coolidge. Chief among them were the former (and future) British prime minister Ramsay MacDonald, who also discussed the case at length with Fuller over dinner in Boston and later said that "the whole affair is just too terrible," and the former (and future) French premier Edouard Herriot, who told reporters in Paris, "To the depths of my soul I am against this punishment."[101]

Early in the summer of 1927 it appeared that Sacco and Vanzetti might be spared after all. The wave of global and domestic protest, now coming from the highest political echelons as well as from activists and intellectuals, finally seemed to be working. Even U.S. Secretary of State Frank Kellogg could not remain indifferent to goings on abroad, and he alerted Coolidge to the fact that "the Sacco-Vanzetti case has aroused ill-feeling against America in foreign countries to a critical point."[102] Fuller himself, bombarded with appeals from abroad and under pressure from political, religious, and business groups at home, announced in late June that the executions, scheduled for July 10, would be stayed for a month so that he could conduct an "independent study" of the case. For this purpose, he took the unprecedented step of appointing a special advisory commission, headed by Abbott Lawrence Lowell, the president of Harvard University and a man favored by many liberals because of his reputation as a champion of free speech and education reform.

No event in the course of the affair sparked as much enthusiasm among Sacco and Vanzetti's supporters as the formation of this commission. Their closed-door investigation lasted three weeks, during which Sacco and Vanzetti's liberal defenders, in particular, believed that justice, finally taken out of the hands of a retrograde provincial judge and put in the hands of an enlightened scholar, would at last be served. When on July 24 Lowell and his more modest associates (MIT president Samuel Stratton and former probate judge Robert Grant) turned in a flimsy report that vindicated the trial and verdict and granted Fuller the legitimacy to refuse clemency, no event, as we shall see, was more devastating to the Sacco-Vanzetti camp, especially its leadership.

Based on Lowell's recommendation, and the results of his own so-called independent study, Fuller announced on August 5 that the execution of Sacco and Vanzetti would go forward. The protest that followed his decision, especially in Europe and Latin America, was the most massive that the affair had provoked until that point.[103] Violence also re-hit the United States. On August 6 bombs went off in the basement of a church in Philadelphia, at the home of the mayor of Baltimore, and on a New York City subway platform. As in 1920 and 1921, the perpetrators were never identified, but the authorities told the press that they thought the bombs "were exploded in sympathy for Sacco and Vanzetti."[104] Less than thirty-six hours before the scheduled August 10 executions, Fuller postponed the date again, to August 23, so that Sacco and Vanzetti's lawyers could attempt one last time to rescue their clients through the courts. Celestino Madeiros, the confessed criminal who was scheduled for electrocution (for another murder) on the same date, was also kept alive, presumably in case he should be needed as a witness in a new trial.

The last thirteen days of Sacco and Vanzetti's lives were an anguished emotional period for everyone involved. The governor received a barrage of petitions, appeals, and visits from prominent citizens and foreign dignitaries. The Federal Council of Churches sent him an appeal two days before the executions stating that "in view of the uncertainty among conservatives as well as radical citizens as to the guilt of Sacco and Vanzetti, we think it would be against humanity and public policy and would shock the moral sense of the nation to allow their execution." Meanwhile, many workers in the United States had finally stirred into action: strikes and rallies in support of Sacco and Vanzetti took place in a number of cities, including New York and Detroit.[105] But the center of tension was Boston, which turned into a militarized zone as thousands of people congregated in the city for a deathwatch, and the authorities cracked down on the protest. The police arrested dozens of protesters, including such young literary stars as John Dos Passos, Dorothy Parker, and Edna St. Vincent Millay. For some it was their first (and in some cases, not their last) significant engagement with the political issues of the day.[106]

Outside the United States, American diplomats and foreign governments had their hands full, to say the least. United States embassies were heavily guarded around the clock. General labor strikes took place throughout Latin America. Huge, often violent demonstrations were held in Paris, London, Berlin, Mexico City, Buenos Aires, Dublin, Geneva, Cape Town, Belfast, Vienna, Copenhagen, Budapest, Brussels, Stockholm, Sydney, and many other cities around the globe. For a brief but crucial moment, the significant ideological and social distinctions between democrats, revolutionaries, anarchists, ordinary workers, and even business magnates, in the United States and elsewhere, blurred into a general catharsis of support for what the *New Republic* called "the two most famous prisoners in the world." In France, for example, warring right-wing royalists and left-wing revolutionaries, who otherwise saw eye to eye on absolutely nothing, both expressed outrage at American justice. In usually peaceful Copenhagen, thousands of protesters rioted in the streets and wounded several policemen. In Geneva, where some of the fiercest violence occurred, a crowd of at least five thousand demonstrators attacked the League of Nations offices (where their wrath was directed in particular at the Woodrow Wilson Memorial Library, an obvious symbol of the new American dominance of European and world affairs), overturned American-made cars in the normally quiet streets, attacked and stoned hotels where American tourists were staying, tried to break into the U.S. consulate, destroyed the American Express headquarters, looted stores selling American goods, and broke into cinemas showing American films. They were dispersed only after firemen began using hoses and the police shot into the crowd; one person at least was killed and thirty-five were injured. To worried observers, Americans and non-Americans alike, it appeared clear that should the Massachusetts authorities insist on going ahead with the executions despite all the appeals and anger from abroad, relations between the United States and the rest of the world might never be the same. The *New York Times* correspondent in Paris warned that "the extraordinary outburst of European opinion on this matter has raised the question whether, even if [Sacco and Vanzetti] are guilty, it might be better not to execute them."[107]

In the last days before Sacco and Vanzetti were finally led to the electric chair, they were failed by the only people in the United States who when all was said and done were in a position to help them. Coolidge remained adamantly silent throughout the national and international storm. He received personal appeals from MacDonald, Herriot, and other foreign leaders, as well as from prominent American citizens, urging him at the very least to follow Wilson's example in the earlier case of Tom Mooney, who, though still in prison for life, had been spared the death sentence. "Those of us long devoted to the Americanization of foreign-born citizens," the social worker Jane Addams implored in a letter from Chicago to the president, "believe that clemency in the Sacco-Vanzetti case would afford a great opportunity for the healing of wounds and for a real reconciliation between Anglo-Saxons and Latin peoples." But Coolidge was a different kind of politician from Wilson, and his nonchalant style included staying out of what he preferred to consider an internal Massachusetts affair. Besides, August was vacation time, and "Silent Cal" was busy in the Dakotas—riding around in a cowboy suit, being made an honorary member of the Sioux tribe, inaugurating the first carvings at Mount Rushmore, and fishing for trout. The unsavory Sacco-Vanzetti business, and the complaints of foreigners, did not merit an interruption.[108]

More crucial, no U.S. Supreme Court justice was found who was willing to grant Sacco and Vanzetti's lawyers a writ of habeas corpus based on Thayer's prejudice against the defendants and overrule the Massachusetts supreme court's upholding of the verdict. Chief Justice William Taft was vacationing in Canada, but no one in the Sacco-Vanzetti camp expected the conservative Taft to save the day anyway. More devastating (and, as it turned out, fatal) to the defendants were the refusals of Louis Brandeis, progressive judicial icon and formerly Frankfurter's mentor at Harvard, who recused himself because his wife (another friend of Elizabeth Glendower Evans's) had temporarily taken Sacco's wife and children into their home, and especially of Oliver Wendell Holmes, the "Great Dissenter," a hero to a generation of American progressives.[109]

The last-ditch attempt to get Holmes to intervene in the case illustrates the drama and tragedy of Sacco and Vanzetti's last days. Their lawyers, Arthur Hill and Herbert Ehrmann, made a trip to Holmes's summer home in Beverly Farms, Massachusetts, where they met on the elderly man's porch. The lawyers pleaded with Holmes, repeating the more outlandish aspects of the case (especially Thayer's out-of-court outbursts) and explaining that he, Holmes, was the only person between Sacco and Vanzetti and the electric chair. Holmes, Ehrmann later recounted, was "deeply moved" and told the attorneys that "there was nothing he would rather do than grant their request," but he saw no way in which he could act: "You don't have to convince me that the atmosphere in which these men were tried precluded a fair trial," he reportedly said, "but that is not enough to give me, as a federal judge, jurisdiction over the case. If I listened to you any more I would do it. I must not do it," he added, then went back inside his house. The visit was over.[110]

For a great jurist, Holmes was applying peculiarly circular reasoning. He could not interfere, as he later explained in an official memo, because he had "no authority to issue [a writ of habeas corpus] unless it appears that the court had no jurisdiction of the case in a real sense . . . but I cannot think that prejudice on the part of the presiding judge . . . would deprive the court of jurisdiction . . . and nothing short of a want of legal power to decide the case authorizes me to interfere . . . with the proceedings of the state court." To Holmes, interfering with the authority of a state court would be a high crime on the part of a federal judge: "The relation of the United States and the Courts of the United States to the States and the Courts of the States," he explained, "is a very delicate matter that has occupied the thoughts of statesmen and judges for a hundred years and can not be disposed of by a summary statement that justice requires me to cut red tape and to intervene."[111] The *New York Times* reporter Louis Stark wrote a decade later (in a period during which Sacco and Vanzetti were widely considered the victims of a primitive justice system and the Red Scare), "To Holmes, the preservation of the fabric of federal-state relations was a principle higher than life. It was what he had fought for as a lad in the Civil War."[112]

But Holmes was not the only powerful figure who would, at the last moment, turn his back on the two doomed men. In the first week of August, Senator William Borah of Idaho, the Republican chairman of the Senate Committee on Foreign Relations, wired to the defense committee in Boston his offer of services if the case were reopened. He believed that Sacco and Vanzetti were innocent, and partly for this reason he would help kill in its infancy Fuller's dark-horse bid to become the Republican candidate for the 1928 presidential election, or even Herbert Hoover's vice-presidential running mate. The newly formed Sacco-Vanzetti Citizens' National Committee in New York wired Borah in desperation, beseeching him to go to Boston. The committee even began making practical arrangements for his trip. But Borah replied by wire that while he would have liked to volunteer his services, "It would be difficult to leave for east before 28th." He would have arrived five days after Sacco and Vanzetti had already been executed.[113]

There was more to Borah's reluctance than just bad timing. Addams, in another eleventh-hour letter, implored the Republican senator to help prevent the executions "on the grounds that to put through the execution in the face of such universal protest might . . . embarrass our relations with other nations"; Borah's reply revealed that for him going ahead with the executions was ultimately a matter of national pride. "The fight for Sacco and Vanzetti can properly be based on innocence or unfair trial and that alone," he wrote back, "[but] it would be a national humiliation, a shameless, cowardly compromise of national courage, to pay the slightest attention to foreign protests or mob protests at home," and added, "This foreign interference is an impudent and willful challenge to our sense of decency."[114]

The last human barriers between Sacco and Vanzetti and their inexorable ends were thus removed. It was now only a matter of time; the deathwatch in Boston and elsewhere continued. Fuller was the only remaining hope, but given the stamp of approval he had received from the Lowell commission he did not seem likely to change his mind, despite the legions of progressive celebrities and notables who made pilgrimages to his office just before the execution, including Congressman Fiorello La Guardia of New York, Paul Kellogg, editor of the *Graphic Survey*, John F. Moors of the Harvard Corporation, and Waldo Cook, editor of the *Springfield Republican*. They all emerged ashen faced. "I watched them leave the Governor's office without hope," recalled Stark. "It was no use, they said. They felt an air of unreality about the whole thing. Never have I seen a more dejected lot."[115]

While the controversy around them swirled to its peak, Sacco and Vanzetti spent their last moments on death row feverishly writing letters to family, friends, and supporters. Vanzetti was consoled somewhat by the dramatic arrival of his older sister Luigia, who made the trip from Villafalletto to plead for his life. Sacco was on his last hunger strike, this one lasting twenty-five days. As the clock wound down, the Italian sections of Boston were put under near-military curfew. Demonstrations around the world grew even more intense. Finally, just after midnight on August 23, 1927, Madeiros, Sacco, and Vanzetti reached the end of the line. Felicani apparently made one last-ditch attempt to stop the executions by bribing an electrician at the prison to shut off the current at the right moment. But the authorities were tipped off, and the electrician was caught and replaced.[116]

Madeiros was electrocuted first; he had eaten so much at his last meal that he became violently ill and did not have much to say when asked for his final words. Sacco was next. Reportedly, his last words were "Viva anarchia!"; then, in English, "Farewell my wife and child and all my friends . . . good evening, gentlemen"; and, just before the fatal current hit him, a mere whisper: "Farewell, *mama.*" Last to the electric chair was Vanzetti. He calmly shook hands with the guards and the warden, who was said later to have wept. "I wish to tell you I am innocent and never committed any crime, but sometime some sin," Vanzetti said to the men present. "I thank you for everything you have done for me." The last thing he reportedly said was, "I wish to forgive some people for what they are now doing to me."[117]

News of Sacco and Vanzetti's executions, with all the lore their final words created, resulted in massive protests, riots, and casualties wherever the two men and their cause had supporters—which was practically everywhere. Six years of unbearable tension exploded at once: the most violent protests (and the most casualties) occurred the day after the executions, and some of the most genteel newspapers in Europe, Latin America, and even the United States could barely contain their shock and outrage at what many saw as both a cold-blooded murder and an affront to justice and decency.[118]

There was a tragic quality to some of the ways that even the most obscure people took the news of Sacco and Vanzetti's deaths. In a mill town in Quebec, a factory worker named Gaetano Pepitone shot and killed another worker, John McNally, with whom he had had a raucous argument over the executions; Pepitone, who believed the two Italians had been innocent, was tried for murder, convicted, and executed in late 1927. And in another bizarre and telling incident, a Venezuelan sailor named Tameto Tesada was stabbed and killed in a Brooklyn poolroom after confronting a group of men whose loud discussion of the Sacco and Vanzetti executions, he felt, was disturbing the quality of his game.[119]

But whether the reactions were major or minor, the execution of the two Italian anarchists was by no means the end of the Sacco-Vanzetti episode; in many ways, it was just the beginning. What had started in 1920 as the local arrest of two seemingly inconsequential immigrant workers had evolved into a traumatic event with profound repercussions throughout the social order, around the world and over time. The affair as a whole—the function of American justice, the political context, the class dynamic, the ethnic factor, the transatlantic relationship, the intellectual engagement, and the day-to-day, year-to-year drama—transcended Sacco and Vanzetti's ordeal and extended beyond their community of supporters. The fallout from the execution came soon and lasted long.[120] And the bitter debates that accompanied the legal and political process went on, as men and women in the United States and abroad grappled with the significance of the case. Sacco and Vanzetti were dead, but the Sacco-Vanzetti affair lived on unabated, perhaps even stronger, without them.

CHAPTER 2

Americans Divided

"Foreign Interference" and the Execution of Sacco and Vanzetti

I n the wake of Sacco and Vanzetti's executions and the powerful worldwide reaction to them, it was easy to forget that only a few months earlier the case had appeared likely to go either way. The first week of April 1927, in particular, had been a palpably tense time for the entire Sacco-Vanzetti camp. The defense committee in Boston was now working nights as well as days. Sacco and Vanzetti were still alive, but time was running out. The case was nearing its conclusion: that month, the Massachusetts supreme court rejected Sacco and Vanzetti's appeal, and their lawyers, led by an increasingly frustrated William Thompson (who would soon resign), were preparing for their clients' return to Thayer's court, where the hostile judge was sure to sentence them to death. It was then, on the brink of what the State Department labeled the global "Sacco-Vanzetti crisis," that a surprising cable from Europe arrived at the defense committee's overcrowded office on Hanover Street. There was nothing unusual about foreigners writing to the committee with words of encouragement, petitions, clippings of supportive editorials, and even money. But this message was different. The Swedish newspaper *Tidningen Vrand*—the unofficial organ of the Social Democratic Party, then in power in Sweden—offered to pay for Georg Branting, a Stockholm attorney and the son of the late prime minister Hjalmar Branting, to join Sacco and Vanzetti's legal team. The defense committee politely declined Branting's services, cabling the Swedes that the defendants were already in capable hands.[1]

But Branting decided to make the trip anyway. In a letter to the defense committee, he explained that "all of Europe takes an enormous interest in the Sacco-Vanzetti affair. . . . Swedish opinion has, however, wanted to go further and decided to send a judicial representative, in order to make an objective study of the case." On his way to the United States, Branting first went to London and then Paris to learn about the repercussions of the case elsewhere in Europe. He then sailed to New York, finally arriving in Boston on May 26. It was perfect timing for such an "objective study": one month after Thayer had sentenced Sacco and Vanzetti to death and shortly before Fuller appointed the Lowell advisory commission. The affair, in the United States as elsewhere, was nearing its climax.[2]

The local press reported widely on Branting's arrival in Boston, where he was greeted—mobbed, according to some reporters—at the train station by "thousands of Sacco-Vanzetti supporters." The city had refused a request to hold a parade in his honor, and the police also foiled a spontaneous attempt to have Branting make a speech to the gathered crowd outside Faneuil Hall. Finally, to inquisitive reporters the visitor from Sweden, who apparently had not expected such an effusive welcome, stated that "America gives an example to the world, so it is natural that there is a widespread attention to her actions." When questioned about his political affiliation, Branting explained to the Boston newsmen, most of whom were not especially well-versed in the nuances of the western European democratic left, that he was "a socialist in the Swedish sense, not at all in the Karl Marx meaning. I am not a communist nor a Bolshevik."[3]

Sacco and Vanzetti's American legal defenders watched all this with some trepidation. For them, Branting's visit created an immediate dilemma. They had already turned down his legal services, but how should they react to his arrival? The defense committee debated whether to hold a welcome reception but ultimately decided to help Branting in his "research" without creating any unnecessary fanfare. As they saw it, his presence in Massachusetts was a distraction from the task at hand; he was stepping into a hornets' nest and could only harm the efforts to save the defendants' lives. They had already embarked on the political process of appealing to the governor, and the pressure on Fuller to reexamine the case was mounting. The main problem with Branting's visit as the defense committee saw it was the potential reaction on the part of people already hostile to the two Italians. Branting was a respectable enough figure, not a radical, but he was also a foreigner. As if to confirm the defense committee's fears, the press reported shortly before Branting's arrival that a group of "Boston citizens" had written to Secretary of State Frank Kellogg, demanding, in vain, that the Swede not be let into the country. "A foreigner," they argued, "has no ethical right to inject himself into a case which is purely domestic."[4]

Branting made things even more complicated for the defense committee when the press reported, just a few weeks after his arrival, that he had cabled a preliminary report to Stockholm proclaiming Sacco and Vanzetti "quite innocent." The quickness of Branting's conclusions may have contradicted his promise to make a "thorough study" of the case but not his unhidden goal of helping the two condemned men. "I can only explain the verdicts [against Sacco and Vanzetti]," he wrote to his Swedish funders, "by prejudice against Italian witnesses and radical defendants."[5]

Still, the defense committee's worries may have been exaggerated. Branting, as it turned out, was surprisingly well received outside the coterie of Sacco and Vanzetti's prominent supporters. The Boston Bar Association, thinking perhaps of its own public relations, asked him to be the first guest at its new club. The *Boston Herald* eagerly described him as "one of the most brilliant lawyers in Sweden" (though it would be hard to see just how the *Herald* could know this) and covered his visit favorably.[6] And the *New York Times,* which had previously been hostile to Sacco and Vanzetti, commissioned F. Lauriston Bullard to cover Branting's trip.

During his stay in Massachusetts, the Swedish lawyer ventured to the scene of the crime in South Braintree, studied documents in the Boston Athenaeum, interviewed Fuller, tried (unsuccessfully) to meet with Judge Thayer and District Attorney Katzmann, and visited Sacco and Vanzetti in prison (where he forged a warm bond with Sacco). Shortly before Branting left the country, Bullard wrote, "In a few days [Branting] returns to Stockholm to render the report of his trip. . . . It should be interesting reading. It may also be important, because European opinion is likely to depend greatly on Mr. Branting's conclusions."[7]

Before leaving, Branting made a last statement to the press that made no secret of where his sympathies lay: "I came here, seeking the truth, unprejudiced, and calm—I studied the records and now each day as I learn more of the truth of the case my indignation grows greater and greater." At the same time, he raised even higher the already lofty expectations among many Sacco and Vanzetti supporters that the two defendants would be rescued: "My hope that these men will not die is strengthened because of my interview with Governor Fuller. . . . His decision will be just." When Branting first came to the United States, he explained, he had believed, based on his talks with outraged sympathizers in London and Paris, that "the majority opinion of your people was against these two men." The few weeks he spent in New York and Boston had changed his mind: "I feel now that there is an increasing reversion of that opinion, as proven by the interest of some of the best minds in America." He even took the opportunity to compliment the Massachusetts prisons, which he found surprisingly modern. The jail in Dedham, he remarked, "is a splendid building, lit, clean, well-managed"; in Sweden, by contrast, "jails are not so human."[8]

Less than two months after Branting's return to Europe, Sacco and Vanzetti—despite the Swede's sunny predictions to the contrary— were electrocuted. In the year that followed, under the shadow of his deep disillusionment with American justice, Branting wrote a summary of his American trip. It was never published in English, however, and as a result his ideas never had any impact on the ways historians have described the receptions of the case in the United States and Europe. Branting drew startling conclusions about the American and European frames of mind concerning the case and the executions sixteen years before another Swedish visitor to America, Gunnar Myrdal, helped publish a celebrated social-scientific study of the problem of race in the United States.[9]

In the international history of the Sacco-Vanzetti affair, Branting was unique among non-Americans in that he actually visited the United States and examined the case up close and at its height. But looking at the affair in broader perspective, he was only one of countless foreigners, particularly Europeans, who became involved with Sacco and Vanzetti's ordeal in a variety of ways—petitions, letters, appeals, strikes, contributions, demonstrations, and, in extreme cases, bombings and other violent acts—and helped transform a local, domestic case into the global cause célèbre that reached its boiling point in the summer of 1927. Because the case was first turned into an *affair* abroad, the controversy over Sacco and Vanzetti in the United States in 1927 became to some degree a debate over how to respond to its powerful repercussions in Europe and elsewhere. In other words, the Sacco-Vanzetti affair in the United States was in some ways a reaction to the creation of the Sacco-Vanzetti affair abroad. The more foreigners protested Sacco and Vanzetti's fate, and the more petitions arrived in Fuller's office, and the more American newspapers carried reports about demonstrations abroad, the stronger the backlash in the United States to that protest grew—especially when it seemed increasingly likely that the international Sacco-Vanzetti campaign might actually work, and the defendants would not be executed after all. This "foreign interference," as Senator Borah would put it in his letter to Jane Addams, became in the summer of 1927 perhaps the dominant component of the controversy over how to resolve the case of the two anarchists. Branting's visit to America touched, then, on two of the most burning questions that came up as the date of the executions neared: Did Europeans—or any other foreigners—have the right to "inject themselves in a case which is purely domestic," as the "citizens of Boston" had put it? And what attention, if any, should Americans pay to opinions about the case coming from abroad?

This was not the same as the well-documented struggle between "internationalists" and "isolationists" that had been at the forefront of the recent fall of Woodrow Wilson, for instance.[10] Nor was it a general debate over whether the United States should be involved in world affairs; from a political and economic perspective, especially after World War I, this was no longer seriously in doubt. Nor was it merely a part of the ongoing debates over immigration, though this too was ultimately an important part of the broader context of the affair. It was also very different from the controversy that arose a decade later over whether the United States should become involved in the new global conflict. At the height of the Sacco-Vanzetti affair, perhaps the most pressing internal issue for Americans was whether to accept the reciprocal, even inevitable, consequence of American global supremacy: the interest and involvement of non-Americans, especially Europeans, in U.S. affairs (and, in the case of Massachusetts, the intervention of out-of-staters in the affairs of the state). In the early morning hours of August 23, 1927, as Sacco and Vanzetti were finally electrocuted, the anti-outsider position enjoyed a momentary triumph, with long-lasting repercussions and implications. But the broader struggle over America's place in the world was far from over.

When Branting visited the United States, Sacco and Vanzetti were no longer championed only, or even mostly, by frightening radicals calling for their immediate release in "a dozen unintelligible tongues."

Their lawyer was a well-connected Massachusetts conservative; their most prominent supporters occupied spacious offices at the Harvard and Yale law schools; their cause had spread from the pages of *L'adunata* and the *Daily Worker* to the editorials of respectable, even mainstream American newspapers and magazines, from the *Atlantic Monthly* to the *New York Times* to *Life*. They even had the cautious but previously unlikely support of a former president of the Boston Chamber of Commerce, Roland Boyden; of Bishop William Lawrence of the Massachusetts Episcopal Diocese; of some of the most influential modernist Protestant clergymen in the nation; and, after much reluctance, of the powerful Boston archbishop, William Cardinal O'Connell. All these men, in their own ways, called on the state authorities to reopen the case and appoint an external review commission, or at least to grant the prisoners clemency.[11]

For the many Americans who took an abiding interest in the case but felt that Sacco and Vanzetti were no more than Red murderers who deserved no sympathy, the situation in 1927 was probably even more disturbing in some ways than that in 1920. If previously the enemy of "one-hundred percent" Americans could be more easily identified as the alien, the militant worker, the revolutionary—the radicals who had stood by Sacco and Vanzetti from the beginning of their ordeal—by mid-1927 that enemy had become much harder to recognize. It was one thing that "eggheads" and "do-gooders" like Felix Frankfurter and the ACLU, as one pamphlet put it, were helping the "red murderers"; civil liberties groups and free-speech advocates had been active in such causes since before 1919. But self-defined "one-hundred-percenters" must have found it dismaying that even the Sons of the American Revolution—a bona fide patriotic group if ever there were one—voted down, at their annual convention in 1927, a resolution to issue a statement of support for Sacco and Vanzetti's death sentence; that Henry Ford, never known as a friend or supporter of radicals, made a plea for Sacco and Vanzetti's lives shortly before their executions (and in return even received a friendly letter from Vanzetti himself); and that, perhaps most confusing, Sacco and Vanzetti's list of supporters in 1927 included the Fascist League of America.[12]

Over the years, historians, journalists, and pundits have referred, usually in vague fashion, to the profound divisions that the case created among Americans in the 1920s, a supposed era of economic prosperity accompanied by deepening "cultural conflicts" and simmering (but repressed) class tensions. Since the late 1920s these divisions have been the particular focus of people who saw the Sacco and Vanzetti executions as a truly dark moment in American history. What those divisions were actually about and what they indicated about American life in the 1920s have remained something of a mystery, however.

In 1928 the young critic Edmund Wilson wrote that the Sacco-Vanzetti case "revealed the whole anatomy of American life, with all its classes, professions, and points of view, and all their relations, and it raised almost every fundamental question of our political and social system."[13] In 1936 an angrier and more radicalized John Dos Passos, in his trilogy *USA*, reflected on the executions and declared, "Alright, we are two nations." And more recently, the late historian Arthur Schlesinger, Jr. (whose family had been engaged with the Sacco-Vanzetti case for eight decades), stated that the case revealed "the deepest conflicts in American life." But what were these divides, these "deepest conflicts"? Who stood on either side of the divide, and what did they stand for?[14]

In 1929, not long before the stock market crash, Wilson made clearer what he meant. The Sacco-Vanzetti case, as he saw it then, was the product of the "combined timidity and capacity for solidarity of the people whose incomes depend . . . on industry, commerce, or finance." The execution of Sacco and Vanzetti "was one of the most conspicuous and terrible triumphs of [the] stupidity and cowardice of the American capitalist mob."[15] Class, according to Wilson, Upton Sinclair, and many other writers, was the primary divider of Americans, in the Sacco-Vanzetti episode as in all other major social and political issues. This interpretation was enshrined in the 1930s by the many young intellectuals who were radicalized first by Sacco and Vanzetti's execution and subsequently by the Depression and who wound up either in or at the margins of the Communist movement. It later became a liberal commonplace: as William Leuchtenberg wrote in 1958, "Since all the forces of upper-class respectability—Judge Thayer, the governor, the president of Harvard, the best old families of the cradle of democracy—had a part in the affair, the execution of Sacco and Vanzetti appeared to be an act of class reprisal."[16]

The other great American divide, so runs a fairly established historical narrative, was over "race" or ethnicity—what one scholar has termed "the ethnic factor in the Sacco-Vanzetti case" and what W. E. B.

Du Bois called "the problem of the color-line." (He did not mean a division solely between the "white" and "negro" "races" in the United States, but rather "the relation of the darker to the lighter races of men in Asia and Africa, in America and the islands of the sea.")[17] In 1920s America, Sacco and Vanzetti were probably on the wrong side of this line. Of equal importance as class, for many of those writing about the case ever since the 1920s, was the fact that Sacco and Vanzetti were Italians, perhaps the immigrant group least liked by early twentieth-century American nativists, especially in New England.[18] Finally, the third factor that spelled doom for Sacco and Vanzetti was the fact that they were avowed radicals at a time when it was particularly disadvantageous to be so. Taken all together, this left the two luckless men—proletarians, Italians, *and* anarchists—with little chance of survival in Red Scare–era America.

These three pillars of interpretation (class, ethnicity, radicalism) were what Sacco and Vanzetti themselves used to explain their predicament. In this sense, writers like Wilson and Dos Passos, struggling after August 1927 to make sense of the case and its awful conclusion, essentially echoed Sacco and Vanzetti's speeches in Thayer's court just before the judge sentenced them to death. Sacco, staunch revolutionary to the end, stressed the first pillar ("I am here today on this bench for having been of the oppressed class"), while the somewhat more flexible and reflective Vanzetti spoke of the other two pillars ("I am suffering because I am a radical and indeed I am a radical. I have suffered because I was an Italian and indeed I was an Italian.")[19]

Wilson, Dos Passos, and Schlesinger Jr. were right: the Sacco-Vanzetti case did reveal fundamental cleavages within American society. Sacco and Vanzetti were also right: their socioeconomic, ethnic, and especially political background played indispensable parts in their ordeal and demise. But as ways to explain the impact their case had on American public opinion in the late 1920s, specifically why the case turned into a national (as well as international) affair, radicalism—or, looking at it another way, antiradicalism—is probably a more important explanation than class and race, both of which worked in this instance on a somewhat abstract level. These latter two categories do not sufficiently illuminate, for example, what occurred in 1927, when the affair was at its height.

The dramatic transition over the course of the 1920s from case to affair meant that the trial occurred in one context—in which class

and ethnicity played more crucial roles—while the execution occurred in another. Wilson and Dos Passos, as well as Schlesinger Jr. and
other historians, never made the crucial distinction between the two
events. In 1921 Sacco and Vanzetti were relatively anonymous and
powerless, their defenders marginalized, their supporters isolated; in
1927 they had friends (and opponents) at all levels of Massachusetts,
and American, society. Their cause did not unite the "working class" in
their favor—or the "ruling class" against them—in any concrete way.
(Leuchtenberg in this sense was wrong: it cannot be said that "all the
best old families" had a part in their executions.) The labor movement
played a relatively marginal role in the campaign on their behalf, as we
have seen. And not even the Italian community was in agreement over
the issue.[20]

Nor was there much of a connection made, by the public generally or among black intellectuals specifically, between the Sacco-
Vanzetti case and the plight of African Americans. Du Bois himself
published two articles about the case (after the executions) and even
wrote a short, striking, unpublished drama about Sacco and Vanzetti,
whom he saw as victims of the same systematic persecution and injustice that plagued blacks in the United States and elsewhere. But he
also acknowledged that although for him the Sacco-Vanzetti case was
"significant," this was true of "few other Negroes."[21]

The trial of Ossian Sweet—the Detroit black man accused and
later acquitted of killing a white man who had attacked his home—took
place in 1925, two years before the execution of Sacco and Vanzetti, but
the main activists in that case, drawn from the ranks of the "talented
tenth" (elite black intellectuals like James Weldon Johnson and Walter
White), were not to be found in or around the Sacco-Vanzetti affair.
Indeed, there was little political or public overlap between the two
cases, which can be seen as having different origins and implications for
different publics; nor did the Sweet case reverberate nationally or internationally the way the Sacco-Vanzetti case did.[22] The few other black
activists and intellectuals who were notably affected by the Sacco-
Vanzetti case primarily became adherents of the Communist Party: the
International Labor Defense (ILD) leader William Patterson, who
would describe the Sacco-Vanzetti case as "a turning point" in his
"conversion" to communism (and who lamented, like Du Bois, that
"most of my Negro friends couldn't see the political significance of all
this"), was perhaps the best example of this phenomenon.[23]

Already while Sacco and Vanzetti were still alive, and even more so after they were executed, their case was imbued with as many meanings as there were people moved by their story. On a deeper level, class and race (or ethnicity) were probably primary causes not only for why Sacco and Vanzetti were tried and convicted but also for why they became such totemic symbols during the decades that followed. Their execution may seem to historians like an event predetermined by the broad forces that shaped early-twentieth-century American history, and thus not surprising. But for a brief period in 1927 their execution was not at all a sure thing. Scholars have to answer a question that has never really been posed in isolation: Why, in fact, were Sacco and Vanzetti executed?

It is not enough to say that the executions in 1927 followed directly from the convictions in 1921 and that Sacco and Vanzetti stood no chance in 1920s Massachusetts; simply put, too much had happened on the way from conviction to execution, and too much had changed in the context of the case. Scholars have not yet examined the impact of the various receptions of the case—the affair—on the figures of power who were in positions to help stop the executions. In this regard, one of the most common assumptions about the history of the case is that Sacco and Vanzetti were executed in spite of all the worldwide protest on their behalf. But a closer look at the controversy immediately before and after they were led to the electric chair suggests that they were put to death in part because of it. It was not only a matter of punishing radical workers, as so many protesters insisted. Nor was it just another case of nativism flaring up against two undesired immigrants. The tumultuous reception of the case among Americans in 1927 brought into sharp relief a fundamental (but not always clearly articulated) nationwide conflict between those willing or eager to take into account foreigners' or outsiders' opinions, and those who rejected them, or, more broadly, between a view of the United States as part of an international community in which ideas (as well as things) were meant to move freely across borders and a view that insisted on the country's principled separateness from the rest of the world.

It would be an exaggeration to state that the issue of class did not enter the Sacco-Vanzetti controversy at all. It did, in various ways: because of Sacco and Vanzetti's background, this aspect of the case was obvious from the start. But as a source of actual conflict, class featured mostly within the Sacco-Vanzetti camp itself, which was basically split into two contrasting views—radical and liberal—of what the case meant and what the campaign should be about. Both sides would later offer passionate and mutually accusatory explanations of why the campaign ultimately failed.

Radical and liberal supporters more or less agreed that Sacco and Vanzetti had found themselves on trial, then on death row, because they were working-class immigrant radicals. The dispute was over how to connect this fact to the legal and political realms, how to translate it into strategy. There were, of course, many Sacco-Vanzetti protesters in the United States for whom class was almost everything in the case—more important perhaps than Sacco and Vanzetti themselves. The 1921 trial, viewed this way, did not stand on its own as a single judicial aberration in a provincial state but was rather part of the ongoing oppression of the American working class. The socialist leader Eugene V. Debs, nearing the end of his tumultuous life, declared in his late-1926 "Appeal to American Workers" that Sacco and Vanzetti were tried and convicted because they were "agitators," as capitalists see labor leaders, "too rigidly honest to be bribed, too courageous to be intimidated, and too defiant to be suppressed."[24] What made their case unique, if anything, was the remarkable reaction it had sparked worldwide. Many radical activists in the United States might have wondered why the Sacco-Vanzetti case received so much attention while the case of Tom Mooney was relatively ignored.[25]

The younger socialist leader Norman Thomas, just ten days before the executions, similarly insisted that the Sacco-Vanzetti case was "an example of class justice or rather injustice." In an editorial released by the League for Industrial Democracy, Thomas argued that the liberal leaders of the defense campaign, while "useful," were misguided; Sacco and Vanzetti's ordeal could be explained only by "the rooted determination, conscious or subconscious, of the dominant class . . . to uphold its immediate interests and passions at all costs." And within the Sacco-Vanzetti camp, as Thomas saw it, the great divide between radicals and liberals was over the fact that "the presuppositions and preoccupations of the dominant class, even when it apparently gropes after fairness, are not the presuppositions and preoccupations of the workers. . . . When all is said and done, in a world without class divisions and without class prejudice, Sacco and Vanzetti would not now face death."[26]

Less prominent radicals than Debs and Thomas shared their outlook, even if they couched it in somewhat less sophisticated terms. Mainstream newspapers tended to caricature these protests; and the authorities, in some places, treated them as a form of insanity. Early in August 1927, for example, the press carried a story about an eighteen-year-old Chicago teenager, Aurora D'Angelo, who made a name for herself as a popular leader of Sacco-Vanzetti protests in the city. During one such rally in the south side of the city, D'Angelo jumped on a truck and screamed for the crowd to follow her to city hall. The Chicago police violently dispersed the protest with tear-gas bombs, and D'Angelo was arrested for disturbing the peace. That night she gave an interview in prison. Laughing in the face of a condescending reporter who compared her to Joan of Arc, she replied, "Joan of Arc? Uh! Emma Goldman was ten times better than Joan of Arc. . . . I'm sick of this darn jail. Why don't they book me? They said they might keep me here a week before they book me. I'd stay two years in jail if it would help Sacco and Vanzetti any. . . . Sacco and Vanzetti—no, they're nothing to me. It's the masses, labor! Action—that's what we got to have." She was next sent to the "psychopathic laboratory," where, as the *Chicago Tribune* nonchalantly pointed out, "persons causing undue trouble to the police are taken these days," before winding up on trial.[27]

But D'Angelo's story was something of an exception. In her own city, Chicago, historically a center of radical labor activity (and where the Haymarket bombings, police riot, and subsequent public executions of four anarchists had taken place in 1887), no major labor leader took charge of any large organized Sacco-Vanzetti protest. The rallies and strikes that took place immediately before the executions were small consolation to militant labor groups who had had so much more success in organizing, if not in achieving their goals, just one or two decades earlier. The press treated D'Angelo and others like her as a source less of menace than of bemusement. And according to a report in the *Chicago Tribune*, just two days before the executions the city's workers were relatively uninvolved in the Sacco-Vanzetti protests, leaving much of the task to "intellectuals" like Jane Addams: "Local proletarians seemingly have subsided into silence and inaction, either because of lack of enthusiasm or police readiness, leaving only the amateur Bolsheviks to carry on with the aid of their bourgeois allies from the east [coast]. Union labor has disowned the 'issue'; radicals of the unions have deserted or excused themselves from the 'cause.' " In its issue of the following day, the same paper added, not without a certain satisfaction, that the impending execution of Sacco and Vanzetti was ignored by the business session of the labor federation "and was greeted only by shrugs and indifference," while "peace and harmony prevailed" at the annual outing of Chicago's Italy-America Society, attended by about two thousand Italian-born Chicagoans.[28]

Because of its preeminent position in the Sacco-Vanzetti camp, the defense committee in Boston was consistently at the heart of the liberal-radical strife. Sacco and Vanzetti had all sorts of friends and supporters, but there was always a hierarchy: above all, they trusted their Galleanista comrade Aldo Felicani, Vanzetti's close friend. Ultimately, Felicani was responsible for the transformation of the militant campaign of 1921 to the more mainstream effort of 1927 by opening the door to such people as Gardner Jackson and Felix Frankfurter and by pushing out Fred Moore (the "blatherskite from out west," as Frankfurter would condescendingly call him). As the cause gained momentum in the mainstream, previously prominent radical supporters like Carlo Tresca, Elizabeth Gurley Flynn, and Eugene Lyons slipped (or were pushed) somewhat out of sight. The ILD and other Communist groups, to their frustration, were not allowed in the central campaign. All these sidelined supporters, however, continued their activities in earnest.

The defense committee in Boston, with its 1927 leadership that teamed a veteran Galleanista like Felicani with a hobnobbing liberal like Jackson, and its headquarters on Hanover Street, just down the road from the symbolically loaded Paul Revere House, can be seen as a sort of late-1920s precursor to the antifascist patriotic Popular Front of the 1930s. But because at the height of the affair the defense committee eliminated any ideological dimension from the Sacco-Vanzetti campaign and refused to connect it to any broader social or political struggle, the more militant left loathed it and refused to accept its premier status in the camp.

In 1927 the goal of the defense committee and its liberal friends was, simply, exclusively, to save the defendants. As they saw it, social criticism was not their business; many of them liked and benefited from capitalism quite a bit. Operating under the still-heavy shadow of the Red Scare, often as terrified and contemptuous of Communists or anarchists as any ordinary *Main Street* American, many liberal Sacco-Vanzetti sympathizers were driven by their persistent fear of public opinion, which, they assumed, tilted heavily against the defendants. This led them to reject Branting's help, to seek legitimacy at the highest levels of state and national power, to discourage demonstrations and other popular protests, to engage in wars of words with Communists, and to hope against hope for Sacco and Vanzetti's salvation from a businessman-turned-politician like Fuller. The liberals' seemingly unshakable faith in the system (and their fear of the "masses") drew the ire of militants, who demanded a "class-based" struggle on behalf of two "revolutionary comrades." As an ILD pamphlet put it after the executions, the proletariat had been cruelly cheated out of the chance to create "a movement to defend all workers ... a unified, non-partisan class defense movement upon which all elements in the labor movement could find a common platform." To such radicals—who probably never believed that Sacco and Vanzetti stood much of a chance at clemency—a potentially great cause had been hijacked by lily-livered social climbers who were cozy with the fat-cat establishment.[29]

These radicals, in turn, filled Sacco and Vanzetti's legal team and their liberal fellow travelers with dread. In 1927 the Sacco-Vanzetti controversy was accompanied by a sharp rise in violent acts—including the bombing of the home of one of the original jurors in June and a supposed attempt on Fuller's life in May, along with numerous attacks on American targets abroad—all of which, as the liberals saw it, had the effect of setting back Sacco and Vanzetti's cause in general public opinion. Many of Sacco and Vanzetti's progressive supporters also shared Walter Lippmann's deep distrust of the "public," which he saw as irrational and easily manipulated.[30] But progressives like Lippmann, rather than distinguish between violent acts and the legitimate anger of radical protesters, often made connections between them instead. Lippmann's own newspaper, the *New York World,* spent nearly as much energy attacking the radicals in the Sacco-Vanzetti camp as it did criticizing the injustice done to Sacco and Vanzetti. As late as August 13, well after the Lowell commission had broken liberal hearts on both sides of the Atlantic, a *World* editorial argued that even more than Fuller or the Lowell commission, "there is no question ... that the activities of the communists and anarchists are the greatest of all obstacles now in the way of a reconsideration of the Sacco-Vanzetti case." The editorial railed against "those demented creatures who think they can help Sacco and Vanzetti by blowing up innocent people." The extremists were "egotistical fools more concerned with their own irrelevant propaganda and with relieving their own emotions than they are with the course of justice and the fate of the two men. If the radical movement . . . has leaders with any sense whatsoever . . . they will stop exploiting this case for their own end. . . . They have not influenced by a hair's breadth the processes of the law in favor of Sacco and Vanzetti. They have, if anything, made them stiffer." And, revealing the profound antiradicalism that went hand in hand with the liberal criticism of the Red Scare, the editorial concluded by hoping that "respectable" people would not stop fighting for Sacco and Vanzetti regardless of the radicals: "Annoying as the behavior of the communists and the anarchists is, they can no more threaten the security of the state than they can fly to the moon."[31]

The tension between the liberals and the radicals came to a head after the executions. Communist activists felt vindicated by what they saw as the proof of the futility of having worked for Sacco and Vanzetti's freedom within the bourgeois system, and their contempt and fury poured forth in a flurry of pamphlets and articles. The Comintern sent Sacco-Vanzetti "speaking materials" from Europe worldwide in an apparent effort to make some kind of propaganda coup; but American Communists, more familiar with the case than the Stalinists in Berlin or Moscow, did not require such instructions.[32] Max Shachtman, an ILD activist, pointed to those responsible, in his view, for Sacco and Vanzetti's deaths: the "careful liberals, gentlemen of the pulpit, kindly and well-bred ladies, worried professors, men of law and learning, good Christian men and women." These people, he charged, "for five or six years had said nothing, and by their silence permitted the springing of the trap that was to kill Sacco and Vanzetti." The only chance to save the two Italians had been through a "mass workers' movement," but the defense committee's insistence on legalities and appeals killed this option since "they demanded the substitution of the movement of the masses by the movement of the lawyers. . . . They were confidently content with polite statements, public discussions; they would even go to the length of expressing indignation and surprise. . . . Being essentially well bred they would countenance no 'misguided action' by 'ill-advised and irresponsible people.' And this meant no action by the working class." To hammer home his point, Shachtman repeated Sacco's description in one of his letters of his Brahmin champion Elizabeth Glendower Evans: "Poor mother! She is so sincere and faithful to the law of the man that she has forgot very early that the history of all the government it were always and every-time the martyrdom of the proletariat."[33]

But the ILD's interpretation of the case was based on a good deal of wishful thinking. There had been no mass workers' movement to save Sacco and Vanzetti in the 1920s, nor could there have been; Communists, who had little strength in the period (despite the imaginings of both 1920s Communists and 1960s anti-Communist conservatives), could not do much for the defendants and had little influence among American workers; liberal Sacco-Vanzetti defenders were sharper and more determined than the ILD gave them credit for; and in any case, liberals could hardly be faulted for the lack of a mass workers' protest. Besides, Sacco and Vanzetti's own letters showed that the two anarchists had welcomed the support of liberals, Brahmins, and intellectuals, and consistently supported and trusted the defense committee; for Sacco and, especially, Vanzetti, the support of famous bourgeois intellectuals was not only a pleasant surprise but even a point of pride. And as committed anarchists, they viewed the Communist movement (and the Soviet Union specifically) as hierarchical, oppressive, and an imprisoner of the proletariat.[34]

Another post-execution, class-based assessment of the affair, its tone more elegiac than angry, came from the shattered, declining IWW. That group had been in the thick of the Sacco-Vanzetti action in 1921, but after Moore's departure from the case in 1924 it was increasingly marginalized in the campaign. Generally, the 1920s were not kind, to put it mildly, to militant labor groups in the United States. So-called welfare capitalism—the ensemble of divide-and-conquer techniques devised by industrial employers to co-opt the unions and avoid the labor demands and debilitating strikes of earlier years—combined with ruthless union busting, the conservative and employer-friendly leadership of the American Federation of Labor (AFL), and the widespread mainstream notion that unionism was inherently revolutionary, effectively put an end to successful militant labor organizing, at least until the New Deal revived the unions in the 1930s. In 1927, at their low point, IWW activists could feel only despair at the defeat of their goals—owing, in their view, to the lack of class consciousness on the part of the American workers on the one hand and the brutal determination of the ruling establishment to deny workers their rights on the other.[35]

The Colorado miners' strikes of 1927 may have been the IWW's

last tragic hurrah. On August 7, the employees of the Colorado Fuel &
Iron Company (owned by John D. Rockefeller) went on a strike organized by the Wobblies, protesting both their own dismal working
conditions and the upcoming Sacco and Vanzetti executions. It was
probably the most significant labor protest in the United States in
(partial and indirect) response to the Sacco-Vanzetti case. It did not
stop the executions, but in November, three months after Sacco and
Vanzetti's deaths, the IWW-led miners went back on strike—this time,
nearly eleven thousand men (according to the IWW) refused to return
to the mines. Not surprisingly, the company, along with the Colorado authorities, reacted with a brutality that recalled the worst of the
1919–1920 period: the (first) so-called Columbine Massacre occurred
in Serene, Colorado, on November 21, 1927, when six strikers were
killed and several more injured by state policemen who fired machine
guns on a crowd of about five hundred picketing miners and their
families. In the end, the miners won a dollar-a-day increase in salary, at
a terrible price.[36]

It is against this background—the violent suppression of the Colorado miners' strike, the deaths of Sacco and Vanzetti, and the general sunset of militant labor—that the late-1927 IWW pamphlet *The
Bloodstained Trail* appeared and should be understood. The pamphlet's striking cover showed droplets of blood falling into a vesicle,
and the text depicted the Sacco and Vanzetti executions as the culmination of more than fifty years of murderous repression of the American proletariat by the capitalist ruling class. Workers in industrialized
1920s America, according to the authors of the pamphlet, had not
grasped the Sacco-Vanzetti case's deeper meaning: "In the U.S., [class
warfare] is perhaps more pronounced than in any other place in the
world . . . but in America, unfortunately for the working class, the
workers are perhaps less educated to their class position than any place
in the world. . . . The appalling ignorance of this condition . . . was
displayed by the millions of workers who failed to realize the class
significance of the Sacco-Vanzetti case."[37]

Yet despite their harsh view of the liberals who after the executions had wound up with egg on their faces, the IWW did not try to
claim that radicals could have done any better—certainly not without
the massive workers' support that, the IWW readily conceded, was
simply not there and could not have been under the circumstances.[38]
Little, after all, could be expected from American workers at large

if the hesitant AFL president, William Green, ostensibly the formal leader of the entire labor movement, waited until the final two weeks before the executions to finally join in the growing calls for clemency. Other, more conservative labor figures had refused to support Sacco and Vanzetti at all, arguing that they represented a menace to decent, ordinary American workers.[39]

By blaming each other for the failure to save Sacco and Vanzetti, neither their liberal nor radical supporters—both of whom, in their own ways, wanted to prevent the executions—provided a convincing answer to the question of why Sacco and Vanzetti were executed despite the impressive campaign on their behalf and the fact that their trial had been clearly shown to have been unfair. It is worth stressing the obvious point that neither side in the camp could make an actual decision about the executions one way or the other. But looking from the Sacco-Vanzetti camp outward, rather than inward, provides a more fruitful perspective for historians trying to make sense of the case's outcome.

By 1927 Sacco and Vanzetti's most devoted opponents in the United States were no longer worrying about a working-class uprising or the menace specifically presented by Italian immigrants as much as they were about the foreign, radical aspects of the campaign on the anarchists' behalf. Indeed, the terms *foreigner* and *radical* (or *Red*) were often used interchangeably, and this fixation with the two perceived threats came to a head after Judge Thayer's verdict in October 1926, when European and Latin American protest began to reach unprecedented proportions. For the Henry Ford–owned *Dearborn Independent,* for instance, there was not much of a difference, when it came to foreign involvement in the Sacco-Vanzetti affair, between planting a bomb at a U.S. embassy and signing a petition. Nor, for that matter, did Ford's newspaper make distinctions between protest at home and abroad or between revolutionaries and liberals in the Sacco-Vanzetti camp. In a December 1926 piece entitled "Government by Bomb," the editors declared that "because Sacco and Vanzetti happen to be members of a revolutionary party a great hue and cry is raised on their behalf. . . . Demands for their freedom are made by radical organizations and newspapers throughout the land. . . . Bombs are exploded in front of United States embassies the world over. American diplomats are menaced. The homes of witnesses who testified against

Sacco and Vanzetti are blown to atoms. The judge and jury who tried them are victims of retaliatory acts. Governor Fuller, visiting in Paris, is threatened with death unless he accedes to the demands. Substitution of the bomb for ordered law . . . is a dangerous experiment."[40]

The piece, though exaggerated, captured a homegrown, conservative perception of the Sacco-Vanzetti campaign as simply an attempt to destroy America from within and without. At the same time that many liberals and radicals were jolted into action by what they saw as a terrible injustice, other Americans could not help obsessing over the most violent features of the worldwide Sacco-Vanzetti campaign (which were dutifully reported by the mainstream press and trumpeted by the Bureau of Investigation under Hoover) and the danger that the "Reds" supposedly still presented to the American people. The intellectual support for the two anarchists had, for the most part, begun later than the threats and bombings that accompanied the case since its beginning; and for many, even in 1927, support for Sacco and Vanzetti simply meant more "red" violence, new wine in old bottles.[41]

The worries of Sacco and Vanzetti's liberal defenders about public opinion may have been understandable, and some historians of the case have assumed that they were right to be concerned. "Public opinion" is notoriously difficult to measure even after the advent of scientific polls, and there is no way to determine with any clarity what the majority of the citizens of Massachusetts, Americans more generally, or even people around the world thought about the case in 1927.[42] But many conservative-minded Americans saw with worry a growing support for the two anarchists among broad swaths of the public. As far as they could tell, the postwar national drive for "law and order"—which had led to the election in 1924 of President Coolidge, taciturn crusher (as Massachusetts governor) of the 1919 Boston police strike—was being sacrificed on the altar of false gods like "civil liberties" and "free speech." The support for Sacco and Vanzetti among intellectuals and other elites was particularly angering to those who claimed to speak on behalf of "ordinary" Americans.

In the preface to his 1950 collection of essays *The Liberal Imagination,* the literary critic Lionel Trilling remarked that conservatives in America did not usually express real ideas but rather "irritable mental gestures which seek to resemble ideas." And a generation of liberal scholars more or less agreed with Richard Hofstadter's complementary observation that because "in its politics the United States has been so reliably conservative a country during the greater part of its history, its main intellectual traditions have been, as a reaction, 'liberal.' " Conservatives, in other words, did not need to develop a full-bodied system of thought because they basically controlled the country. In this respect, the Sacco-Vanzetti affair, on its face, seems to vindicate Hofstadter's intuitive view. For all the protests, essays, and petitions of major intellectual figures in the United States in support of the Sacco-Vanzetti cause, there was relatively little articulated intellectual justification of the Sacco-Vanzetti trial, verdict, and executions. There was no equivalent counterweight to prominent defenders like Frankfurter or Lippmann; presumably there was no need for it, since political power was in the hands of the executioners.[43]

The most prominent public attacks on the Sacco-Vanzetti campaign had a decidedly populist flavor, even when voiced by supposedly strict conservatives. In April 1927, John Henry Wigmore, dean of the Law School at Northwestern University, an erstwhile progressive and reputedly the nation's leading expert on evidence, published in the *Boston Evening Transcript* what many of Sacco and Vanzetti's opponents had hoped to see in print: a furious attack on Felix Frankfurter, who had published his influential article on the case in the *Atlantic Monthly* a month earlier. Relatively little of Wigmore's much-anticipated piece, however, dealt with the legal matters that Frankfurter had discussed, or even with Wigmore's own area of expertise, evidence. Instead, Wigmore focused more on what he called the "international aspect" of the case—a topic that Frankfurter had raised only cursorily. Wigmore was so upset at Frankfurter's intervention in the Sacco-Vanzetti affair that he could not even bring himself to mention the Harvard professor by name. Instead, he repeatedly referred to Frankfurter as "the plausible pundit"—who, Wigmore charged, "fails to tell us the reason [the case] has aroused such international interest." The reason, in Wigmore's view, was that "the two accused appear to be valued members of an international fraternity or cabal or gang who have . . . sought to give aid to their convicted associates by the most extensive system of international terrorism that the world has known for a century." He warned that "if [this terrorism] had succeeded, justice in the United States would be at its mercy." Wigmore followed this accusation with a laundry list of every attack or violent act committed against Americans at home and abroad since the Sacco-Vanzetti case began—all of them, in his view, in direct response to the case—and concluded: "Is not this an intolerable state of things, that American justice should be subjected to the dictates of international terrorists? This insensate resort to violence is invoked in a case which has been misrepresented, by the cabal, all over the world, as a case of persecution of radicalism. The dangerous thing to American justice is that the local representatives, by pressing a button, can set this international force in motion to secure immunity for any one of its members who is charged with any serious crime." Frankfurter, to Wigmore, was perhaps even worse than the cabal itself, because, as he saw it, "the plausible pundit . . . knowingly enlists himself in their support and appeals to the public at large to excite popular sympathy in favor of . . . this international terrorist gang."[44]

On reading Wigmore's attack, the well-connected Frankfurter immediately contacted his friends in the Boston press and published a response that appeared on the same day in both the *Transcript* and the *Boston Herald*, sticking to his legal critique, pointing out Wigmore's errors of detail, avoiding discussion of the case's "international aspect," and refraining from name-calling. Wigmore then wrote a second article, largely reiterating his points about the "plausible pundit" and the international Sacco-Vanzetti "cabal." There were no great new legal insights to this exchange; Wigmore did not know nearly as much about the case as did Frankfurter, and this plainly showed. What it demonstrated, rather, was the nature of the Sacco-Vanzetti affair as it looked to Wigmore and those who shared his view: that the United States was under attack, and a straightforward Massachusetts legal issue had turned into a matter of national defense.[45]

The tussle between the two law professors spilled out from the pages of the Boston dailies—already an unusual forum for what was supposed to be a legal debate—and into the broader public sphere, revealing just how deep into the national mainstream the Sacco-Vanzetti case had moved. In May, the National Civic Federation (NCF)—a group founded in 1900 by progressive business and labor leaders seeking to eliminate conflicts between industry and organized labor and whose honorary president that year was Elihu Root, with members that included Theodore Roosevelt (until his death in 1919) and Columbia University president Nicholas Murray Butler—asked Fuller to sponsor a public debate between Frankfurter and Wigmore, to be held in New York City and broadcast nationwide by radio. The NCF suggested that such a debate could help the governor decide how to re-solve the Sacco-Vanzetti case. But Fuller did not take up the offer, and so neither Frankfurter nor Wigmore had the opportunity to accept or refuse.[46]

There are additional sources that reveal something of the thinking of what Richard Nixon, had he been in politics at the time, might have called "the silent majority," though in this case the voices were far from silent. At the same time that Fuller received countless petitions for clemency, he was also sent letters by lawyers, professors, doctors, and some calling themselves "ordinary people," demanding that he uphold the verdict and, after the formation of the Lowell commission in June, expressing disappointment or even anger that he did not re-main resolute about the executions.[47] U.S. Congressman Charles L. Underhill (Republican of Massachusetts) made a fiery speech in Wash-ington denouncing "red activities in this country" (further evidence that the Red Scare was not completely over) and made a direct appeal to Fuller, demanding that the governor "show courage" and not give in to the growing requests for clemency.[48] And the *Boston Herald*'s mild criticism of Sacco and Vanzetti's treatment, beginning in late 1926, provoked a particularly angry batch of responses from readers. Ac-cording to one typical letter, the anarchists' defenders were "lily-fingered highbrows, professional publicity seekers and chronic sym-pathizers who simply cannot bear that anyone, anywhere, at any time, should ever be punished for any crime, no matter how heinous." Writ-ing on behalf of what the he called "the plain people," this indignant citizen felt that Sacco or Vanzetti's actual participation in the South Braintree crime was "unimportant," since the murders were carried out "by some ones who had the same objects, the same ideas of social life, the same beliefs and purposes. . . . They had all the same disregard of social obligation. . . . They were potential murderers all." Sacco and Vanzetti, "whether or not they actually fired the shots . . . are just as guilty." This was an absurd assertion on many levels (to begin with, Sacco and Vanzetti were tried and convicted for the nonpolitical crime of banditry), but its lack of internal logic was beside the point; the issue was whether the Massachusetts authorities would go through with the executions or buckle under the pressure of foreigners and subversives.[49]

Perhaps the purest expression of this public sentiment came from a Massachusetts state functionary by the name of Frank A. Goodwin, appointed in 1919 to the newly created position of state motor registrar by then-governor Coolidge. Goodwin made something of a name for himself in 1927 by widely delivering a speech that he ominously called "Sacco-Vanzetti and the Red Peril" to such captive audiences as the Lawrence, Massachusetts, Kiwanis Club and the Cape Cod Lodge of Odd Fellows. Goodwin had little to say about Sacco and Vanzetti's original trial, to which he devoted just a few words. Nor did the dignity of the state's courts much concern him, as he often showed elsewhere with considerable contempt. Instead, Goodwin focused on Sacco and Vanzetti's public defenders at home and their radical supporters abroad and the threat that these groups together represented to ordinary, hard-working, God-fearing Americans.[50]

The speech was a perfect cocktail of populism and jingoism. "The Sacco-Vanzetti case," Goodwin informed his audience, "is a blessing in disguise. It has dragged out into the open the enemies of our country, not only those who openly plot to overthrow it by force, but those who are insidiously tearing down the institutions that have made it possible for us to become the greatest nation in the world." The way he (and probably his audience) saw it, Communists or other open radicals were far less dangerous than those, like Frankfurter and the ACLU, who posed as patriotic Americans but actually represented totally un-American values. Sacco and Vanzetti to him were merely two additional names on a long list of Reds championed by subversive eggheads in New York.[51]

Those who had appealed to Fuller on behalf of the two "red crooks" were, in Goodwin's view, "all in the same boat: the sob sisters, who believe that the community should not protect itself from the degenerates and the criminals; the pacifists, who teach internationalism . . . and who believe we are citizens of the world, rather than of our country, and the Reds, whether they are the type that throw bombs, or the intellectuals, who now have control of our colleges, and are teaching nonsense to our children." Goodwin also urged his listeners to "send your children where one-hundred percent Americanism is taught." The defenders of Sacco and Vanzetti were not just out to save two Reds but to wage war against the sacred American institutions of home and family. After a sordid description of deteriorating sexual norms at colleges, especially women's institutions, Goodwin added that "almost 100 percent of the presidents and teachers in these [women's] colleges have signed petitions for the release of Sacco and Vanzetti."⁵²

Goodwin's speech does not fit with the familiar historical portrait of the 1920s as a period in which complacent conservative values and an unchallenged business ethic ruled supreme over cowed consumers, frightened fundamentalists, shattered unions, flighty flappers, and escapist intellectuals. The "do-gooders" and supporters of "Reds," in Goodwin's worried worldview, were both wealthy and powerful; they were quite willing to use "mobs" to achieve their goals; and, most alarmingly, they were winning the battle against the one-hundred percenters. The only forces within American society that could block their way to complete victory, Goodwin warned, were such groups as the American Legion, the Daughters of the American Revolution, the Elks, the Odd Fellows, the Knights of Columbus, and patriotic business organizations like Kiwanis and Rotary.⁵³

Ultimately, it was a matter of defending the American people against dangerous foreign and subversive influences. As Goodwin put it, "It is an impressive fact that that the nearer we get to the scene of the murder, the more convinced are the people that these men are guilty." On the other hand, "in those domains where foreign and un-American principles are in vogue, such as Russia, Harvard, Argentine [*sic*], Wellesley, China, and Smith College, they are sure these men are innocent."

Despite the demand of many Americans that foreigners keep their noses out of the "internal" Sacco-Vanzetti affair, many non-Americans obviously did not keep quiet on the issue. This was particularly true of British observers, for whom it was easy to jump directly into the public fray. As opposed to, say, French or Latin American critics, British intellectuals wrote in English, had fast access to American newspaper and journal editors, and were generally much more familiar with the networks of American political, cultural, and intellectual life. The professional intimacy that already existed between many British academics and journalists and the American universities and journals that hosted them helped, ironically, to create a unique degree of friction and criticism. We might also speculate that the colonial past of the United States and the "special relationship" between the two countries had something central to do first with the quickness and volume with which British intellectuals wrote critically about the Sacco-Vanzetti case (and about American faults and foibles generally) and second the touchiness that many American readers (especially in New England) demonstrated on reading them.[54]

Britain did not experience the same remarkable degree of popular and political response to the Sacco-Vanzetti case as did, for example, France. But in that country, too, the reception of the case was noisy and violent enough that even a political leader like former and future prime minister Ramsay MacDonald felt it necessary to make direct appeals to Coolidge and Fuller on behalf of the two anarchists. British critics—unconstrained by the control of a Mussolini, as in Italy, or by the language barrier, as in Argentina—made some of the most angered and controversial commentaries on the case. And perhaps no British (or European) writer was better situated to make his feelings about the Sacco-Vanzetti issue known to an American public than H. G. Wells. Familiar to a general educated public in the United States as the author of such utopian and science fiction novels as *The Time Machine* and *The War of the Worlds,* Wells also carried weight as a political thinker, social critic, popular historian, and founder of the Fabian movement. For many American progressives and social reformers, in particular, Wells wielded enormous influence as a strong critic of unrestrained industrial capitalism and a consistent champion of the modern benevolent experimental state. He was one of several European public figures who went beyond the acts of signing petitions and sending cables to American leaders. Like the French authors Anatole France and Romain Rolland, for example, who shared his pan-European and internationalist sensibilities, Wells tried to join the internal discussion of the case by writing directly for the American public—in his case, in the *New York Times* (which reprinted articles he published first in the *London Daily Express*). Some Americans would consider this in itself an act of provocation.[55]

Wells began to pay attention to the Sacco-Vanzetti case in 1926, following Thayer's rejection of the Madeiros appeal. And as it was for many other Europeans of his background, the prime fuel for his engagement was the dissemination of Frankfurter's *Atlantic Monthly* article and book on the Sacco-Vanzetti trial. Not only did Wells's tone become more agitated with each article he wrote, but he refused to stick to the topic, moving from a criticism of the process—with which he was not intimately familiar and whose legalities did not particularly interest him—to an examination of present-day American ills. In reading his comments, it is worth imagining the ways in which American readers with a developed sense of national pride might have reacted to them.

For Wells, the Sacco-Vanzetti affair was "more dismaying from some points of view even than the long tale of atrocities on which the fascist dominion in Italy rests today." No less than the most momentous event in recent history, the affair called for "the closest study on the part of every one who is concerned with the present development of our civilization." He presented a distinctly European point of view, first by casting the net of responsibility for the case on all Americans and barely mentioning the state of Massachusetts; second by contextualizing the case in the dramatic rise of U.S. global power and the country's newly unchallenged place in the world after the Great War; and third by emphasizing the idea that Sacco and Vanzetti were persecuted for their radical politics. "The case," he stated, "has passed out of the purview of courts and persons, and become a challenge to every American citizen. The fact, plain as day and staring the world in the face . . . is that the greatest, most powerful, and modern state in the world is now confronted with the question of whether it will permit these men to be killed upon a false accusation because of their political beliefs. Is their blood to stain Old Glory?"

Wells shared the common liberal obsession with Thayer, now an almost cartoonishly villainous figure to many people around the world, but whereas American liberals tended to see the elderly Massachusetts judge as an aberration, Wells saw him as "tremendously normal," typical of Americans of the day. He wrote contemptuously of "Thayerism," a mindset that had "taken over American society" and was closely related to the rise of fascism in Italy. The most characteristic traits of Thayerism, perhaps surprisingly, were honesty, integrity, and a deep sense of obligation to one's country. Thayerism was not evil or corrupt but rather human and even sympathetic. Wells was "quite willing" to credit Thayer and the other Americans who shared his way of thinking with "intelligence, integrity, and public spirit." But, he added, "it is crude intelligence, dull integrity, and sentimental public spirit. They have under-developed minds; the minds of lumpish overgrown children. They have had no fine moral and intellectual training. They have lived in an atmosphere where there is no subtle criticism of

conduct and opinion, where everything is black and white . . . everything is overemphasized. To be bad or wrong . . . is to be outlawed and
not given a dog's chance."

All in all, Wells assured his readers, Thayer and his ilk "mean well.
That is the tragedy of the situation. . . . The Judge Thayers of the
world, just as much as the Saccos and Vanzettis, want the world to be
fair and fine . . . but Thayerism has the upper hand." Wells ended his
first *Times* article with a bleak warning: too many people in the United
States "believe that a little blood-letting is good for their civilization.
So did the Aztecs before them. But blood is a poor cement for the
foundation of a civilization. . . . There have been civilizations before
the present one in America, and for all the blood they shed so abun-
dantly upon their high places they have gone and are buried and stuff
for the archaeologist."[56]

This article, and the next one Wells wrote, went too far for the
editors of the *New York Times,* who had merely asked for his assessments of the Sacco-Vanzetti case but had gotten a lot more than
they bargained for: not only a highly unflattering appraisal of the
American people with their "minds of lumpish overgrown children"
but even the prediction that the American imperial republic would go
the way of the Aztecs. Wells was unceremoniously informed that his
articles would no longer be published stateside.[57]

One of those most displeased by Wells's writings, and by similar
speeches he made on the subject, including an address at the Sorbonne
in Paris, was Senator Borah, who in an essay of his own in the *New
York Times* assailed Wells as an enemy of American democracy. Later,
as we have seen, Borah declined Jane Addams's request that he intervene with Fuller or Coolidge before the executions because it would
be "a national humiliation . . . to pay the slightest attention to foreign
protests or mob protests at home."[58]

There were others in the United States who responded angrily to
Wells's commentaries. One reader of the *Boston Evening Transcript*
warned that "Americans will not readily forget or forgive the noisy
intrusion of many prominent literary men of Britain into a matter into
which they had no concern." The letter added that "the leaders of
British thought and letters really have for us a deep contempt, as if
we were a people without national pride. . . . The wagging finger of
a scolding, preaching, half-informed Englishman can do more harm
to Anglo-American relations than all the propaganda of all the Irish

republican societies, and for that harm Britain even more than America can pay."[59]

After Sacco and Vanzetti were executed, and in reaction to these kinds of heated responses, Wells wrote an even more provocative essay that dealt with what he saw as the American "over-sensitivity" to foreign criticism. This touchiness, he charged, had ultimately doomed the two Italians. And in Wells's opinion, it was a hypocritical form of sensitivity since Americans, in high places as elsewhere, did not have similar qualms about criticizing European societies, and did so frequently. "Are Americans a sacred people?" he rhetorically asked; "Is international criticism restricted to the eastward position?"

His new essay—which the *New York Times* refused to publish and which instead appeared in Wells's next book—concerned "the right of British and European people generally to have and to express opinions about American affairs. The converse right has never been questioned, and is exercised freely by Americans throughout the world. . . . I maintain my right to think freely about the affairs of the United States, and to say what I think to be true and proper about all or any of these affairs. I refuse to regard the people of the United States as in any way a Holy People." At this point, for Wells the Sacco-Vanzetti case represented part of more general and severe problems with the United States. The reactions to his article revealed, in his view, "the extraordinarily bad temper certain types of Americans display at the mere shadow of discussion of the [Sacco-Vanzetti] case—and indeed, of any discussion of things American. One can scarcely let a sentence that is not highly flattering glance across the Atlantic without some American blowing up. No other people have so acute a sensibility." The "Sacco-Vanzetti business" was bad enough in itself, but its real significance was that it "has brought this testy impatience to its head."[60]

As an aside, one case would later prove Wells's assertions in concrete fashion. In 1929, the Icelandic author Halldor Kiljan Laxness, a future Nobel Prize winner for literature who was then living in Los Angeles, wrote a positive review of Upton Sinclair's *Boston* (which depicted Sacco and Vanzetti as the victims of an unjust capitalist society) for an Icelandic literary journal. Reportedly, although Laxness wrote the review in Norse, the Immigration Bureau in Washington, D.C., found out about it and ordered an investigation into the author's stay in the United States. Laxness was summarily summoned to the

Bureau of Investigation office in Los Angeles and, according to him, was told that only foreigners "contented with the [U.S.] government" were wanted in the country. He was then deprived of his visa and faced deportation proceedings.[61]

In Wells's view, Americans could no longer claim by 1927 that the Sacco-Vanzetti affair was strictly a domestic matter. How could it be, when government officials abroad were scratching their heads trying to figure out how to protect American diplomats and businesses, control rowdy demonstrators, prevent bombings, and deal with the growing clamor to make official appeals to U.S. leaders on behalf of the two Italians?

In the world of British letters, when it came to Sacco and Vanzetti, Wells was not alone. Replying in part to Borah's disparaging comments about foreign interference (disseminated quickly and widely in Europe), the influential journal *New Statesman and Nation* argued that "America may plead her isolation, but in fact she is not, and cannot be, isolated." The fact that authorities in London were forced to dispatch thousands of policemen, whose salaries were paid by the British people, to protect the U.S. embassy around the clock made Sacco and Vanzetti the business of any British citizen. "We cannot help but be concerned at the matter," the editorial pointed out. "Certainly it is in theory no business of ours. The Americans may kill as many of their Italian citizens as they please. . . . But if their methods lead to serious trouble in London, not to mention other civilized cities [in the world], we have every right to complain and to criticize."[62]

For Wells, too, this "right to criticize" was a matter of principle and extended beyond the immediate issue of maintaining law and order. The Sacco-Vanzetti affair had an enormous impact on the rest of the world, whether Americans were aware of it or not, because of the postwar strength and influence of the United States. It was not only the Sacco-Vanzetti issue that bothered Wells; that case, in his view, had its roots in deeper problems that he saw in postwar American society. Most crucial, the American people, with their provincial proclivities and nativist notions, were not keeping up with the loftiness of their new international station. Indeed, they seemed to be unaware not only of their place in the world but even that a world outside the United States existed at all. Wells identified the basic education of Americans as the most urgent matter in this regard: "It is a matter of concern to the whole world that the general level of education in America should be high," he wrote; but "the level of American elementary school education in America is not high enough for her immense possibilities and her limitless aspirations. . . . The insufficiency of the American common school is a danger to the peace of the world." He ended his article with a telling (and prophetic) remark: "The world becomes more and more one community, and the state of mind of each nation has practical reactions upon all the rest that were undreamt of half a century ago. The administration of justice in Massachusetts or Italy concerns me almost as much as in London. Particularly when the lives of aliens are involved . . . the world becomes my village, and whether Senator Borah likes it or not, part of me walks down Main Street and defies all America to expel it."[63]

It is tempting to dismiss Wells's criticism of American justice and society as the venting of an elitist, displaced, disgruntled British intellectual who had no impact on actual goings-on in American politics (and no direct knowledge of the case itself). But along with Frankfurter's article and book, Wells's articles were probably the most significant intellectual contribution to the Sacco-Vanzetti controversy for what they implicitly revealed about American reactions to the case as much as for what they said explicitly.

There were some crucial differences between Frankfurter's and Wells's interventions. Whereas Frankfurter's writing—cautious, legal, and politically noncommittal—had the effect of galvanizing influential liberals, without whom the Sacco-Vanzetti case would never have become an affair, Wells's impassioned and cutting writing had perhaps an even more powerful effect in a negative sense. Unlike Frankfurter, who wrote as an insider, Wells intervened in the affair as an outsider. The reactions to his engagement with the case showed how difficult it was for powerful American figures in the 1920s to come to the aid of two controversial radical—and *foreign*—defendants who were championed so publicly and prominently by left-wing foreigners, and how tempting it was to deny those appeals in order to make political gains at home. After the executions, another high-profile Sacco-Vanzetti supporter, the playwright George Bernard Shaw, confessed privately that in spite of their best intentions, foreigners who tried to pressure the Massachusetts authorities to show lenience to Sacco and Vanzetti had ultimately underestimated Americans' resistance to "outside opinion." Shaw even partly agreed with Borah that "the foreign declarations that Sacco and Vanzetti's execution would be a 'judicial murder' of two innocent men were insulting and indefensible, to say nothing of their making it impossible for the authorities to reprieve the condemned men."[64]

Wells's writings indirectly revealed what may have been at the heart of the transatlantic controversy over the Sacco-Vanzetti case. They represented, to a large degree, a post–World War I mindset popular in some European circles that saw an increasing global interlinking as both inevitable and desirable (though within a decade or so that vision would come to seem remarkably quaint). In this brave new world, as enthusiastic internationalists like Wells saw it, the American people would play a major role whether they liked it or not, and his articles thus chastised Americans not only for their alleged sensitivity to foreign criticism but also for the fact that they seemed unwilling to lead this new international community or even to participate in it. The executions of Sacco and Vanzetti—which entailed ignoring so much pressure and so many appeals from abroad—seemed retroactively to prove Wells's points.

If Wells considered Sacco-Vanzetti an international affair with American national-cultural origins, many American critics of the case, especially liberals in the Sacco-Vanzetti camp, believed that the episode had a narrower cause: the depressing transformation of Massachusetts, once the jewel in the nation's cultural crown, into a provincial, paranoid, bigoted, infighting backwater. As the progressive writer Horace Kallen put it, the state that in its "Golden Day" (between about 1830 and 1890, he estimated) had produced Emerson, Longfellow, Thoreau, and Hawthorne, and in which "very little that was spiritually significant in the national life failed to have its starting point," had become only a generation later "the laughingstock of the civilized world"—a place characterized, in Kallen's stark psychological terms, by "delusions of grandeur, delusions of persecution, economic, social, and political, and a consequent homicidal attitude toward men and ideas." These pathologies, Kallen believed, could be seen in the state's treatment of its two most famous prisoners: "Freethinking immigrant radicals of Catholic origin became the victims of a gigantic persecution complex involving in its prejudices and indecencies not only the Tory machinery of Massachusetts justice, but the presidents of Harvard and M.I.T. and the whilom Governor of the state."[65]

Scholars have long assumed that the origins of the Sacco-Vanzetti

case were to be found in the social history of Boston and Massachusetts. The story of the region has been oft described: the replacement
of much of the state's original Yankee rural population, lured away
primarily by the promise of the western frontier, by waves of poor
Catholic immigrants, particularly from Ireland, Poland, and Italy, who
flocked to the cities; the gradual but marked decay and stagnation of
the state's industry and economy; the sharpening of class and ethnic
hostilities; the ensuing rise of intolerance, censorship, and repression.
Sacco and Vanzetti's defenders saw the recent history of the state as
leading directly to the persecution of the two men, and historians have
tended to agree.[66] But scholars have not looked at how the ways that
Massachusetts was seen by people outside the state (and even by many
people from inside the state) in this period might have affected the
Sacco-Vanzetti legal and political process itself—or, to put it another
way, at the state's place in the transformation from case to affair and
the effect of that transformation on the state itself.[67] Beginning in 1927
many newspapers and journals outside Massachusetts, especially in
New York, bombarded their readers with harsh assessments of the
cultural and moral collapse of the state (and of New England generally). "In all truth," wrote Heywood Broun in his popular syndicated
column, "New York is the mental capital of the Nation. Boston's claim
to high thinking has been dead and gone these many years."[68] Two
weeks before the executions, Kathleen Millay (younger sister of Edna)
captured a widespread sentiment when she claimed, "New England as
a whole hates the rest of the United States. And New England is the
stubbornnest place in the world. The real New Englander never admits he is wrong."[69] And as the editors of the *New Republic* saw it,

> The agitation for a review of [the Sacco-Vanzetti] trial touches the Back
> Bay [of Boston] on its . . . most vulnerable spot. It is composed of an
> ethnic minority which still rules . . . by virtue of wealth and social
> prestige. It resents the idea that the processes of this rule should be chal-
> lenged by representatives of other, and, in their opinion, inferior, peo-
> ples. . . . The first article in the creed of Back Bay is that descendants of
> the early English settlers are entitled by a species of divine right to rule
> this country and particularly Massachusetts. Its apologists associate the
> welfare and security of the commonwealth with the unimpaired exercise
> of this sacred privilege. At present, however, the descendants of these
> early settlers . . . are hopelessly outnumbered. They are afraid of being
> overwhelmed and submerged. . . . They consider their own prestige and

that of their class compromised by the challenge of the Sacco-Vanzetti verdict. Thus their stubborn and impassioned defense of a doubtful conviction is chiefly a matter of pathological class consciousness.[70]

This is essentially another way of seeing the division among Americans over the case in 1927: Boston (or Massachusetts or New England) versus critics of that city (or state or region) in the rest of the country. This tense adversarial setup was psychically connected to the hostile reaction of many Americans to critical foreign opinion generally; in Massachusetts, this outlook translated into a hostility even to critical opinion coming from outside the state. For it was not only Greenwich Village bohemians and uptown liberals in New York who wrote such caustic commentaries. Some of the firmest support for the Sacco-Vanzetti cause (and the harshest attacks on Massachusetts politics and culture) came, for example, from the *Haldeman-Julius Weekly,* based in tiny Girard, Kansas.[71] In Georgia, the *Macon Telegraph* called on its readers to "make a lot of noise" about "this rotten business up in Massachusetts." The *Southern Maryland Press* likened the upcoming executions to the crucifixion of Christ. And a resident of Pikesville, Kentucky, in a letter to the *Boston Evening Transcript,* even displayed some ironic schadenfreude: "I have business in your state which I am now forced to abandon because I fear to set foot in the bloody state of Massachusetts where witches are burned and radicals are executed upon slight pretext. . . . Kentucky surrenders the title of 'bloody' to Massachusetts."[72]

Probably the most damning anti-Massachusetts feeling vis-à-vis the case was expressed by those who knew the place best. In this conflict, not even residents of the state—insiders, in other words—could be counted on to stand firm against the criticisms of outsiders. Some had escaped what they saw as the backwardness and intolerance of their home state for new vistas. "Alas for Massachusetts and Boston," wrote William Sloane Kennedy, a friend and biographer of Walt Whitman's, "for fifty years my adopted state and city—but no longer mine in spirit. Alas that I cannot now utter the names without a shudder and a feeling of shame."[73] "Throughout Europe," wrote the expatriate poet Elliot Paul, "the word 'Massachusetts' brings forth at once the words 'Sacco and Vanzetti.' Whenever a foreigner asks me where my home was and I am obliged to say Massachusetts, I feel my cheeks flushing and I realize they are thinking of Lowell, Fuller,

Thayer, and the rest of the smug company who have made the state infamous all over the civilized world. . . . The details of the case are well understood by Europeans generally, and are thought to be as grotesque as the antics of the early Puritans or of the Western moving picture stars." A typical conversation in Europe, he recounted, ran like this:

> "Where is your Home?"
> "Massachusetts."
> "Ah. That is where the witches were burned, where Sacco and Vanzetti were killed, and where books are forbidden. It must be very odd, there."[74]

Those who remained in the state were not of one mind about the case. According to Bruce Bliven, writing in the *New Republic,* Boston itself was in a virtual state of civil war. Families were divided, longtime business partnerships had broken apart, and in Back Bay social clubs all conversation about Sacco and Vanzetti was forbidden because "the arguments have been so acrimonious." Indeed, Bliven claimed, in the whole of American history, "perhaps nothing since the slavery dispute before the Civil War has created such violent differences of opinion among persons who would ordinarily think alike."[75] Likewise, Robert Lincoln O'Brien, the publisher of the *Boston Herald,* later wrote that "there has never been in this state anything like the inflamed feeling that attended this case. Newspaper circulations ran to astonishing totals. I was not here in the days of the slavery issue, but I am convinced that the disputes of that day were not more bitter than those evinced in the Sacco-Vanzetti affair." And the progressive journalist and publisher William Allen White, editor of the Emporia, Kansas, *Gazette* and the so-called "Dean of American Journalism," wrote in an open letter to Fuller: "I sprang from New England stock—as old New England stock as there is. I have just returned from New England . . . and I was surprised beyond words to find the bitterness and hate which had sprung up . . . particularly in Massachusetts, among those who fear that Sacco and Vanzetti will not be executed. Until I went to Massachusetts, into the homes of my ancestors . . . I had no idea that men could let their passion so completely sweep their judgment into fears and hatreds, so deeply confuse their sanity. I know now why the witches were persecuted and hanged by upright and Godly people."[76]

The last paragraph of White's open letter to Fuller revealed, in a sense, what was at stake in the Massachusetts-American controversy. "This is a tremendously important case for America," he wrote. "This case seems to be wider than your state. It is America, and America's justice, which is on trial."[77] For White, as for many others, this type of appeal was meant to make Fuller and other high-up authorities realize the errors of their ways in dealing with the case. But it most likely had the unintended effect of reinforcing Fuller's impression, first, that state (and even national) public opinion demanded that the executions go through, and second, that to many people calling off the executions would mean giving in to "foreign" pressures—from outside the United States generally and from outside Massachusetts specifically. Bliven in the *New Republic* described the "overwhelming demand" that he heard and saw in Boston and Massachusetts "that 'outsiders' not interfere in the [Sacco-Vanzetti] case." When John C. Hull, the Speaker of the Massachusetts House of Representatives, at a banquet of self-described best citizens remarked, "We would respectfully ask you [outsiders] to mind your business," the approximately 750 guests reportedly leapt to their feet and broke into wild, lengthy applause.[78]

One of the state's most celebrated sons (and an original product of its nineteenth-century Golden Day) was U.S. Supreme Court Justice Oliver Wendell Holmes, known as the Great Dissenter to a generation of progressives because of his groundbreaking legal opinions of earlier years. By the late 1920s, however, his brand of progressivism, heavily influenced by social Darwinism, came to many of his liberal admirers to seem increasingly intolerant, cranky, repressive, and outdated. In the 1927 case of *Buck v. Bell*, for example, the elderly Holmes ruled that he could find no constitutional grounds to bar the compulsory sterilization of a mentally retarded woman, crudely reasoning that "three generations of imbeciles are enough."[79] That same year, to his chagrin, he became embroiled in the Sacco-Vanzetti case, when a few days before the executions Sacco and Vanzetti's desperate lawyers asked him to save their clients by granting a writ of habeas corpus and overruling the Massachusetts supreme court's decision supporting Thayer's verdict. But Holmes refused to intervene, citing the strict autonomy of state legal authorities.[80] In his official statements, Holmes stood behind the letter of the law, which, he argued, allowed him to do absolutely nothing for the two condemned anarchists. But his extensive correspondence with the young British intellectual Harold Laski is highly instructive about what Holmes thought of the case aside from its formal legalities.[81]

Holmes and Laski were unlikely pen pals—for one thing, in 1927 Holmes was eighty-six and Laski thirty-four—and nowhere was the gulf between them as wide as it was over the Sacco-Vanzetti executions. Like H. G. Wells, Laski was a Fabian. He was also a political theorist, an economist, and a future leader in the British Labour Party. He knew the United States (or at least its northeastern corridor) and was no remote foreign critic: he had taught at Harvard for five years between 1915 and 1920, made numerous American friends, and written for a score of American journals.[82] Laski admired Holmes as one of the founding fathers of transatlantic reformism and regarded him as a paternal figure.[83] Like Wells and other progressive British and European writers, Laski was shaken by Frankfurter's analysis of the Sacco-Vanzetti case, and he wrote about it to Holmes repeatedly, hoping perhaps that his powerful friend would help prevent the upcoming executions.[84] After the Lowell report sent shockwaves among liberals in both the United States and Europe and provoked riots around the world, Laski vividly conveyed this anger: "With us, as I expect with you, everything is obliterated except the decision of the [Sacco-Vanzetti] case. . . . Frankly, I do not understand it. . . . The whole world revolts at this execution; and it will remain . . . one of those judicial murders which make the mind reel. I agree fully with all that Felix [Frankfurter] says of Lowell in this case. Loyalty to his class has transcended his ideas of logic and of justice."[85]

Five days before the executions, after the meeting with Sacco and Vanzetti's lawyers on the front porch of his summer home, Holmes complained in a letter to Laski, "I have not escaped the Sacco-Vanzetti case." Defending his decision not to grant the writ of habeas corpus, he made the distinction between Sacco-Vanzetti and another case, *Moore v. Dempsey,* in which he had done just that: "There had been a mob outside the court ready to lynch the man, the jury, counsel, and possibly the judges if they did not convict, and made the trial a mere form."[86] Sacco and Vanzetti's lawyers argued that their clients, in a different way, had also been tried under extreme prejudice. Holmes disagreed: "The line must be drawn between external force, and prejudice, which could be alleged in any case." The result of his decision, he informed Laski, "has been already . . . letters telling me that I am a monster of injustice." Holmes added that "the house of one of the [Sacco-Vanzetti] jurymen was blown up two or three nights ago," thus making a connection between dissent from the Sacco-Vanzetti rulings and terrorist violence. Holmes did not mention that the authorities did not know for certain who was behind the bombing, nor did he explain what that incident had to do with his actions in, or opinion on, the Sacco-Vanzetti case.[87]

Laski wrote his next letters to Holmes from Geneva, where he witnessed firsthand the furious reaction to the executions in that city: "I wish you could realize the immense damage [this] action has done to the good name of America. This case has stirred Europe as nothing since the Dreyfus case has done. And to me . . . it seems that [Sacco-Vanzetti] is indeed another Dreyfus case . . . the executions deeply affected me. The riots . . . were very bad; and both in Geneva and Paris the ill-feeling against Americans is . . . profound." Referring to Borah's statements, which had expressed in more jingoistic terms sentiments that were otherwise similar to Holmes's, Laski added: "What has angered thinking people [in Europe] most is the incredible remark that it would be 'a national humiliation if any account were given to the European protests.' As one Frenchman said to me, 'if we have to mobilize five thousand troops to protect American lives and property, we are at least entitled to consideration.' "[88]

Holmes's response directly addressed the anger Laski described. For the Great Dissenter, simply, the foreign protest over the Sacco and Vanzetti executions boiled down to a misplaced sympathy with Communists and radicals at the expense of other Americans who deserved it more: "Your last letter shows you stirred up like the rest of the world on the case. I cannot but ask myself why this so much greater interest in red than black. A thousand-fold worse cases of negroes come up from time to time, but the world does not worry over them. It is not a mere abstract love of justice that has moved people so much. . . . I see no adequate available reasons for the world outside the United States taking up the matter and I think your public and literary men had better have kept their mouths shut."[89]

Holmes's response raised a valid point: scholars still need to face the question of why the Sacco-Vanzetti cause enjoyed the kind of national and global attention that anti-lynching activists in earlier days, for instance, could only have dreamed of. On the other hand, the justice did not give an example of "cases of negroes" that went ignored

by Europeans, nor did he explain why injustices done to blacks justified the fate of Sacco and Vanzetti or rendered protest over their executions hypocritical. The letter revealed, rather, Holmes's difficulty
in adapting to some of the changing conditions of American political
and social life. The *Moore v. Dempsey* he had referred to had its origins
in a 1919 incident, typical of that year; by the late 1920s, circumstances
had changed to a certain degree. Other scholars have shown that lynchings—obviously and understandably Holmes's point of reference for
American judicial abominations deserving attention—were in gradual
numerical decline, having been largely replaced by legal, institutionalized state executions, which continued to primarily target blacks and to
which Holmes did not necessarily object.[90] Ossian Sweet, the black
man tried in 1925 for killing a white man in Detroit, had been acquitted;
it would have been hard to envision this happening just a decade or so
earlier. It was evidently easier for Holmes, whose outlook was shaped
primarily by the abolitionist movement and the Civil War, to acknowledge the injustices done to blacks. But it was harder for him to recognize the possibility that Italian immigrants and proletarian radicals
could also be on the receiving end of similar injustices and prejudices
(as Du Bois, another erstwhile Victorian progressive, saw things).[91]
Holmes also could not in the end tolerate outsider opinion, harsh or
otherwise, on what he ultimately considered an internal American, and
even an internal Massachusetts, matter.[92]

Why, then, did Sacco and Vanzetti die? Was it because of the
determination of the "ruling class" to see them dead, as the socialist left
argued? Was it due to racism or nativism? Was it the intransigence of
the trial judge? The conservatism of the legal authorities? The fears and
prejudices of the community? After the executions, many attempted to
provide answers. To the horrified Edna St. Vincent Millay (author of
some of the most passionate, futile last-minute appeals to Fuller's conscience), it was clear that the two Italians were executed not for murder,
nor even because people thought they were murderers, but because
"these men were castaways upon our shore, and we, an ignorant savage
tribe, have put them to death because their speech and their man-
ners were different from our own, and because to the untutored mind
that which is strange is in its infancy ludicrous, but in its prime evil,
dangerous, and to be done away with."[93] To the angered Heywood
Broun, Sacco and Vanzetti were killed "because they were radicals and

foreigners."[94] To the distressed Jane Addams, men in power (she was thinking primarily of Borah) "had grown confused between love of country . . . and the orthodox form of patriotism, which unhappily assumes that one's own country is always in the right and the other countries uniformly in the wrong." To the self-defined "neutral" Robert Lincoln O'Brien, "the momentum of the established order required the electrocution of [Sacco and Vanzetti]."[95]

But perhaps the most revealing answer may have been provided by the man who actually made the final decision. In 1930, former governor Fuller, his political career over and thus freed from the obligation to spout niceties, told the prestigious German left-wing journal *Weltbuhne* (probably without realizing exactly to whom he was talking) that Sacco and Vanzetti "had both confessed to being anarchists and to rebelling against the present social order. They had belonged to a band of conspirators who attacked peaceful citizens with bombs and dynamite. They were for socialism and godlessness. The American people repudiate such frivolous ideas." Fuller did not couch the case and the executions in legal terms and did not even mention that Sacco and Vanzetti had been tried and convicted for robbery and murder and not for their political activity. Instead, he stated that "the tendentious prejudice and general bitterness [in Europe] against the United States only damaged the two men. Perhaps without such pressure from outside another solution might have been possible. . . . The widespread support that Sacco and Vanzetti enjoyed abroad proved that there was a conspiracy against the security of the United States and that we should have to defend ourselves with every means at our disposal."[96]

Scholars might read this as a convenient pretext for a discredited governor seeking to blame foreigners and outsiders for the end result of the case (which from the perspective of the 1930s seemed increasingly like an injustice rooted in the Red Scare). But there are good reasons to take Fuller at face value. The veteran reporter Louis Stark, who covered the case for the *New York Times,* reiterated in 1937 that the common thinking among the beat newspaper writers assigned to the story in 1927 was that Fuller had been inclined to grant clemency to Sacco and Vanzetti but after learning of Coolidge's decision not to run for re-election in 1928, suddenly changed his mind. According to Stark, Fuller hoped to become Herbert Hoover's vice-presidential running mate in the 1928 election or even the Republican presidential nominee (on the same "law and order" platform upon which Coolidge had been elected three years earlier) and, convinced that the majority of the voting public was against saving Sacco and Vanzetti, opportunistically decided against clemency. Soon thereafter, Fuller's political ambitions were killed by Borah and other influential Republicans who thought that Sacco and Vanzetti were probably innocent and at any rate did not wish the issue to feature in the upcoming presidential race. Fuller, according to this theory, had gambled and lost. "[The Republican Party] would have to assume the burden of defending Fuller's actions in the Sacco-Vanzetti case, which was 'political dynamite,'" Stark explained.[97]

Like the question of Sacco and Vanzetti's guilt or innocence, establishing the veracity of this thesis is beyond the aim of this study. (Fuller never made such a point explicitly, and historians are not mind readers.) But Stark was merely reviving a story that had been widespread in political and media circles in the period immediately after the execution. "By the 1930s," he wrote, "the idea that Sacco and Vanzetti had been sacrificed in the name of 'law and order' was pretty entrenched among mainstream liberals and New Dealers."[98]

Even Robert Lincoln O'Brien, the *Boston Herald* publisher, could not help but notice the suddenness and strangeness of Fuller's turnabout: as O'Brien recalled, all signs had pointed to clemency for the two anarchists. In his written summary of the case in 1928, he told of his long encounter with Fuller at the Boston University commencement ceremony in May 1927. Fuller had talked freely about Sacco and Vanzetti and sounded, to O'Brien, quite hostile to the prosecution: "He told me that he should settle this case so as to live with his own conscience, as the one great determining factor in his deliberations." People close to Fuller and the state authorities, O'Brien added, expected the governor to grant Sacco and Vanzetti a new trial. One politician told O'Brien that "[Fuller] was internationally minded," that "he liked to go to Paris better than anywhere else, and to be thought of well there, and in other world centers," and that "to him the sentiments which were cropping out in European newspapers would have a substantial, even though unconfessed, influence. Now what happened?" O'Brien's answer: "A surprising number of groups and elements and factions of the community came to regard leniency for Sacco and Vanzetti as an assault upon the honor of the Commonwealth. . . ." Everywhere the tide ran with the fury of a torrent." The general public, he added, "was outraged at the possibility that Sacco and Vanzetti would be pardoned." This, in O'Brien's opinion, was enough to cause the ambitious Fuller to change his mind at the moment when under other circumstances he might have gone the other way.[99]

Georg Branting, the once-optimistic visitor from Stockholm, spent a grim year after his visit to Boston writing on the meaning of the Sacco-Vanzetti executions for Europeans. He was in a good position to reflect on what had happened in the United States: he had met with some of the main protagonists of the story, had observed the affair from within, and, writing in Sweden, he could look back on the case from a tranquil yet critical distance.

In Branting's view, the case "ended in tragedy" because "foreign opinion was robbed of much of its power [in the United States]. . . . It had nothing to lean on except moral pressures." Indeed, these "foreign pressures" may have worsened Sacco and Vanzetti's already dire situation. The main problem to Branting was that Americans, a decade after the world war and during a period of decline for the European powers, were not facing any real global foe or competition. And yet this new American feeling of omnipotence was mixed with a striking sense of fragility: "We quite knew what sort of feelings now began to awaken in the young American power, how conscious one is of one's empire's strength . . . how touchy over every feared attack on American self-determination and independence."

In order to explain the American attitude toward the world at the time of the executions, Branting asked his readers to "imagine being a young nation, perhaps the strongest in the world, the richest in the world, the most virtuous, the most energetic. . . . Imagine a great land which the gods have never allowed to suffer any veritable, large catastrophe—if we except the Civil War—and which, wherever it looks toward the horizon can distinguish no serious foe, no real danger! Think of being lifted up on a powerful wave of perpetual material betterment, of seeing the nations of the world as borrowers at its doors . . . of seeing the oceans traversed by intrepid American fliers." In this ambience, European activists on behalf of Sacco and Vanzetti had felt, as Branting put it, "like someone trying to save some trembling victim from between a lion's paws, but who dares not irritate the wild beast into ending with one blow the victim's life."[100]

Ultimately, in the debate over whether individuals or a system were the downfall of Sacco and Vanzetti, Branting came down firmly on the latter side. He assigned little personal responsibility to Thayer, Lowell, Fuller, or others. In his opinion, Sacco and Vanzetti were executed because of "mighty forces that were in motion"; the Lowell commission, in which American and European liberal intellectuals had placed such enormous hopes, was merely a tool for these forces. No other outcome, Branting now wrote in contradiction of his hopeful public statements in June 1927, could seriously have been expected. To his mind, the questions that the legal and political authorities in the United States and Massachusetts were asking themselves in the heated days of 1927 were: "Should the ruling party, with the presidential campaign impending, yield to the radicals' demands? Should one risk . . . being suspected of weakness toward the 'reds'? The answer: never, it must not happen! Foreign countries, let them go to the devil."[101]

It is safe to assume that Branting, who was back in Stockholm, did not read the self-satisfied editorial that appeared in the *Boston Evening Transcript* on August 24, 1927, the day after the executions, but it showed how correct his assessment probably was. "The Sacco-Vanzetti case," wrote the editors, "has been the vehicle of as vicious propaganda as ever deluged a community. Radicals the world over . . . saw here an opportunity to further what they call their cause. Without their meddling interference the case never would have assumed unusual proportions. . . . Many well-meaning [American] citizens either thought these foreign agitators were in earnest or were afraid of what they might do. . . . Massachusetts could not pay the slightest attention to European protests or the sentiments voiced by the journals and public men of distant lands."

In this, the editors of the *Transcript* faithfully captured the jingoism and anti-outsider feeling that ultimately did in Sacco and Vanzetti, and the editorial reinforces the impression that Sacco and Vanzetti were executed because men in positions of power made the choice to allow it happen. And these choices were made in a political context that made it seem to these individuals that clemency for Sacco and Vanzetti would mean a surrender to foreign pressures and subversive activities. These figures did not act in unison or even for the same personal or political reasons. But they either genuinely agreed with what they considered the broader public sentiment about foreign interference (as did Borah) or simply calculated that it would be better to agree with this sentiment than to gamble that saving Sacco and

Vanzetti would not jeopardize their own futures (as did Fuller). This is not to reduce the explanation for the end of the case to the machinations and calculations of a few specific people in power. Rather, given the public context within which they operated, it helps answer both the specific question of why Sacco and Vanzetti were executed and the broader question of how, and over what, Americans in the late 1920s were divided when it came to the fate of the two Italian anarchists.

In all, the Sacco-Vanzetti affair presents historians with a paradox. On the one hand, without the appeals and protests of non-Americans, there would have been no "affair" to speak of, and probably not much hope for Sacco and Vanzetti; their executions would have been carried out but without as much national and international controversy. On the other hand, these pressures and protests ultimately had the effect of damaging their chances at survival.[102] But the paradoxical quality of the reception of the case in the United States also points to the most powerful divisions that the affair ultimately created among Americans. Reactions in the United States to reactions in other countries (as well as reactions in Massachusetts to reactions in other states) set the primary terms of the Sacco-Vanzetti debate, resulting, on August 23, 1927, in a temporary anti-outsider triumph. But those more accepting of "foreign interference" would later be able to refocus attention on the case in a way that increasingly made the decision to execute Sacco and Vanzetti seem like a judicial error or political miscalculation at best, a judicial murder and political killing at worst.

Nicola Sacco and Bartolomeo Vanzetti (foreground, second and third from left) being led to the courthouse in Dedham, Massachusetts, June 1921 (AKG-Images, London)

Massachusetts judge Webster Thayer, a villain to Sacco-Vanzetti supporters worldwide, a hero to their opponents in the United States (TopFoto/Roger-Viollet)

Vanzetti (left), Sacco, and Sacco's wife, Rosina, at the prisoner's dock in the Dedham courthouse. During the trial the defendants were seated in a barred metal cage, a symbol of the menace they presented to respectable society. (Bettmann/Corbis)

Elizabeth Gurley Flynn, one of Sacco and Vanzetti's earliest supporters, addresses a rally on their behalf in New York's Union Square, August 9, 1927 (Bettmann/Corbis)

A visibly unenthusiastic meeting in support for Sacco and Vanzetti at the Danilov Factory in Moscow, 1927. Workers throughout the Soviet Union were instructed to attend sympathy meetings for the two Italians even as the authorities intensified their campaign to destroy the anarchist movement in the Soviet Union. (Roger-Viollet)

A member of the Comité Sacco-Vanzetti collects signatures for a petition to be sent to President Coolidge and Governor Fuller, Paris, May 1927 (Photograph by Henri Manuel; Courtesy of the Trustees of Boston Public Library/Rare Books)

Sacco-Vanzetti demonstration, New York, July 1927. Under the direction of the defense committee, the campaign in 1927 was aimed at an increasingly mainstream audience. (Courtesy of the Trustees of Boston Public Library/Rare Books)

Activists canvass London in anticipation of a mass Sacco-Vanzetti rally in Hyde Park, July 1927 (Bettmann/Corbis)

Harvard University president A. Lawrence Lowell, 1927. No event
in the course of the affair sparked as much enthusiasm among Sacco
and Vanzetti's supporters as the formation of the Lowell commission,
and no event was more devastating to them than the publication of
the commission's report. (Harvard University Archives, call no. HUP
Lowell, A.L., 33)

"Bestial Act of Cruelty!" Demonstrators in Berlin, May 14, 1927. (AKG-Images, London)

"Save Sacco and Vanzetti!" German protesters announcing an upcoming rally, June 1927. After Sacco and Vanzetti were executed, many in Germany viewed the United States as the "lost leader" of a free, democratic world. (Courtesy of the Trustees of Boston Public Library/Rare Books)

Sacco-Vanzetti protesters in New York, 1927 (Roger-Viollet)

Chicago teenager Aurora D'Angelo (center) at her court hearing after being arrested during a Sacco-Vanzetti rally on the city's South Side, August 1927. She was next sent to the "psychopathic laboratory," along with other protesters. (Chicago History Museum)

Sacco-Vanzetti defense attorneys William Thompson (right) and Herbert Ehrmann leaving the Massachusetts State House after meeting with Governor Fuller, June 1927 (Bettmann/Corbis)

U.S. Supreme Court Justices Oliver Wendell Holmes (left) and William Howard Taft, 1926. Holmes, known as the Great Dissenter to a generation of admiring progressives, met with Sacco and Vanzetti's lawyers but refused to stop the executions. Chief Justice Taft considered Sacco and Vanzetti "murderous anarchists" and claimed that their defenders were "closely in touch with every Bolshevist movement in this country." (Bettmann/Corbis)

While the Sacco-Vanzetti affair was reaching its height, and appeals on behalf of the two men were pouring in from national figures and world leaders, President Coolidge was on vacation in South Dakota, where he visited a Sioux reservation, inaugurated the carving of Mount Rushmore, and spent much of the rest of his time fishing: "President Catches Eleven Trout" was the headline in the *New York Times* the day after the executions (AP/World Wide Photos)

Mourning armbands were worn in Boston and elsewhere following the execution (Courtesy of the Trustees of Boston Public Library/Rare Books)

One of a series of striking cartoons on the case by Fred Ellis published in the *Daily Worker* in 1927 (Communist Party of the United States Photographs Collection, Tamiment Library, New York University)

At 56–58 boulevard Sébastopol, north of the Paris city center, a crowd gawks at a destroyed kiosk and two stores whose windows were smashed and merchandise looted in the August 23, 1927, riot following the execution of Sacco and Vanzetti (Préfecture de Police de Paris tous droits réservés)

"A Thriller for the Truth": West German publicity poster for Giuliano Montaldo's
Sacco e Vanzetti (1971), which had an enormous impact on a generation of
Europeans, many of whose knowledge of the case was based on this impassioned
but stagy film (AKG-Images, London)

CHAPTER 3

"This Frightful America Whose Heart Is Made of Stone"

The Transatlantic Affair

Sacco and Vanzetti's most bitter American opponents, men as disparate as Frank Goodwin and John Henry Wigmore, were right in one sense: from beginning to end, this was an international story. The Sacco-Vanzetti case may have taken place mostly in Massachusetts, but the Sacco-Vanzetti affair was born abroad, most specifically in Europe. Even the term *affair* itself was first used by French commentators. As in the United States, Sacco and Vanzetti attracted relatively little public attention in Europe between 1922 and 1926, when the legal process lagged and the death sentence had still not been pronounced. By late 1926 and early 1927, however, European fascination grew not only with the case itself but through it with the United States more generally. Even on a continent still ravaged and deeply divided nine years after the end of the World War I, it appeared at the peak of the affair that Sacco and Vanzetti represented a rare common denominator. Harry Elmer Barnes, a political science professor at Smith College who was in Europe when Sacco and Vanzetti were executed, later wrote of that period that "the only subject that uniformly interested all classes, from ex-emperors to communists, and upon which there was approximate unanimity of opinion, was the treatment of Sacco and Vanzetti."[1]

Concern over the case was naturally strong in Italy, the homeland of the two protagonists; but there, after the fascists' seizure of power, much of the reaction, as we have seen, was bound up with Mussolini's political interests, his ambivalent attitude toward Sacco and Vanzetti themselves, and particularly his delicate dealings with U.S. leaders and diplomats. Italy's press increasingly represented the voice of the new

fascist dictatorship, while the left was muzzled, and many of the sur-
viving radicals fled the country.[2] But although all western Europe was
affected to some degree by the case, the epicenter of European engagement with Sacco and Vanzetti was probably France; as one activist put
it, "It was as if the prisoners themselves were French."[3] Outside the
United States, Third Republic France, with its colorful press, loosely
democratic institutions, polarized political life, and lively polemical
tradition, was the site of arguably the case's most widely, diversely, and
powerfully felt reverberations. It thus offers historians the richest context for examining the ramifications of the Sacco-Vanzetti affair in its
global context: through the French responses to the Sacco-Vanzetti
case, we can get a sense of the deeper dynamics of the European and
worldwide dimensions of the affair.

There were various reasons for the broad and powerful engagement in France with the Sacco-Vanzetti case, most importantly the
legacy of the Dreyfus case, the particular (and peculiar) fascination
with the United States, and the numerical and organizational strength
of the left. However, French criticism of American justice in the Sacco-
Vanzetti case was not confined to the left. One French historian has
argued that after the popularity enjoyed by the United States in France
in the early 1920s thanks to the decisive U.S. intervention in the Great
War, the Sacco-Vanzetti affair marked the beginning of a durable
French anti-Americanism in the twentieth century. Many of the events
and reactions in France in the late 1920s and beyond bear out this
assessment. In the years following the executions a remarkable outpouring of what we might call anti-American literature emerged from
all parts of the political spectrum, although how much of this was a result of the Sacco-Vanzetti affair is unclear.[4] At the same time, Barnes's
observation about "unanimity of opinion" was wrong: French opinion
on the case was far from monolithic, and many people held views that
were favorable toward the United States and even to the authorities'
handling of the case. French responses to the case did not constitute a
simplistic anti-Americanism, at least not in the sense that this prob-
lematic term has been understood in recent years.

In broader context, it should be remembered that 1927 was a year
in which America was a source of fascination for many in France,
much of it negative but some of it quite positive.[5] To make matters more complicated, 1927 was also a crisis year for diplomacy be-

tween France and the United States, mostly as a result of official anger in France over U.S. policies on the war debt and foreign loans, and over the Americans' growing isolationism and refusal to side with the French government in its continual disputes with its newly revived archenemy Germany. In May, immediately after the French government turned down an invitation from the Coolidge administration to participate in the Geneva conference to promote international disarmament, U.S. Secretary of State Frank Kellogg described Franco-American relations as "bitter."[6] But that same month, just as intellectual anti-Americanism seemed to reach its peak, Charles Lindbergh completed his celebrated solo flight from the United States to France, sparking a renewed (and to U.S. diplomats, astounding) wave of popularity for America in the French public imagination. For academics and intellectuals in both countries, perhaps the most celebrated publication of the year was André Siegfried's *Les Etats-Unis d'aujourd'hui* (translated as *America Comes of Age*), a critical but not unsympathetic analysis of American society and economics by a major French social scientist.[7] And in September, just a few weeks after the executions, the American Legion, the national right-wing veterans' organization, held a celebration in France—hosted by the French government—commemorating the tenth anniversary of America's entrance into the world war. This event would also become central to the Sacco-Vanzetti controversy.

The Sacco-Vanzetti affair did not just burst upon the French scene in 1927, however. Serious engagement with the case in France began in 1921, when the two anarchists stood trial: that year, two French citizens, separated in age by fifty-four years, made their feelings about the trial known in noteworthy but different ways. Together, their responses represented two of the principal forms that "l'affaire Sacco et Vanzetti" would take in France: radical action and intellectual indignation.

On October 19 a twenty-three-year-old anarchist named May Picqueray—who, according to her memoir, wanted to force the mainstream French press to pay attention to the case—delivered a bomb to the Paris home of the longtime U.S. ambassador in France, Myron T. Herrick. Herrick's American servant, a veteran of World War I, received and opened the package (which was innocuously marked "perfume") and alertly managed to throw it away, but the explosion caused severe damage to the house, and the servant was wounded. By chance, however, the ambassador was not in, having taken his grandson to a grand reception at the Hôtel de Ville for General John J. Pershing.[8]

One month later, the seventy-seven-year-old Anatole France—who received the Nobel Prize for literature later that year—published "To the People of America" in the *Nation*.[9] And along with three other literary figures, Madame Séverine, Romain Rolland, and Henri Barbusse, he also sent a petition on behalf of Sacco and Vanzetti to President Warren G. Harding.[10]

"To the People of America" was written in the tradition of the calls for justice issued during the Dreyfus affair by Emile Zola and other intellectuals, including France himself. Besides being about six years ahead of its time (France was perhaps the only writer of his stature, in either Europe or the United States, to write about the case so early on), the piece is striking in two other respects. First, France did not settle for an audience of outraged French readers. Rather, setting an example that would be followed by others, he chose to address the American people directly, in a way that would bypass diplomats and elected officials, the usual vehicles of communication between foreign nationals. Second, by referring to the injustice as occurring "in one of your states," France was early to articulate a difference between the way French critics and most American critics were to see the affair at its height. For him, Massachusetts itself was of no particular importance. The responsibility for righting the terrible injustice (his piece did not entertain the possibility that the two men were guilty) fell upon all citizens of the United States.[11]

This view was shared by relatively few American critics, many of whom saw the Sacco-Vanzetti case as the specific product of the political culture, social history, and legal institutions of the state of Massachusetts. The scathing analyses written by Horace Kallen, Edna St. Vincent Millay, and other Americans did not resonate with Europeans, for whom the distinction between the federal republic and its individual states was meaningless. It is important to note in this context that most European petitions and cables protesting the Sacco-Vanzetti case were first sent to President Coolidge; only when European organizers learned that their urgent messages to the White House were forwarded, unopened and unread, to the governor of Massachusetts, did they begin to address their cables, letters, and petitions directly to Fuller.[12]

For French intellectuals, in particular (even those with a more substantial knowledge of the political structure of the United States), it was logical and natural to write to the head of the republic—the person with the highest authority, political and, supposedly, moral. Aside from their obvious projection of the French political model, they were perhaps still impressed by Woodrow Wilson's vigorous internationalist activism—a trait that the subsequent Republican presidents, Harding and Coolidge, did not share. French intellectuals and political figures often found incomprehensible the Americans' explanation that the president of the United States did not have the authority to intervene in the case and that Sacco and Vanzetti were under the sole jurisdiction of the state of Massachusetts. Unlike many of their American counterparts, they eventually turned to Fuller not in order to protest the state's handling of the case, or to ask that he redeem its "good name" (as did several Boston liberals), but because they had learned that he was the only political figure with the power to change the course of the legal process. In this sense, French activity concerning Sacco and Vanzetti was characterized not by helpless rage but by a sincere belief that the two could be saved. After the executions, however, the tone of criticism changed considerably.

Although the Sacco-Vanzetti trial had already galvanized many French radicals and literary intellectuals in 1921, the case became an affair in France, as in the United States, when the radicals campaigning in favor of Sacco and Vanzetti were joined by growing numbers of prominent intellectual and political figures, when the case drew the attention of the mainstream press and public, and, most important, when it became an issue of law and order—when violence surrounding the affair forced state and local authorities to intervene.[13] And, as in the United States, much of the activity on behalf of Sacco and Vanzetti in France took on an early form of the Popular Front of the 1930s.

In October 1926, after Thayer's final rejection of Sacco and Vanzetti's legal appeal, the energetic libertarian and pacifist activist Louis Lecoin, along with the Ligue des droits de l'homme (Human Rights League; LDH)—the pioneering organization that grew out of Alfred Dreyfus's defense in the late 1890s—began organizing a large-scale campaign of protest over the case.[14] Lecoin, in a sense, was the French version of Aldo Felicani, the principal figure in the Sacco-Vanzetti defense committee in Boston: an anarchist organizer eager to make alliances across political lines. Lecoin helped form the Comité Sacco-Vanzetti (mirroring the name of the American group), whose principal goal was to collect 5 million signatures that would be sent to

Coolidge and Fuller. The petition, tellingly, was relatively mild and
free of revolutionary language: "In the name of humanity, in the name
of justice, free Sacco and Vanzetti as innocent men. The voice of universal conscience needs to be heard." According to one estimate, 1.5
million signatures were collected by June 15, 1927, and by the time of
the executions, according to another, later estimate, there were approximately 2.8 million. Lecoin was also a primary mobilizer of fashionable intellectual opinion, collecting the signatures of the playwright Georges Courteline, the biologist and author Jean Rostand, the
Romanian-French writer Panait Istrati, the authors Romain Rolland,
Victor Margueritte, Georges Duhamel, Madame Séverine, and Henri
Barbusse, the painter and sculptor Amedeo Modigliani, the political
leader Edouard Daladier, and numerous other writers, politicians, and
artists. Signing this petition, and thus joining—even marginally—the
Sacco-Vanzetti protest was the first explicitly political act of two of the
future giants of French intellectual life, then unknown eighteen-year-
olds—Simone de Beauvoir and Claude Lévi-Strauss.[15]

There was a considerable degree of ingenuity and eclecticism to
the committee's public campaign. Going beyond the somewhat predictable effort of recruiting left-wing intellectuals, artists, and politicians to the cause, Lecoin and his associates, in an attempt to capitalize
on Lindbergh's enormous transatlantic appeal, courted famous aviators, in the belief that their support would help sway both American
and French public opinion. Lecoin, according to his own account,
took the petition to the grieving mother of Charles Nungesser, the
French pilot and war hero who had reputedly shot down forty-three
enemy planes during World War I but disappeared in May 1927 along
with his co-pilot, François Coli, while attempting to fly across the
Atlantic to the United States. Lecoin believed that the pilot's name
would have enough clout in the United States to help save Sacco and
Vanzetti; as he himself later recounted, "I was terribly naïve."[16]

Lecoin also came up with the idea of enlisting the support of
Lindbergh himself, who had succeeded where Nungesser and Coli had
failed (by flying in the opposite direction). The problem was how to
approach the celebrated young aviator: the State Department had decided, in light of the wildly enthusiastic response to Lindbergh's arrival in France, to try to make a diplomatic coup of it. During the
aviator's stay in Paris, he lived inside the U.S. embassy and was accom-

panied at all times by an entourage that included Herrick, the ambassador whose home had been bombed six years earlier.[17]

Lecoin's opportunity arose when he learned that Lindbergh was to be received by the president of the Chamber of Commerce in Paris. Lecoin persuaded a left-wing député from Marseille, who was invited to the reception, to present the committee's petition to Lindbergh. Lecoin, who according to his account managed to get into the building but not into the reception, witnessed Lindbergh reading the short letter, pausing, and then taking a pen out of his pocket. Then, according to Lecoin's uncorroborated account, just as the aviator was about to sign, Herrick yanked the paper out of Lindbergh's hand and after reading it angrily stuffed it in his pocket.[18]

Like Felicani and Jackson in the United States, Lecoin's ultimate goal, beyond collecting signatures, was to create a network of support for Sacco and Vanzetti that would extend across seemingly impenetrable political camps. This was a particularly complicated task in the late 1920s. The main ideological divide within the French left during this period mirrored the one in the United States and elsewhere, namely between what we might term revolutionaries and democrats. The French republican left (of which the LDH was an integral part) maintained a certain confidence in the American judicial system and saw the Sacco-Vanzetti case as a latter-day, American version of the Dreyfus affair—a matter of justice for two innocent people in the court of world opinion. The revolutionary left, by contrast, saw the case as part of the war waged by the capitalists against the working class; for them, the fight for Sacco and Vanzetti was not a humanitarian or legalistic one but inextricably linked to the fight to overthrow the bourgeoisie. Another important difference is that while moderates highlighted the demand for mercy, the radicals made a principle of Sacco and Vanzetti's innocence. As we have seen, these two opposing positions can be traced to the personalities of Sacco and Vanzetti themselves, with the latter representing a cautiously optimistic belief in the ability of the system to redeem itself and the former embodying an unwavering, exclusive reliance on the proletarian struggle.

Even within the revolutionary left there were irrevocable differences. The two main constituencies for protest, the anarchists and the Communists, not only held clashing views of what the Sacco-Vanzetti case meant but saw each other as rivals, even enemies, and could not be counted on for common action. While the radical left in its entirety was much stronger in France than in the United States, for example, its power in the 1920s should not be overestimated. In the late 1920s, the French Communist Party (PCF) was still young (having been created at the 1920 Congress of Tours, in which the French socialist movement was permanently split) and already in numerical decline, relying to a large degree on the activism of immigrant workers, many of them from Italy. The older—and now smaller—anarchist movement, uneasily centered in the Union anarchiste, was even more fragmented and in typical anarchist fashion unable to agree even on basic policies. Its heyday, when anarchists could create real problems for the French state (including the killing of President Sadi Carnot in 1894 by an Italian comrade), was long behind it.[19]

Not surprisingly, then, the Sacco-Vanzetti campaign in France was marked throughout by factionalism and infighting. Anarchists in France as elsewhere saw Sacco and Vanzetti as flesh-and-blood comrades and felt a personal affinity with the two condemned prisoners. Resenting both the rise of international communism and the long eclipse of their own movement, anarchists accused Communists of treating Sacco and Vanzetti as symbols, rather than as real people to be saved, and of exploiting the case for their own purposes. The Communists, for their part, accused all their rivals on the left—anarchists, syndicalists, and socialists—of seeking alliances with capitalists and reactionaries and selling out the working class to the bourgeois governments of France and the United States. These sorts of internal tensions existed elsewhere, including the United States, but in France they were more significant since the French radicals possessed a capacity for action that their American counterparts did not. At the same time, this relative size and strength created problems for French radical protesters that the American radicals never needed to deal with. The anarchists were tormented by the need—or the injunction—to collaborate with democratic, nonrevolutionary groups like the LDH on the one hand and with their bitter revolutionary rivals the Communists on the other. This prompted a long letter written to them from prison by Vanzetti himself and published in Le libertaire, encouraging his French anarchist comrades to cooperate with whoever was working on behalf of his (and Sacco's) freedom regardless of their politics.[20]

The Communist position on Sacco and Vanzetti was somewhat convoluted: the PCF leadership was eager to tap into what was rapidly

turning into a popular worldwide struggle but needed to justify political action on behalf of two ideological opponents. It did this by linking
the case to party dogma. French Communists, as elsewhere, refused
to see Sacco-Vanzetti as strictly an American case; since to them it
was part of the worldwide class war, their fight was as much with
the French government (and any bourgeois government) as with the
United States. In principle, they also rejected the link—made so strenuously by the Ligue des droits de l'homme, for example—between the
Sacco-Vanzetti and Dreyfus cases. Dreyfus had been an army officer,
therefore a bourgeois; hence, that affair, according to the PCF, had
been an internal dispute among the ruling classes. As one writer for
L'humanité put it, the Dreyfus affair represented "the last spasm of the
radical petite bourgeoisie in France in its long war with clerical reactionaries and against the absolute domination of the military clique."
Sacco and Vanzetti, on the other hand, were hounded by the Americans, according to the Communist newspaper, purely because they
were proletarians. Nor could the PCF support the appeals for mercy
and against the death sentence—one of the main features of the campaign for Sacco and Vanzetti in France and elsewhere—since capital
punishment and the punishment of political crimes generally were
basic staples of the Bolshevik regime. (Indeed, the anarchists attacked
the PCF for its hypocrisy on this point.) Instead, the Communists
described the Sacco-Vanzetti case as a new stage in the revolutionary
struggle.

Whereas, in the Communist view, the Dreyfus case had been
strictly an internal French matter, the Sacco-Vanzetti case had much
more significant world import; it had originated in the United States
not because of the special cultural and social tensions that existed there
but because that country exemplified the most advanced form of Western capitalism. "It is not by accident," *L'humanité* explained, "that the
[Sacco-Vanzetti affair] occurred in the country where capital is most
powerful, where the bourgeoisie is the most stable, where technique
helped decide the result of the Great War, where ready-made plans like
[the Dawes plan] are made for Europe's sake, and where the desperate
heads of all the financially ruined countries have turned for help." In
order to prove this last point, *L'humanité* mentioned Senator Borah's
disparaging comments on "foreign interference," although the quota-
tion was distorted, making it seem as though Borah had said that
whether Sacco or Vanzetti were guilty or not they should be executed

because the "American bourgeoisie should not succumb to the protests of the working class."[21]

The long-standing tension between French anarchists and Communists would come to a head in the second half of 1927 as a result of
two overlapping events: the execution of Sacco and Vanzetti, a traumatic moment for the left the world over, and the Comintern's decision, at the behest of Joseph Stalin, to move the entire Communist
movement "leftward," abandoning the previously official ideology of
"socialism in one country" and adopting the new goal of "world revolution," thus abolishing collective action with other groups on the left.
In effect, this meant an end to unified radical protest over the case.[22]

Still, the importance of this left-wing infighting over the case
should not be exaggerated. Even in France, where the radical left
was stronger than elsewhere, any major success for the Sacco-Vanzetti
campaign in general public opinion was due more to the humanitarian
appeal of the case, particularly the powerful memory of the Dreyfus
affair, and to the involvement of respected public and political figures
than to the actions or opinions of either Communists or anarchists. A
case in point: one of the largest Paris rallies for Sacco and Vanzetti took
place on June 12, 1927, outside the Panthéon in central Paris, and the
featured speaker was Joseph Caillaux, one of the major politicians of
the Third Republic. Caillaux, a moderate republican and erstwhile
prime minister, had once seen his career fall apart under the burden of
scandal and was tried for treason (and nearly executed) in 1918 during
the height of the war fervor, but later made a remarkable comeback. In
his speech he compared Sacco and Vanzetti's imprisonment to his
own. No anarchist or Communist leader spoke at this occasion.[23]

Indeed, the eventual failure to stop the executions put the frustrated and already weakened Communists and anarchists at one another's throats. From the Soviet Union came the news that the Bolshevik authorities, following the logic of the leftward turn, had increased
their efforts to eradicate the last vestiges of the anarchist movement in
Russia and Ukraine, a campaign begun by the Bolsheviks soon after
the October Revolution (this repression was promptly reported by
anti-Soviet libertarians in Paris, including the exiled Alexander Berkman).[24] After the executions, the two groups blamed each other for
Sacco and Vanzetti's deaths: the anarchists claimed that the Communists, by constantly and militantly depicting the case as part of the
worldwide class war, had alienated the American public to the extent

that it had become impossible to save Sacco and Vanzetti.[25] The Communists responded with a counteraccusation: the anarchists' collaboration with "reformers" and "social fascists" was what killed Sacco and Vanzetti; had the struggle been based on "broad working class protest," as the Communists demanded, it might have succeeded. For the rest of 1927, while the Sacco-Vanzetti protest in France became more anguished, *L'humanité* and *Le libertaire* constantly attacked each other's camps at the same time that they both attacked American justice, bourgeois capitalism, and, most severely, the French government, for hosting the festivities honoring America's entry into the Great War.

Since the Communist and anarchist movements were on the defensive, on the decline, and bickering with each other (and among themselves) during this period, historians must seek out additional, more crucial causes for the remarkable degree of agitation in France over the Sacco-Vanzetti case. Communist anxiety and anarchist distress were not enough to create a cause célèbre. Rather, two motives combined to give the French engagement with the case its impressive drive and volume: the lingering effects of the Dreyfus affair and the distinct power of both Americanism and anti-Americanism—a combination that we could call "conflicted Americanism"—in French intellectual, cultural, and political life.

The Dreyfus affair was the dominant backdrop to the public conversation in France over the Sacco-Vanzetti case. It, in particular, linked to the case people who otherwise wanted nothing to do with radical left-wing politics, who helped transform the case from a matter of interest primarily to revolutionaries into a broader public affair.[26] There was perhaps no better example of this than the intervention of Alfred Dreyfus himself. The rehabilitated army officer was now an aging, ailing man, but he emerged—at least in spirit—from his sickbed to publicly plead for the lives of the Italian anarchists. Dreyfus was a rather conservative and politically insipid figure (as his public defenders learned to their chagrin during the 1890s, when he resisted many of their efforts on his behalf), but his rarely heard voice carried considerable weight with American and French audiences alike. French activists on behalf of Sacco and Vanzetti had already attempted to recruit his support for the cause, and he had steadfastly refused, citing his hatred of anarchists, before finally stepping into the fray on August 21, 1927, two days before the executions. Dreyfus was quoted in both the

American and the French press as saying that the impending electrocutions "would be the greatest moral disaster of many years, fraught with terrible consequences to American justice." His oldest son, Pierre, made the statement even more dramatic by explaining that "Captain Dreyfus is sick in his bed, his condition having been made worse by thoughts of those two men waiting in the electric chair. . . . The Sacco-Vanzetti case has been his constant preoccupation for months." (This depiction was somewhat *too* dramatic, as Sacco and Vanzetti were not actually waiting *in* the electric chair but rather in their prison cells, but the point had been made.)[27]

Beyond the former officer's personal involvement, the Dreyfus affair largely shaped the way different French groups approached the Sacco-Vanzetti case. One such group was the legal community. In an ironic reversal, Francophone legal experts now attacked American justice in terms nearly identical to the ones that had been used by indignant American jurists and commentators to describe the Dreyfus case in the late 1890s and early 1900s.[28]

The law professor Fernand Collin, for example, wrote a study of the case based in part on Frankfurter's article in the *Atlantic Monthly,* by then widely disseminated in France. Collin compared the "Anglo-Saxon" and "continental" legal systems and argued that the Sacco-Vanzetti affair could not have occurred in France because of the provisions in the French legal system, put in place after the Dreyfus case, that prevented a judge from abusing his power and deciding in appeals of his own verdicts. In Collin's view, Americans took pride in the fact that defendants in the United States were presumed innocent until proven guilty, and likewise believed that in Europe the opposite was true. But, he argued, "can one imagine that in Europe one single legal affair should be brought seven times before one single judge; that this magistrate would have to evaluate his own ability to preside over a trial; that any appeal would depend on this person's goodwill in admitting or refusing any revision; and all this under the pretext that only this judge has enough substantial knowledge about the case?"[29]

Too much in the American system, Collin continued, depended on the individual judge; the French system, on the other hand, took into account the "imperfections of men." In America, he complained, the magistrate alone is responsible for that guarantee, whereas continental Europeans (specifically the French) had a more humane and wise system of checks and balances. Anglo-Saxons put all their confidence in the judge, while continental legislature put restrictions on his power. "Which is the better system? Can we ever know?" he asked. "Yet let us suppose that Sacco and Vanzetti are innocent. Wouldn't they, even in a time of crisis, find a better justice with us Europeans?"[30]

One of the most notable results of the Dreyfus affair was the emergence of the *intellectuels,* first defined as such in the late 1890s (initially in a negative sense, by their conservative opponents). Projecting freely from the recent French past, these intellectuals saw in Sacco-Vanzetti another clear-cut Dreyfus case and consequently expected American intellectuals to behave the way Emile Zola, Anatole France, Georges Clemenceau, and others had a generation earlier. They made these demands upon their American counterparts apparently without realizing that significant changes in the political world, specifically in the relationship between intellectuals and state power, and the growing fragmentation of intellectual authority, rendered such interventions (especially in America) less effective. In addition, they often failed to make the distinction between the place and role of intellectuals in Third Republic France, with its centralized political and cultural life based in Paris and their own relative proximity to the political elite, and the far more marginal role played by independent American intellectuals in the much more culturally, socially, and politically decentralized and heterogeneous United States of the 1920s.[31] They evidently were also unaware of the growing number of American intellectual and public figures who were already actively engaged with the Sacco-Vanzetti case by 1927. One such example of this mindset was the communiqué written by a group of French intellectuals addressed to "our fellow American intellectuals" and published in *Le quotidien* three weeks before the executions. Dreyfus himself was cited as the spiritual patron of this appeal. The message was clear: if Sacco and Vanzetti were to die, "there would be between us a chill, a shame, that neither you nor we could understand. . . . This is not a threat against American tourists, just a warning of what might happen. A country which heretofore has been known as the cradle of fair play, must take into account the world's opinion."[32]

American intellectuals, according to the communiqué, had the power to change the course of legal affairs if they so wished: "We ask you intellectuals that the Sacco-Vanzetti executions be postponed until a complete revision of their case is made." The writers also explained that Dreyfus had considered coming to the United States "at the last moment" to plead for the lives of Sacco and Vanzetti but was prevented from doing so by his failing health. The communiqué captured a simultaneous admiration and hostility toward America; it conveyed disappointment and fear rather than rage. The managing editor of *Le quotidien*, Gustave Terry, explained to American reporters that the executions would be "bad for Franco-American relations. . . . Are we going to lose at one blow . . . all that the heroic noble prowess of Lindbergh has won?"

In the same Dreyfusard-republican vein, and displaying the same sort of conflicted Americanism, some French critics of the Sacco-Vanzetti case wished to appeal directly to the American citizenry, whose collective sense of justice, they felt, could overcome the blindness and bigotry of their politicians and judges. In this regard, however, the situation of French and other continental intellectuals was totally unlike that of their British counterparts, such as H. G. Wells and Harold Laski, who wrote in English and possessed a more natural and immediate familiarity with the networks of American intellectual and cultural life. Wells, for example, whose scathing critique of the Sacco-Vanzetti case and American society were published in the *New York Times,* could appeal easily and without mediation to a relatively wide American readership (that is, until the *Times* refused to publish his articles), while Laski regularly corresponded for nineteen years with one of the most important public and legal figures in the United States, Supreme Court Justice Oliver Wendell Holmes. British journals such as the *New Statesman and Nation* and the *Spectator* commented on the Sacco-Vanzetti case almost as frequently and anxiously as did liberal American venues like the *Nation* or the *New Republic,* and were read in the United States as well, as indicated by the letters sent to those journals by often-disgruntled American readers.[33] French intellectuals, on the other hand, relied on translation, and their cultural and political distance from the United States was greater. Their potential American readership was inevitably more restricted.

Some French writers, however, did have a captive, albeit small, audience in the United States. One such intellectual with a devoted American following was Romain Rolland, the pacifist writer and historian. Rolland was admired by such antiwar American intellectuals (and Sacco and Vanzetti sympathizers) as Jane Addams for his refusal during World War I to join the chorus of intellectual jingoism that accompanied the war effort—a disturbing phenomenon that occurred in every major nation involved in that war, including the United States. "It is hard to convey to you the sense of rescue which your challenge to the war brought to many of us in the United States throughout the dark years of violence and denial," Addams wrote to Rolland in 1925.[34]

Rolland was especially revered by the so-called Young America intellectuals, Waldo Frank and Lewis Mumford, who rebelled against the dominance of pragmatism in American thought and embraced communitarianism as the path to national and cultural rejuvenation. Frank saw his own relationship with Rolland as emblematic of the cultural and spiritual connection and inspiration that the Young America group sought across the Atlantic.[35]

One of Rolland's American friends, the *Boston Globe* journalist Lucien Price, suggested that Rolland write an essay for the *Nation,* which championed the Sacco-Vanzetti cause and had published Anatole France's "Appeal to the American People" six years earlier.[36] Rolland's essay, subtitled "A Message to America on the Massachusetts Tragedy" and written in the form of a personal letter to Price, appeared in September 1927, after Sacco and Vanzetti had already been executed, but his ambition had always been broader than merely trying to save two lives; he wanted American readers to know about the deterioration of America's image in Europe.[37]

Rolland's main point of reference was the Dreyfus affair, but he combined this theme with a passionate reflection on America's past, present, and future. To him, a dark chapter in fin-de-siècle French history had repeated itself in America, this time without the happy ending. Thirty years earlier, at the height of the Dreyfus controversy, Rolland, then a music-history professor at the Ecole Normale Supérieure, had refused to take sides in the great national dispute, later explaining: "I thought that, whatever happened, the cause of justice would be compromised and that the *patrie* ran the risk of being destroyed, so that there would be nothing left of either." This position was in line with his philosophy of remaining "above the *mêlée,*" one he followed two decades later during the war.[38]

But over the years Rolland grew more critical and pessimistic, and by the 1920s, after the gruesome experience of the war and perhaps owing something to his sense of guilt over not having protested Dreyfus's fate, he was prepared to take a clear stand. His passion over the Sacco-Vanzetti case can thus be seen as a form of latter-day breast-beating, not entirely dissimilar from the case of American liberal intellectuals who in 1927 defended the two anarchists while also implicitly lamenting their former support for America's participation in the war.

Speaking of "the killers of Sacco and Vanzetti," Rolland wrote: "I am not astonished that these bloodthirsty souls should exist. We knew similar ones in our Dreyfus affair. The great judges, lay or military, are both of the same species. . . . After passing judgment [they] would have let the whole world crumble rather than admit that they had made a mistake. . . . If there exists a Hell, the place of honor in it is reserved for such pride as that." Other Americans, in Rolland's view, did not necessarily have to share in the responsibility for the killing of Sacco and Vanzetti, because "the crime of such men [as the judges] involves only themselves. It does not involve their nation and community." But at the same time, Rolland insisted, "It is the duty of these latter [American people] to dissociate themselves from it. Thus did the better France in the Dreyfus affair. The better France, after years of struggle and suffering, snatched the victim from the torturers. It was this that the Defense Committee for Sacco and Vanzetti tried to do—without success—in the United States."[39]

Rolland here expressed a recurring French theme, according to which support for Sacco and Vanzetti was not a matter of the class struggle but rather a simple matter of mercy. With the possible exception of the Communists, even propaganda emanating from the radical left in France often stressed the humanitarian aspect of the affair over class and capitalism: one widely distributed anarchist pamphlet, for example, expressed the hope that as a result of the Sacco-Vanzetti case, people in the United States would realize that "despite their economic power, [Americans] are well behind European civilization from both a moral and humane point of view." These criticisms derived their language not from propaganda officials in Moscow, nor from the ideological principles of anarchism, but from the lessons of the Dreyfus episode.[40]

Rolland's essay highlighted the significance of American history, specifically the example of its democratic model, for French intellectuals. And it revealed an acute awareness of American sensibilities, as, for example, when the author made a point of identifying himself as a nonradical, "a friend of America . . . a man who has long held himself aloof from political parties; who has acquired the habit of looking and thinking beyond the passions of the day; and . . . a man who is by certain traits as well as of temperament more akin to the Anglo-Saxon than to the Mediterranean." These clarifications (namely, the need to show that the writer was neither a radical nor of Mediterranean temperament) were a necessary prerequisite for Europeans trying to reach a broad American audience. (H. G. Wells had made similar claims.)

After the polite introduction, Rolland laid out a harsh critique that looked beyond the Sacco-Vanzetti case itself and into "the soul of America." The most terrible aspect of the whole story, to him, was not the execution of Sacco and Vanzetti, who by death had "finally escaped torture," but rather "the abyss which this offense has now dug between the United States and the rest of the peoples of the world." For Rolland, the question of Sacco and Vanzetti's guilt or innocence was secondary. Much more important was the cruelty they had endured, "such as the most barbarous in our world today, Bolshevik, Balkan, or Fascist, would have thought too cowardly, too inhuman." Rolland recounted that he had cabled Governor Fuller on August 20 saying that "one simple solution is demanded: mercy. A friend of America entreats you to spare Sacco and Vanzetti. Even if guilty, humanity would demand [it]."

Who constituted Rolland's "better America"? Certainly not its political and legal elites. As he saw it, "The most overwhelming and heartbreaking of all this drama, this disaster in the eyes of the world," was that "not one of the notable official personages who represent the government of the United States intervened to give audible expression to the voice of humanity. [President] Coolidge found the hour propitious for his annual vacation (perish the thought of disturbing him!) while they were assassinating Sacco and Vanzetti. [Supreme Court Chief Justice and former U.S. President] Taft did not find it worth the trouble to return from Canada. [Senator] Borah—and this is the bitterest of all—said . . . that it was merely a question of facing down the insolent clamor from abroad. . . . Thus the most vulgar sentiment of *amour propre,* of national pride, tramples humanity underfoot!"

As for the resentful American responses to the European criticism, Rolland acknowledged that "it is not pleasant for a nation to receive the objurgations [*sic*] of foreigners." This, however, was no excuse for ignoring them or worse, for using them to justify denying clemency to two innocent men, as Borah had done: "Despite the acts of violence that have accompanied the protest, you know well, all of you in America, that those most overwhelmed by the judicial crime in

America have not been the violent in Europe. They have been the moderates . . . the liberals, the Christians, all the saner and better balanced elements of Europe. And the majority of protests . . . came from sincere friends of the United States, who, like myself, were heart-broken when they saw such a crime soil the honor of the great nation they love, and destroy the ideal image which they had made it."

America, the "great nation," had failed: "A strong nation possesses imagination. It takes thought. Yours should have done so. For your nation owes to itself and to the world to scorn the threats made against it; but not the supplications of its friends, not enlightened counsel." Rolland reserved his deepest contempt for the American politicians: "The pitiless hardness of heart of all the leading public officials in America, their absolute insensitivity . . . have produced a most sinister impression throughout the entire world. It was a question not of justice, but rather of simple, humble, divine humanity." And the result of this failure was that "moderate" Europeans like himself could no longer in good faith defend the "better America" on whose existence he still insisted.

Ultimately, to Rolland, the Sacco-Vanzetti affair was a "world tragedy . . . no more American than the Dreyfus affair was French alone. This calamity . . . has shown the crushing supremacy—from afar one might almost say the unanimity—of this frightful America whose heart is made of stone, of this America for whom humanity does not exist." And he summed up bleakly: "What is to be done? The abyss yawns. I know too well the peoples of Europe, and the travail that is going on within them, not to perceive that from this day on a state of moral warfare exists between them and the United States. And, should it be six years, or twenty, or fifty, or a century, this state of moral warfare will be realized one day indeed. For the conscience of the world has received a blow. And, alas! A blow received in history is always sooner or later given back."

Was this essay an example of "anti-Americanism," a category into which scholars have tried to fit a wide variety of political phenomena? On the one hand, Rolland complimented American traditions, insisted on the existence of a "better America," and called himself a "sincere friend" of a "great nation" he loved; on the other, he described the United States as the new enemy of the civilized world and on behalf of all Europeans threatened "moral warfare." We might rather argue that the essay conveyed a "conflicted Americanism," neither anti nor pro—

a western European sense of America's importance to the world, not only in creating the dismal Sacco-Vanzetti case but also in setting a moral example to all nations.

Perhaps what most troubled Rolland was that whereas he had considered the democratic United States a sort of national kindred spirit to France, the executions of Sacco and Vanzetti (in contrast to the eventual rescue of Dreyfus) had destroyed this illusion. Indeed, for him, the starkest difference between the two countries could be distilled to the fact that whereas French intellectuals were able to redeem France's national reputation after terrible injustices, the same had not happened in the United States: "Although in the pantheon of the martyrs of the civilized world one will speak for centuries of Sacco and Vanzetti as one still speaks of Jean Calas," he lamented, "[Sacco and Vanzetti] have not found in America their Voltaire!"[41]

Among Rolland's archived papers there are examples of the displeasure that the French version of his essay caused to grassroots radical protesters in France, who had an entirely different conception from his of what the Sacco-Vanzetti case meant. Two teachers in Marseille, a married couple who had in the past written Rolland admiring letters, now sent him an angry message in which they chastised him for ignoring the "class struggle" aspect of the case: "Your background, your economic situation, your social station, all of these no doubt prevent you from knowing, from personal experience, what the real situation of the worker is in relation to the forces of capital." What particularly irked these teachers was that Rolland had called Sacco and Vanzetti "poor insignificant Italians." They much preferred a celebration of the two men's martyrdom, since they had defied the capitalist machine even at their deaths: "They battled and they triumphed!" One sign of Sacco and Vanzetti's ultimate success, in their eyes, was the fact that Governor Fuller, when he came to France after the executions, had been obliged to stay in the country under an assumed name and with police protection. Quoting one of Vanzetti's famous last statements— that in death, he and Sacco would become more important than they would have been had they lived out the rest of their lives in obscurity ("this agony is our triumph!")—the teachers wrote to Rolland that Sacco and Vanzetti "did more for humanity than a hundred inventors and a thousand philosophers!"[42]

Rolland did not lose interest in the case in the years to come. He remained in contact with the principal organizers of the Sacco-

Vanzetti campaign in France, such as Lecoin and the leaders of the
LDH, as well as with Lucien Price and other Americans, some of
whom led the posthumous efforts to clear Sacco and Vanzetti's names.
And in the 1930s—like so many of the American writers and artists
similarly shattered by the executions of Sacco and Vanzetti—Rolland
became something of a Communist fellow traveler, a position he had
deplored as late as 1927.[43]

In lamenting the implications of the Sacco-Vanzetti case, especially the depths to which America's moral standing in the world had
fallen, Rolland was not writing just as a French intellectual. True, his
"Message to America" made several references to the recent French
experience, but by the 1920s he was living openly, self-consciously, as a
European—"au dessus de la mêlée," supposedly above the fray of national jingoisms that had led to the horrors of the war. Rolland made
his home outside France, in Villeneuve, Switzerland; he spoke and
wrote German, English, French, and Italian; his own journal of letters
was called *L'Europe;* he had friends all over the continent and overseas (including the pacifist Indian leader Mahatma Gandhi, one of
his biggest influences beginning in the 1920s). And he made his critique of America in the Sacco-Vanzetti case on behalf of "the peoples
of Europe." Indeed, Rolland can be seen as an important intellectual
precursor to the late-twentieth-century drive for a unified European
identity.[44]

Rolland's essay is thus important not only because of its caustic
analysis of the Sacco-Vanzetti case itself or because it carried the moral
weight of the Dreyfus affair but also because in writing about Sacco
and Vanzetti, Rolland represented a broader, cross-national, more general European phenomenon. He was not the only French writer to
speak of a European sense of horror at the case, as we have seen. And
France was surely not the only European country where America was
a source of fascination and dismay in the 1920s. Although probably
the most vibrant national arena of reaction to the Sacco-Vanzetti case
outside the United States, it was not the only such arena.[45]

As the affair reached its climax, Rolland's warnings of an abyss
and moral warfare between Europeans and Americans were echoed by
politicians and protesters across the continent. Editorials about the
Sacco-Vanzetti case in France, Italy, Germany, Switzerland, Sweden,
Denmark, Holland, and Belgium regularly spoke of European (rather

than just national) outrage at American justice. Georg Branting, as we have seen, had traveled from Sweden to the United States to study the case on behalf of "European opinion." Outside the Continent itself, even British intellectuals shared this pan-European identity: Wells wrote his Sacco-Vanzetti articles as a "friendly European critic," as he put it, and Laski, in his correspondence with Justice Holmes, described himself as a worried European. The French response to the case should thus be seen as part of a broader European response. The European context can help us make sense of the French reception of the case, while the specifically French reactions allow us to get at the deeper dynamics of the European (and implicitly international) reception.

Sacco and Vanzetti's ordeal took place during a pivotal moment in transatlantic history; their case would not have achieved prominence in France (or elsewhere in Europe) were it not for this particular historical timing. The rise of the United States to nearly unrivalled global strength at the same time that the traditional European powers—Britain, France, and Germany—faced crisis and decline was dramatic enough a shift. But the changing of the geopolitical guard was not merely symbolic: after the war, the imperial European nations also became the Americans' debtors. Wrote one disgruntled critic: "The America of idealism, democracy, and internationalism had turned into the America of debt collectors."[46] This new and humbling state of affairs was made more complex by the economic and cultural inroads that American elites made in the 1920s into bourgeois Europe, especially through the influx of consumer goods, films, and other forms of material and popular culture. The response to "Fordism"—one catchphrase for this American corporate invasion—was an important part of the backdrop to the European, specifically French, response to the Sacco-Vanzetti case. It helped forge a European identity based on the resistance to, or accommodation of, the growing American presence in Europe: after the war, it became clearer to European elites that the question of which nation or empire would dominate Europe had become moot, superseded by the more urgent question of how Europeans as a whole would deal with the big, young, entrepreneurial, and very different power across the ocean.[47]

The late-1920s fascination with all things American produced a flurry of books in France that tried to make sense of *l'outre-Atlantique* by juxtaposing American and European sensibilities (a French intellectual tradition that even today shows no signs of decline).[48] The

French social scientist and essayist André Siegfried, whose 1926 *Les Etats-Unis d'aujourd'hui* was rapidly translated into English and received a surprising amount of attention in the United States in the spring and summer of 1927, presciently put the case in rather unflattering context. In America—where he spent about a year researching his book—Siegfried saw a mortal collision between "Nordic Protestants" (who were hard, money-loving, and crass) and "non-Nordic elements" (Catholics, Jews, and other outsiders, heirs to the "magnificent civilization" of Europe). "The herd sentiment," he wrote, "tends to engulf America, throwing her into violent contrasts with the liberty-loving Latins." Siegfried also believed that freedom of opinion in the United States was disappearing and that the press was too tied to capitalist interests. Offended by William Jennings Bryan's anti-Darwinian stance at the Scopes Monkey Trial, Siegfried added that many Americans held "primitive Protestant beliefs," which he contrasted with the richness of Catholic and Latin traditions. As for the immigrants who came to America, they often lost "the rich heritage of magnificent civilizations"; that is why no Frenchman, in Siegfried's view, could ever accept the spirit of what he called the American "herd psychology." "The idea that his personality is being constantly suppressed is almost painful to a Latin," he concluded. "He cannot comprehend the Calvinist point of view that the group and not the individual is the social unit."[49]

Other observers were even more scathing. Many saw links between the persecution and deaths of Sacco and Vanzetti and the rise of right-wing extremism and authoritarianism in postwar Europe. The prominent Viennese journalist Karl Kraus—who, perhaps not knowing where else to turn, had implored Czech president Thomas Masaryk to appeal to the U.S. government for clemency for the two Italian anarchists—denounced Sacco and Vanzetti's executioners as "monsters" and, drawing a parallel with the Austrian government's brutal suppression of working-class demonstrations in Vienna in 1926, identified the killing of Sacco and Vanzetti with the "martyrdom" that results when judicial processes are subordinated to "the authority of violence." Kraus, like many Europeans on the interwar liberal left, judged the Sacco-Vanzetti affair in terms of the universalizing of the principles of civil law and international justice, which meant, to him, applying the same standards to the United States as to Europe.[50]

Many Europeans on both the right and left believed that America represented the future of the rest of the world. The way America went would thus determine Europe's destiny as well, especially given the ease with which so many Europeans seemed to be accepting, and even encouraging, American influence. And to many interwar European intellectuals, from Wells to Duhamel to Kraus to Gramsci, this was a disturbing thought. They felt much like the Swedish critic Carl Laurin, who, shortly before Sacco and Vanzetti were executed, wrote that "the Americanization of the world is . . . the most horrible of future perspectives."[51] To many Europeans the Sacco-Vanzetti case revealed an America that was frighteningly out of touch with the moral compass of the rest of the world, threatened extinction to the European way of life, and seemed impervious to any foreign influence, yet at the same time was determined to export its way of life across the ocean.[52]

But these bleak thoughts were largely reserved for after Sacco and Vanzetti's electrocutions. In France, the more optimistic belief that Sacco and Vanzetti were not doomed and that the essence of the French engagement with the case should be to speak directly to Americans and appeal to their basic sense of justice remained dominant until the moment Sacco and Vanzetti were executed. Many French observers, much like their American counterparts, had believed that the formation of the Lowell advisory commission marked the end of Sacco and Vanzetti's ordeal and the coming triumph of justice; the commission, according to this optimistic view, would provide an exit strategy for American officials who knew (or so these observers believed) that the two men were innocent and had had an unfair trial but who also needed a pretext for releasing them without losing face in the eyes of the world.

When on August 10, just before the second scheduled date of the executions, Fuller announced a temporary reprieve, much of the French press was prematurely convinced of a happy ending. The editorial in *Paris soir* exclaimed: "Sacco and Vanzetti are saved! The citizens of the United States have ended by understanding. . . . They have been unable to remain insensible to the formidable current of opinion that has traversed the whole world."[53] The radical press celebrated the defeat of Sacco and Vanzetti's bourgeois tormentors, and *L'humanité* and *Le libertaire* each proclaimed (while giving all or most of the credit to their own camps) that "American capital" had backed down in the face of mass proletarian protest. Less radical organs simply saw Fuller's reprieve as a sign that the Americans had finally come to their senses.

During this period, "l'affaire Sacco et Vanzetti" dominated the news pages and editorials even of the conservative and right-wing press, which until then had usually associated the Sacco-Vanzetti cause with the menace of a leftist revolution. Some editorialists expressed concern for the future of France's relationship with the United States, still perceived by many as their savior in the war and a bulwark against the threat of socialism. And the different types of reactions to the case show that anti-Americanism was by no means a uniform sentiment in France. The August 11 editorial in *Liberté*, written immediately after Fuller's temporary reprieve, proclaimed: "Enough of hysteria. The campaign in favor of Sacco and Vanzetti led by the 'French' press of the extreme left has been simply abominable. . . . Are there no laws in our [legal code] to punish such incitements for murder?" The Sacco-Vanzetti affair "is perhaps unfortunate for America," the editorial continued, "but we assure [you] that it is equally unfortunate for France. When one seeks alliances, when one wishes for credit, when one desires peace, one ought not to display hysteria in front of the entire world."[54] Nor did *L'intransigeant* appreciate the campaign in France on behalf of two faraway radicals: "The French and American peoples think with different mentalities. . . . Every people has the right to administer alone its own affairs. And if the state of Massachusetts does not consult the state of New York in the administration of its justice, the more reason it will have for repulsing suggestions from across the Atlantic."[55]

Still, these opinions were written during the brief period when it was widely believed that Sacco and Vanzetti would be granted clemency. When Fuller eventually authorized the executions, the main reaction in the French press was rage and indignation. With some exceptions, this can be said of the left, center, and right. What united the different groups across the political spectrum was the sense of horror at the idea of executing Sacco and Vanzetti after they had spent more than six years in prison (even Pope Pius XI was finally persuaded on these grounds to appeal for "God's clemency" for Sacco and Vanzetti); according to this view, even if the two men were guilty, more than six years of waiting for death was punishment enough.[56]

The protest now came from the highest echelons of the republic;

the former (and future) premier Edouard Herriot (of the center-left Radical Party) stated: "To the depths of my soul I am against this punishment." *Liberté*'s editorial declared: "The burial of this deplorable business would be certainly better from every point of view than the burial of the two victims. The symbolic torch which the Statue of Liberty carries in her hand must not be replaced by two half-scorched scarecrows." The mainstream daily *Paris soir,* which just a few days previously had complimented the American people on rediscovering their wisdom and maturity, now insisted: "The whole conscience of the world revolts and finds it impossible to believe such a monstrous deed will be performed. Is the image of Christ absent from the American courts? If America allows Sacco and Vanzetti to go to the electric chair she will dishonor herself in the eyes of the whole universe. Their death will be murder, and their blood will be upon the heads of all Americans."[57]

And while Sacco and Vanzetti were compared to Christ, their executioners were seen as reincarnations of tyrants past. From beyond the grave, Anatole France was again involved in the affair, when *L'humanité* republished his short story "Le supplice de la mort différée," in which a young mother in early-eighteenth-century Paris is sentenced to death for killing her child, but the royal executioner, overcome with emotion at the woman's plight, repeatedly fails to execute her. Eventually the king pardons the woman. The posthumous morale: as opposed to Fuller and Coolidge, even the despotic King Louis XV had a human, merciful side. (It is not clear whether the Communist editors were aware of the irony of their using the ancien régime as a positive example.)[58]

And as the executions drew near, even the extreme right drew startling conclusions from the case. For the veteran royalist movement Action française, the main issues in the Sacco-Vanzetti affair were the long period between the conviction and the execution of the two men, which even they found cruel and unusual by "European" standards; their fear (also expressed, as we have seen, by Benito Mussolini) that the American authorities were providing leftist revolutionaries with invaluable fodder for their propaganda needs; and especially their profound contempt for American liberal democracy, which, they argued, had created the whole sordid affair though its inherent weakness, indecision, and hypocrisy.

The royalists' interest in the Sacco-Vanzetti case, incidentally, began earlier: in 1921, Action française members had been informants for the U.S. embassy in Paris concerning anarchist and Communist activity in protest of the Sacco-Vanzetti trial. In a letter to Washington, Ambassador Herrick praised the leaders of the movement, "whose secret service on political developments," he enthused, "is very extensive and has frequently proved accurate." Apparently, Action française supplied the Americans with such information because the royalists believed, at least in 1921, that the protest was the work of German agents seeking to destabilize France.[59]

By 1927 the royalists had developed a more clearheaded interpretation of the case; indeed, Charles Maurras, the movement's leader and principal thinker, probably made some of the most astute observations about the affair to come out of France. For Maurras, the Sacco-Vanzetti affair was another unfortunate product of the Dreyfus legacy in France, although as one of the most committed and controversial anti-Dreyfusards in French intellectual and political life, his position was the inverse of the opinions of Dreyfusard intellectuals like Romain Rolland. As Maurras bitterly put it, "Our nation has suffered too much from the intervention of foreigners in the Dreyfus affair for us to . . . allow ourselves to express an opinion on the judicial aspects of the [Sacco-Vanzetti] affair." Like the radical left, Maurras was indignant at "the unbelievable length of moral and emotional torture that ha[d] been inflicted" on Sacco and Vanzetti, and through his journal, *L'Action française,* he called for their immediate release: after six years of imprisonment, he felt, those who would order their execution "would be crossing over from the zone of the odious into the zone of the ridiculous."[60]

Nonetheless, the royalists had some original things to say about the case, particularly about what they saw as its ethnic origins (an aspect that went almost totally ignored by the French left). The persecution of Sacco and Vanzetti, *L'Action française* argued, was the result of the fact that immigration to the United States had become increasingly "Latinized," especially since the turn of the century, while the "American establishment" wished it to remain an Anglo-Saxon state, and to be the most powerful in the world. Indeed, for *L'Action française* the case was primarily about Sacco, who was from southern Italy (Vanzetti, though the poorer of the two men, was from the wealthier North), and the journal referred to it as "l'affaire Sacco." Americans, in the editors' opinion, were still insecure in their station in the world, despite their singular rise to global power, and they resented the protests and pressures over the case emanating from Europe; the "humanitarian crusade" launched by intellectuals and the left in France, the royalists argued, probably correctly, did more damage than good to the effort to save the two anarchists. And in principle, they agreed with their enemies on the left that the main effect of the affair was to "create in the entire world an unabashedly unfavorable feeling toward the Americans."[61]

Still, the main conclusions Maurras himself drew from the affair adhered closely to his virulently antidemocratic worldview. The American justice system, as the product of mass democracy, and with its many options for appeals, was slow, inefficient, cumbersome, and run by foolish, unmanly bureaucrats. Indeed, the lengthiness of the entire process, for Maurras, was what had provided the left with the opportunity to conduct its nefarious activity. At the same time, Maurras did not dismiss the danger that postwar America now posed to the French. And even this ultra-nationalist royalist expressed a sort of pan-Europeanism vis-à-vis America akin to that of Rolland or Wells: what Europeans really needed to understand, as Maurras saw it, was that the United States was not and could never be an ally; rather, it was a rival and wholly alien imperial power with interests and values completely opposed to those of the European nations.[62]

The most violent French protest over Sacco and Vanzetti occurred on the night of August 23, 1927, in direct response to the executions. Through the efficient network of information that had been created around the case, news of Sacco and Vanzetti's death the previous night in Massachusetts arrived in France first thing in the morning on the 23rd, in time for angered radicals to prepare a countrywide confrontation with the authorities. In the afternoon, as the daily newspapers hit the streets, Parisians heard the sound of newsboys screaming "Sacco et Vanzetti electrocutés!" and other such headlines. That evening in Paris and practically every other major city in France there were massive riots, as thousands of mostly Communist protesters clashed with police. Older bourgeois Parisians, caught completely off guard by the wave of protest, were suddenly reminded of the bloody days of the 1871 Commune. They had come to believe over the years that because the government had outlawed popular demonstrations within the city limits and banished working-class and immigrant groups to the new suburbs (leading to the rise of the so-called Red Belt), bourgeois Paris was safe from the hazards of "undesirables" and militants. Left-wing protesters were expected—by the authorities and by residents—to stick to their usual demonstration sites on the eastern and northern parts of the city or in the working-class suburbs. This time they headed straight to the city's center and even into the heart of the comfortable bourgeoisie, the grand neighborhoods of western Paris. This in itself completely changed the nature and outcome of the protest.[63]

A severe rainstorm that began that evening and a massive police turnout did nothing to calm the anger. Many did march peacefully in the direction of the U.S. embassy, but they were not allowed near it and were quickly dispersed by police. Others were not satisfied with this kind of protest. Shouting such slogans as "Death to the Bourgeoisie!" these demonstrators, turning up in separate groups all over the city but especially in the north, set up barricades in some of the main central boulevards, especially Sébastopol; broke into shops; attacked cafés, brasseries, and clubs (especially those frequented by American tourists, such as the Mikado, the Select, and the Moulin Rouge); overturned cars and trams; and tried to storm police lines. At the Champs-Élysées and the Arc de Triomphe, the protesters were able to temporarily drive back the gendarmes and attempted to destroy the Tomb of the Unknown Soldier. Americans in Paris who had been leading sheltered lives on the Left Bank rudely discovered that their French idyll was over; some of the rage was directed against them. One unwitting expatriate later wrote of the day's events in his memoir:

> Having put the baby to bed, my wife and I had gone down to the little river-front café that we frequented. . . . We found the place packed that night with men whose eyes glared at us from all corners of the room. Their gestures as well were menacing. . . . The proprietor, who knew us well, came up. "If Monsieur-Madame will pardon me," he said, "I would suggest that they go. It is dangerous." We thought it strange; but as there was a stir at the nearby tables and . . . a movement in our direction, we decided to leave without asking any further questions. . . . [Later,] coming down along the boulevard Raspail on the bus, we noticed signs of tumult as we neared the Carrefour Vavin. There was a large crowd milling about in the square, and we could see residents of the Quarter, many of whom we recognized, running in all directions.

As we alighted in front of the *Rotonde* and glanced down the boule-vard Montparnasse, we saw what was happening. We saw, but we did not understand. The cafe terraces were in turmoil; they were being invaded. . . . Tables were being overturned, chairs were being hurled, there was a crash of china and glassware, and customers male and female were being tossed into the street. Someone ran past and shouted: "Get out! Get out of here, quick!" We acted on this advice.[64]

The city police, headed by the infamously repressive Préfet Jean Chiappe, who had apparently made it his personal mission to rid the city of militant protesters once and for all, joined in some of the worst political street violence Parisians would see until 1934, when France found itself on the verge of civil war between right and left. In their zeal to stop the protest, Chiappe's police did not bother to make distinctions between random looters, angry protestors, peace-ful marchers, or innocent bystanders; anyone who stepped into their path was clobbered by batons. By midnight the protest had been forc-ibly subdued; by morning the municipality reported 250 arrests, 124 injured policemen, and at least 800 injured protesters. (*L'humanité* claimed that all these numbers were too low, and accused police of beating to death a disabled war veteran.) Other cities experienced simi-lar events: in Montpellier, in the South, several bombs were exploded, two of them at the central police station and next to the municipal jail; several policemen were injured.[65]

The riots in Paris were part of a larger general pattern of interna-tional violence in response to the Sacco-Vanzetti case. Similar (though smaller) riots took place in London, Berlin, Brussels, and other capital cities. In Europe and Latin America, bombings and attacks against American targets drew the attention not only of local authorities but also of the United States government. This sort of activity was perhaps the darker side of the globalization of political protest, of which the Sacco-Vanzetti episode was probably the first and premier modern example. But whereas most such violence (especially, but not only, in Latin America) was more explicitly anti-American, the anger in Paris (and other European cities) seemed to be aimed at no one in particular, since the revolutionary left, particularly the Communists, blamed the entire world bourgeoisie, not merely the U.S. government, for Sacco and Vanzetti's deaths. For many of the Communists in France, the executions and their violent aftermath were part of the "revolutionary moment" Stalin was describing that year.

But even many in France who deeply sympathized with the Sacco-Vanzetti cause felt that this time the radicals had gone too far, especially by attacking such politically sacred sites as the Tomb of the Unknown Soldier, and the backlash was instantaneous. For a crucial moment, much mainstream public opinion turned partly away from the Sacco-Vanzetti cause, even though the rioters clearly did not represent everyone in the camp. The fact that many Italian Communists and anarchists had come to France in recent years to escape Mussolini's repression had a lot to do with the ugly mainstream reaction to these riots.[66]

The Paris riots took place in the context of a raucous debate in France over immigration that would have been easily recognizable to Americans: on the one hand was the longstanding economic need for foreign manual labor, on the other were racism and xenophobia and the political baggage that many immigrants, particularly Italians, brought with them. In the wake of the riots, the latter side gained the upper hand; it would have been difficult to find in mainstream American newspapers and politics the sort of language that Parisian politicians and editorialists used to describe the street protesters in the last week of August 1927. Some of those who had publicly appealed to the Americans to show mercy to the two imprisoned Italians now turned on their own "foreigners" with rabid fury (and the rich irony of their shift was apparently lost on them). The minister of the interior, Albert Sarraut, described the demonstrators as "a mob of foreigners," "common criminals," "scum," who were "more interested in laying waste than in anything else." The mainstream press, while remaining critical of the executions, reacted to the riots with alarm and in some cases horror. The editorial in *Le temps* on August 24 warned: "We have here in Paris a gang of rioting, of armed violence, of vandalism, all organized and staffed. Yesterday's events must have political consequences." *Paris midi* was more shrill, and racist, describing the demonstrators (not all of whom were foreigners) as "a bunch of foreign subjects, undesirable refugees, and Wops of all colors," who, "having escaped persecution and poverty in their own countries, have taken advantage of our hospitality, our freedom, and our offers of work [in order to] break into shops, loot as they please, and steal cars, all the while screaming in twenty different languages their godless hatred for France."[67] Both newspapers—along with the nationalist and Catholic press—called for the arrest or even the head of Paul Vaillant-Couturier, the principal editorialist of *L'humanité*, who, they charged, had incited much of the Paris violence with his incendiary editorials; they also called—in vain—for the dissolution of the PCF and an end to diplomatic relations between France and the Soviet Union.[68]

The right-wing press, such newspapers as *Petit bleu* and *Gaulois,* forgot for a moment their derision toward America and focused on what they saw as the biggest scandal facing France: the state's de facto granting to its Italian immigrants of permanent asylum from Mussolini's regime. Whereas all other foreigners in trouble with the law would be automatically deported back to their country of origin as soon as they had served their time in prison, Italians were usually released back into French society, in the understanding that they were political refugees. Chiappe and other authorities did their best to present the riots as the product of Italian immigrants' revolutionary ingratitude toward their hosts, but the police's own records show that the issue was a red herring. The Paris police, who took it upon themselves after the riots were long over to seek out and arrest "undesirables" and revolutionary activists who might have been involved in them, ultimately pressed charges against ninety-two people for their roles in the August 23 riots; of these, only fourteen were foreigners, and eight were Italians (among the group were two Americans in their early twenties, who were promptly sent back to the United States). The rest were French natives, residents of Paris or the outlying area, usually workers in their twenties and thirties, more often than not members of the PCF.[69]

The arrival of the American Legion in France shortly thereafter only exacerbated these internal tensions. Scheduled to take place on September 19, a mere three weeks after the executions of Sacco and Vanzetti, the French-sponsored celebration of the American veterans' organization associated by many with the reactionary right (and especially with Mussolini, who was invited in the early 1920s to speak at American Legion conventions) and with the freshly remembered horrors of the war was simply too much for some to bear.[70] The protest that preceded the Legion's arrival worried the government to the extent that it considered moving, rescheduling, or even canceling the event. As the date of the celebration neared, the left again agitated for action, led by the radical press. *L'humanité* ran daily articles on the American Legion, describing it ominously as a "fascist organization" and charging—based on a report from John Dos Passos in Boston—

that Legion leaders had informed Fuller and Coolidge that they would "step in to stop any disturbances" that might occur after the Sacco-Vanzetti executions, a charge that to sensitive European leftists implied an imminent coup d'état, Mussolini-style. *Le libertaire*'s headline of August 29, 1927, was "Stop the Macabre Celebration!" and the editorial furiously attacked the French government for going ahead with the ceremonies: "How can the leaders of France not understand the total lack of taste and dignity in holding a Franco-American celebration such as this now?" From the editors' point of view, hosting the American Legion in Paris so soon after the trauma of August 23 would be "like assassinating Sacco and Vanzetti for the second time."[71]

Strong French opposition to the American Legion's visit came from other quarters as well. The LDH called for a boycott of the Legion and organized the campaign against it. The protest was not marginal. The mayor of Lille refused to call a municipal holiday on the day of the ceremonies, ordering instead that flags in the city be lowered to half-mast. The president of the Fédération héraultaise des anciens combattants républicains, a veterans' association, wrote to the American Legion representative in France that in protest of the Sacco and Vanzetti executions he would decline the invitation to be a delegate at the congress. The same intellectuals who had been approached by the LDH and the Comité Sacco-Vanzetti before the executions were now asked to sign petitions against the Legion.[72] And, as always, others demonstrated their sentiment more directly: the government announced just a few days before the celebration that train tracks on the Côte d'Azur railway had been sabotaged at Juan-les-Pins and Cap d'Ail, and the perpetrators, who had hoped to derail coastal trains carrying sightseeing members of the Legion and their families, had left behind them written slogans protesting the "barbaric" executions of Sacco and Vanzetti.[73]

The Legion stepped, then, into a highly contentious fray, the result both of the left's strong opposition to its arrival and of the conservative backlash against the violence of August 23. The LDH found itself under attack from right-wing editorialists who accused the organization of cooperating with revolutionaries. *Le gérant,* for example, charged the LDH with ignoring political crimes in the Soviet Union and neglecting the economic plight of veterans in France, choosing instead to "support the cause of criminals." In general, however, the nationalist and Catholic press criticized the LDH not so much out of love for the United States but because in their view it was unhealthily obsessed with Sacco and Vanzetti and as a result was helping French radicals in their fight against the government. The right wing's anti-Americanism did not contradict its persistent fear and hatred of the left in both its republican and its revolutionary form.[74]

The French government, determined to stop any disturbances to the Legion events, came into more criticism after the celebration was over. Louis Lecoin, who even after the Sacco-Vanzetti executions was being watched (at least according to his own account) by police at all times, had "disguised" himself as a legionnaire and attended the main rally at the Trocadero, "sitting with the delegates from Massachusetts," as he recalled in his memoir. As the president of the Legion was about to begin his speech, Lecoin rose and shouted, "Vivent Sacco et Vanzetti!" and was promptly dragged away by the police. His subsequent arrest and weeklong imprisonment angered the left-center press, which had not liked the riots and violence that followed the executions but did not see much wrong with an activist briefly interrupting the American Legion rally. *Paris soir* attacked not only the government for arresting Lecoin but also others who did not share their outrage at the incident: "If our press were capable of independence in the face of power," the editorialist complained, "it would vigorously protest this scandalous arrest."[75]

The French government got its wish and aside from Lecoin's arrest and a few other skirmishes managed to prevent major embarrassments to the Legion parade. Some historians have since described September 19 as a loud and uniform Parisian cheer for Lindbergh-era America, drowning out meager voices of protest.[76] But the Sacco and Vanzetti executions and their tumultuous aftermath would continue to echo in French life for years.[77]

The many Americans living or traveling in Paris in the 1920s were in a privileged position to witness these developments, both before and after the executions. Jane Addams, who cultivated transatlantic relationships throughout her career, spent much of 1926 and 1927 in Europe and recalled being "continually interrogated about Sacco and Vanzetti, the questions showing a detail of information which only a few people in the United States then possessed." It was clear to her that many people in France saw the Sacco-Vanzetti case as a new Dreyfus affair; for Addams, the comparison was particularly evocative because in 1900, when the conspiracy against the Jewish captain had fallen apart and the aftermath of the affair was convulsing French society, she had spent time in Paris as a juror on social economics at that year's World's Exposition.[78]

Much has been written about the presence of disaffected young American artists and hangers-on in 1920s Paris, the legendary Lost Generation who fled what they considered a backward, conformist, and culturally impoverished America after the war for the haven of modernism and individuality (and then began to return to the United States once Paris sank into recession in the early 1930s).[79] Several of them were marginally involved in the protest over the Sacco-Vanzetti case, which only reinforced their disgust with American society. This, too, was part of the context for the reception of the Sacco-Vanzetti case in France, though not the most important part. American poets and painters were but a small, well-documented part of a major, as yet understudied, transatlantic phenomenon. There were approximately forty thousand American citizens living in Paris alone in the late 1920s: diplomats, journalists, bankers, senior citizens, business-men, artists, shopkeepers, barflies, and people of virtually every pro-fession and orientation, making for a remarkable American presence in the city's social, cultural, economic, and intellectual life. There were also unprecedented hordes of shorter-term American tourists, drawn to France by the dramatic fall of the franc against the dollar (from 5.45 francs to the dollar in January 1919 to 50 francs to the dollar in July 1926) and especially by the fact that they could consume alcohol openly and readily; these Americans were viewed with contempt by both resident Parisians and American expatriates.[80] According to one estimate, the combined spending of American tourists and residents in France in 1928 totaled more than $137 million—nearly half of the entire spending of Americans in all of Europe that year—creating a veritable "American economy in Paris."[81]

Not surprisingly, many Americans in France could not avoid re-sponding to the case or even belligerently confronting one another about it, just as they did in the United States. The lively American press in Paris eagerly reported one symbolic encounter between two very different types of Americans. Shortly before her death on Sep-tember 14, 1927, the dancer Isadora Duncan was reported to have had a public spat over the case with an American judge, Jacob Hopkins of

Chicago. Duncan had been living in self-exile in Europe since 1900 and often could be heard expressing her disgust with American culture and society. Hopkins was staying in Paris that August and wished to hear what he called the "leftist take" on the case, so he went to a noted "Bohemian" (his word) café popular with the American expatriates, the Select. There he saw Duncan sitting with a group of admirers and overheard her saying that "the [Sacco-Vanzetti case] is a blot on American justice. It will bring a lasting curse on the United States, a curse deserved by American hypocrisy. Fuller's name will go down in history with that of Pontius Pilate." Duncan's reference to Scripture was apparently too much for Hopkins, who intervened in the conversation with an impromptu defense of American justice: "If the original sentence of death had been pronounced on Sacco and Vanzetti in any country of Europe," he told the surprised Duncan, "they would have been executed and buried six years ago." The ensuing debate between Duncan and Hopkins, and others who joined in, went on for hours and ended with Hopkins inviting Duncan to join him for dinner with his friend Clarence Darrow, himself a Sacco-Vanzetti supporter, who also happened to be in Paris at the time.[82]

One of the many self-exiles in the so-called American Paris was a young writer, Elliot Paul, who was originally from Massachusetts and was a friend of Gertrude Stein and James Joyce, among others. In a 1929 essay, Paul pointed out how vivid the memory of Sacco and Vanzetti remained in Paris after their execution. Fuller had been a frequent traveler to the city until 1927, but he had to cut down on his visits when the French government informed him that it could no longer guarantee his safety. The ultimate humiliation for Fuller came after his bid to become the 1928 Republican Party candidate for president had been killed by Senator Borah and other influential Republicans, when he was also denied the post of U.S. ambassador to France.

"What a laugh there was in the editorial offices of the American newspapers published in Paris when Fuller's name was suggested," Paul later wrote. "One of my friends who covered the embassy said that he would get himself a suit of mail at once." The former governor, according to Paul, now had to deal with the fact that "in the French press, Fuller's name is never mentioned without being coupled with those of the men he allowed to be killed. On the streets of Paris men and women speak of his arrival in hushed voices, expecting trouble. The railroad station is packed with extra police, soldiers and plainclothes men.... [Fuller] is spirited away secretly and conceals his address."[83]

What, ultimately, was the context of the reception of the Sacco-Vanzetti case in France? Or, to look at the issue another way, what was the main driving force of the French responses? Reactions in France to the case were so different and often contradictory that identifying a single major cause may prove impossible, although the Dreyfus affair comes close to qualifying. We can quickly discard one explanation that has made too much headway in the scholarly conversation over the affair, however: the notion that the Sacco-Vanzetti campaign was secretly orchestrated by Communist operatives working at Stalin's bidding to dupe gullible liberal intellectuals (the other and complementary side of this argument is that the liberals and intellectuals enthusiastically allowed themselves to be duped). There were simply too many nonrevolutionary—indeed, nonleftist—aspects to the Sacco-Vanzetti affair for this argument to hold true, in France as anywhere else. The case appealed to various stripes of public, political, and intellectual opinion for a variety of reasons that often had little or nothing to do with the objectives of the Communist International or the anarchist movement, although adherents of those movements were consistently part of the protest and responsible for its most violent components.

For many people in France—radicals, democrats, conservatives, even nationalists—the Sacco-Vanzetti case represented a number of things: a miscarriage of justice, a humanitarian issue, deep flaws in the American political and legal systems. But the variety of the French responses did not constitute a simplistically defined anti-Americanism. Rather, a conflicted Americanism, and even a sense of betrayal, were more dominant sentiments. There were also those willing to defend the United States or indignant that what they saw as a purely internal American matter could cause such consternation and conflict in faraway France, which had considerable political and social problems of its own.

And yet a stubborn question still remains. There were many other well-known cases of documented injustices in the United States during this period, as we have seen—Mooney's ongoing imprisonment in California, the lynchings of African Americans, and the 1925 Sweet murder trial are only some examples. Why, then, Sacco and Vanzetti?

What was it about this case that made it reverberate so powerfully in the streets and journals of Paris?

One answer to this question might have been provided by an American who probably knew the case better than anyone: William Thompson, the Boston establishment lawyer for Sacco and Vanzetti between 1924 and April 1927. After leaving their legal defense, Thompson made an eye-opening statement to the press. Frustrated by his inability to save his clients, angered by what he saw as a jingoistic response by Americans to criticism from abroad, he did not see a difference between, say, French, British, and Italian reactions to the case. There was only a "European" response, he believed, and it was based on the origin of the defendants: "Europeans, gentlemen, these men are Europeans. That is the whole story. It is impossible for an American to understand fully their European turn of mind." To make his point, Thompson asked the reporters to imagine a scenario in which Harvard president A. Lawrence Lowell was arrested and put on trial in the Soviet Union: "How would the Russians get [Lowell's] point of view? He would immediately be denounced as the president of a bourgeois college, a friend of capital, an enemy of the working class, and before the trial had progressed far, bullets would be flying in the back of the court house."[84]

Thompson's assessment rings essentially true: the identification by Europeans with the plight of other Europeans on non-European soil might have been, in some cases, a prime motivator for the protest, a shared sentiment that could unify the likes of Maurras and Rolland, anarchists and republicans, politicians and workers, elites and masses. The fact that Sacco and Vanzetti were themselves Europeans also helps answer the question of why they, rather than American victims of injustice, became the major cause célèbre in France.

Sacco and Vanzetti's imprisonment and execution dramatized and personified a stark new postwar world in which Europeans, once mighty world players, had become helpless, so it seemed, in the face of American power, and even captive to American whims. More fearful critics reasoned that having completed its westward expansion and established its empire in the Pacific and Latin America, the United States was ready to extend its control to the rest of the world, including Europe itself. This dismay was exacerbated by the suspicion, especially after the executions, that even progressive Sacco-Vanzetti sympathizers in the United States could not abide European criticism, and

that Americans in power would not even listen to the opinions of
Europeans or, worse, that even the friendliest European opinions had
ultimately stiffened American isolationism and doomed Sacco and
Vanzetti. (This suspicion was reasonable.)

But European critics might have had other reasons for worrying
about Sacco and Vanzetti. One historian has argued that as opposed to
Americans, who saw the Sacco-Vanzetti case in "ethnic" terms, "Europeans saw the issue in terms of the worldwide struggle between revolution and capitalism." It was a matter of example; European democracies faced similar tensions, and especially after World War I looked
to the United States as a model: "Conservative, liberal, and radical
Europeans all agreed that America was the bulwark of capitalism and
democracy. Could the United States contain radicalism and still retain
its democratic tolerance? This question was of direct importance to the
Europeans. If even the powerful United States could not strike a moderate pose between reaction and revolution, how could European democracies hope to do so?"[85]

Viewed this way, the interest in Sacco and Vanzetti represented
mainly European concerns, on both the left and the right. A prominent Danish newspaper, for example, concluded that "liberal" Europe
saw its own social institutions at stake. European liberals feared that
since the United States showed in the Sacco-Vanzetti case that it had
abandoned its liberal tradition, and since America represented the future, "the execution would undermine the 'bourgeois' ideals of humanity and justice" in Europe as well. And like Mussolini in Italy,
other European conservatives and nationalists, according to an American diplomat in Belgium, "deplored the sentence of execution [for
Sacco and Vanzetti] . . . because it would furnish much ammunition to
radical agitators everywhere."[86]

And yet this interpretation, while capturing understandable interwar anxieties in much of Europe, does not give enough weight to the
precise historical moment in which the Sacco-Vanzetti affair occurred.
Nor does it pay enough attention to the differences between individual
European states. European democracies may have been fragile and
may have looked to America for inspiration. But not all democrats felt
equally vulnerable, and by the end of the 1920s any admiration for
American democracy was tinged with, and even overwhelmed by, fear
and disillusionment (sentiments perhaps best captured, somewhat in-

advertently, in Franz Kafka's novel *Amerika,* published in 1927, three years after the author's death).

In the end the center of attention for all those in France who responded in one way or another to the Sacco-Vanzetti case was the United States. This can even be argued of the Communists, the least American-oriented of the French protesters, who considered capitalistic America the most formidable obstacle on the path to the dictatorship of the proletariat. In his 1929 *World Politics,* the American political scientist Harry Elmer Barnes attempted to explain the global significance of the affair, with special reference to Franco-American relations. "The most important aspect of the Sacco-Vanzetti case," he argued, "was that it wiped out at a stroke with the vast majority of foreigners what remained of our once laudable reputation as a country that afforded an asylum for the persecuted and down-trodden and provided an opportunity for all, irrespective of social status, opinions, or beliefs. . . . The [case] did more to destroy abroad our ancient reputation of being a 'land of the free' than all of the other historical incidents of the last century." Barnes, who was in France during the frantic summer of 1927, concluded: "It is scarcely possible to exaggerate the unfortunate effect of the case upon [European] opinion of American justice."[87]

In 1928 the British journal *Nation and Athenaeum,* in a review of the newly published collection of Sacco and Vanzetti's letters—the volume that helped establish the two men's latter-day reputations as soulful utopian martyrs—argued that the case became an international cause célèbre not because America was seen as worse than other places but because it was supposed to be much better. "Many of those who protested most loudly against this execution would themselves, if they attained power, attempt to exterminate all opponents of their theories," wrote the young critic Raymond Mortimer. But the Sacco-Vanzetti affair, he explained, "caused much more anxiety [in Europe] than the wholesale political executions in Russia, Hungary, and Italy, partly due to our expecting a very different standard of justice and tolerance from Americans." Bertrand Russell, the British celebrity-philosopher who moved back and forth across the Atlantic, was similarly disappointed: "One is not so surprised at occurrences of this sort in Hungary or Lithuania. But in America they must be matters of grave concern to all who care for freedom of opinion."[88] In

Germany, too, many radicals, as well as liberals, viewed the United States after the Sacco-Vanzetti affair with more sadness than rage, as a "lost leader" of a free, democratic, progressive world.[89]

It is not possible, of course, to speak of a common European position on the Sacco-Vanzetti case, given the myriad tensions and conflicts between different nations and political and social groups, which made a common European position on anything impossible in this period. If even radicals in France fought bitterly among themselves over the Sacco-Vanzetti case, there should be little surprise that French and German nationalists did not put aside their differences to unite around the case. And the pan-European, transnational mobilization around the case that occurred at the grassroots and among intellectuals did not necessarily translate into cross-governmental action.[90]

But at least in France, on the general question of the United States, as well as on the specific issue of Sacco and Vanzetti, we can discern a clear sentiment. From left to right, intellectuals and activists, political figures and ordinary people, even violent rioters on the streets of Paris and Lille and Marseille, juxtaposed an ideal, timeless America with its more horrifying, time-specific reality—a reality that produced a case such as that of Sacco and Vanzetti, an even grimmer sequel to the Dreyfus affair.

CHAPTER 4

The "Mob of Broadcloth-Coated, Heavy-Jowled Gentlemen"

The Lowell Commission and the Aftermath of the Affair

For many in the Sacco-Vanzetti camp, Americans and non-Americans alike, the formation of the Lowell advisory commission in June 1927, one month before the original scheduled date of Sacco and Vanzetti's executions, was proof that the system worked after all: the unfortunate affair, it appeared, would have a happy ending. When on June 29 Fuller announced a thirty-day delay of the executions the optimists seemed to be vindicated; the next step, many believed, would be clemency. Even a conservative politician like Fuller, the former bicycle-repairman-turned-salesman and millionaire representative of the business class, could not resist, they believed, the flood of letters, petitions, appeals, and protests that were sent to him from within and outside the United States, especially since Thayer's pronouncement of the death sentence in April.

Fuller's decision to conduct an independent study of the case was unprecedented and unusual, and it provided internationally minded progressives, especially those who had been in contact with horrified European intellectuals, with the comforting sense that the American political class was not entirely detached from the rest of the world. It won him praise from such worried venues as the *New York World,* whose editorial proclaimed that Fuller showed "characteristic courage. . . . [He] is a man of liberal views and not afraid to stand up for his convictions." Fuller, the *World* editorial added, "though a millionaire . . . sympathizes with labor. . . . There can be no doubt that he will bring perfect integrity and independence to the case." The *Nation* flattered him even more directly: "You have won a reputation . . . for independence and courage. . . . [This] embolden[s] us to believe that as an honest and fearless man you will face the great issues presented to you . . . without shrinking and with a determination to get at all the facts." New York Congressman Fiorello La Guardia, probably the most prominent Italian-American politician in the country, told the press, "[Governor Fuller] is free from bigotry and prejudice and will investigate fairly and fully. There is no prejudice in his makeup. I so judge from my knowledge of him in congress." The Stockholm lawyer Georg Branting, who had studied the case on behalf of the Swedish Social Democrats, told the press before he left that "my hope that these men will not die is strengthened because of my interview with Fuller. . . . His decision will be just." And even Vanzetti himself, always capable of surprising optimism as well as political gloom, told supporters that the governor, who had interviewed him in prison, struck him as kind and sympathetic.[1]

All these compliments, whether genuine or tactical, were misplaced. Fuller's moves were dictated not by enlightened awareness but by purely political considerations and pressures, and they reflected the growing doubt about the case both in the United States and abroad that after 1926 went beyond the protest of anarchists and other radicals and was expressed by mainstream figures and conservative groups. Fuller, evidently loath to make a decision for fear of its effect on his own career, probably saw this as a win-win situation: an advisory commission would allow him either to grant the anarchists clemency without appearing to be weak or to go ahead with the executions with the imprimatur of an impartial intellectual authority.

Fuller's advisory commission consisted of three Massachusetts establishment men, but only one of them mattered in the long run: Abbott Lawrence Lowell, the president of Harvard University since 1909. The two other members, former probate judge Robert Grant and MIT president Samuel Stratton, were public nonentities in comparison, far less well known, influential, and impressive; Lowell easily dominated the committee, which was named after him even though he was not formally its chair. (Lowell himself insisted that Grant hold that position.)[2]

The seventy-one-year-old Lowell, a veteran educational reformer, Harvard Law School graduate, and former president of the American Political Science Association, was a quintessential Boston Brahmin. He came from one of New England's most famous families and was a paragon of the educated elite in which some of the most influential members of the Sacco-Vanzetti camp put their faith (and to which several of them belonged). Colder-eyed critics, especially in later years, would note that as Harvard president Lowell had a mixed record, to say the least: in the early 1920s he had presided over the creation of the quota system designed to limit the growing number of Jews at the university, and he had promoted segregation in student freshmen dormitories (where there were few black students to begin with). Indeed, many scholars would now argue that Lowell—not unlike many men of his background, as well as leaders of other elite American universities at the time—was an anti-Semite, a snob, a misogynist, and a homophobe by today's standards.[3] Still, segregation, quotas for Jews, and expulsions of homosexuals were not policies that outraged most white progressives in the 1920s, and Lowell, a pioneering social scientist in his day, was no small-town police chief or ignorant provincial judge, the two great scourges of the Sacco-Vanzetti camp thus far. Liberals in particular were pleased with Lowell's appointment, even willing to overlook his former vice presidency of the National Immigration Restriction League, in the hope that his avowed nativist sensibilities would not prevent him from making a fair-minded investigation into the case.[4]

For many progressive Sacco-Vanzetti supporters, perhaps the most formative political and legal experience of the previous decade had been the struggle over free speech, and in this regard Lowell's public career seemed exemplary. He might also have reminded veteran progressives, in a good way, of another ambitious academic: Woodrow Wilson, once the reform-minded president of Princeton University. Unlike his fellow Massachusetts Brahmin, the powerful senator Henry Cabot Lodge, Lowell had been an enthusiastic supporter of the U.S. entry into the League of Nations.[5] Perhaps more important, unlike many university leaders, he had stood up for academic freedom in the face of considerable pressure. In 1919 he had protected the young left-wing British political scientist Harold Laski—who as an untenured Harvard lecturer publicly supported the Boston policemen's strike—threatening to resign if the university overseers fired Laski.[6] Lowell acted similarly in 1920 when a group of Harvard Law School graduates demanded that Professor Zechariah Chafee be fired for publishing an article in the *Harvard Law Review* condemning the policies of Attorney General A. Mitchell Palmer.[7] Earlier, during World War I, when German, German-American, and pro-German university professors across the country were fired or harassed, Lowell defended the psychology professor Hugo Münsterberg—who had openly embraced Germany's position—despite the reported threat of a Harvard alumnus to withdraw a ten-million-dollar legacy contribution. As late as 1927, despite his own personal animosity toward Frankfurter, Lowell, in a tense meeting with some angry Harvard overseers, defended the law professor's right to speak out in favor of Sacco and Vanzetti, reportedly demanding: "Would you have wanted [Frankfurter] to wait in expressing his views until the men were dead?"[8]

Lowell's principled and consistent defense of free speech won him fans as unlikely as the socialist muckraker (and Sacco-Vanzetti supporter) Upton Sinclair, who complimented him on this point only in his otherwise blistering critique of American universities, *The Goose-Step*.[9] Lowell, many Sacco-Vanzetti defenders hoped, would bring to bear on the case the calm, rationality, and learning that befitted his lofty position and that had been so sorely missing from their trial during the nativist atmosphere of 1921. Expertise and education, rather than fear and ignorance, would now determine Sacco and Vanzetti's fate. To the *Nation* and the *New Republic*, best representatives of this hopeful mindset, the Lowell commission represented more than just the chance to save Sacco and Vanzetti from death; more important, it was being given the opportunity to rescue America's rapidly dwindling reputation abroad. Harold Laski revealed his hopes in a letter to Oliver Wendell Holmes: "Lowell, I imagine, would be fair." Laski expected that the members of the commission would read Frankfurter's article or book on the case and that the result of their investigation would be nothing less than "a full pardon." "It would be terrible," he added, "to have an unsatisfactory ending . . . before the attention of Europe." Even Jackson and Felicani, the principal figures in the Sacco-Vanzetti defense committee in 1927, were so confident at first in the results of Lowell's investigation that they asked radical activists in the United States and abroad to abstain from protests and demonstrations while the advisory commission was in session. They also prevented other Sacco-Vanzetti activists from pursuing alternative options: Roland Sawyer, a Congregational minister and a member of the Massachusetts state legislature, unsuccessfully tried to persuade the defense committee to support his proposal to ask the state house of representatives to set up a special commission of judges to review the case. And even the most critical European commentators became relatively cheerful at this juncture: newspapers in France, for example, predicted that the formation of the Lowell commission marked the end of Sacco and Vanzetti's ordeal.[10]

Given this degree of anticipation on both sides of the Atlantic, it is easy to understand the disappointment, anger, and embarrassment that eventually greeted the advisory commission's report in some quarters —and the relief that met it in others. In an underwhelming and selective text, reportedly written by Lowell himself, the commission vindicated the trial, the judge, and the death sentence. For many Sacco-Vanzetti supporters, this was more astounding than anything that had previously happened in the entire course of the affair. The now-imminent execution of Sacco and Vanzetti could no longer be portrayed as the act of bigoted backwater officials; it had now been stamped with Harvard's prestigious *Veritas* seal.[11]

The repercussions began almost immediately and continued long thereafter. The negative reactions to the report certainly did not come only from "socialists, communists, and anarchists here and abroad," as Lowell's official biographer later wrote.[12] Lowell's report should be seen as the dividing line between the first part of the Sacco-Vanzetti affair and its second, longer part—its afterlife. In the wake of the report's publication, Lowell received dozens of letters from judges, writers, lawyers, businessmen, politicians, Harvard graduates, and ordinary citizens, representing a broad swath of public opinion. These letters reveal its powerful effect on political, judicial, and intellectual elites in the United States and help explode the lingering notion that the late 1920s was a relatively apolitical period in American history. Indeed, the Sacco-Vanzetti affair preceded the November 1929 economic crash in creating a sense of crisis for many American intellectuals. The reactions to the Lowell report also helped move issues such as expertise, psychology, and education to the forefront of public debate and sharpened fears that the United States had isolated itself from foreign opinion. Finally, the report helped push a significant group of American progressives and public figures toward a more radical political and social stance. Since this group was later predominantly responsible for the popular and scholarly depiction of the Sacco-Vanzetti case, at least through the 1960s, their responses to the report, and to the executions that followed it, marked the beginning of Sacco and Vanzetti's path in memory, politics, and culture—the ways in which Americans and many non-Americans presented, perceived, and gave meaning to the two men's lives and deaths in the decades that followed.

Regardless of how one viewed the Sacco-Vanzetti question, the Lowell report itself came as something of an anti-climax: there was little in it by way of explanation. Lowell evidently saw himself as an "umpire," as he later put it, but he did not appear to be a fair one. Aside from the thin and mostly circumstantial evidence presented against Sacco and Vanzetti at their trial—which appeared even more flimsy as new details and confessions came to light—two of the most controversial aspects of the case were the conduct of Judge Thayer and the xenophobic, anti-radical atmosphere in which the trial was held. The Lowell commission heard and read testimony that Thayer had talked freely about the case and mocked both the defendants and their attorneys outside the court, boasting of his treatment of "those anarchistic bastards." William Thompson had looked Lowell in the eye and told the commission that Thayer, whom he had known all his adult life, was "a narrow-minded man . . . a half-educated man . . . an unintelligent man . . . full of prejudice . . . violent, vain, and egotistical."[13] The committee also learned that the jury foreman had exclaimed, on hearing of some potentially exonerating evidence, "Damn them, they ought to hang anyway," and that the prosecutor had made open use of Sacco and Vanzetti's radicalism while arguing his case in court. Many legal experts like Frankfurter were sure that all this was enough to overturn the verdicts and at least earn the defendants a second trial. The commission, however, was not fazed by these accounts:

> It has been said that while the acts and language of the judge, as they appear in the stenographic report, seem to be correct . . . his attitude and emphasis conveyed a different impression. *But the jury do not think so* [emphasis mine]. They state that the judge tried the case fairly; that they perceived no bias; and indeed some of them went so far as to say that they did not know when they entered the jury room to consider their verdict whether he thought the defendants innocent or guilty. . . . To the committee the jury seemed an unusually intelligent and independent body of men. . . . Each of them felt sure that the fact that the accused were foreigners and radicals had no effect upon his opinion. . . . From all that has come to us we are forced to conclude that the judge was indiscreet in conversation with outsiders during the trial. He ought not to

have talked about the case off the bench, and doing so was a grave
breach of official decorum. But we do not believe that he used some of
the expressions attributed to him, and we think that there is an exaggeration in what the persons who spoke to him remember. Further-
more, we believe that such indiscretions in conversation did not affect
his conduct at the trial or the opinions of the jury, who indeed, so stated
to the committee.[14]

This eyebrow-raising statement was followed by an equally controversial conclusion. After dismissing Sacco's alibi and positing that
he was guilty beyond a reasonable doubt, Lowell and the committee
added that "on the whole, we are of the opinion that Vanzetti also was
guilty beyond reasonable doubt." The first three words of this sentence, ambiguously phrased and maddeningly open to interpretation,
epitomized for many the somewhat strange logic that ran through the
report. Particularly striking to many was the sloppiness with which
Lowell, much like Thayer, confused socialists, Communists, and anarchists, indiscriminately calling them all Reds, and displaying a lack of
understanding not only of the nuances and realities of radicalism but
of the Red Scare.

The Lowell report hit liberal Sacco and Vanzetti sympathizers
in the United States and Europe hardest. Supporters who mobilized
around the case, as we have seen, were divided into two main groups:
those who chose a legalist approach, stressing proper procedure and
confidence in the existing system, and those who opted for a politicized, extralegal approach that emphasized protest and radical action.
The appointment of the Lowell commission and Fuller's decision to
study the case had been the culmination, even the vindication, of the
legalist-pragmatic approach; but the report itself bore out the predictions of the radical camp and brought forth a stream of scorn for
the liberals who had thought that Sacco and Vanzetti could be saved
through legal channels. "The investigation of the governor and his
commission was the sheerest fraud," an angry International Labor
Defense (ILD) pamphlet declared after the report was published. "It
was all stage scenery, rosily decorated, behind which the final prepa-
rations for the executions [were] being organized." With regard to
Fuller, ILD writer Max Shachtman continued, "The liberals were in a
fine fettle. Here was an honest and independent executive! Here was a
man who could be approached by the 'right' people in the 'right' way.
They made Fuller's name synonymous with hope and justice. They

never had a doubt about him, only joyous faith; and they severely scolded those rude, vulgar, noisy rebels who were annoying the governor and embarrassing him with their demonstrations and incessant protests."[15]

If Communists like Shachtman and other militants could partake of a bit of anti-liberal schadenfreude over the results of the Lowell investigation, the report came as a complete disaster to the liberal-legalist camp. But there was still the matter of saving Sacco and Vanzetti; they had gambled that Fuller would come through, and until the last moment—as Communists and other radicals never failed to mockingly point out—they did not stop trying to change his mind. During the few weeks that passed between the release of the report and the executions, stunned liberals in the Sacco-Vanzetti camp tried desperately to persuade the governor to call off the executions despite Lowell's report. The *New York World* and the *New Republic* both implored Fuller to commute the death sentence to life imprisonment. When Fuller granted Sacco and Vanzetti temporary reprieves on August 10 so that their lawyers could make one more round of the courts, the liberals' enthusiasm briefly revived; even harsh French observers became convinced once more that the authorities had finally seen the light, and Sacco and Vanzetti would be freed.[16] These hopes too were short-lived. After Sacco and Vanzetti were executed, the liberal-legalistic camp broke apart, and the tone of its commentary changed permanently, as did the focus of its critical attention. The disillusionment did not come immediately, however, and the reactions to the Lowell commission's report need to be understood in their complexity.

In the United States, unlike in Europe or Latin America, much of the press greeted the Lowell report and the subsequent executions with quiet and sometimes self-congratulatory acceptance, while to those for whom the entire affair was little more than the creation of radicals, eggheads, and foreigners the report even came as something of a relief. For the same reasons that liberal Sacco and Vanzetti defenders had been optimistic, this group had been gloomy; the Harvard president, they feared, would surely save the two anarchists. Even appointing such an advisory committee was in their opinion a surrender to foreigners and subversives—especially foreign subversives. But the report—and executions—enabled them to rest easier.[17]

The *Boston Evening Transcript*, consistently hostile to Sacco and Vanzetti, explained in its editorial of August 23, which appeared a few hours after the executions, that "the Sacco-Vanzetti case has ended in the only way it could. . . . Any other conclusion would have been sheer surrender to the forces of anarchy and disorder and an abject admission that trial by hysteria—which is nothing else than lynch law—had prevailed." Less jingoistic but more typical, and thus significant, was the response of the *Boston Herald*. This mild-mannered mainstream newspaper had played a key and unexpected role in strengthening the public campaign that had pressured Fuller to form the commission. But after the release of the Lowell report, the editors of the *Herald*, seeing the case as closed, decided to relegate all coverage to the back pages. They were praised for this in a letter from a police superintendent in Boston who complained that excessive attention to Sacco and Vanzetti had made New Englanders "too afraid to come to Boston to do their shopping."[18]

And on August 24, one day after furious demonstrators in European and Latin American cities clashed with police, attacked American companies and tourists, set cars on fire, and called for vengeance, and even usually moderate newspapers in France and Argentina screamed on their front pages that Sacco and Vanzetti had been murdered, the *Herald* published an editorial entitled "Back to Normalcy." There was no Europe-bashing or Red-baiting here. Instead, the editors, paraphrasing Warren Harding's English-mangling but election-winning slogan of 1920, urged their readers to put the Sacco-Vanzetti affair behind them. "The asperities which have attended the Sacco-Vanzetti case . . . should be forgotten as promptly as possible," they wrote. "Let us get back to business and to the ordinary concerns of life. . . . It has been a famous case. It has attracted the attention of the world. . . . But the time for all discussion is over. The chapter is closed. The die is cast. The arrow has flown. Now let us go forward to the duties and responsibilities of the common day with a renewed determination to maintain our present system of government, and our existing social order."[19]

But not all the American press was willing to bury the issue so casually; cracks in the "normalcy" consensus had appeared even before the executions. Immediately in response to the Lowell report, the *Springfield* (Mass.) *Republican*—which had been in favor of clemency —highlighted the commission's bias toward the prosecution.[20] The editor of the *New Republic*, Herbert Croly, called on Fuller to "satisfy demands for justice," to stop the executions as "a way of escape" between "executing two men who many people believed were unfairly

convicted, and not executing people who were found guilty and condemned by his own commission and by the court." That compromise
meant keeping Sacco and Vanzetti in prison but alive—perhaps with
the assumption that future judicial review would get them released.[21]
Even Henry Luce's popular new magazine *Time* criticized the verdict
and the executions as the products of intolerance, nativism, and the
bizarre laws of Masschusetts.[22]

The editors of the *Nation,* Oswald Garrison Villard and Freda
Kirchwey, were more distressed. "We are shaken to the core," they
wrote; "we had not believed such a decision possible." Making a comparison between Sacco and Vanzetti and another deeply controversial
figure, the radical 1850s abolitionist John Brown, who was hanged,
they warned that the decision to execute Sacco and Vanzetti "no more
closes [the case] then the hanging of [Brown] ended the Harper's Ferry
raid and condemned him to execration and oblivion. . . . The people
saw behind [Brown] issues of far-reaching moment that soon thereafter tore this country apart and for four long years drenched it in
blood."[23] For the *Nation,* the Lowell report marked the passing not
only of liberal dreams but of values as old as the American republic
itself: "It is *not* the radicals alone who fought for Sacco-Vanzetti. Noble souls have given years of their lives and their money to this cause
who are neither Reds nor foreign-born Americans; nor have they belonged to those holding the anarchist views of the condemned. If there
are finer types of our citizenship, or men and women of older American lineage, we should like to have them pointed out to us. . . . An
incredible tragedy is being finished before their eyes: a judicial murder
is being committed . . . . Let those who would uphold the present
system by force beware lest . . . August 10, 1927 [the original date
of execution], be forever recorded as the day of a great American
change."[24]

The *New York World*'s reaction was equally noteworthy. Edited
by Walter Lippmann, one of the most important American political
writers of the 1920s, and published by the Pulitzer family, the *World*
had lost much of its circulation and clout since its muckraking heyday
in the 1890s, but in the 1920s it was still a persistent and influential voice of East Coast progressivism, or what remained of it. When
the Lowell report was released, Lippmann conceded at first—reportedly, without reading it—that it "satisfied demands for justice," and
that "the lingering doubts" about the case had been "quelled."[25] But

shortly thereafter he changed his mind; his initial editorial had outraged his friend Felix Frankfurter, who reportedly rushed from the
Harvard Law School to Lippmann's New York office for a meeting
that consisted mainly of the jurist loudly reprimanding the editor.
Lippmann never again defended the Lowell report and instead—
perhaps too late—became one of its most relentless critics.[26]

Croly's *New Republic,* so cautious before the executions, quickly
changed its tone afterward. It is telling to contrast the journal's August 24 issue (written before the executions), which criticized the
Lowell report but dutifully maintained the liberal belief that Fuller
would save the defendants, with the August 31 issue, whose headline
was "An Ominous Execution." The executions, the editors now felt,
"can only be described as judicial murder . . . one of the most sinister
events which has as yet taken place in the life of the nation." After an
unsettling description of the electrocutions, which were "brutal and
sordid," the editors turned their attention to the "executors," primarily Lowell.

Disillusioned and bitterly disappointed, yet freed, now that Sacco
and Vanzetti were dead, from the obligation to appeal to the powers
that be, the editors observed that "the comfortable gentlemen, Thayer,
Fuller, Lowell, and the rest, who from their seats on high had elected to
end the lives of these two poor victims, did not attend the ceremony.
That task was delegated to paid employees." The formal judicial process that doomed Sacco and Vanzetti was "just a veneer," but "there are
[those] who see the matter in a different light. They see a group of men,
their hearts filled with bitter black rage against something, identifying
that something with the persons of the obscure fish peddler and the
factory hand. They see these men filled with an almost sadistic satisfaction, venting their deep-seated grudge by fulfilling the forms of legal
procedure against the individuals who have become . . . the symbols of
a struggle between classes, between social ideals, between philosophical systems."

To the editors of the *New Republic,* the executions were "ominous" because they represented "a clear case of the failure of a temper-
ate and reasonable public agitation to produce any sufficient effect
upon official action. . . . If this condition of mind continues, the America of our fathers is rapidly passing away." The inevitable result, they
warned, would be "a dangerous and unstable America." In another
column in the same issue, entitled "Penalties of the Sacco-Vanzetti

Execution," the journal lambasted Lowell for "a betrayal of the faith in reason which is inherent in the composition of a liberal and humane state" and predicted that "the shades of Sacco and Vanzetti will harvest their revenge": the executions would drive liberals to the idea of class warfare and make aliens radicals again after more than a decade of "Americanization."[27]

The *Nation,* in an issue entitled "Massachusetts the Murderer," echoed these sentiments in starker terms, stressing America's ruined reputation abroad. By killing Sacco and Vanzetti, the editors argued, American authorities had awarded a gift to revolutionaries the world over. The members of the advisory commission "outraged the opinion of the foreign world. . . . They struck at the reputation of the whole nation. . . . They everywhere strengthened the hands of violence and of all those persons who believe that the world can be reformed only by bombs and bloodshed. Everywhere they have made peaceful men and women despair that progress may be achieved without force."[28]

It is difficult to assess public sentiment in an era before the advent of modern opinion polls. But it is also clear that looking only at the press reaction to the Lowell report provides an overly superficial understanding of the Sacco-Vanzetti affair in the public sphere. Personal correspondence gives a fuller picture. Written out of the public eye, beyond the constraints of respectability or commercialism, and allowing the correspondent to unleash more honest and intense political and personal feelings, private letters are among the most revealing indicators of public opinion.

The Lowell papers in the Harvard University archives, which were closed for thirty years, contain dozens of letters written in response to Lowell's role in the Sacco-Vanzetti case. These papers have a fascinating and troubling history of their own. They were deposited in the archives by Lowell's official biographer, Henry Yeomans, in December 1948, with the stipulation that the archive remain closed until December 1977. Yeomans had barely quoted from them, perhaps because their contents would not have fit with his largely doting portrait of Lowell (reportedly, Yeomans wanted to destroy the papers but was dissuaded by a conscientious Harvard librarian). Over the years, these closed papers became something of an obsession for historians of the case, who, concerned almost exclusively with the question of Sacco

and Vanzetti's guilt or innocence, speculated that they would con-
clusively exonerate or incriminate the men.

In the summer of 1977, toward the fiftieth anniversary of the executions, Mayor Al Vellucci of Cambridge and the amateur researcher
Robert D'Attilio sued Harvard to have the papers opened to scholars,
citing the recently passed Freedom of Information Act, under which
another amateur researcher, Lincoln Robbins, had successfully petitioned the Department of Justice to have the FBI's Sacco-Vanzetti
files made public. "There is something that . . . Harvard is hiding,"
Vellucci ominously told the press, while Harvard argued, with some
justification, that opening the papers earlier than the date promised the
donor would compromise the possibility of obtaining future archival
donations.[29]

A Suffolk County judge ruled against the plaintiffs at the end of
August, but four months later the Lowell papers were finally opened
on the originally stipulated date, to much media fanfare (archivists are
not generally accustomed to the presence of television cameras). But
Sacco-Vanzetti scholars and buffs alike were bitterly disappointed to
find no minutes of the advisory commission's deliberations (apparently none had been kept), nor the long-awaited smoking gun that
would settle the case once and for all. As a result, they have since
ignored the papers' broader implications. While the documents do not
prove whether Sacco and Vanzetti "did it," they do show that a substantial part of the public refused the urgings of various groups to
return to "normalcy" after the Lowell report was published.[30] The
Lowell papers also do much to refute the popular image of the late
1920s in the United States as an era of a detached professoriate, intellectuals interested primarily in modernism and escapism, and a politically indifferent citizenry complacently shopping for needless goods
and following frivolous trends, all unwittingly headed toward economic disaster and social upheaval.[31] There were in 1927 strong por-
tents of the sharp conflicts to come in the 1930s. The responses to the
Lowell report also put to rest the common perception that the division
over Sacco and Vanzetti followed class lines. In general terms, as we
have seen, the more marked conflict was over Americans' reaction to
foreign interference in the affair. As to the Lowell report specifically,
the most striking chasm was within the elite, rather than between a
powerful establishment and a marginalized working class.

Relatively few of the letters in Lowell's papers were from radicals or workers—although one writer, presumably a fan of Heywood Broun's column, addressed an irate letter to "Hangman's House," Broun's term of derision for Harvard after the executions.[32] Many of the letters were from what historians like to call ordinary people, including a surprisingly large number of church pastors. Some were supportive of the report, but many were critical, often very much so. The correspondents as a rule took pains to distance themselves from Sacco and Vanzetti's politics. One pastor, from the First Methodist Episcopal Church in Upland, California, informed Lowell that "your best fellow citizens, including many church men, feel like there must be something done which will clear up the darkness which veils [the case] . . . in spite of the fact that [Sacco and Vanzetti] hold and have propagated ideas altogether opposite to those we hold."[33]

Many of the angriest letters were from Harvard's own. Some of Sacco and Vanzetti's most committed advocates, including Broun and Dos Passos, were former Harvard students, and their opinions were shared by less prominent alumni. A resident of Petersburg, Virginia, identifying himself as a "Harvard M.A.," wrote of his "shame and amazement" at the report. "I am not one of those 'socialists' or 'communists' whom you so carelessly confuse [in your report]," he began. "I am . . . as heartily opposed as you are to the Sacco-Vanzetti Utopia— but what has that to do with justice or with the *veritas* emblazoned on Harvard's seal? I believe, sir, that many Harvard graduates are today abashed to see their university represented before the world by a man who so emphatically fails to typify the independence of mind and devotion to truth that have for centuries spelled Harvard."[34]

Another former student, writing after the report was published but before the executions took place, implored Lowell to change his mind while there was still time and stressed the international resonance of the affair: "The world now thinks that the smug, conservative element of the United States . . . is fighting to save its self respect, and that the life of two radical 'dagoes' counts for nothing in the balance." The responsibility for righting the injustice, in his view, fell not on Fuller, who "is not big enough to feel that more is at stake than the legal process in Massachusetts," but rather on Lowell: "Chance has put you in a position where . . . you could save Sacco and Vanzetti. It is a terrible responsibility, but we Harvard men have faith in you."[35]

Lowell received similarly chagrined letters from some Harvard faculty. Three days before the executions, Albert Sprague Coolidge, a chemistry professor at the university and a member of the Socialist Party, wrote a detailed letter on the points in the case that he felt were ignored by the commission. It struck Coolidge that Harvard's symbolic place in the affair was critical. "The matter is peculiarly vital to me," he explained, "because I am a Harvard man. . . . It was because you were president of Harvard that you were appointed, and it will be a long time before the Harvard crimson will not be popularly identified with the blood of the two Italian anarchists." He too reminded Lowell of the effects of the case abroad: "You must be aware that their execution will be regarded by millions of men and women, including many of the world's most civilized minds, as a piece of barbarity ranking America with, let us say, Turkey or Roumania."[36]

Of course, many Harvard graduates and faculty did not share these sentiments and were still concerned, as they had been in 1919 and 1920, with the menace posed to Americans by "Reds," both at home and abroad. A member of the class of 1898—perhaps not the most gifted writer the college ever produced—complimented Lowell: "Had those men been allowed to go free where would the civilization of the whole world gone to it would have been Red rule all over the world, i think this is one of the greatest decisions that has ever been handed down and ranks on a par with the Bolicemens strike in Boston."[37]

The background to much of this correspondence had as much to do with what was happening at Harvard as with the case itself. The university, and Lowell as president, had experienced serious financial and political trouble in the preceding ten years because of the unpopular stance on various political and legal issues of some of its faculty, whom Lowell had valiantly defended in the name of academic freedom. But his report on the Sacco-Vanzetti case redeemed Lowell in the eyes of many who had previously thought him too soft on subversives. One New York businessman, once a generous contributor to the Harvard Endowment Fund, according to his own testimony had cancelled his donations in 1922 because, as he explained in a letter to the Endowment Fund Council, he had been angry that Lowell had prevented "Americanization meetings" at the end of the war. But he was in a much better mood now. Writing from a New York Yacht Club cruise around the time Sacco and Vanzetti were executed, the businessman let Lowell know that he was now ready to renew his donations to the university.[38]

All of these letters underline the principal challenge that Lowell had faced since the war: balancing the demands of the trustees and donors, the lifeblood of an expanding and dynamic private elite university like Harvard, with the increasingly vulnerable principles of academic freedom and free speech. But the Sacco-Vanzetti affair, for Lowell, was a challenge of a different order, and one that proved insurmountable. Defending Harvard professors from the charge of treason was one thing; standing up for two Italian immigrant working-class anarchists convicted of murder in a Massachusetts court was quite another. In retrospect, it is clear that Lowell could never have been an objective arbiter in the case, primarily because it was too deeply intertwined with his own public career. Despite the liberals' pronounced faith in him, he indeed proved himself incapable, as one of his own friends later remarked (and as radical supporters of Sacco and Vanzetti had insisted all along), "of seeing that two wops could be right and the Yankee judiciary could be wrong." But it never occurred to him, as it should have, to refuse appointment to the commission.[39]

This is the backdrop to a particularly aggressive and intriguing letter sent to Lowell after the executions by Harold L. Ickes, at the time a brash progressive Republican lawyer in Chicago, and within a few years the secretary of the interior in Franklin D. Roosevelt's cabinet and one of the chief policymakers of the New Deal. Ickes's letter is important because, among other things, it links the reaction to the Sacco-Vanzetti case—specifically the Lowell report—to the New Deal itself; it is logical to assume that one of the goals of policymakers like Ickes in the 1930s was to change the circumstances of American life so that a case like Sacco and Vanzetti's would never again occur.[40]

Later famed for his abrasive and even insulting verbal style, the still relatively unknown Ickes did not mince his words. Lowell, Ickes wrote, should have disqualified himself from serving on the commission. Indeed, in Ickes's view, by accepting the role Lowell had committed no less than a crime. He had always thought the Harvard president "a fearless and intellectually honest man," but then "disquieting rumors came to me" that Frankfurter's public defense of Sacco and Vanzetti had cost the Harvard Law School more than a million dollars in donations. "You as president," Ickes wrote to Lowell, "must have known of it." When Lowell took on the role of arbiter in the Sacco-Vanzetti case, "consciously or unconsciously it must have been on your mind that if . . . Frankfurter, in pleading for a fair trial for these two men, had been detrimental to Harvard how much more would it injure Harvard if you, the president of that institution, should find from all the evidence not only that Sacco and Vanzetti had not had a fair trial, but that they were in fact not guilty of the crime?"

As Ickes saw it—though he never provided any proof—Lowell was "probably not free from prejudice" when he agreed to head the advisory commission and when he re-condemned Sacco and Vanzetti. And if the Harvard president really were prejudiced when he accepted the appointment, he was, according to Ickes, "guilty of a more terrible crime than the supposed crime for which Sacco and Vanzetti were so lightly sent to the electric chair by yourself and your associates. For you cannot seek refuge behind the trial court which originally found these men guilty and imposed the sentence of death. . . . You and your associates had this case before you de novo. You were the jury that found them guilty and Governor Fuller was the judge who put on the black cap and pronounced sentence of death against them in accordance with your verdict."

Fittingly, Ickes ended his letter by combining a radical critique of the establishment with a simultaneous renunciation of radicalism. While he himself identified with the political and social elite of which Lowell was an integral part, he now saw a deep breach within it: "I am neither an anarchist, philosophical or otherwise, nor a socialist. . . . I have been by inheritance and inclination a republican in politics. In both lines my [American] ancestry goes back to pre-Revolutionary days. I have no sympathy for the mob that with torch and dagger in hand would attempt to destroy our civilization. I despise mobs of all sorts. And particularly abhorrent to me is the mob of broadcloth-coated, heavy-jowled gentlemen that with a calm demeanor that barely disguises suppressed fears and a hardly controlled hysteria carries out cold-bloodedly and relentlessly its sinister purposes in the name of 'law and order.' "[41]

It is difficult, even impossible, to determine whether Ickes's charges against Lowell were correct. There is no reason to believe that Lowell would have made his decision solely out of fear of trustees and donors; he had already held out against them during and after the war in the struggles over academic freedom. But it is also safe to assume that to argue *himself* that Sacco and Vanzetti were the victims of an injustice at the hands of the Massachusetts courts was beyond his capacities. If Lowell ever answered Ickes's letter, there is no record of it in his papers.

He did, however, civic-mindedly take the trouble of answering nearly everyone else who wrote to him, including most of his severest critics. His responses are as telling as the letters he received. Over time his skin thinned considerably. His early letters are brief and nearly identical. When writing to congratulators, Lowell complained that "there has been much misrepresentation," without adding much explanation. When replying to critics, he took the tone of a man who had stood up to a hysterical pack. Those who had advocated for Sacco and Vanzetti were not much different, in his view, from those who condoned lynchings. In response to one of the dismayed Harvard graduates, Lowell insisted, a month after the executions, that "the fact that by propaganda a large number of people had been led to doubt their guilt does not seem to me a reason why justice should not be done. . . . Criminal trials should be conducted by the constituted authorities, not by popular sentiment. It is the opposite view that has led to lynching in portions of our country."[42]

A recurring theme in Lowell's responses was what he called "mob psychology." To James Mickel Williams, a professor of economics at Hobart College who criticized the report: "Have you not been carried away by the mob psychology provoked by energetic propaganda?" To Frederick Lewis Allen, an editor at *Harper's,* he explained: "It has been a curious instance of mob psychology artfully inflamed by not too scrupulous methods." Lowell did not clarify what he meant here by "it," but elsewhere he explained that the belief in the innocence of Sacco and Vanzetti was based on "the logical process [that] the prisoners were Reds. There was a violent prejudice against Reds in the U.S. . . . therefore the men were unfairly tried. Therefore it was judicial murder for political reasons."[43]

But many of Lowell's correspondents found bewildering (and infuriating) his unwillingness to explain the commission's reasoning and his inability to understand why anyone would even question its conclusions. Lowell habitually replied to his critics that if they were to see all the evidence he had seen, they too would become convinced of Sacco and Vanzetti's guilt, but he refused to specify what that supposedly damning evidence included (and the opening of his archives in 1977 indicated that Lowell did not possess any such evidence besides that already used by the prosecution at the trial). Coolidge, in response to Lowell's cryptic letter, explained to the Harvard president that "Trust me" was simply not a good enough answer: "The spirit of democracy prohibits citizens from accepting without challenge the opinions of experts on public affairs, [and] requires them to take an active and well-informed part in political activities."[44]

Robert L. Hale, a professor at Columbia Law School, had once worked for Lowell as a research assistant, but this did not stop him from writing his former mentor one of the harshest letters the Harvard president must have received. Hale accused Lowell of ignoring evidence in favor of the defendants and went on to give an explanation of why: "I suspect that a natural reluctance to countenance so serious an indictment of the judicial system in its relation to radicals may have had its influence." Hale, the dominant figure behind what became known as the first "law and economics movement," was particularly worried about the effect of the Lowell report, and Sacco and Vanzetti's executions, on the legitimacy of the courts in the eyes of ordinary Americans, especially workers and immigrants. "Many of us will think," he wrote to Lowell, "that the whole investigation was conducted for the purpose of reconciling the public to the carrying out of the sentence. . . . Our conviction will be strengthened . . . by . . . the social and intellectual background common to all three members of the committee. It is distressing . . . that incalculable class bitterness is to be aroused against the courts."[45]

Lowell, in his response, appeared mystified by Hale's demand that he justify his conclusions: "Are you not on somewhat the wrong track? The people who believed in the innocence of Sacco and Vanzetti, or felt doubtful, asked for an umpire. . . . To convince those [who disagree] is what no umpire . . . can do, or ought to be expected to do." Hale countered that "you may perhaps say that the matter is closed and there should be no further discussion. If so, I cannot agree; for if . . . the men were innocent . . . then not only has a horrible wrong been done (and that cannot be undone), but there is also something calling for . . . greater public skepticism as to the soundness of judgment of those in high educational position, and greater self-criticism on the part of those men themselves."[46]

There is a striking gap in these letters between Lowell's self-perception as a referee whose authority should not be questioned and his critics' demands for explanations, accountability, and transparency.

"It was not the business of the committee to attempt to prove the correctness of their opinion but to report it," Lowell wrote to one correspondent, "and . . . it is rarely possible to change the opinions of those who have already formed them."[47]

To Lowell's challengers, this was an unacceptable position. But while many of them described the Sacco-Vanzetti affair as a struggle between the haves and have-nots, their own reactions show that the deeper rift was, as Ickes implicitly grasped, among elites. They may have been younger (in most cases) than the seventy-one-year-old Harvard president, but like Lowell they were part of powerful social, economic, educational, legal, and political milieus. Lowell's responses to their harsh criticisms reflect his surprise that of all people they—not Italian Americans, or workers, or anarchists—would call into question his intellectual authority.

When the Sacco-Vanzetti affair re-exploded as a public issue in the early 1960s, Michael Musmanno—formerly a Sacco-Vanzetti activist and later a Pennsylvania supreme court justice—speculated that Lowell "believed himself a super-intellectual and was satisfied that he would be hailed as a hero by the Brahmins for his cleverness."[48] Indeed, Lowell's letters raise the suspicion that he never dreamed that he would be called upon to explain or justify himself. Because his analysis of the case was so insubstantial, he was unprepared for learned criticism of his report; his answers were rich in indignation but poor in detail.

As he tried to deal with the barrage of letters criticizing his report, Lowell seemed to find some comfort and sympathy with like-minded friends, preferably abroad. In particular, he appeared to have a fondness for rather snobbish, conservative British men of his own age, class, temperament, and outlook. "The propagandists," he wrote to one such British friend, "have told the world that it was a case of racial and political prejudice, and have tried with considerable success to set the working men against employers." Who were these so-called propagandists? The Sacco-Vanzetti defense committee and their friends, Lowell explained in a second letter to his British friend, "have carried on an active propaganda to which the court and the prosecuting attorneys could not have properly replied, and their propaganda has been very misleading." Lowell also felt it "somewhat curious" that the defense committee "asked for a commission to inquire into the case and approved of my appointment thereon, but the decision not being in their favor, they merely attack us as they have everyone else who did not agree with them."[49]

In all these responses Lowell failed to explain where the "mob" of Sacco-Vanzetti defenders was or why their behavior was more "hysterical" then that of those who wanted to see the anarchists executed. Nor was he willing to give an example of what he continually called propaganda. Neither the report nor Lowell's subsequent correspondence attempted to deal with the question of racial and ethnic prejudice or the political context of the 1921 trial, or to show that these did not play a part in the convictions, except in the report's assertion that the jury members considered themselves unprejudiced. And by repeating himself constantly, as if he were copying responses from one letter to the next, Lowell dodged—or willfully misunderstood—some of the more thoughtful and novel critiques put to him.

His exchange with Williams, the Hobart College economist, is a case in point. Lowell, in earlier days, had pioneered some important trends in the development of the social sciences in the United States. Now he was severely chastised for his own lack of scholarly rigor. Williams criticized the Lowell report not only for its conclusions but also for its lack of expertise. Why were no specialists (perhaps Williams himself) invited to testify? The members of the commission, he pointed out, had no experience in criminal matters. "Among the aspects which discredit your report," Williams wrote, "are the assumptions you make from beginning to end, which have no basis other than the opinions of minds untrained in these technical matters." It was "regrettable" that the commission did not include "experts in analyzing testimony in criminal courts, . . . who also understand the effects on a jury of judicial prejudice." The whole basis of the report was "an attitude against the defendants." The word *attitude,* Williams further explained, "has come to have a technical meaning in social psychology," and, somewhat condescendingly, he directed Lowell to his own *Foundations of Social Science,* which had recently been published. "Your report," Williams concluded, "is an example of a kind of judicial attitude to which I there refer . . . a judge subservient to certain unconscious attitudes." With this emphasis on expertise, psychology, and recent trends in the academic disciplines, it was as if a new model of American social scientist were toppling over Lowell's nineteenth-century academic establishment.[50]

Lowell may have found his younger colleague's attempt to teach him scholarly lessons irritating, to say the least, but he responded by again invoking the "propaganda" over the case and asking Williams whether he had not been overly influenced by it. Williams did not relent: "Do you not owe it to us who have regarded you as·a scholar to give us an extended analysis of the case, not mere assumptions but all the evidence which you say is little known to the public?"[51]

On a similar note, Lowell was further taken to task by Julian Mack, a U.S. circuit court judge. Mack, also a Harvard Law School graduate, was perhaps the most important member, along with Frankfurter, of the Jewish and progressive circle of jurists who were protégés of Supreme Court Justice Louis Brandeis. Mack and Lowell did not enjoy a warm relationship, to say the least: Mack had been a Harvard overseer from 1919 to 1925, and he and Frankfurter had confronted Lowell (who might not have been prepared from a psychological standpoint to deal with a Jew in such a high position) over the quota system devised to keep down Jewish enrollment at the university. The tension between Lowell and Mack could also be traced to Lowell's opposition to Brandeis's candidacy to the U.S. Supreme Court in 1916, supposedly on the grounds that Brandeis did not have the support of the Massachusetts Bar.[52]

But Lowell could not well ignore a letter from Mack, who had presided over some of the most controversial trials of the 1920s, including Marcus Garvey's mail-fraud case in 1923, H. L. Mencken's obscenity and censorship trial in 1926, and, perhaps most significant, the trial of Harry Daugherty, former attorney general under Warren Harding, who was prosecuted twice, in 1926 and 1927, for his role in the corruption scandals that were the Harding administration's undoing.

Mack was not known for extralegal writing; Frankfurter, a much more prolific writer, liked to joke that Mack suffered from "paralysis of the pen." But the Lowell report was enough to shake him temporarily out of this condition. In a letter to Lowell written shortly before the executions, Mack argued that the Sacco-Vanzetti case had become a national and international crisis: "The feeling of doubt which seems to exist in the minds of millions . . . is not the result of any 'Red' agitation. . . . It is a genuine feeling of doubt both as to whether or not these men had a fair trial and as to whether or not their guilt has been established beyond a reasonable doubt."[53]

Mack had not written merely to castigate but also to plead for the lives of the two defendants. Lowell, however, did not write back until six days after the executions—he had been enjoying a hiking trip when Sacco and Vanzetti were electrocuted. He seemed, or pretended, to miss the point of Mack's letter, and his response was slightly, and perhaps disingenuously, incredulous: "Is it not true that I have been occupying temporarily a judicial position, as you do permanently? I am sure that, if your decision in the [corruption] cases was not approved by both parties, it would surprise you if I were to write asking you to modify your decision." Mack replied that he was "unable to reconcile your view that you were temporarily occupying a judicial position with the action of the advisory commission." He then remarked what should have been obvious to the Harvard president: that the Lowell commission had called crucial witnesses like Judge Thayer without the presence of Sacco and Vanzetti's counsel, whereas in the Daugherty case, Mack had not allowed judges to testify without being cross-examined in open court. But openness was one of the chief components missing from both the Lowell report and his justifications of it, and Lowell had no convincing answer to Mack's complaint.[54]

In the days immediately preceding Sacco and Vanzetti's executions, while a seemingly endless parade of public figures and foreign dignitaries appealed to Fuller to spare the defendants, and protest in both Europe and Latin America grew ever more anguished and violent, a flurry of telegrams and letters arrived in Lowell's office, begging him to help stop the executions that his report had sanctioned. The majority of these appeals, like most of the letters, came from members of the socioeconomic, cultural, and political elite. Lowell's correspondents, not unlike Lowell himself, showed a tendency to fit the Sacco-Vanzetti affair into categories that they easily recognized. They understood the case as part of the "class struggle" in America, a concern that may have been more relevant in political terms a decade earlier. They could not have seen what the historian now can: that the Lowell report had a much stronger—and more devastating—effect on progressives and liberals, the supposed ruling class, than on workers and radicals, whose expectations from a man like Lowell had always been low.[55]

"This wire is from a hater of anarchism, bolshevism, and all forms of isms," wrote, for example, James Ernest King from New York. "We are members of the New York Stock Exchange and deal in longtime investments, therefore believe in ordered government. . . . For God's sake do not canonize two saints for future generations of Reds." King called the Lowell report "woefully inadequate. . . . It leaves a much stronger suspicion of innocence than guilt. A manly admission of error in procedure is the only thing left to restore confidence in integrity of purpose." And lest Lowell think that the letter represented a single, wayward voice, King added, "These last sentences I have heard on the lips of at least fifteen conservative thinkers in the last fortnight!"[56]

Lowell was not present to receive these messages, and on his return from vacation he remained unperturbed by the appeals waiting on his desk. Nor did he understand the outrage, especially strong in Europe, over the six-year wait that Sacco and Vanzetti endured between conviction and execution. This delay was what had primarily driven European figures as unlikely and diverse as Benito Mussolini and Pope Pius IX to ask the American authorities to spare the two anarchists. Lowell, by way of response, repeatedly put the blame on Sacco and Vanzetti themselves for the delay in their own executions; if their lawyers had not repeatedly appealed the verdict, he pointed out, they probably would have been put to death in 1921.

The French right-wing intellectual Charles Maurras, leader of the royalist movement Action française, saw the Sacco-Vanzetti case as the product of inherent American weaknesses—the lack of swift justice, the sluggishness of unmanly bureaucrats, the softness of liberal democratic institutions. Lowell, in one of his letters, unknowingly agreed with the ultra-reactionary from Paris: "The long delay [in the executions] which was . . . inexcusable, was due to the American habit of thinking that every chance, reasonable or unreasonable, should be given to the accused and this has been used by motions for a new trial on newly discovered evidence of a less and less substantial value." Sacco and Vanzetti had to wait seven years in prison "because their counsel took advantage of these methods." Lowell also argued, in a letter to Albert Shaw, editor of the conservative *American Review of Reviews* (which offered its readers a lengthy defense of Lowell and Fuller along with an attack on Sacco and Vanzetti's defenders), that Sacco and Vanzetti were protected and even exalted precisely because they were outsiders: "If they had been Yankees they would have been executed long ago, and would have had no sympathy." Lowell did not point out (or perhaps did not realize) that if Sacco and Vanzetti had been Yankees they would never have found themselves in such a situation to begin with.[57]

In retrospect, it is clear that Lowell was so entrenched in his position, so convinced that he was fighting "propagandists" and "mass hysteria" (which he repeatedly linked with lynchings), that any shift on his part was inconceivable. It also becomes more evident that any other conclusion on the part of the Lowell advisory commission, given its composition and background, would have been highly unlikely. But the progressives and liberals who had seen (or wanted to see) Lowell as one of their own and had had such high hopes from him preferred to see his report as the exception and not the norm.

In this respect, perhaps the most imploring and hopeful letter to arrive at Lowell's office just before the executions came from Oswald Garrison Villard, editor and publisher of the *Nation*. Villard, though from a very different background, was probably as much of an elite figure on the national level as Lowell. He owed much of his influence to his pedigree: he was the grandson of the nineteenth-century abolitionist leader William Lloyd Garrison and the son of the railroad baron-turned-newspaper-magnate Henry Villard.[58] Villard, a pacifist and an internationalist, saw in the Sacco-Vanzetti affair a major source of embarrassment for the United States and a menace to its relationship with friendly European nations, and the *Nation* put forth these ideas forcefully and frequently, especially by covering reactions to the case abroad.[59] Behind the scenes, however, Villard was prepared to lay aside the rhetoric and the politics and communicate privately with Lowell, man to man, elite to elite, if that was what it would take to save Sacco and Vanzetti.

Villard explained in his letter that he was "not writing in my capacity as editor of the *Nation*, but as one American citizen who tried to serve his country to another who has conspicuously done so. I appeal to you . . . on behalf of domestic peace and good will among all Americans." As he saw it, if the Sacco-Vanzetti case ended in death for the two anarchists, it would mean no less than class war in the United States. It was thus a matter of urgency that Lowell ask Fuller to commute the men's sentence to life imprisonment, at least: "I cannot . . . recall anything else in our American life which has so set apart the working classes from . . . the capitalistic classes. The consequences of this trial I dread to contemplate if the men are put to death, because millions of our people—not merely foreign-born radicals but solid American citizens—feel that they have an intense personal stake in the issue."[60]

Villard raised the interesting specter of what would happen if Sacco and Vanzetti were pardoned. He predicted a return to the political climate of 1919: "Extremists on the conservative side will feel similarly outraged. . . . They literally thirst for blood. We shall see bitterly hostile legislation against aliens . . . and a drag-net investigation of all foreign-born who are not citizens." Before the American people, then, lay two unpleasant possibilities, class warfare or a new Red Scare. The first option, Villard argued, was the worse of the two: "I believe the working class . . . are in the majority, and the majority is supposed to rule in America. Clemency after the findings of the court have been upheld would have a tremendously soothing effect upon great masses of people. . . . It is hard to over-emphasize the bitterness of spirit which . . . will permeate American life if these men are done to death."

Beyond speaking for immigrants and workers (who probably would not have chosen him as their spokesman), Villard also wanted Lowell to know the extent of the damage that the affair was doing to America's image abroad. He wrote that "even conservative newspapers in Britain and France are against the executions" and argued that the American Legion should cancel their scheduled trip to France, where protest over the Sacco-Vanzetti case was nearing fever pitch. "In Berlin, in Rome, everywhere else, there is a unanimity of sentiment," he added. "Mussolini has appealed for them—the despot himself." Villard recounted the meeting he had witnessed between Fuller and the former British prime minister Ramsay MacDonald, in which the latter informed the governor over dinner that "British opinion is that even if the men were guilty, they have expiated their crime and should now be released."[61]

Villard clearly represented the view that foreign interference in the case, and in American matters generally, should not be ignored, rejected, or denounced. If many Americans, particularly in Massachusetts, saw the intervention of foreigners in the affair as an incentive to press forward with the execution of Sacco and Vanzetti, Villard viewed it as welcome. He beseeched Lowell to pay, as Thomas Jefferson had put it in the Declaration of Independence, "a 'decent respect to the opinions of mankind.' . . . In all my experience, I have never seen such unanimity of sentiment in Europe." Comparing the Sacco-Vanzetti case to the Dreyfus affair, he added: "I cannot forget that I was one of those who with the [New York] *Evening Post* led the American side on behalf of Dreyfus, and I know what a tremendous influence foreign opinion was in settling that case. . . . Must we add to the hatreds we have earned in Europe and South and Central America by the conduct of our foreign affairs?" Villard even offered Lowell a creative solution to the dilemma. Sacco and Vanzetti, he suggested, could be deported to Italy, where "their punishment will be continued. . . . The United States will be rid of them, the warning will be there so that all who run may read."[62]

But Villard's pleas, like those of others, were in vain. It took Lowell six weeks to answer Villard's letter, by which time Sacco and Vanzetti were long dead. Ignoring practically everything Villard had put to him, Lowell once again replied briefly, mechanically arguing that "lynching . . . is the result of criminal administration of public administration" in the United States."[63]

Much as Lowell attempted to deflect the issue, it refused to go away. Well after the executions, the Lowell report drew into the Sacco-Vanzetti controversy people who previously had not been much engaged with the case. And the criticism raised against Lowell in the private letters inevitably spilled out into the public domain. If many in the Sacco-Vanzetti camp had been stunned by Lowell's report, Lowell, as it turned out, was the one in for the real shock. In the social and intellectual world and in the America with which he was familiar, his report was supposed to be accepted without reservations. Instead, it—and he—came in for incessant attack.

In November 1927, three months after the executions, while Lowell was still answering letters, the *New Republic* published an article about the report by John Dewey, the most influential American public philosopher of the 1920s. Dewey was a relative latecomer to the Sacco-Vanzetti affair, but he distilled many of the ideas communicated in the private letters to Lowell into a strong criticism of the Lowell commission. The article, "Psychology and Justice," caused the Harvard president yet more embarrassment among liberals and progressives, to many of whom Dewey was a voice of intellectual authority.[64]

To Dewey, perhaps typically, the fates of the two individuals at the center of the drama were of little importance: "Sacco and Vanzetti are dead. No discussion of their innocence or guilt can restore them to life." Unlike many of his intellectual peers, he had not published a word about Sacco and Vanzetti while they were still alive. The Lowell report, rather than the fate of the two anarchists, drove Dewey's belated entry into the fray: instead of dwelling on the case, he preferred to look to the future, to discuss "our methods of ensuring justice." He was not particularly interested in the individuals who had prosecuted and convicted the two anarchists, or in Sacco and Vanzetti themselves. The important issue, as Dewey saw it, was "the psychology of the dominant cultivated class of the country as revealed in the report of the advisory committee."[65]

Dewey saw in the Sacco-Vanzetti episode a watershed event in American life. As he put it, "The condemnation and death of two obscure Italians opened a new chapter in the book of history." And in his rather inelegant prose, Dewey set out to understand "the tone and temper of American public opinion and sentiment, as they affect judgment and action in any social question wherein racial divisions and class interests are involved." Lowell's report fascinated him because "The future will recognize that the document . . . is typical and symbolic, a representation of the state of mind that must be widespread [among] the educated leaders of the American public in the third decade of the twentieth century."

Both the principal sides of the Sacco-Vanzetti controversy increasingly used psychology to explain the evolution of the affair, and a number of prominent writers, Horace Kallen and Edna St. Vincent Millay in particular, focused closely on the psychological aspect of the case.[66] To both Lowell and his critics, albeit in different ways, "hysteria" and "mob psychology" were central motifs in the case's history, and these took diverse, bizarre expressions.[67] But whereas Kallen, Millay, and others like them were concerned primarily with the psychology of fear among the people of Massachusetts, where Sacco and Vanzetti in their opinion had basically stood no chance, Dewey wanted to analyze the "attitude, the mental disposition" of the educated elite— the authors of the Lowell report themselves.[68]

Dewey attacked some of the report's most glaring inconsistencies. His starting point was the commission's own statement that in finding Sacco and Vanzetti guilty the members had applied a "cumulative" principle. "As with . . . fingerprints," Dewey explained, "no one . . . line has by itself much significance, yet together they may produce a perfect identification; so a number of circumstances—no one of them conclusive—may together make a proof beyond reasonable doubt. . . . In deciding the men guilty, it is not each item by itself in isolation that counts, but the cumulative effect of all in their mutual bearing." But, Dewey pointed out, whereas this principle was strictly upheld when finding the two defendants guilty, the commission did not apply the same standard when it came to potentially exonerating evidence. There "matters are segregated, both at large and in detail; every item and topic is treated as an isolated thing, to be disposed of by itself without regard for anything else." The "cumulative principle," then, was "not only disregarded; it [was] deliberately departed from." Dewey asked why, noting that "men of disciplined and cultivated minds . . . do not reverse their criterion and procedure without a cause."

Dewey examined the three principal questions the commission had posed to itself: "First, was the trial fairly conducted? Second, was the subsequently discovered evidence such that . . . a new trial ought to have been granted? Third, are they, or are they not, convinced beyond reasonable doubt that Sacco and Vanzetti were guilty of the murder?" The three questions, he argued, could not be treated in isolation—as the Lowell commission had done—since they were closely connected to one another. The result was that "the main issue, as it stands before the world, is not faced. It is not even mentioned. That issue is whether, *taking all considerations together,* there was or was not reasonable ground for doubt as to a miscarriage of justice in case of the men's immediate execution." The method chosen by the commission "fails to face the fact that . . . a miscarriage of justice was reasonably possible if the sentence of death were put into effect forthwith."

Why, then, did the commission treat these questions in isolation? The answer, according to Dewey, "can be found only in the attitude with which the issue was approached." Indeed, not only were these questions dealt with in isolation but even the six points that made up the first two questions were dealt with separately. He found this incredible: "Are the six points treated as having a force such that, while each by itself is 'inconclusive,' when taken together they have a probative force as to reasonable doubt? Such a treatment is not even hinted at. Systematically, each is kept apart from every other, so that the question of cumulative effect may not even arise." For example, new evidence about the supposed identification of Sacco's cap—an issue that defense lawyers had repeatedly introduced in their appeals—"is disposed of by saying that it is 'so trifling a matter in the evidence in the case that it seems to the committee by no means a ground for a new trial'—as if it had been argued that, taken by itself alone, it did afford such ground."

But Dewey reserved perhaps his harshest criticism for the fact that rather than function as a public, extrajudicial committee with the license to examine the case in larger, nonlegalistic perspective and to take into account public opinion, social tensions, class conflict, and the political context of the trial, Lowell and his associates chose instead to simply retry the original case against Sacco and Vanzetti, only this time in secret and without either a jury or the right of cross-examination: "Although the question at issue is whether there was ground for a new trial, with a new jury, the committee themselves assume the function of a jury in dealing with new evidence so as to deny the new trial."

One of the Lowell report's most important and controversial conclusions was that the jury had not been prejudiced against the defendants. Dewey found this ludicrous since on the one hand the commission conceded that the trial had taken place during the Red Scare, when Americans everywhere (especially in Massachusetts) lived in fear of radicals and foreigners, and that the prosecutor had taken advantage of this hysteria during the trial, and on the other the commission insisted that this atmosphere had not affected the outcome of the trial. How did the group arrive at this conclusion? By asking the jurors themselves whether they had been influenced. Their answer, not surprisingly, was no. Dewey mocked the Lowell report's assertion that "each [juror] felt sure that the fact that the accused were foreigners and radicals had no effect on his opinion": "These men . . . are now sure . . . that *they* were immune to the prevailing contagion of 'fear and credulity,' and immune although they had not 'little evidence' but convincing proof of 'dangerous opinions.' Believe it he who can . . . if, in such an atmosphere, they had been aware of the influence of this force upon their beliefs, they would have been extraordinary men, even more unusual than the members of the committee."

Public intellectuals in America who involved themselves in the Sacco-Vanzetti case, thus helping transform it into an affair, obviously viewed it through the lens of their primary philosophical or political concerns and obsessions, which usually superseded the specifics of the case itself. For Villard, for example, the case was about the destruction of America's image in the world, especially among Europeans; for W. E. B. Du Bois, it was about "the problem of the color line." For

H. L. Mencken, Sacco and Vanzetti were victims of the Puritan spirit and the cultural poverty of what he liked to call the booboisie.[69]

Dewey, for his part, worried about rationality, education, experimentation, and social progress. His essay did not really explain, as he had promised to do, "the psychology of the advisory commission." But it reveals nonetheless the severe breach that the Lowell report had opened within the educated progressive elite to which both he and Lowell belonged. While Dewey, like other Lowell critics, began by expressing his concern with "racial divisions" and "class tensions," he ended by confessing his deep sense of shame at being part of the "cultivated dominant class" that had produced a document like the Lowell report and confirmed the prejudices that in the eyes of many people in the United States and around the world had doomed Sacco, Vanzetti, and many others. This was the final message of Dewey's article. "One is profoundly humiliated," he summed up, "at the revelation of an attitude which, it is submitted, the record amply sets forth, the record placed before the bar of history. The sense of humiliation is akin to that of guilt, as if for a share in permitting such a state of mind as is exhibited in the record to develop in a country that professes respect for justice and devotion to equality and fraternity."[70] It is also evident that for Dewey, as for many other progressives, the belated support for the Sacco-Vanzetti cause and the criticism of the two men's persecutors (in the shape of the Lowell commission) were a form of breast-beating, atonement of sorts for his earlier enthusiastic support for America's entry into World War I, which spawned the Red Scare and which he had come to regret.[71]

Dewey's essay created considerable controversy. Quoted extensively in the post-execution campaign to vindicate Sacco and Vanzetti and clear their names, it also provoked angered responses from those who resented Dewey's intervention. Lowell had powerful defenders. Grant, the only member of the commission who eventually produced a memoir, quoted a letter he received from William Howard Taft, chief justice of the Supreme Court and former president of the United States. Referring to himself as "one of the too often forgotten public," Taft assured Grant that the participation in the advisory commission "concerned the welfare of society here and the world in an unusual way." The former president added that "it is remarkable how [Felix] Frankfurter with his [*Atlantic Monthly*] article was able to present to so large a body of readers a perverted view of the facts and then through the worldwide conspiracy of communism spread it to many, many countries. Our law schools lent themselves to the vicious propaganda.... It was a bubble and was burst by the courage of the governor and his advisors."[72] Although Taft's thin conspiracy theory would have been more accepted wisdom in 1921, when Sacco and Vanzetti first stood trial, by 1928 it was already becoming outdated.[73] In the 1960s, it would be revived.

For years after the executions, Lowell was dogged by his role in the Sacco-Vanzetti affair. Despite the best efforts of censors in Boston and elsewhere, Sacco-Vanzetti became the case that would not go away. The public aftermath of the affair was not kind to Lowell's reputation, and the hardest blows, again, came from within the elite. In the end, Sacco and Vanzetti were not the only victims of his report. Lowell remained president of Harvard until 1933, but Fuller's political career was over by 1928; Borah and other Republicans, suspecting that Sacco and Vanzetti had been innocent and fearful that the case could become a damaging issue in the 1928 national election, killed the governor's bid to become their party's candidate for vice president or even president. After he was subsequently denied the post of ambassador to France because of the objections of the French government (which would not guarantee his safety), Fuller left politics and returned to business, later showing his true political colors by reemerging occasionally into the public spotlight to grant interviews about Sacco, Vanzetti, and the radical menace.[74] Frank Goodwin, maker of the xenophobic speech "Sacco-Vanzetti and the Red Peril," was booted out of office by Fuller himself. Even the Massachusetts Bar came under embarrassing attack from its own president, George R. Nutter, who in an interview in the *New York Times* described it as a provincial body that "has been deteriorating for forty years."[75] The Massachusetts law that forced Sacco and Vanzetti to appeal to the same trial judge who had convicted them—an issue that the Lowell commission had not even addressed—was not changed until 1939, but the State Judiciary Council, the board of jurists who studied the state's system of jurisprudence and made recommendations to the legislature, published its recommendation to do so in January 1928.[76] Nor did it much help the reputation of the prosecution that one of the Bureau of Investigation's agents who had been involved in the case was sentenced to twelve years in prison for highway robbery; that the state attorney general was im-

peached for extorting $25,000 from an organization he had been inves-
tigating; and that the court interpreter at the 1921 trial was sent to
prison for the attempted bribery of a judge.[77]

More important, new information about the criminal case that
appeared after 1927 made many of those involved in the convictions
look less than ideal, and Sacco and Vanzetti themselves less guilty.[78]
The trial of Harry Canter (the Workers' Party candidate for secretary of state of Massachusetts) for publicly calling Fuller a murderer
(he had carried a placard with the words "Fuller—Murderer of Sacco
and Vanzetti" in a demonstration in front of the state house fourteen
months after the executions) had the effect of keeping the case in the
public eye; in a sense, as it turned out, Fuller and Lowell were the ones
who seemed to be on trial.[79] *The Letters of Sacco and Vanzetti*, first
published in 1928, documenting the two men's sensitive, hopeful, and
humane natures (while downplaying their more explicitly political,
militant, and angry attitudes, including Vanzetti's vow to see "Thayer
death" before his own), began to establish their posthumous reputations, especially among liberals, as gentle utopian dreamers mar-
tyred by a reactionary establishment.[80] Upton Sinclair's novel about
the case, *Boston,* also published that year, portrayed Sacco and Vanzetti as the victims of a capitalist conspiracy. Perhaps more significant,
The Sacco-Vanzetti Case: Transcript of the Case Record, an exhaustive
compilation of the case documents (including the Lowell report), was
also published in early 1928; the project was supported and funded by,
among others, Elihu Root, former U.S. secretary of state and the head
of the American Bar Association; John D. Rockefeller, Jr.; Newton D.
Baker, the former secretary of war in Wilson's cabinet; John W. Davis,
ambassador to Britain during the Wilson presidency and a former
Democratic candidate for president; and Charles Nagel, former secretary of commerce in President Taft's administration. These were all
unlikely Sacco and Vanzetti sympathizers, but they put their names to
a preface that stated that the case promised "to be the subject of controversy and discussion for many years to come," and they donated
sets of the volumes to the most important libraries of the United
States.[81]

Transcript of the Record was particularly awkward for Lowell
because it made clear that the possible rehabilitation of Sacco's testimony (an issue repeatedly introduced by the defense in the courts) had
not even been raised in the commission's hearings. The publication

provoked a new batch of letters to Lowell's office, including one from a Harvard graduate who claimed to have accepted the Lowell commission's conclusions back in 1927 but now joined the ranks of the critics: "You challenged us back in student days to high citizenship. . . . I raise, Sir, this question. If you should ever reach the point when you are not certain that those men were guilty would you have the courage to tell the people . . . that fact? I would rather die in the electric chair, conscious that I had been wrongly sent to death, than die in my bed with a conscience that searched me for an answer I dared not give."[82]

Lowell was subjected to renewed attacks, especially in the disillusioned liberal journals. More national public Sacco-Vanzetti committees were formed after the publication of *Transcript,* consisting of numerous well-known figures dedicated to clearing Sacco and Vanzetti's names. (One of these groups, the Sacco-Vanzetti National League, boasted an advisory board that in 1929 included Jane Addams, Morris Cohen, Clarence Darrow, Floyd Dell, John Dewey, John Dos Passos, Will Durant, Bishop Paul Jones, Joseph Wood Krutch, Fiorello La Guardia, Jeanette Marks, A. J. Muste, Eugene O'Neill, Upton Sinclair, and Oswald Garrison Villard.)[83] Anti–death penalty activists, fighting an uphill battle during this period, reported that membership in the League to Abolish Capital Punishment had doubled by 1928, and they attributed this—perhaps overconfidently—to the public repercussions of the Sacco-Vanzetti executions; at the league's annual meeting in 1928 the criminologist George Kirchwey optimistically (and prematurely) declared that in their deaths Sacco and Vanzetti "struck a death blow at capital punishment in America."[84] Under increasing pressure to account for the advisory commission's methods, Lowell stood his ground: "I do not care to enter into any public controversy on the subject of [Sacco and Vanzetti]," he wrote to a critical young writer from the *Harvard Progressive.* "I have done my duty as a citizen with honesty and courage."[85]

But the damage had been done, and the tone for future evaluations of the case was set by articles with titles like "Lessons for Liberals" in the *New Republic.*[86] The veteran progressive historian Charles Beard summed up an increasingly common mainstream attitude when he expressed the wish of "seeking to discover, by study, the significance of this trial and its outcome for the whole process of justice."[87] Gardner Jackson, in his 1929 article "Was President Lowell Conscious," absolved Fuller and other political functionaries of the "judicial murder" of Sacco and Vanzetti while laying practically all the personal responsibility for the failure of justice at Lowell's doorstep. "They are politicians," he explained of Fuller and his ilk, "products of a commercial age, men of limited intellectual development and of emotions shaped to the mass level." Lowell, on the other hand, represented intellect, reason, and knowledge; and thus the abject failure of his authority had a much more traumatizing and radicalizing effect.[88]

Similar lessons were drawn by Paul Kellogg, editor of *Survey Graphic*, veteran social reformer, and within a few years a key architect of the Social Security Act under the Roosevelt administration. Like Ickes, Kellogg represents a direct link between the liberal reaction to the Lowell report and the advent of the New Deal. He is also emblematic of the shock that the Lowell report created among previously optimistic progressives. In a *Survey Graphic* editorial in October 1927, Kellogg argued that "for fifty years, under the spur of the scientific spirit, our colleges have been building a body of standards in the discovery of truth. [President Lowell was] in a sense [a] steward of these newer resources of intelligence, matching the older tradition of the courts as an agency for sifting fact from falsehood and assertion." But instead of drawing on the knowledge of experts, Kellogg lamented, Lowell and his commission "reverted to the narrowest of legal conceptions; fell short of that, applied it upside down."[89]

Two years later, Kellogg returned to the aspect of competing authority in the Sacco-Vanzetti case. Two members of the Lowell commission were university presidents, he pointed out, and even though "they had economists, jurists, historians, engineers, sociologists, and psychologists at their call," they "did not employ the technique of these professions as implements for arriving at truth in the face of hysteria": "University men and women were among those who stood out against the execution, but we have had as yet no cleansing facing of these facts by the educational leaders involved in this miscarriage of the scientific spirit as devastating as the miscarriage of justice."[90]

The fallout from the Lowell report extended to Europe, where for some intellectuals Lowell himself—now seen in many quarters as a major culprit in Sacco and Vanzetti's deaths—came to embody all that was wrong with modern postwar America. Bertrand Russell, who freely traveled between Britain and the United States and was a lifelong critic of various aspects of American (as well as British and European) life, despised Lowell, whom he had first met in 1914. He later wrote in his autobiography, "I am proud to say that I took a violent dislike to Professor Lowell, who subsequently assisted in the murder of Sacco and Vanzetti."[91] Russell visited the United States in September 1927, shortly after the executions, and lectured at a series of colleges on the eastern seaboard. What he had to say there adhered closely to the kind of "conflicted Americanism" that characterized so much of the European reaction to the case, and which Russell himself personified: a constant presence in American academia and letters, where he felt quite comfortable, he was also an outspoken, highly critical observer of American politics and society.

As Russell saw it, Lowell and his cohorts were the unfortunate products of a once glorious American tradition. Of his own parents, who as Victorian aristocratic radicals visited the United States in 1867 and befriended New England abolitionists, Russell wrote, "They could not foresee . . . that these men and women whose democratic ardor they applauded and whose triumphant opposition to slavery they admired were the grandfathers and grandmothers of those who murdered Sacco and Vanzetti." As Russell saw it, if the United States was so opposed to Bolshevism, it ought not to have behaved like the Soviet Union. And since America represented the future, what happened there was immensely important to the rest of the world, especially to Europeans. Lowell was not Thayer, a provincial judge, or Fuller, a mediocre politician; therefore his role in the case was infinitely worse. But most important, for Russell, Harvard was supposed to be a center of enlightenment; the conclusion of the Sacco-Vanzetti case, in which the university's president played a key part, thus represented a terrible dereliction of its duty. "If you cannot liberalize the colleges there is no hope for America," Russell said in one interview. "Liberals in the United States need to realize that America dominates the world. To liberalize the United States is to liberalize the world. Liberals everywhere feel this keenly and it explains their intense interest in the Sacco-Vanzetti case. . . . American liberalism must show the way, and liberalism's greatest hope is in the colleges."[92]

Into the late 1930s, Lowell continued to receive letters about the commission's report, many of them critical, some aggressive, most asking for simple explanations. He was also peppered with requests to appear at talks and on panels, write articles, and answer his critics—in vain. Gardner Jackson even invited Lowell to speak at the 1929 Sacco-Vanzetti memorial in Boston, but the Harvard president understandably refused. He did not see himself as participating in any public discussion of the case; as the "umpire," he had ruled, and there was nothing further to discuss. He now wished to see himself as having been untouched by the passions of the time. In a 1929 letter to a former Harvard student Lowell explained that "no doubt . . . feeling about Sacco-Vanzetti ran high, but I am sure that neither I nor my colleagues on the committee were in any way affected by any feelings of the kind." Ironically, his report had said more or less the same about the jury that had convicted Sacco and Vanzetti in 1921.[93]

Lowell's position became more rigid and bitter as the years passed and Sacco and Vanzetti's public standing grew. "I have learned a lesson," he wrote to a friend in 1929; "a public service does not always bring reward in the form of recognition. On the contrary, an unpopular act of righteousness brings severer condemnation than an evasive compromise between conflicting opinions." The reaction to the commission's report was no different in his mind from that of 1919, when he "was hounded by alumni and others because I would not bow to their fanatical cries about Reds in our colleges."[94]

In 1936, at Harvard's tercentenary celebration, Lowell's role in the Sacco-Vanzetti affair was again thrust into glaring public light at what was supposed to be a moment of personal glory for him. A group of twenty-eight Harvard alumni, including Malcolm Cowley, John Dos Passos, Heywood Broun, Charles Angoff, Powers Hapgood, and Granville Hicks, mailed a pamphlet entitled *Walled in This Tomb* to all the invited guests. The pamphlet recapitulated—in one-sided fashion—the history of the case and especially Lowell's decisive role in it and illustrated the impact of the Sacco-Vanzetti affair on a younger generation of American intellectuals. These writers, all of whom had been radicalized by the executions and perhaps even more so by the Lowell report, wanted their fellow alumni to discover, as they themselves had, "what happened to the mental processes of their alma mater's president. . . . Out of such discovery, will come an awareness of the incredible and destructive twists of men's minds—even the mind of a president of Harvard." Of course, times had changed: the economy had since collapsed and the political world seemed to have turned upside down. The pamphlet made a direct link between the Lowell report and the rise of fascism overseas: written as Europe and the United States began to head toward (as yet) unimaginable violence, the pamphlet, according to its authors, was intended to "be of value in the struggle to keep this nation from being torn asunder by that mass of unreason which has been so skillfully developed by power-mad individuals and cliques in Europe. No one looking at the fate of intellectual and cultural pursuits in Germany and Italy can escape an intense feeling of the immediate peril confronting our own universities."[95]

According to the authors' plan the pamphlet would reach each recipient before September 18, the day Lowell, as former university president, was to introduce President Roosevelt at Harvard Yard. But when they heard of the protest the university authorities created awkward and self-defeating publicity for it by intervening with Harvard's internal postal service and destroying as many copies of the pamphlet as they could find.[96]

In their statements to the press after the tercentenary, the twenty-eight alumni demanded to know why Harvard had not lived up to President James Conant's declaration that the university stood for the "spirit of tolerance which allows the expression of all opinions however heretical they may appear." The destruction of the pamphlets, they argued, offered "a curious contrast" to Roosevelt's words in the Harvard Yard: "In this day of modern witch-burning, when freedom of thought has been banished from many lands, it is the part of Harvard University and America to stand for the freedom of the human mind and to carry the torch of truth."[97]

These and other protests did nothing to change Lowell's viewpoint. In a 1936 letter to Bruce Bliven, the *New Republic* editor who was writing an article on the after effects of the Sacco-Vanzetti case a decade after the executions, Lowell expressed no regrets and insisted that there was not even any need to change the state laws so that appeals would not be made to the original trial judge.[98] In December 1938, at Lowell's eighty-second birthday party, the head of security at Harvard "prevented him from seeing a hand-lettered placard that virtually hid his gigantic birthday cake: 'Sacco and Vanzetti Might Have Lived to Be Eighty-Two, Too.' "[99] That same year, Musmanno, who was writing a book about the case, interviewed Lowell at the latter's summer home in Massachusetts. According to Musmanno, the aging Lowell was extremely irritated at the growing image of Sacco and Vanzetti as martyrs: "It is all poppycock to say that these were poor honest working men. They were bandits." Apparently not noticing that his comments might appear bigoted, particularly to an interviewer of Italian descent, Lowell further explained that "no one could mistake

Vanzetti, because he had an odd-looking face. Sacco, on the other hand, had a face like every other Italian." Realizing then that perhaps he had said something inappropriate, Lowell tried to correct himself: "Sacco's face was like hundreds of other Italians." When asked why one of the defense witnesses would falsely testify on behalf of Vanzetti, a man he did not know, Lowell answered—perhaps jokingly— "Why, everybody knows that Italians make up alibis. They tell me that they come in with their alibis on a tray."[100]

By 1938 statements like this, even if they were slightly facetious, made Lowell appear to belong to another era; to see how the climate regarding the case had changed in just a few years, one need only compare Frederick Lewis Allen's 1927 letter to Lowell with his 1931 history *Only Yesterday,* aimed at the general public. In the letter Allen had agreed with Lowell about "the hysterical attitude of a large part of the public toward the case," and added: "Let me congratulate you on the thoroughness and calmness of [the report]. . . . [It] has set my mind at rest; I now have as little respect for the people who keep on yapping about the decision as for those who thought the men ought to hang because we have too many radicals anyway."[101]

Four years later, Allen had changed his tune. In *Only Yesterday,* he had this to say: "Whether [Sacco and Vanzetti] were actually guilty or not will probably never be definitely determined—though no one can read their speeches to the court and their letters without doubting if justice was done." The division over the case among Americans was "between those who thought radicals ought to be strung up on general principles and those who thought the test of the country's civilization lay in the scrupulousness with which it protected the rights of minorities."[102] Allen, himself a scrupulous follower of the winds of public opinion, could have been describing the main conflict between Lowell's supporters and critics; it was not difficult to determine where the book's sympathies lay.[103]

It would be rash to argue that by the late 1930s the Sacco-Vanzetti controversy had been publicly resolved in favor of the two dead anarchists. But as more state and national political power was now in the hands of progressive bureaucrats and thinkers like Ickes and Kellogg, the New Deal framework in which they operated brought with it an interpretation of the Sacco-Vanzetti case that would remain dominant at least until the early 1960s. It was encapsulated in classic fashion in

1937 in the WPA guide to Massachusetts, prepared by members of the Federal Writers' Project, which served as a sort of official government history of the state. The authors noted that "Sacco and Vanzetti had become . . . the classic example of the administering of justice to members of unpopular minorities." The guide also described the case as the product of the long-standing struggle of the working class under capitalism and asserted that Sacco and Vanzetti were found guilty "despite their alibis" and "the highly circumstantial nature of the evidence." The authors concluded provocatively: "It was widely believed that although legal forms were observed, the determining factor in the case from start to finish was the affiliation of the two men with an unpopular minority political group."[104] Although the publication of the *Guide to Massachusetts* provoked raucous public debate and opposition within the state, it also clearly articulated and helped establish the dominant, long-lasting vision of what the Sacco-Vanzetti episode meant: the persecution of two probably innocent men on the basis of their class, ethnic, and political backgrounds.[105] Indirectly and in the long run it also brought into sharper relief something more specific about one of the episode's principal figures. Lowell may have thought when he took up work on the advisory commission that his report would bring the Sacco-Vanzetti affair to a close. Instead, like so many others, he was swept up in it, and even fueled it. It was far more powerful than he, and he was never able to live it down.

CHAPTER 5

"A Kind of Madness"

The Return of Sacco and Vanzetti

Three decades after the execution of Sacco and Vanzetti, the issue of the two Italian anarchists had settled for many into a largely unchallenged narrative that depicted the case as a product of the post–World War I Red Scare and the preference given by American legal and political authorities to "law and order" and the status quo over the principles of justice. It is not true, as some have suggested, that Sacco and Vanzetti were forgotten, or even obliterated from public memory, over the course of the 1940s and early 1950s. But neither can it be said that their case was a hotly contested topic during these years. Nor, by any means, was their innocence uniformly accepted; rather, as the journalist Murray Kempton put it in 1955, "very few of Sacco and Vanzetti's enemies [felt] in a position any longer to dispute the major cantos of their epic—poverty, false witness, testament, and crucifixion."[1]

In an intellectual context, liberal American scholars of the 1950s, including Richard Hofstadter, Frederick Hoffman, Arthur Schlesinger, Jr., and Robert K. Murray, were highly influential in portraying the Red Scare as the product of nativist hysteria. This scholarly view essentially corroborated the older left-wing interpretation of the Sacco-Vanzetti case that had emerged at the time of the executions and their aftermath. The most thorough studies of the Sacco-Vanzetti case until the 1960s—by Felix Frankfurter (1927), Osmond Fraenkel (1931), Herbert Ehrmann (1933), and G. Louis Joughin and Edmund M. Morgan (1948)—had all been sympathetic to the defense (and, in the cases of Frankfurter and Ehrmann, actually penned by activists *in* the defense). This was also true of the two best-known American novels on Sacco and Vanzetti, both written by bona fide radicals: Upton Sinclair's *Boston* (1928) and Howard Fast's *The Passion of Sacco and Vanzetti*

(1953). And Maxwell Anderson's *Winterset*—a successful Broadway play in 1935 and a Hollywood film in 1936, both starring Burgess Meredith—indirectly dealt with the Sacco-Vanzetti case and championed the two men's innocence.

The so-called consensus historians of the 1950s, as well as journalists and memoirists such as Kempton, also did much to promote the idea that the Sacco-Vanzetti affair was a critical impetus for the transition of an entire generation of young American intellectuals from the escapist, apolitical alienation of the 1920s to the political engagement (and leftist radicalism) of the 1930s.[2] This idea was not new to the 1950s; it had already appeared in a brief but important essay, "Echoes of a Crime," published in the *New Republic* in 1935 by Malcolm Cowley. Written at the height of the Great Depression, at the start of the Popular Front phase in American political life and the dawn of radicalism's most significant moment of popularity in the United States until the late 1960s, Cowley's article was perhaps the first retrospective discussion of the Sacco-Vanzetti case's effect on what he called the intelligentsia. According to Cowley, intellectuals of the 1920s were stirred by the case because of, first, "the situation of two men tried unjustly and sentenced to death, the old story of innocence endangered"; second, the fact that "these men were radicals and had been arrested during the Palmer raids, when the liberals had also been threatened"; third, "the high smugness of Massachusetts officials, who turned themselves into caricatures of everything that artists hate in the bourgeoisie"; and fourth, "the international interest in the case." But the fifth and most important reason for the intellectuals' indignation, to Cowley, was the personalities of Sacco and Vanzetti themselves.[3]

Cowley gave intellectuals collective credit—perhaps too much—for mounting the Sacco-Vanzetti campaign: "It was the intelligentsia rather than the labor unions that conducted [Sacco and Vanzetti's] defense. . . . They held meetings, raised funds, issued statements, suggested new appeals. . . . At the very end, the intellectuals even came out into the streets and got themselves arrested, like workers on the picket line of a strike that is being broken." In the cause, Cowley saw intellectuals coming together to take a stand, but then separating after the bitter defeat of August 23, 1927, "each back into his own orbit." After the executions things quieted down at once: the newspapers "quit talking about" the case, and "the intellectuals were trying to save their private souls by love and psychoanalysis and running away from the machine age. Their only group manifestations were literary teas; their only political platform was a cocktail tray." Still, the cause had not really died: "The effects of the Sacco-Vanzetti case continued to operate, in a subterranean style, and after a very few years they appeared once more on the surface."

The real meaning of the case for Cowley was manifested in the political (and specifically radical) awakening of young intellectuals like himself and his friends in the 1930s. Regarding the radicalism of the Depression years, he noted that "almost nobody mentioned the obvious fact that, whatever else it might be, it was also a sequel to the Sacco-Vanzetti case, a return to united political action. This time, however, the intellectuals had learned that they could not accomplish anything unless they made an alliance with the working class. . . . In an unexpected way, they were carrying out the prophecy that Sacco made to his son."

Twenty years later, even Arthur Schlesinger, Jr., champion of the so-called vital center in American politics, could agree with this radical (and overly self-involved) assessment of the case. Cowley's essay was not useful as a history of the affair in the late 1920; those years were far more political, and divided, than Cowley and his 1930s cohort would have one believe, and they boasted more than their fair share of politically engaged intellectuals. But Cowley did crystallize a point of view that turned into a commonplace over time: because the trial and execution of Sacco and Vanzetti had been unjust and irrational, by extension the ensuing radicalization could be seen as justified and logical. Liberal historians of the 1950s also implied that American political culture had come far since the 1920s, but dangerous long-term trends, such as anti-intellectualism and hatred of foreigners and nonconformists—or the lingering power of what Hofstadter, thinking primarily of McCarthy, memorably termed "cranky pseudo-conservatism"—were endangering that progress.[4]

But despite the apparent public accord that had developed over the Sacco-Vanzetti case following their executions, the other side of the debate had never really disappeared, and as the 1960s began the dispute erupted again, in an entirely different political, intellectual, and cultural context. This renewed furor had as much if not more to do with the political and cultural battles of the 1950s and the early 1960s as with the Sacco-Vanzetti case itself. The dramatic re-explosion of interest in the affair in the United States during the Cold War era on

the part of intellectuals, politicians, students, journalists, artists, activists, and ordinary people is illuminating not only because of the different ways in which Sacco and Vanzetti themselves were remembered
a generation after their executions but because of how their case was
adopted or co-opted, used or appropriated, championed or vilified in
order to promote competing and sometimes bitterly conflicting political, social, and cultural visions. More specifically, this was the first
time, since the late 1920s, that the question of Sacco and Vanzetti's
innocence or guilt came powerfully to the fore, and the dominant
interpretation of the case came under furious attack from the rising
conservative movement, culminating in a cantankerous controversy in
the United States and Europe that was shaped by the experiences of
the Cold War and by the struggles over McCarthyism—a controversy
that, in many ways, continues today.

In 1958 the first significant attempt was made by Massachusetts
politicians to persuade the governor to pardon Sacco and Vanzetti (an
effort that eventually resulted in Michael Dukakis's decision in 1977 to
grant the two anarchists what amounted to a posthumous pardon, by
officially declaring that their trial had been unfair). It was a failed
attempt at first, and one that raised much antagonism within the state:
the hearings were noisy, and occasional violence broke out among the
spectators, and ultimately the bill was defeated. But at least it had
gotten through to the legislature; earlier attempts to jump-start this
process had been rebuffed by prominent American public figures who
might have been able to move it forward. Eleanor Roosevelt, for example, in response to a letter from Gardner Jackson and Aldo Felicani in
1952, claimed that the time and circumstances were not yet favorable
for such an initiative: "I really think it would be unwise to call more
attention to the Sacco-Vanzetti case. It would just give rise to new
attacks by the reactionaries. This is an election year and a bad one." (In
1952 the Republican candidate Dwight D. Eisenhower was preparing
to face off against the liberal Democrat Adlai Stevenson; it was the
height of the Cold War, the U.S was mired in the war in Korea, and
Julius and Ethel Rosenberg had been convicted of treason the year
before and sentenced to death.) By the end of the 1950s, though, these
circumstances were clearly changing. For one thing, as the harshest
effects of McCarthyism abated somewhat, the notion that Sacco and
Vanzetti had been tried and executed unjustly was gaining more main-

stream respectability. It did not hurt, either, that some of the most active former Sacco-Vanzetti defenders were avid Communist hunters during the McCarthy period and thereafter.[5]

Also in 1958, CBS devoted an episode of its flagship television serial *Camera Three* to a sympathetic portrayal of Sacco and Vanzetti. A sense of the coming shift in public opinion can be discerned from the (highly) positive viewer responses to the show. In a typical letter, a Brooklyn man wrote to the network, "I would like to commend you for your very interesting program today on Sacco and Vanzetti. . . . I am as fierce a partisan for Western programs as any other TV viewer, however I find that it keeps TV from 'fading' to be able to see a stimulating and provoking program of this kind."[6] Two years later, in June 1960, as television sets were becoming more widespread through-out the country, NBC aired a two-part special program, "The Sacco-Vanzetti Story," written by Reginald Rose. The once-radical idea that Sacco and Vanzetti were innocent men who had fallen victim to the class warfare, ethnic intolerance, and political repression of the Red Scare era was now showcased in a medium that had captured the national imagination, and more than any work of historical scholar-ship could ever do, it sparked renewed public interest in the case.[7] Perhaps not surprisingly, right-wing pundits did not like these pro-grams one bit. By broadcasting shows sympathetic to the executed anarchists, the indignant columnist Westbrook Pegler wrote, "CBS and NBC . . . give moral aid and comfort to the enemy and . . . exalt murderers as pathetic victims of persecution."[8]

Pegler and others like him had good reason to be disturbed: Sacco and Vanzetti, it seemed, had never enjoyed such broad public respect-ability. The director of the NBC special, Sidney Lumet, was one of the most promising filmmakers in the country; Sacco and Vanzetti were portrayed, respectively, by two talented young actors, Martin Balsam (who that year also appeared in Alfred Hitchcock's horror classic *Psycho*) and Steven Hill (cast a few years later in the lead role on the smash TV hit *Mission Impossible*). The program was made with the help of former members of the Sacco-Vanzetti defense committee, especially Aldo Felicani; it was a strange irony that just a few years after the McCarthy period, when numerous mainstream writers and artists were blacklisted by Hollywood studios, the recording industry, television, and radio, a renowned Galleanista was named "special con-sultant" to an NBC program. Robert Alan Aurthur, the executive producer for the network, even sent the script to Felicani and Michael Musmanno for approval before the broadcast. Felicani attended the filming and was encouraged to intervene if he felt that the actors were not properly capturing the personalities of the protagonists, whom no one had known more intimately. He did not hesitate to do so, at one point interrupting the filming to urge Hill to convey more of Vanzetti's famed pathos and emotion.[9]

The NBC special is a good example of the influence of a close-knit circle of Sacco-Vanzetti defenders and activists on the way in which the case was presented to the general public. Oddly, there is no study of what we might call the "Sacco-Vanzetti community"—including Felicani, Jackson, Musmanno, Mary Donovan, Tom O'Connor, Ehrmann, and to a lesser extent, Frankfurter—that maintained contact over decades, united by their devotion to the memory of Sacco and Vanzetti and their hatred of Communists (which, for them, went hand in hand). This group was first forged in 1926–1927, when they rallied around the Sacco-Vanzetti cause; in later years they were usually the first people to be contacted by journalists, artists, and students interested in the case. They occasionally bickered over how best to commemorate Sacco and Vanzetti and to represent their cause publicly, and the mood within the group depended largely on Sacco and Vanzetti's posthumous public profile. At the time of the NBC broadcast, for example, the correspondence between them was self-congratulatory, nearly euphoric: "These last few weeks," Musmanno wrote to Felicani, "have been incredible. . . . Being with you as [NBC] produced the television show . . . made me almost believe that we were back together in Boston in 1927. . . . As the camera ground in the filming . . . I could feel myself transported back to the heart-tearing months from April through August 1927."[10]

In 1963 an even bigger artistic monument to the Sacco-Vanzetti legend was in the works: a high-budget transatlantic film with the Italian Dino de Laurentiis as producer and the American Richard Fleischer as director. The filmmakers corresponded eagerly with Felicani, Ehrmann, and others of the Sacco-Vanzetti community, and screenwriter Edward Anhalt (*Panic in the Streets*) put together a 243-page screenplay. But because of internal financial disputes, the project was dropped in favor of Fleischer's next film, *Fantastic Voyage,* a naughty science fiction adventure starring the less controversial and decidedly more crowd-pleasing Raquel Welch.[11] These plans, though aban-

doned, were a clear sign of the growing public interest in the case, on
both sides of the Atlantic; neither de Laurentiis nor Fleischer was one
to consider film projects without commercial appeal. A less expensive
but commercially successful Italian film, Giuliano Montaldo's *Sacco e
Vanzetti,* was eventually released in 1971, featuring music by Ennio
Morricone, including "Here's to You (Nicola and Bart)" sung by Joan
Baez, who also wrote the lyrics. (One of Baez's heroes, the folk artist
Woody Guthrie, had recorded an album called *Ballads of Sacco and
Vanzetti* in 1946.) Montaldo's film had an enormous impact on a gen-
eration of interested Europeans, many of whose knowledge of the case
was, and is, based on this impassioned but stagy film.[12]

This growing interest was especially true of Italy, where Sacco
and Vanzetti were belatedly rediscovered—perhaps as a result of the
lengthy postwar reckoning there—as lost native sons killed on hostile
foreign soil during one of the darkest periods in Italian history.[13] Particular interest was given to Sacco and Vanzetti's rural Italian roots: in
1960, the American composer Marc Blitzstein, who was awarded a
Ford Foundation grant for the purpose, went to southern Italy to
write a three-act opera about Sacco and Vanzetti—a project he had first
considered doing in 1934, while he was working with the Federal Arts
Project. (The work was commissioned and optioned by the Metropol-
itan Opera in New York, but Blitzstein was killed by burglars while
working on it in Martinique in 1964; the opera was eventually completed by another composer and finally performed in 2001.)[14] That
same year, in Rome, the Paroli Theater presented a new stage hit about
Sacco and Vanzetti, co-written by Mino Roli and Luciano Vincenzoni.
After its successful run in Italy, the play was shown in Germany,
France, Britain, and various Latin American countries. In New York, a
loose musical version of the play, *The Shoemaker and the Peddler,* was
well attended by off-Broadway crowds.[15]

One of the least enthusiastic spectators at the Paroli production
was Robert Clements, a professor of comparative literature at New
York University and frequent traveler to Italy, who later delivered a
lecture in New York titled "The Triumph of Sacco and Vanzetti." It
was a triumph that the rather conservative Clements was none too
happy about. In his view, Roli and Vincenzoni's play was a display of
pure left-wing European anti-Americanism: the defendants were portrayed as doomed from the start because they were anarchists, pacifists, draft-dodgers, and, worst of all, Italians (all this, of course, was

no different from what many Americans of various political stripes had been saying since the 1920s). After the show, Clements reported, the capacity Roman audience applauded for a full ten minutes. The professor also took a look at what spectators wrote in the guest book; the results there were mixed. One wrote, "If this is American justice, let's keep it out of Italy." Another jotted, "The one exclusive, single purpose of this play . . . is to revile America to the audience." Another reaction was "Viva Italia!"—an ironic statement, Clements duly noted, considering Sacco and Vanzetti's own views on the national question.[16]

The Italian press, Clements observed, also helped generate enthusiasm for the play. Critics were not interested in the play as history but rather, as a writer for *Paese sera* noted, as "an important document for present-day concerns," particularly the growing objection in Europe to capital punishment. A writer for *L'unità,* the Communist newspaper, remarked: "Many times during the play . . . our thoughts went back to the fate of [the executed] Ethel and Julius Rosenberg, in so many ways painfully like that of Sacco and Vanzetti."[17] The play also received substantial attention in the popular press, including a six-page spread in the March 1961 issue of the mass-circulation magazine *Oggi.*

Clements did not restrict his investigation to the theater itself; he also wanted to capture the mindset of the man in the street—or, barring that, the man in the corridor of power. One of his more interesting interviewees was an unnamed judge in the Palazzo di Giustizia, "with an anti-fascist and pro-American record," as the author made sure to note. Clements asked him whether the play "leaves you uneasy about American justice today." "Yes," the judge answered, "I'm afraid that this revival of the old case will remind us Europeans of the Rosenbergs, the Scottsboro boys, McCarthy, Caryl Chessman . . . leaving us with the impression that American justice has these unfortunate recidivisms much too often."[18]

Clements, in response, tried to make the case for social and legal progress in the United States. He argued, for example, that the death penalty had been abolished by most states, that changes in Massachusetts law would have surely granted Sacco and Vanzetti a new trial in 1961, and that the Massachusetts voters had since elected two Italian-American governors (Foster Furcolo in 1956 and John Volpe in 1961)—an unimaginable occurrence in the 1920s. Clements might have added that capital punishment in Massachusetts was finally struck down by the state legislature in 1959, in part because of the after-effects of the

Sacco-Vanzetti executions. But the "pro-American" judge was not very impressed: "Every country in Europe will have some sensitivities offended by this play. Here in Italy death sentences are unpopular, because they remind us of fascist justice."[19]

Clements continued to follow the reawakening of interest in Sacco and Vanzetti in Europe. In 1965, four years after his trip to Italy, he reviewed a new book on the case for the *New York Times*. Still hypersensitive to what he saw as the automatic linkage made in Europe between the Sacco-Vanzetti affair and American society as a whole, Clements noted that it was not only the European left but also the right that kept the case alive, for what he called "their anti-American propaganda needs." "Arriving in Paris last year," he wrote of his most recent visit, "during one of Mr. De Gaulle's anti-American ebulliences, the first thing I heard at turning on my radio was the national network presentation of a tearful drama, 'Le Procès Sacco et Vanzetti.' "[20]

Clements might have overstated his case somewhat. As a general rule, the controversy over Sacco and Vanzetti in Europe in the 1960s did not reach the level of rancor it did in the United States. The cataclysmic experiences of the 1930s, World War II, and the war's gloomy aftermath had changed the culture, psychology, and nomenclature of European political life to such an extent that the memory of Sacco and Vanzetti, who had stirred so much emotion in the 1920s, had somewhat dimmed. As early as 1947, Albert Einstein (who had lived through the Sacco-Vanzetti episode in Europe but had since moved to the United States) put it this way: "At that time [of the Sacco-Vanzetti case] the desire for justice was as yet more powerful than it is today, although it did not triumph. Too many horrors have since dulled the human conscience." After Hitler and Auschwitz, in other words, Sacco and Vanzetti had lost much of their relevance, and their cause could seem in retrospect more quaint than powerful, particularly since anarchism no longer existed as a viable mass movement and their story had little to do, at least at first glance, with the dreadfulness of totalitarianism.[21]

Still, curiosity and passion about the case in Italy and a similar revival of interest in France, West Germany, and elsewhere in Europe in the 1960s and 1970s suggest that memories of the Sacco-Vanzetti affair were still strong on the European side of the Atlantic. But this interest, or memory, had a peculiar flavor: Sacco-Vanzetti came to be seen as almost strictly an American story, perhaps with an additional Italian dimension. In France, for example, where the controversies over Sacco and Vanzetti in the 1920s were arguably more intense than in any other country outside the United States, even the echoes of the case were seen in American terms, overlapping somewhat with the history of the Italian diaspora. The executions of the Rosenbergs in 1953 and of Chessman in 1960, rather than the Dreyfus affair, were now the main French point of comparison with Sacco and Vanzetti, thus sharpening the focus on the distinct *American-ness* of the story. And the varied engagement with Sacco and Vanzetti in Europe was largely forgotten, except for rare mentions of distant riots and official appeals to American leaders.[22]

In the United States, on the other hand, the picture was quite different, and the more vivid public and artistic interest in the Sacco-Vanzetti case in the late 1950s and 1960s was expressed in a variety of forms. As in Europe, one primary venue was the theater: in addition to *The Shoemaker and the Fishpeddler,* a number of plays were produced in this period about Sacco and Vanzetti, including *The Advocate,* written by Robert Noah and first staged by the Bucks County Playhouse in Pennsylvania. In October 1963, the opening of the play on Broadway was broadcast live on national television. It focused on a character named Warren Curtis, based on William Thompson, Sacco and Vanzetti's upper-crust Boston defense attorney, who had been shaken by the treatment of his clients; like almost all artistic representations of the case in this period, it was sympathetic to Sacco, Vanzetti, and their supporters.[23] It was also popular: this was the first time that a Broadway play was screened on television, live and free of charge, while it was running on the stage. The play itself was an immediate hit: the Broadway debut drew a capacity audience of 1,177 to the ANTA theater. The Westinghouse Broadcast Company, which had financed and produced the television broadcast of the play, estimated that the number of viewers "at any given moment" reached about two million; according to the *New York Times,* "There was general agreement among viewers that the play was a welcome relief from domestic comedies, cowboys, and hospital corridors."[24] By the end of the decade, the outpouring of artistic works on Sacco and Vanzetti would become so prodigious that the critic Alfred Kazin remarked that he was waiting for "the inevitable musical to be made out of the [case]." Kazin was being facetious, but there already had been more than one musical staged about Sacco and Vanzetti.[25]

A less visible but equally telling form of renewed focus on the case in these Cold War years was the curiosity about it of students, teachers, and even children. At the college level, one early and typical example of this phenomenon was a thesis written by a Harvard undergraduate in 1955 titled "The Failure of the Lowell Commission in the Sacco-Vanzetti Case." As the title made clear, the young author was critical of his school's administration and particularly of former university president Lowell himself; he argued, not without merit, that the negative reactions to the report among progressives eventually brought about a reevaluation of the place and rigor of higher education in American social life.[26] In 1963 the *Harvard Crimson* published an article even more critical of Lowell and his committee. The author studied the report and concluded that it was "a disappointing document. . . . A conglomeration of unsupported conclusions, and each conclusion seems to be the same: prosecution witnesses were to be believed, defense witnesses were not. . . . The committee seems to have first reached the judgment that Sacco and Vanzetti were guilty and then to have interpreted the evidence so that it would best support this conclusion. . . . The best of people with the best intentions managed to do the worst of deeds—kill two men who did not deserve to die."[27]

Students became interested in the case beyond the gates of Harvard as well. One sign of this could be seen in the New York Public Library: the Sacco-Vanzetti materials there, wrote the former *New Republic* correspondent and Sacco-Vanzetti supporter John Beffel in 1965, were in "terrible shape." Many pamphlets were missing, some were torn, and it had become nearly impossible for students to conduct proper research on the topic. Beffel spoke to the information desk librarian about this problem and discovered that "each October, teachers assign pupils to write papers on the case, and apparently they come in droves."[28] At Hunter College in New York, Vanzetti's last speech in Thayer's court ("I do not wish to a dog . . .") was used in a course titled "Public Speaking and Oral Interpretation" alongside quotations from such figures and sources as Lincoln, Emerson, Whitman, Shakespeare, both Roosevelt presidents, Keats, and the Bible. According to college records in 1965, between five hundred and a thousand students enrolled for the course each semester.[29]

But the most enthusiastic students did not settle for an analysis of pamphlets or the celebrated letters of Sacco and Vanzetti. Many wanted to meet and discuss the case in person with people who had been involved in it. Members of the Sacco-Vanzetti community thus received numerous invitations from schools and colleges to talk about the case. One student at the University of Massachusetts at Amherst invited Ehrmann to speak to her history club by explaining that "the officers of the Club feel that students should be made aware that even in a democracy the legal code is subject to the machinations of corrupt and misguided men." Ehrmann and Felicani also received numerous letters from children asking them to write back about their remembrances of the case. Understandably delighted to be receiving so much attention in their twilight years, the two men rarely turned down these requests, except when increasingly failing health prevented them from traveling. Their activity helped to further disseminate the increasingly accepted idea that Sacco and Vanzetti had been unjustly sent to their deaths by narrow-minded, bigoted reactionaries. By 1962, in Musmanno's words, "Public opinion had become pretty well convinced that Massachusetts executed two innocent men."[30]

In order to understand the ensuing backlash against Sacco and Vanzetti and their cause, it is important to take into account not only the frequency and sympathy with which their story was presented at the start of the decade but also the historical weight that accompanied it. One important aspect of the affair was its inevitable link to communism: Kempton and many other Sacco-Vanzetti sympathizers had observed that the most immediate intellectual beneficiary of the case had been the CPUSA. The lesson of the Sacco-Vanzetti affair for many young American intellectuals was that liberals had badly misunderstood the significance of the case, specifically the determination of the establishment to execute Sacco and Vanzetti regardless of evidence or justice, and that the radicals' diagnosis of the case had been essentially correct. As a result, these intellectuals moved further to the left, ending up in or near the growing Communist movement in the 1930s. As Kempton put it, "After the final defeat [of Sacco and Vanzetti], it was very hard for some of these violated innocents not to believe that the communists had been right in one thing . . . liberalism had been blind in proclaiming that they could hope for justice from peaceful appeal to the conscience of established society." Kempton also made the observation (echoing Cowley) that for a lot of these young people, "the myth of the thirties began at Charlestown Prison in Boston with Sacco-Vanzetti," and did not, as is now more common, identify it with the collapse of the stock market in 1929 or even with the election of Franklin Roosevelt to the presidency in 1932.[31]

Yet even if we agree with Kempton about the lasting centrality of the Sacco-Vanzetti affair, scholars still face the question of how and why the issue survived over decades in the United States during which Americans experienced grave economic depression, enormous social upheaval, world war, nuclear anxiety, and the assassination of a popular president. Arthur Schlesinger, Sr., in his 1963 memoir *In Retrospect,* recognized the importance of this question: "By [our] time so many horrors [have] afflicted the world," he wrote, "that it seems as though the lot of two insignificant individuals in Massachusetts back in the 1920s could no longer prick the public conscience." Schlesinger went on to suggest an answer which can be described as self-congratulatory and even self-serving but not necessarily wrong: "This did not prove to be the fact, probably because, whatever the malpractices of totalitarian regimes, Americans could not escape a sense of responsibility for what they themselves had permitted to happen."[32]

Schlesinger's view had essentially not changed since 1929, when he had written that "history never lets bygones be bygones. . . . As the Sacco-Vanzetti case recedes into the past and the miasma of hate and prejudice lifts, the failure of the commonwealth and its legal system to render justice without fear or favor becomes increasingly plain. History already sees Sacco-Vanzetti as the victims of a faulty judicial system administered by men blinded by postwar hysteria and passion."[33] This, in a nutshell, was the classic late-1920s liberal narrative of the case that continued to dominate public conversation from the 1930s through the 1950s, according to which Sacco and Vanzetti were the victims of ethnic hatred, class prejudice, political indifference, and an unreformed legal system. This view deemphasized Sacco and Vanzetti's radicalism, their political aims, and especially the international dimensions of their cause. The complementary aspect of this attitude in the United States was the emphasis on "better morality in public affairs," as Einstein put it in 1947: "Everything should be done to keep alive the tragic affair of Sacco and Vanzetti in the conscience of mankind. They remind us of the fact that even the most perfectly planned democratic institutions are no better than the people whose instruments they are."[34] By 1960 these were the most commonly accepted interpretations of the case, especially among American liberals. For these reasons, it becomes clearer why nearly four decades after their deaths Sacco and Vanzetti became prime symbolic targets for attack.

In 1960, William F. Buckley, Jr., the rising young star of the American Catholic right and founder of the *National Review,* was still shaken from the defeat of his hero Senator Joseph McCarthy by what Buckley saw as an array of godless forces tolerant, if not supportive, of communism. Following *God and Man at Yale,* his brash 1951 attack on his alma mater—and the book that first made his name—Buckley wrote *McCarthy and His Enemies* in 1954 with another young Catholic conservative, his brother-in-law L. Brent Bozell. Buckley and Bozell portrayed the disgraced politician as having been fundamentally correct about the state of American politics and unfairly maligned by his nefarious left-wing enemies; McCarthy had not in their view created a "reign of terror," as the Tydings Committee of the Senate had concluded after studying his allegations—but even if he had, it would have been justified under the circumstances. Most important, McCarthy had been an indispensable leader in the ongoing fight against communism, and Buckley and Bozell still insisted that "on McCarthyism hang the hopes of America for effective resistance to communist infiltration."[35]

The historian George Nash pointed out in his sympathetic study of the conservative intellectual movement that "the McCarthy episode had a traumatic importance for the American intellectual Right."[36] Buckley was the perfect example. He was not impressed by the drubbing that the quintessential liberal Adlai Stevenson suffered at the hands of Eisenhower and the Republican Party in the presidential elections of 1952 and 1956. Rather, in 1960, Buckley was still deeply disturbed by the downfall of McCarthy, which he attributed to the dominance of liberalism in American political life, and that year he helped found Young Americans for Freedom, the national right-wing student movement.[37] He also found ideological ammunition for his cause in *Sacco-Vanzetti: The Murder and the Myth,* published by a seventy-one-year-old Boston lawyer, Robert Montgomery. It was the first new nonfiction book on the Sacco-Vanzetti case to appear since the 1940s.

Montgomery's goal was straightforward: he wanted to shatter what he called "the Sacco-Vanzetti myth." According to him, Sacco and Vanzetti had been guilty, their trial had been fair, and the fuss over the case was nothing more than disingenuous radical anti-American

agitation. Making clear where his sentiments lay, Montgomery dedicated his book to "all those who believe in and are dedicated conform-
ists of law and order." When it came to Arthur Schlesinger, Jr., Montgomery turned especially ill-tempered. He could not understand why
the celebrity scholar, in his *The Crisis of the Old Order,* had described
Sacco and Vanzetti as "two obscure immigrants about whom no one
cared," when they had been the focus of so much national and international attention. Completely disregarding the fact that Schlesinger was
referring to the time of their 1921 trial, when the two were relative
unknowns, Montgomery snapped: "How, in the face of the worldwide
support of the defense by law professors, lawyers, law students, college presidents, college professors, journalists, preachers, poets, playwrights, authors, labor unions, civil liberties unions, church councils,
picketers, demonstrators, dynamiters, and do-gooders, Schlesinger had
the effrontery to write that 'no one cared' would pass my comprehen-
sion if I knew less than I did about his standards of scholarship."[38]

Aside from the bilious tone, this passage reveals much of what
was to characterize much of the revisionist-conservative attack on
the Sacco-Vanzetti "myth": a failure to distinguish between the stages
of the Sacco-Vanzetti history (most crucially, between the situations
in 1921 and 1927 or between case and affair) and among the various
types of activity on behalf of the defendants (between, say, exploding a
bomb and signing a petition). More broadly, it made more marked the
tendency to write the history of the case from a transparently partisan
viewpoint and to base that viewpoint primarily on the presumed guilt
or innocence of Sacco and/or Vanzetti.

Montgomery's account, like later revisionist writings, lumped
Sacco and Vanzetti's defenders into a single anti-patriotic group. "The
case," he argued, in precise and probably unintentional repetition of
Frank Goodwin's xenophobic "Red Peril" speech of 1927, "would
never have become a cause célèbre unless the Reds had made it one."
The "exploitation" of the case, as he saw it, began as early as 1920, with
the ACLU joining in 1921 and the Communist ILD in 1925. "With
a multitude of front organizations, radical labor unions, the radical
press, paid publicists, and volunteer agitators," the protesters "joined
in an exploitation of this ordinary murder trial for revolutionary purposes and propaganda, mass agitation, and the breaking down of the
American judicial system and American institutions generally. That so
many men and women of good will and supposed intelligence . . .

should have joined in this shameful exploitation is a measure of the success of the techniques which have set a pattern of exploitation *for cases of the same kind which were to follow*" (emphasis mine). After this simplistic description of the transformation of the case into affair, Montgomery ended in a decidedly unscholarly manner: "I have told the truth about Sacco-Vanzetti, but I am not in the least confident that the telling of the truth will destroy a myth so dear to the credulous who had deified Vanzetti and so valuable to the powerful forces throughout the world who still use it for their evil purposes. The truth is mighty but it will not prevail against a Great Lie, and the Sacco-Vanzetti Myth is the greatest lie of them all."

Quick to strike the iron while it was hot, Buckley published his own article on the Sacco-Vanzetti affair not in his *National Review* but in the more widely disseminated *American Legion Magazine.* Borrowing from Montgomery's book, Buckley also aimed his fire at the Sacco-Vanzetti Myth. He picked up on Montgomery's central theme: that all forms of Sacco-Vanzetti protest were connected, starting in 1920 and ending in the present, and that the support for Sacco and Vanzetti's cause was never about either Sacco and Vanzetti themselves or about justice but rather was about the legitimacy (or lack thereof) of American institutions. In other words, to defend Sacco and Vanzetti was to have been in cahoots with Communist revolutionaries. To Buckley the Sacco-Vanzetti Myth was an important foundation of the contemporary liberal American left. Like Montgomery, Buckley focused on the 1921 trial, exonerating the jury, the judge, and the prosecution of any wrongdoing. According to him, the case began to attain its lasting meaning only after the conviction, when "[Fred] Moore and his committee encouraged international expressions of resentment over the verdict, and there followed during the summer months demonstrations and parades and strikes and explosive editorials all over the world. In the excitement all touch with reality was lost. . . . For one thing, the communist party moved in. . . . The communists and the ideologues never took over the Sacco-Vanzetti case in the sense that it can be said they took over the Scottsboro case a few years later; but they did, by their rabid distortions, create a hysteria and recklessness which caught on in saner circles, which continues . . . to characterize most of the rhetoric on Sacco-Vanzetti."[39]

Drawing on the reputation of Oliver Wendell Holmes, Buckley quoted, out of context, the former Supreme Court justice's remark to Harold Laski that the case "was turned into a text by the Reds" and attempted to connect it to his own more immediate concerns: "It became about as difficult to maintain the guilt of Sacco-Vanzetti in fashionable quarters—or the innocence of the executors of justice in Massachusetts—as, much later, it became to suggest that Senator McCarthy had something important to say about security standards in government."

Buckley's main concern was with the events and legacy of the 1950s—specifically, his wish to salvage conservatism from the collapse of McCarthyism, or, more precisely, to rehabilitate McCarthyism in the aftermath of McCarthy's downfall. He spoke of Communists, but his real enemies were liberals. In the rise of postwar conservatism, much depended on the destruction of so-called liberal ideals, and the Sacco-Vanzetti case was supposedly one of the most cherished of these.[40] By tying Sacco and Vanzetti's history to the circumstances of the Cold War years, Buckley's article represented, in a sense, the flip side to the work of the liberal historians, who also wrote about the Sacco-Vanzetti case from the vantage point of their mid-1950s political sensibilities.

Buckley's main argument was with Arthur Schlesinger, Jr. Following Montgomery's lead, Buckley catalogued a number of errors of fact made by Schlesinger (while making as many, if not more, of his own) and compared the accusations of framing in the Sacco-Vanzetti case to one of the more sordid episodes of the McCarthy period, the downfall of Alger Hiss: "[It is] the kind of madness which at a later time seized some otherwise responsible Americans who have gone about charging that the Justice Department and the FBI joined hands in a project to forge a typewriter with which to frame Hiss."[41]

After asserting the clarity of Sacco and Vanzetti's guilt, Buckley rhetorically asked, "Why are we constantly being told that justice itself was sick in Massachusetts, when in fact justice ruled reasonably on the basis of the evidence in hand, and ground out a verdict which the facts—as known—all but compelled?" In his opinion, even if it were to be discovered that Sacco and Vanzetti had been innocent, this would not vindicate their defenders, then or now, "for their obligation would still be to point back to the trial and say why the jury should have voted otherwise . . . or show where the trial judge abused his role as arbiter; or indicate why the . . . courts should have suspected it was not Sacco-Vanzetti, but someone else. . . . But no such demonstration has been made. Not a single change in the rules of evidence or procedure in Massachusetts law is traceable to the distilled criticisms of the handling of Sacco-Vanzetti."

It is difficult for a historian to determine whether Buckley was exhibiting feigned or real ignorance. His article, like Montgomery's book, ignored the fact that Thayer had ruled on all the appeals and had refused to recuse himself from the case even though he had never made a secret of his disdain for the defendants; that there was in fact a subsequent confession to the crime by Celestino Medeiros (whose story was not believed by the judge or the authorities); and that Massachusetts law was indeed changed as a result of the case in 1939. Buckley added that "[no criticism of the trial] was indicated, in the opinion of the responsible authorities, nor in the opinion of a considerable number of interested bystanders, who included the great John Henry Wigmore, the ranking authority on evidence in America. Sacco and Vanzetti were fairly tried, they said." It is not clear what Buckley meant here by "the responsible authorities," but he may not have known that beginning in late 1926 and certainly in 1927 the proceedings were criticized by prominent political, legal, and intellectual figures, not all of whom belonged to the radical left.

Buckley's statements were particularly tendentious in light of the fact that Frankfurter's *The Case of Sacco and Vanzetti*, first published in 1927, remained the most influential study of the case well into the 1950s. Wigmore made his opinions on the case known in the context of his public attack on Frankfurter, which sparked the aggressive exchange between the two law professors in the Boston press; and in that debate, most of Wigmore's criticism had to do with what he saw as the subversive and foreign nature of the protest and not with the substance of the Sacco-Vanzetti case, about which he knew little.[42] Buckley also made it seem as though Holmes had supported the verdict and the execution, but Holmes's primary reasoning for not intervening in the case was not approval of Thayer's conduct or even the conviction that Sacco and Vanzetti were guilty but rather his belief in the legal autonomy of the individual states and, less officially, his aversion to the foreign and outside pressures put on the Massachusetts and U.S. authorities.[43]

More generally, Buckley was wrong on the evolution of the Sacco-Vanzetti affair at both the national and international levels. In this regard, too, he was merely copying Montgomery's mistakes but for a larger readership. The explosion of world opinion did not occur before 1926–1927; until then the protest over the case mostly emanated from the radical left, whose influence and power were negligible at best. Whereas in 1921 the case was relatively obscure, by 1927 it had become a cause célèbre in much wider political and intellectual circles, irrespective of the actions or opinions of Communists and anarchists, who remained weak, divided, on the defensive, and with little impact, except perhaps in the negative sense, on public opinion in the United States.

Toward the end of his article, Buckley got to his real point. The controversy over the Sacco-Vanzetti case, he argued, was but one manifestation of a long and unfortunate twentieth-century American tradition that reached its climax with the struggle against McCarthyism: "Why the continuing fever? Beyond the personal appeal of the poor and illiterate fish peddler and his friend the shoemaker, there was everywhere the virulence of men who despised this country and its institutions. Here was a human vehicle through which to indict the existing order, condemn our institutions, dramatize the cause of proletarian socialism, scrape away at the Puritan ethic, tear and wrench the nation and cause it to bleed across the pages of history. Their success has been considerable, and they do not give up, just as they will never give up on Alger Hiss. But they face the formidable opposition of common sense, and the toughminded honesty of Anglo-Saxon jurisprudence."

To Buckley, the Sacco-Vanzetti affair was a myth that needed to be debunked so that future generations of Americans would not have to live under its shadow. To this purpose he ridiculed even the defendants' most hallowed characteristics: "The functional pidgin English of Vanzetti was transmuted in some of his letters into a dirge on our time of almost overpowering eloquence." Of Sacco's famous last letter to his young son Dante, in which he asked him to remember to "help the weak ones that cry for help, help the persecuted and the victim, because they are your better friends," Buckley had this to say: "This is a lesson for all of us, surely, murderers and non-murderers alike. These clearly were mythogenic men. . . . From the beginning, the anguish was unrestrained. There was even a book of poems, including the titles 'Two crucified,' etc. . . . This is bathos, and sacrilegious bathos at that."

Montgomery's book and Buckley's article were the first shots in what would soon become a wider long-term right-wing crusade to explode the Sacco-Vanzetti Myth in American political culture. But

Buckley's essay had a more visceral effect on the Sacco-Vanzetti community. While Montgomery's book could be seen as a last hurrah for the vanishing reactionary Boston milieu that had produced intellectually limited men like Thayer and Fuller, Buckley was a new, younger voice on the scene: his audience was larger, his influence more considerable. Hence, responding to him was more urgent.

Tom O'Connor, a former reporter who had volunteered to assist in the Sacco-Vanzetti defense campaign in 1927 and later devoted much of his life to preserving Sacco and Vanzetti's memory, was a particularly energetic (and slightly eccentric) correspondent. His belief in Sacco and Vanzetti's innocence did not diminish over the years; in addition to numerous letters to fellow former activists in the community, O'Connor was quick to respond to anything written on the case. In an angry letter to Buckley, O'Connor reiterated the view of the case as America's ignominious version of the Dreyfus affair. Thirty-three years after the execution, he still shuddered at the memory of how "a spineless court and a multi-millionaire automobile salesman, cheered on by the great majority of an ignorant, church-ridden public, flouted the pleas, not only of communists, who, on your thesis, wanted Sacco-Vanzetti executed as 'martyrs,' but of the leaders of the civilized world." O'Connor also corrected several of Buckley's errors (among them, the latter's claim that Thayer had never conducted himself inappropriately outside the court) and informed Buckley that Massachusetts law *was,* in fact, changed as a result of the case; as O'Connor made sure to explain to Buckley, the amendment passed by the legislature in 1939 was proposed to allow the Massachusetts supreme court to review cases and render verdicts based on "the interests of justice" and not simply on the rules of evidence—the restriction that had prevented the court from overturning Thayer's rulings in 1926 and 1927.[44]

Corrections like these, however, did not give Buckley pause. In a letter to an unnamed professor at Columbia University, which he published in the *National Review* a few months later, Buckley added to his litany of antiliberal criticisms his suspicion that Sacco and Vanzetti's last oral testaments were fake, ghostwritten by one or more of their supporters. He based this view on the "incompatibility of the syntax" of these speeches (especially Vanzetti's) with that previously used by the defendants. In Buckley's opinion, those who insisted that Sacco and Vanzetti were innocent did so because they were so impressed with their eloquence; as he put it, "Many of these people shrink from believing the evidence because they are so overwhelmed by the beauty of the prose, which they flatly conclude is inconsistent with the suggestion that Sacco-Vanzetti were murderers." Indeed, several of Sacco and Vanzetti's defenders had made such arguments, and the defendants' moving words as they neared their demise had become an important part of the Sacco-Vanzetti legend. Buckley hoped that his recipient at Columbia would read all the material and study the hypothesis that Sacco and Vanzetti "used a ghost—heaven knows there were enough of them around—every litterateur in the country paid court to them." There is no record of such a study ever being conducted.[45]

Another facet in the conservative attempt to defeat the supposedly entrenched Sacco-Vanzetti Myth was the role of pre–World War II leftists, some of them former supporters of Sacco and Vanzetti who were now right wingers eager to use their past experience in the service of anti-communism. One such figure was the erstwhile Trotskyist and founder and editor of *The Masses* Max Eastman, who was anxious to enter the fray because he wished to share information that he hoped would shatter the myth for good: a brief, interrupted conversation he had had in 1941 with the former anarchist leader Carlo Tresca, in which the latter "confided" to Eastman that Sacco had been guilty.[46]

Encouraged by Buckley, Eastman wrote an article on the subject, but it was turned down, he claimed, by *Reader's Digest,* the *Saturday Evening Post, Time,* the *New Leader,* and *Esquire.* In March 1961, still unable to find a publisher, he wrote to a friend, "I think [William] Buckley would have published it, but I was loth to have it look like a conservative argument. . . . I must say the facts are, as I see them, a conservative argument, or a pretty severe indictment of the 'Reds' and myself among them."[47] Eventually, Buckley published Eastman's piece in the *National Review* and wrote in a preface that Eastman had tried to get the article published "in a half dozen more leftward papers, because I thought it would be more effective if published there; but they all shied away from it." His explanation for that was simple: "American liberals grew up on the myth of Sacco-Vanzetti, and do not want to ruffle it—the ensuing emotional and intellectual readjustment would be too painful." It did not occur to Buckley that perhaps this was not the result of a left-wing conspiracy but rather that editors had not yet caught up to the reemerging interest in Sacco and Vanzetti.[48]

In his article, "Is This the Truth About Sacco and Vanzetti?" (the answer, of course, was an emphatic yes), Eastman, too, focused on the "myth" of the men's innocence, concluding—based on his reported aborted conversation with Tresca—that Sacco had been guilty and Vanzetti went to his death covering for his comrade. More broadly, Eastman sought to delegitimize the Sacco-Vanzetti cause and link it to the anti-patriotic mania already outlined by Buckley. Echoing Cowley, as well as the 1950s liberal historians, but from a right-wing standpoint, Eastman described the Sacco-Vanzetti case as "a principal cause of the stampede of the American intelligentsia to the cause of 'proletarian revolution' in the 1930s. . . . It also gave its first impetus to that anti-American sentiment which, nourished by . . . the communists, is to be found today in many parts of the world." As for his own involvement in the Sacco-Vanzetti cause, Eastman remembered it as part of his "youthful Marxist idiocy" (though it should be noted that he was a ripe forty-four years old when Sacco and Vanzetti were executed). He had just completed his "pilgrimage" to Russia, as he recalled, and on his return to the United States (in 1923), "I made no study of the case myself, but was swept along by a mixture of revolutionary dogma and pure emotion into the general outcry against their 'martyrdom' and against class rule in America."[49]

To Eastman, the Sacco-Vanzetti affair was one more example of how misguided and dangerous the entire American left was. By mixing the Sacco-Vanzetti cause with his own former "revolutionary dogma," he meant to show that protesting the conviction and execution of the two Italian anarchists had been thoughtless, reflexive, and unpatriotic. The fact that Eastman himself had supported the cause (albeit never in any central or visible role) could be seen as a boon for the revisionist, right-wing agenda and was particularly galling to those who continued to uphold the principle of Sacco and Vanzetti's innocence. O'Connor, for one, sent Eastman an even more bellicose letter than the one he had sent Buckley, challenging all Eastman's assertions and concluding, "You are a victim of your own complete ignorance of the case and—I suspect—of your disillusionment with radicals."[50]

A more intelligent revisionist article than Eastman's appeared in the journal *Commentary* in January 1962. The author, James Grossman, following Eastman's lead, argued that Sacco was guilty and Vanzetti probably innocent. His article also treated Sacco-Vanzetti as a hallowed myth badly in need in destruction, but he did a superior job than either Buckley or Eastman at explaining why its enduring power was so troublesome to the right. "Since their deaths," Grossman wrote, "[Sacco and Vanzetti] have transcended human nature. Their literary remains . . . have taken on the precious beauty of words of saints and martyrs. As in so many canonizations, the harshness of reality has fallen from them." His task, therefore, was to expose the real Sacco and Vanzetti. Grossman was explicit about wanting to focus on the question of guilt or innocence as something separate from the fairness of the trial, since "whether they committed the act of which they [were] accused is a question of little importance in determining the unfairness of the legal proceedings but of great importance independently of it. These two men have so large a place in American culture that their lives and deeds are a part of American history and should be examined like any other historical question."[51]

While these articles, especially Buckley's, are riddled with factual errors and questionable assumptions, they did make two general points that have both endured as integral to the ongoing debates over Sacco and Vanzetti and in an indirect way pushed scholars to develop a fuller picture of Sacco and Vanzetti the men and the political actors, rather than Sacco and Vanzetti the legends. First, they were right to intuit (as Buckley did) that liberal historians such as Schlesinger had in essence adopted the 1930s left-wing interpretation of the case. Second, and perhaps more important, they contributed to the understanding that the reinvention of Sacco and Vanzetti as benign utopian dreamers was largely false and that in fact the two were committed (not just theoretical) anarchists, devoted to the violent overthrow of Western bourgeois governments.[52] Even in this regard, however, the revisionist view was exaggerated; Sacco and Vanzetti's defenders had never denied that the two men had been involved in revolutionary politics before their arrests. In addition, the eventual reevaluation of Sacco and Vanzetti as real political individuals, and the general shattering of such liberal "myths," had as much, if not more, to do with developments on the American left since the 1960s.[53]

Still, this issue is primarily why it became so pertinent for conservatives to focus on the guilt of one or both of the defendants. Since Sacco and Vanzetti had been considered morally and philosophically incapable of committing a violent crime, it became important to show that this was nothing more than a myth, that in fact they were very much capable of violence. There were different ways of proving such

guilt, however. Grossman made the case that Sacco was guilty based on
a supposed "consciousness of guilt," though of a different sort from
the one used to convict the two defendants at their trial. Sacco, Grossman observed, had never clearly denied the act of killing; instead, he
had proclaimed his "innocence" in general terms while ranting and
raving about the evils of capitalism and bourgeois justice: by *innocent*
Sacco could have meant only that he did not recognize the legitimacy
of a bourgeois court to determine his fate (this was probably true).
Vanzetti, on the other hand, repeatedly professed his innocence in
concrete rather than abstract terms, by making it clear that he had
never personally killed anyone. Grossman thus argued that Sacco had
committed the crime in the context of war—in 1920, the Galleanisti in
the United States believed that they desperately needed money to
protect themselves from the government, which was deporting and
even killing their comrades.[54]

But while these debates of the early 1960s led eventually to a
partial and belated reexamination of Sacco's and Vanzetti's political
biographies, specifically their insufficiently recognized radical background, they also helped give rise to the single most unfruitful aspect
of Sacco-Vanzetti scholarship (and public discussion) of the past five
decades: the obsession with the question of one or both men's guilt or
innocence of the robbery and murder at the expense of the social,
political, intellectual, and global context and ramifications of their
case, which have been neglected.

In this respect, no other work on Sacco and Vanzetti has been as
important—and as prototypical—as Francis Russell's *Tragedy in Dedham,* first published in 1962.[55] Russell's correspondence at the time
he was working on it demonstrates how hotly anticipated (and later,
hotly contested) his book was. Russell, it seems, did a masterful job
of impressing upon his various interviewees and correspondents that
his study would vindicate their own particular view of the Sacco-
Vanzetti case. One such correspondent was the indefatigably enthusiastic O'Connor, who believed that Russell's reexamination of the case,
including an extensive analysis of ballistics remains and other such
criminal paraphernalia, would produce what O'Connor hoped would
be "the classic book on the case," a definitive vindication of the pro-
Sacco-Vanzetti position; after all, Russell's earlier writing had reiterated the general view that the two men had been both innocent and
unfairly tried.[56] To this purpose, he helped Russell extensively with his

time and documents. But O'Connor's hopes were dashed, spurring him to begin dispatching chagrined letters to Russell and others.[57]

A far more intriguing Russell aide in the early 1960s was John Dos Passos, whose 1927 tract *Facing the Chair* was one of the earliest and most important literary condemnations of the Sacco-Vanzetti trial, and whose 1936 trilogy *USA* showed the traumatic effect of the executions on the Depression-era American left—most memorably in his stark vision of an America divided into "two nations," one the innocent "haters of oppression," the other, "strangers who have turned our language inside out, who have taken the clean words our fathers spoke and made them slimy and foul."[58] Like many other idealistic left-wing intellectuals of the interwar period, Dos Passos became disillusioned with Marxism as a result of his experience fighting for the republican side in the Spanish Civil War, and he fell out with the Communist movement in the course of the 1930s, precisely at the moment when its popularity peaked in the United States and the rest of the Western world.[59] In the 1940s and 1950s, driven by his hatred of the Soviet Union, Dos Passos drifted further to the right.[60] By the 1960s his literary prestige was not nearly what it had been twenty or thirty years earlier, but his ideological trajectory, similar to that of Eastman and many other radicals of his generation, makes his retrospective views on Sacco and Vanzetti valuable to scholars seeking to understand the shifting meanings of their case, especially for those who had been active in their cause.

Despite his move from radical left to radical right, Dos Passos, perhaps because he knew the details of the case much more intimately than Eastman, was not so easily willing to renounce his belief in Sacco and Vanzetti's innocence. At the same time, his letters to Russell are startling in their total lack of the pathos that had once characterized his writing on the case. "I realize that the possibilities of error are endless," he wrote in 1960. "At the time I was naturally friendly disposed toward Sacco-Vanzetti because they were anarchists. . . . I talked to both men, and, although I could imagine their nerving themselves up to such an attempt for political purposes . . . I just didn't think they were the men to do it."[61]

As Dos Passos remembered it—perhaps selectively—the Sacco-Vanzetti affair predated the war in Spain as the beginning of his break with the radical left. While he remained skeptical about Eastman's assertions of Sacco's guilt, since this was for him a matter above politics (or so he now claimed), he had no problem attacking the mobilization around the Sacco-Vanzetti cause: "The propaganda use of the story is quite another business. It was the last gasp of the international anarchist movement. The way the communists gradually took it over was a preview of what was to happen in Spain a decade later."[62]

The case, which to Dos Passos once signified an irreparable breach within American society, a casus belli between "two nations," now boiled down to the question of whether Sacco and Vanzetti's trial had been technically fair and whether one of the men had pulled the trigger on that drab industrial street in South Braintree. Even the matter of intellectuals' engagement in political and social causes, a staple of 1930s left-wing culture, meant little to him now, and in a 1961 letter he offered Russell "just one piece of advice . . . don't put too much faith in the testimony of 'intellectuals.' They are changeable as water." Probably no one knew this better than Dos Passos himself.[63]

Still, Dos Passos remained fundamentally conflicted. Russell shared with him the results of his ballistics investigations, which implicated Sacco as a perpetrator of the crime. Dos Passos was now willing to concede that perhaps Sacco's innocence was not a sure thing after all. Writing to Russell in late 1961, he called Eastman's *National Review* article "excellent"; the new information Russell gave him on the evidence Dos Passos found "fascinating." "It makes me feel," he added, "how remiss I was not to look into the whole story more carefully. . . . Though obviously an activist . . . Sacco did not seem to me to be the gunman type."[64]

But while he did not object to the idea that one of the defendants (namely, Sacco) might have been guilty, Dos Passos still believed that their trial had not been fair. In a subsequent letter to Russell, he pointed out (correctly) that if Sacco were indeed the gunman, the two defendants should have been tried separately, and that since the case against them relied heavily on Vanzetti's prior conviction for the attempted robbery in 1919 in Bridgewater, trying them together made Judge Thayer, and the entire legal process, look even worse.

To the contradiction between his Cold War right-wing views and his lingering doubts about the Sacco-Vanzetti case, Dos Passos found a solution, or solace, in a strange and ultimately unconvincing balance between extremists on both sides. Rather than focus on the more disturbing and important events of 1926 and 1927 Dos Passos chose to emphasize the origins of the case in 1919 and 1920, before he had become involved. By focusing on the case rather than on the affair, he could explain away the entire Sacco-Vanzetti episode as the result of radicalism gone awry, a favorite Cold War theme. The whole country, he wrote to Russell, had been suffering in the aftermath of World War I from collective insanity, for which the radicals and the government were equally responsible. He urged Russell to take into account the atmosphere in the country at the time of the Red Scare and recommended that he read *The Deportations Delirium,* the 1923 account by Louis F. Post, assistant secretary of labor in the Wilson administration.[65] "Don't neglect the hysteria on both sides," Dos Passos wrote. "The radicals were in a state about the Palmer raids etc. . . . such Massachusetts buogers [sic] as Judge Thayer were in a state—about such things as the Wall Street bombing, the rise of Bolshevik power in Russia—all the after war unrest."[66] As for Buckley, who had led the charge against the Sacco-Vanzetti Myth (and who had provided him with an intellectual home at the *National Review*), Dos Passos considered him a "fairminded fellow" but also a man who "just couldn't imagine the state of mind of postwar America in 1919–1920. . . . Take the 'liberal' hysteria against McCarthy, turn it upside down, and multiply it by ten and you'll have [an idea] of the state of mind of 'good citizens.' The radicals, pacifists, IWW sympathizers were equally hysterical—they were the foxes with the hounds at their trail."[67]

Dos Passos was not the only original Sacco-Vanzetti intellectual supporter to look back at the case through the prism of completely changed political beliefs. Others who had walked a similar ideological path shared his ambivalent attitude toward the case and their involvement in it. The New York intellectual James Rorty, another former radical who had been marginally active in the cause in the 1920s, first became doubtful of Sacco and Vanzetti's innocence (or so he claimed) after reading Montgomery's *The Murder and the Myth,* and he wrote a positive review of that book in the journal *New Leader.*[68] Still, though signs now pointed, in his view, to the guilt of one or both of the defendants, he did not agree with Eastman's account of a "youthful idiocy" tempered by age and conservative wisdom. In a 1961 letter to Russell, Rorty insisted that involvement in the case was still something to be proud of, since "our reasons were decent and honorable."[69]

Dos Passos himself would finally find a formulation that allowed him to reconcile his radical involvement in the Sacco-Vanzetti camp with his postwar conservatism. To him, the disillusionment with the left began and ended with the Communists' cynical, opportunistic, Soviet-directed takeover of "good causes" like the Spanish Civil War and the Sacco-Vanzetti case. Thus, the evils of such histories could be distilled to the intrusion of the Communist movement into the arena of protest, not necessarily the conditions against which the protest was directed. He expressed this view neatly in a 1963 West German television program on Sacco and Vanzetti by contrasting American justice with its Soviet counterpart. "At a time when the Anglo-Saxon ideas of justice are in great jeopardy," he rationalized, "you could look back on the agitation of the Sacco-Vanzetti case with a certain satisfaction because [at least] there was justice to appeal to."[70] For the Cold War–era Dos Passos, in other words, the Sacco-Vanzetti case no longer represented the destruction of the American dream, as it did in the 1930s, but was rather an example of its enduring strength. And the emphasis on Communists and the Soviet Union as the real villains who doomed Sacco and Vanzetti before they went on to doom republican Spain would later be echoed by other writers who had been similarly pained, and politically confused, by the executions, including Katherine Anne Porter, whose brief 1977 memoir of the affair, *The Never-Ending Wrong*, contained a similar message.[71]

Former Sacco-Vanzetti supporters like Dos Passos, Rorty, Eastman, and Arthur Schlesinger, Sr., were not the only ones to revisit the case in the 1960s. One figure on the side of the prosecution of Sacco and Vanzetti to become involved in the new-old debate was Michael E. Stewart, who as the Bridgewater police chief had set up the police dragnet that had first ensnared Sacco and Vanzetti in 1920. For the controversial Stewart—accused over the years by Sacco and Vanzetti campaigners of conspiring with the Department of Justice and the local prosecution to frame the two anarchists by manipulating or planting evidence—the controversies of the 1960s were nothing new. He was still furious over what he saw as a pernicious campaign against law, order, and morality that had begun in the 1920s and was still going strong. As we have seen, one of the less-expected outcomes of the Sacco-Vanzetti case was its adverse affect on some of the political and legal figures who had been responsible for the convictions and executions of the two men. Several who had probably expected their role in the case to further their careers had fallen into obscurity or failure, and for some Sacco-Vanzetti defenders (like Musmanno, now a

Communist-hunting state supreme court justice in Pennsylvania) this had been a source of satisfaction. This view had also seeped into the thinking of conservatives like Buckley, who saw the Sacco-Vanzetti Myth and its exploiters as victorious at the expense of important American institutions.

Stewart, now an octogenarian, wrote a bitter piece in which he tried to settle old scores. Although the article was never published, his voice represents the outrage of an ordinary law enforcement official whose identification with the Palmer raids and the political culture that produced them was complete and uncompromising, even after forty years: "The fair name of Massachusetts was sullied and her institutions bitterly assailed, throughout the world, by men of ungodly beliefs, whose chief purpose was, and still is, the destruction of rational government. . . . Many . . . respected citizens were to become sometimes rabid sympathizers, their better judgment dwarfed by the constant drum beats of hate and false propaganda emanating from the twisted minds of the [Sacco-Vanzetti] defense committee." Whom exactly did Stewart have in mind? He noted "two intellectuals, both professors at one of our oldest institutions of learning." We may assume that one was Frankfurter, but the identity of the second is unclear; it might have been William Hocking, Arthur Schlesinger, Sr., Roscoe Pound, or a number of the Harvard professors who shared Frankfurter's opinion. "The writings of these gifted men," he charged, "added much to the flames of hate, as much of the material in their books was not alone untrue." Stewart ended his polemic by lauding the people who had finally written the truth about the case, particularly Robert Montgomery.[72]

Whereas Stewart wrote out of unabated hostility to Sacco and Vanzetti and their defenders, some ardent Sacco and Vanzetti supporters also attacked Frankfurter at this time, many of them aging progressives who felt continuing anguish over their failure to stop the executions. The eighty-year-old Roland D. Sawyer, a congregational minister and a former member of the Massachusetts state legislature, was a member of the Committee for the Vindication of Sacco and Vanzetti in 1962. Almost four decades after the executions, he still criticized "Frankfurter's baleful influence," without which, as he saw it, the Sacco-Vanzetti defense committee in Boston would have supported his proposal in 1927 to ask the Massachusetts House of Representatives to set up a special commission of judges to examine and review the proceedings. He claimed that he had won the support of defense attorney William Thompson for this step but that Frankfurter's "domination" of the defense committee prevented him from going forward. Whether or not this was true, Sawyer believed that such a commission would have eventually led to Sacco and Vanzetti's acquittal. In his view, the defense committee's decision to rely solely on the Massachusetts politicians and the Lowell commission sealed Sacco and Vanzetti's fate, and he called it "a sad blot on Frankfurter's distinguished career" since the Harvard law professor had "forced the defense . . . to leave the fate of [Sacco and Vanzetti] in the hands of Governor Fuller, inept and prejudiced as he proved to be."[73]

Even those somewhat closer to Frankfurter expressed skepticism in the 1960s about his role in the case. Roscoe Pound, for example, who had been dean of Harvard Law School at the time, claimed in later years to have arrived at the conclusion that Sacco and Vanzetti had been guilty after all. Pound had important free speech and civil liberties credentials: he was one of Palmer's strongest critics in the legal world after World War I and an advocate of Jacob Abrams, an anarchist who had been convicted under the Espionage Act for criticizing the government during the war—an involvement which created a tense relationship with his own university. In a 1962 letter to Herbert Ehrmann, Pound explained that after reading Frankfurter's *Atlantic Monthly* article in 1927 he had assumed that the Sacco-Vanzetti case was another Abrams case, based on repression of dissent. Later, as he recounted, he studied the case himself and concluded that Sacco and Vanzetti were guilty, "and I have held that conclusion ever since."[74] But, Pound claimed, because of his friendship with Frankfurter, Thompson, and Ehrmann, he had refrained from making any public statement to that effect. In private, he also implied that Frankfurter was remaining publicly silent on the Sacco-Vanzetti issue in the 1960s because he had changed his mind about their innocence.

Considering, however, that Frankfurter's *The Case of Sacco-Vanzetti* had been republished as recently as 1954 and that in his correspondence he adamantly stood by all his assertions, these were puzzling statements on Pound's part. It is true that during the period of renewed interest, Frankfurter refused to comment publicly on the case (he was by then a long-standing U.S. Supreme Court justice) and instead directed inquisitive reporters and students to Ehrmann, his former protégé, or to Musmanno. But he also encouraged the two men in his letters "not to let the revisionists [get away] with anything." Pound's comments should be read rather in the context of his tense and deteriorating relationship with Frankfurter. Despite Pound's claim, the two men were anything but good friends. Frankfurter had once greatly admired Pound, one of his mentors, but during the 1920s his attitude had chilled considerably because of what he saw as Pound's timidity on political, legal, and social questions—in particular, the Sacco-Vanzetti case. Pound had objected to the publication of Frankfurter's *Atlantic Monthly* article, and Frankfurter, in response, wrote a furious letter to his own mentor, Louis Brandeis. Pound and Frankfurter also clashed on faculty hirings at Harvard, especially of Jews, and on various private issues. By the 1930s, they were in a virtual state of war. As one Frankfurter biographer has written, his relationship with Pound "never recovered from the cumulative weight of their controversies during the late twenties."[75]

Russell's *Tragedy in Dedham*, which concluded that Sacco was probably guilty and Vanzetti most likely innocent (but with foreknowledge of the crime) and was based on his examinations of ballistics evidence and the unreliable hearsay opinions of three controversial former Sacco-Vanzetti advocates (Tresca, Sinclair, and Moore), elicited anxious responses from the Sacco-Vanzetti community and middling reviews from scholars.[76] Despite its lack of notes and its unscholarly approach, *Tragedy in Dedham* was seen by many in the world of letters as the final word on the topic. And over time it became the source of a particular orthodoxy regarding the case that offered a symbolic compromise of sorts: by positing that one of the men (Sacco) had been guilty and the other innocent, troubled former Sacco and Vanzetti supporters could have it both ways: they could now believe that their youthful cause had not been entirely based on a lie but that the establishment was not wholly corrupt.[77]

In the early 1960s, however, the initial reaction was far more agitated. Already distraught by the wave of revisionism that had preceded and accompanied Russell's book, the Sacco-Vanzetti community reacted to its publication by launching Operation Ambush: a "counteroffensive against the defamers of Sacco-Vanzetti's memory," in the words of former ILD head James Cannon. Musmanno, in a typically choleric piece ("The Armchair Theorists Begin to Comment on the Sacco-Vanzetti Case"), dismissed the new wave of revisionism as a superficial but "dangerous" trend and argued that by the start of the

1960s, "it was clear to any right thinking person that Sacco and Vanzetti had had an unfair trial and were wrongly executed." Especially after the NBC program, he felt, public opinion had "become pretty well convinced that Massachusetts executed two innocent men."[78]

This counteroffensive had begun relatively early. In 1960, even before the publications of Montgomery's *The Murder and the Myth* (whose conclusions the community knew well in advance) and Buckley's *American Legion* article, Ehrmann reissued his own 1933 book on the case, and he and other Sacco-Vanzetti supporters made a concerted effort to disseminate it as widely as possible; one of his recipients was the young presidential candidate from Massachusetts, Senator John F. Kennedy. Ehrmann also began work on a new large-scale book based on his legal work on the case, which was eventually published in 1969 as *The Case That Will Not Die*.[79]

Indeed, the revisionists touched a raw nerve among Sacco-Vanzetti's veteran defenders, and their personal correspondence reveals the depth of emotion involved. Much of the anger was directed at defectors like Eastman and Dos Passos. As Felicani wrote to Rose Pesotta, another former activist in the cause, in language reminiscent of the ideological wars of the interwar years, "We are confronted by a gang of people without scruples." Musmanno, in a letter to Felicani, announced, "I am now preparing [a] reply to Grossman, whom I despise even more than Eastman. Grossman is vicious and must be devastated directly and particularly." Musmanno and Ehrmann both wrote angry responses to Grossman's article in *Commentary*, but these were rejected by the editor, Norman Podhoretz, who wrote to Ehrmann that "the controversy has almost completely died out" and that Russell's book had settled the debate. In response, Ehrmann pointed to the attacks on Russell's book, as well as to the flurry of public and artistic interest in the case, and added, "I should have thought that [*Commentary*'s] first concern should have been with the manner in which two foreign-born radicals were treated under the American system of justice, and not whether the men were guilty or innocent."[80]

Another testament to the hold Russell's book had over many editors in 1963 is the fact that Ehrmann had great difficulty finding a publisher for *The Case That Will Not Die*. Still, the community found ways to make its voice heard. Musmanno wrote spirited critiques of Russell's book in the *New Republic*, the *American Bar Association Journal*, and the *Kansas Law Review*, while some rebuttals were direct and personal: Russell, in *Tragedy in Dedham,* had claimed that James Cannon had later decided that Sacco was guilty; in a letter to the *New Republic,* Cannon flatly denied this.[81]

And there was another form of counteroffensive. Some of those who had been involved in the Sacco-Vanzetti cause in the late 1920s were spending their golden years doing more sleuthing of their own in legal and police archives, occasionally even uncovering important new bits of information. In late 1960 the officially silent Frankfurter circulated a letter from his friend Lindsay Rogers, a retired professor of public law and political science at Columbia University, in which Rogers claimed that he had once heard Lowell remark at his club that the Sacco-Vanzetti case had gone "so far" that someone had to become "the goat." "There are only three possible goats: the state of Massachusetts, Webster Thayer, and Sacco-Vanzetti," Lowell had supposedly said, implying that the choice of the latter was obvious. Rogers also reported to Frankfurter (who then spread the word) that in 1953, in the papers of the Massachusetts judge John Aiken, he found a 1920 letter from Thayer in which he asked to be assigned to the Sacco-Vanzetti case, explaining that he was a "stern and righteous judge" who would see that the defendants "got what they deserved." And for every article that provided supposed proof of Sacco and/or Vanzetti's guilt of the crime, there was an immediate counter article, such as the one by the reporter Fred J. Cook in the *Nation,* who shed new light on the minutiae of the case in order to show that the two men were innocent.[82]

For Eastman, at least, these "liberal reactions" to the revisionism about the case that he had helped spearhead were not surprising—in a letter to Russell he charged, "We've learned from the Nazis and communists . . . how a 'line' once decided upon can acquire all the emotional attributes of truth"—and the counteroffensive sparked a revisionist counter-counteroffensive. In 1965 the revisionists got a slight, temporary boost with the publication of David Felix's *Protest: Sacco-Vanzetti and the Intellectuals,* a work that was even more historiographically limited and damaging than Russell's. Like *Tragedy in Dedham,* it contains no citations or notes, and it is more concerned with chastising intellectuals who supported the Sacco-Vanzetti cause in the 1920s than with attempting to understand what drew them to it. Nor does the author make any attempt to distinguish between different types of intellectuals in the United States or to analyze non-

American reactions, settling instead for such explanations as "Europeans have the greatest difficulty with the simplest events."[83]

Ultimately, the community did not succeed in totally discrediting the revisionists nor the revisionists the community, but the Sacco-Vanzetti supporters did regain ground in the battle over Sacco and Vanzetti's memory, and the result of this struggle—at least over the question of guilt versus innocence—should be seen as a stalemate of sorts. In many ways, the battle lines over Sacco and Vanzetti that were drawn in the early 1960s have remained in place, including the inescapable question of whether they were guilty.[84]

It is difficult to determine who, if anyone, emerged triumphant from the Sacco-Vanzetti controversies of the 1960s and beyond. Any attempt to answer this question demands a clear set of criteria and focuses. In the media and the arts, and at schools and universities, the belief in Sacco and Vanzetti's unfair treatment remained dominant; in western Europe (particularly Italy and France) this notion appears especially strong and should be understood in the context of complex postwar and Cold War attitudes toward the United States. In the narrower world of American letters, the 1950s consensus on Sacco-Vanzetti became somewhat fragmented by the wave of revisionist writing on the case in the 1960s.[85] And yet there is evidence that even toward the end of the 1960s, the notion that the Sacco-Vanzetti case was unjust had been accepted by much of what we can call the political and legal establishment. One example of this is a 1969 letter from Erwin Griswold, U.S. solicitor general under President Richard Nixon (and former dean of the Harvard Law School), to Ehrmann: "There were times, long ago, when I occasionally had some doubts, but these have long since gone. . . . The thought that [Sacco and Vanzetti] could have been the guilty ones is so implausible. . . . [Their] case is a sad chapter in [our] legal history."[86]

In another sign of the times, the noted poet Robert Lowell, younger cousin of A. Lawrence Lowell and a longtime intellectual activist on the left, stated at a commemorative meeting for Sacco and Vanzetti held in New York in 1967 on the fortieth anniversary of their deaths, "I believe that my cousin was honest, but that he was wrong." At the same event, Mary Donovan linked the fight on behalf of Sacco and Vanzetti in the late 1920s to the civil rights and Vietnam struggles of the 1960s—a link that Dos Passos, for one, had refused to make. It is somewhat surprising, given the seemingly intuitive connection between the two protest movements, that she was one of few to do so, but it is line with the fact that some veteran Sacco and Vanzetti defenders, like Musmanno, could never really abide left-wing radicals and even shared Dos Passos's antipathy toward Communists.[87]

On the political level, advocating posthumously for the two executed anarchists—a desultory process in the 1950s and 1960s—became not only safe but successful: Massachusetts governor Dukakis's declaration in 1977 that Sacco and Vanzetti's trial had been unfair proved that the once subversive idea had become almost a commonplace, even if it did not go unchallenged.[88] Indeed, in 1977, the fiftieth anniversary of Sacco and Vanzetti's execution, the two returned to the international agenda, though on a more modest scale than in 1927. Dukakis's proclamation in the dead men's favor was preceded by requests to the White House from influential figures on the European left. François Mitterrand and Enrico Berlinguer—the leaders of the French Socialist Party and the Italian Communist Party, respectively—jointly asked President Jimmy Carter to grant a posthumous pardon to the long-dead anarchists. And just as in 1927, the issue was immediately sent by the presidential staff to the attention of the Massachusetts governor.[89]

In any case, there are probably more pressing and interesting questions facing historians than "Who won the debate?"—a question that could prove as intellectually limiting as "Did they do it?" What was the controversy about? What was at stake? How did the return of the affair influence the way people thought about Sacco and Vanzetti? In the late Cold War era, liberal historians, leftists-turned-conservatives, Catholic pundits, the Sacco-Vanzetti community—all of these groups and others had compelling personal and political reasons for their stance. To take just two examples, Arthur Schlesinger, Jr., and William F. Buckley, their involvement had much to do with the McCarthy episode and the lessons that each drew from it. At the center of this renewed struggle was the history that had led from the Sacco-Vanzetti affair up to that point. How to interpret that history? For Buckley, the legacy of Sacco-Vanzetti represented an obstacle to the advancement of his ideals, since the twin beliefs in Sacco and Vanzetti's innocence and the unfairness of their trial served as foundational myths, as he saw it, for his enemies; thus, the defeat of McCarthyism was rooted in the defense of Sacco and Vanzetti. To Schlesinger, Sacco and Vanzetti's politics were irrelevant (and perhaps inconvenient); as far as he was concerned, they were destroyed by a nativist, intolerant, reactionary "old order" that he despised and whose political heirs were responsible for the political aberrations of the 1950s. It is probably also significant in his own case that his father had been active in the Sacco-Vanzetti cause in the late 1920s.

And yet there are other, perhaps more illuminating, ways in which to understand the latter-day, Cold War–era Sacco-Vanzetti controversy and its significance. Liberal historians have often seen the early 1960s, particularly after the inauguration of John F. Kennedy, as a period of renewed energy, innocence, and hope in American political life, especially among the newly confident liberals.[90] In this sense, an episode like the Sacco-Vanzetti case became important once again for a generation eager to exorcise the demons of the older generation, whether one looked at the case from the left or the right.

For Schlesinger, Buckley, Dos Passos, and Eastman, as well as for the scores of playwrights, students, television producers, journalists, activists, and others who revisited or even discovered the case beginning in the 1960s, Sacco and Vanzetti were symbols used in a broader struggle over American culture, politics, and memory. Even the European sources from this period show that the Sacco-Vanzetti affair held interest primarily as a precursor to more recent events that sharpened the animosities toward American justice, such as the Rosenbergs' execution in 1953, which some European observers on the left found disturbingly reminiscent of the Sacco-Vanzetti executions. (By contrast, the Rosenberg case was conspicuously missing from the Sacco-Vanzetti debates in the United States in the 1950s and 1960s—a sign that there was little correlation between American support or condemnation of Sacco and Vanzetti and support or condemnation of the Rosenbergs).[91]

For the Sacco-Vanzetti community, however, the two dead anarchists were not abstract symbols. For Musmanno, for example, they were two men with no particular political significance—especially, for him, no *Communist* significance. A letter he wrote to NBC executive producer Robert Alan Aurthur after reading the script for the 1960 television special is telling. True, Musmanno was thrilled that NBC was to highlight the injustices of the trial and bring the Sacco-Vanzetti case to the attention of a new, younger public. But Musmanno feared that NBC was turning the program into an "ideological sermon." He did not agree with the show's message that Sacco and Vanzetti were

killed because of fear of anarchism and class war. He wanted the program to convince Americans not that the upper class had targeted two
members of the working class but that Sacco and Vanzetti were the
victims of individual stupidity, greed, and ignorance.[92]

This was, in a sense, a repetition of the late-1920s debate, both in
the United States and abroad, between those who believed that the
case represented something fundamentally rotten in the American
body politic and those who felt that it was an aberration within a generally workable system, a crime or conspiracy perpetrated by region-
specific, isolated individuals and not by an entire system or society.
Musmanno, a man of the legal establishment and an avowed Communist hunter both during and after the McCarthy period, belonged
to the second category, even while his criticism of those individuals
(Thayer, Fuller, and Lowell) was particularly harsh: "Thayer killed
because he hated Italians and all those who did not conform to his
notions of loyalty," he explained to Aurthur. "Fuller killed because he
was criminally stupid and actually believed that he could become president of the United States by standing on the corpses of Sacco and
Vanzetti. Lowell killed because he felt it was his great responsibility to
protect the fair name of Massachusetts and Massachusetts justice. He
believed himself a super-intellectual and was satisfied that he would be
hailed as a hero by the Brahmins for his cleverness. . . . I followed the
Sacco-Vanzetti case from the beginning, and I was never conscious of a
so-called class war. I was conscious of the greed, hypocrisy, and cruelty with which the prosecutors would destroy two innocent men for
their own selfish gains."

The 1960s controversy can be seen as a struggle between those for
whom Sacco and Vanzetti were real people, to be exonerated and vindicated long after their deaths, and those for whom Sacco and Vanzetti
were part of a collective memory—political symbols. What the symbols stood for depended on what particular political beliefs one held.
But it is evident that the Sacco-Vanzetti affair did not simply end in the
1920s, or even in the 1930s, and was alive a generation later (as it still is,
in a sense, today). A much more crucial question in the long afterlife of
the affair than whether the two men were guilty is to what degree their
execution represented a distinctly *political* phenomenon in American
history. If Sacco and Vanzetti were merely the victims of a few individuals' selfishness and irresponsibility, their deaths mean little in
terms of American society—or even Massachusetts society—in any

meaningful sense. If, on the other hand, their case had broader social, political, and cultural roots and implications, as this book argues, it transcended the actions of a few individuals and can be explained only in both a national and an international context. The dramatic return of Sacco and Vanzetti to the public arena in the 1960s, and again in the 1970s and beyond, makes clear that the case cannot be seen strictly as a finite episode; it remained a part of American and European history long after August 23, 1927.

Postscript

The Place of Sacco and Vanzetti

In the eighty years since their deaths, Sacco and Vanzetti have occupied an array of roles in the public imagination. At the time of writing, however, they seem to have come full circle, even if they are no longer near the center of any political discussion. For many today Sacco and Vanzetti were the innocent victims of America's first ill-conceived "war on terror," their execution an act of barbarism that was rooted in the fear of immigrants, persecution of radicals, and oppression of the working class, at a time when being proletarian, Italian, and an anarchist was perhaps the equivalent of being labeled an enemy combatant after September 11, 2001. For others, they were criminals and terrorists who benefited from a duplicitous worldwide propaganda campaign led by people who despised America and everything it stood for. But beyond these diametrically opposed perceptions the more subtle, or subconscious, aspects of Sacco and Vanzetti's joint afterlife deserve closer attention.

Many of Sacco and Vanzetti's appearances are fairly predictable and revolve around the pet obsessions of half-informed pundits looking to score easy political points. These should not be the focus of scholars. But others are more unexpected, even trivial, and thus more revealing. On *The Sopranos*, a thoughtful (and sadistic) television series about an organized crime family that was avidly followed by millions of viewers worldwide (including me), Tony and Carmela Soprano explain to their children—over a lavish dinner in their New Jersey mansion—that Italian immigrants who came to America received a raw deal, thus implicitly justifying their own Italian-American family's dubious livelihood. "They won't tell you about Sacco and Vanzetti!" Mr. Soprano shouts during his rant. "The two anti-Christs executed in Massachusetts?" asks his young, none-too-bright son.

"They were two innocent men who got the chair because they were Italian," Mrs. Soprano authoritatively explains. In another example, a writer for the magazine *Sports Illustrated,* discussing the National Basketball Association's decreasing popularity, remarked that "the public has given [2005 finalists] Detroit and San Antonio the Sacco and Vanzetti treatment, condemning them before giving them a chance."[1]

Other reminders are more sobering, or ironic. Europe—where the case, though fairly well known to the educated public, has been treated over the years as an almost exclusively American story—provides several examples. In Clichy, a large northern suburb of Paris whose residents are mainly poor immigrants from northern and Sub-Saharan Africa, angry riots took place in the fall of 2005, protesting the conditions of émigrés in France; it is hard to know whether the demonstrators on avenue Sacco-Vanzetti near the city center gave the two Italians, whose deaths were the cause of violent riots by other immigrants eight decades earlier, a second thought. European colleagues whom I told about this book often know nothing about the protests that took place in their cities in the late 1920s but almost invariably bring up the 1971 Italian film *Sacco e Vanzetti* and its theme song, which is easily recognizable to many who lived in France, Italy, or elsewhere on the Continent in the 1970s and the 1980s. In Russia, Ukraine, Belarus, Lithuania, and other former Soviet states, the names Sacco and Vanzetti instantly conjure up images of pencils, because the largest pencil factory in the Soviet Union was named after the two men in 1927. (In a recent sign of the times, the walls of the factory were torn down at the initiative of a developer from Texas to make way for an enormous shopping center called Park City.)[2]

But what are we to make of these disparate cameos on television, in the sports pages, on the streets, in daily life, in fleeting memories? All they seem to show is that outside the ever-shrinking world of radical politics, where the case is still an extremely touchy topic, and U.S. history textbooks, where it usually appears, somewhat misleadingly, in sections on the Red Scare of 1919–1920, Sacco and Vanzetti are iconic but somewhat abstract figures, symbols of persecution or injustices of all sorts, and the Sacco-Vanzetti affair remains misunderstood.[3] Sacco and Vanzetti's various appearances (or reappearances) do, however, show that despite their widespread posthumous ubiquity, and the strong notions that many people still have about them, their place in our historical consciousness, and in our civic life, is not at all clear—and it will never be as long as we continue to focus on the question of guilt or innocence rather than on the broader meanings of their story. The Sacco-Vanzetti affair deserves better: less detective work, more history. Less punditry, more research. Even Tony Soprano's son, and his nonfictional equivalents, should have a clearer idea of who these men were and what their history was about.

We will never know whether Sacco and Vanzetti "did it." It is too late for that. (In the Dreyfus affair, things were more straightforward—even opponents of the Jewish officer knew, after a certain point, that he was innocent.) What is clear, and more important, is that their legal process was unfair and their execution, as a result, an injustice, whether they were guilty or not. In 1929, two years after their deaths, H. L. Mencken wrote that their case "refuses to yield. . . . The victims continue to walk, haunting the conscience of America, of the civilized world."⁴ This was eerily prophetic: despite the passage of eight decades, the execution of Sacco and Vanzetti is still with us—a deeply troublesome event that gnaws insistently at our collective sense of right and wrong. But although Mencken also insisted that "there must be an end, sooner or later, to that abomination," none is yet in sight.

But the vagueness surrounding the Sacco-Vanzetti affair in both the historical record and popular culture is to be expected for another, more contextual reason. Sacco and Vanzetti's ties to our own day are perhaps more symbolic than concrete. Whereas once anarchism inspired many and terrified more, today it is a nostalgic curiosity, more a source of bemusement than of fear. Few people even know exactly what it is, or was. Italians in America—and in Italy, for that matter—inhabit an entirely different universe from that of the 1920s. And revolutionary politics, a key backdrop to the Sacco-Vanzetti episode, seem over—at least for now. But most crucial, Sacco and Vanzetti, and their history, cannot be connected in a direct and obvious way to the main historical preoccupations of the post-1945 generations in Europe or America. They were neither Communists nor fascists; they had little if anything to do with the rise of Hitler, the destruction of Europe's Jews, the rise and collapse of the Soviet empire, de-colonization, the civil rights movement, the sexual revolution, the nuclear age, or the Vietnam War. All this may be part of why Sacco and Vanzetti have in one sense gone back to where they were in 1927, or even 1921. Often it appears—as when a play about their case opens in France, or a blogger revisits their story, or an anti-globalization punk band dedicates yet another ear-shattering tune to their memory—that they have once again become the exclusive domain of marginalized radicals. But this is to miss the larger point of the affair, which transcended the persecution of anarchists or working-class Italians and became a story about the way the United States, the world's first modern superpower, related to the rest of the world.

The beginning of the twenty-first century has reminded historians and commentators of the difficulties that Americans have had in the past in dealing with the rest of the world, and even more so, in the ways that the rest of the world has viewed, and interacted with, the United States in times of dramatic international flux. One of the more striking aspects of the struggle over Sacco and Vanzetti's fate in 1927 was the way that the international opposition to U.S. policies became in itself a reason for many Americans to strenuously insist on continuing these policies, in the face of inconvenient facts and undesirable results. Nearly eight decades later, worried observers could see a similar mechanism at work in the domestic context of the misguided war in Iraq. Many of those in or near power warmly welcomed international support for the war (which grew more meager, then practically nonexistent, as the war turned into a fiasco) but later proved unable to stomach international criticism, which was not only rejected but used as proof that the United States needed to "go it alone," no matter the cost to its global reputation and no matter how badly the war was actually going. (Indeed, the beleaguered 2004 Democratic presidential candidate John Kerry was castigated by a large segment of public opinion because he dared to suggest in a debate with the incumbent president that there was a "global test" that the United States needed to pass before launching preemptive wars. No matter that this had been the official basis for United States foreign policy for generations; during a time of a war it was considered unpatriotic.). Similarly, pleas or suggestions from abroad (as well as from many in the United States) to maintain the decades-long regulation of the financial markets and not to abandon the welfare state were treated by those in authority in the United States, often dismissively, as all the more reason to continue those policies.

In an earlier, different, version of this sort of mentality and comportment, the Sacco-Vanzetti affair showed what happened when certain American authorities proved unwilling to heed the call in the Declaration of Independence to pay "a decent respect to the opinions of mankind," a call that was repeated by a wide array of conscientious Americans, as well as many friendly (and not-so-friendly) critics from abroad, during Sacco and Vanzetti's final days. Then as later, too many Americans in positions of power were determined to forge ahead with what increasingly appeared to be an illegitimate and unwise decision, even in the face of reasonable criticism and disturbing facts, because they believed that to change course would have meant surrendering to the demands of foreigners, subversives, and "terrorists." But at the same time, then as now, other Americans demonstrated an awareness of being part of a wider world, and a willingness to accept, and even embrace, the legitimacy of international interest in the politics of the United States—as shown, most recently, by the 2008 election to the presidency of a multicultural, intellectually curious man whose extraordinary popularity overseas was matched only by the global unpopularity of his parochial, proudly incurious predecessor.

From its inception the Sacco-Vanzetti affair has intersected with the most pressing concerns of the day; it needs to be understood nationally in terms of social and political tensions in the United States, and internationally in the context of America's changing place in the world. The history of the Sacco-Vanzetti affair is also the history of how politics came to function in our world. Only when it receives the attention due to it from scholars—not trying yet again to prove guilt or innocence but exploring its meaning—can justice be done, if not to Sacco and Vanzetti, then at least to their place in history.

Notes

Abbreviations

ALLP A. Lawrence Lowell Papers Concerning the Sacco and Vanzetti Case, Houghton Library, Harvard University, Cambridge, Mass.

BPL-Felicani Aldino Felicani Sacco-Vanzetti Collection, Boston Public Library, Rare Books Department

BPL-Joughin G. Louis Joughin papers, Rare Books Department, Boston Public Library

CPUSA Files of the Communist Party of the United States of America in the Comintern Archives, 1919–1943, Tamiment Library, New York University

Ehrmann Papers Herbert B. Ehrmann Papers, Harvard Law School Library Special Collections, Cambridge, Mass.

FBI SV Federal Bureau of Investigation Sacco-Vanzetti Case Files, Library of Congress, Washington, D.C.

Fonds RR-BNF Fonds Romain Rolland, Département des manuscrits occidentaux, Bibliothèque Nationale de France (Richelieu), Paris

Frank Papers Mrs. Walter Frank Papers, Brandeis University Archives and Special Collections Department, Waltham, Mass.

Harvard Law SV case record Sacco-Vanzetti Case Records, 1920–1928, Harvard Law School Library Special Collections, Cambridge, Mass.

Harvard Law SV news. clip. Sacco-Vanzetti Trial Newspaper Clippings, Apr.–Nov. 1927, Harvard Law School Library Special Collections, Cambridge, Mass.

LDH-BDIC Papers of the Ligue des droits de l'homme, Bibliothèque de Documentation Internationale Contemporaine, Nanterre

O'Connor Papers Tom O'Connor Papers, Brandeis University Archives and Special Collections Department, Waltham, Mass.

Russell Papers Francis Russell Papers, Brandeis University Archives and Special Collections Department, Waltham, Mass.

Introduction

1. This book does not focus on the technicalities and evidence of the case. These have been treated extensively elsewhere. Most of the literature on the legal and criminal aspects of the case can be divided into two basic groups: those sympathetic to the Sacco-Vanzetti defense and those hostile to it. The first group includes Felix Frankfurter, *The Case of Sacco and Vanzetti: A Critical Analysis for Lawyers and Laymen* (New York, 1927); Osmond K. Fraenkel, *The Sacco-Vanzetti Case* (New York, 1931), Karl N. Llewellyn, "The Sacco-Vanzetti Case," in *Criminal Law and Its Administration: Cases, Statutes, and Commentaries,* ed. J. Michael and H. Wechsler (Chicago, 1940), 24–63; G. Louis Joughin and Edmund M. Morgan, *The Legacy of Sacco and Vanzetti* (New York, 1948); Herbert B. Ehrmann, *The Untried Case: The Sacco-Vanzetti Case and the Morelli Gang* (New York, 1933); Ehrmann, *The Case That Will Not Die: Commonwealth vs. Sacco and Vanzetti* (Boston, 1969); Roberta Strauss Feuerlicht, *Justice Crucified: The Story of Sacco and Vanzetti* (New York, 1977); David E. Kaiser and William Young, *Postmortem: New Evidence in the Case of Sacco and Vanzetti* (Amherst, Mass., 1985). The second group includes Robert Montgomery, *Sacco-Vanzetti: The Murder and the Myth* (New York, 1960); Francis Russell, *Tragedy in Dedham: The Story of the Sacco-Vanzetti Case* (New York, 1962); Russell, *Sacco and Vanzetti: The Case Resolved* (New York, 1986); James Grossman, "The Sacco-Vanzetti Case Reconsidered," *Commentary* 33:1 (Jan. 1962): 31–44. For the ballistic evidence, see James Starrs, "Once More Unto the Breech: The Firearms Evidence in the Sacco and Vanzetti Case Revisited," *Journal of Forensic Studies* 31 (1986): 630–654, 1050–1078, and Joseph B. Kadane and David Schum, *A Probabilistic Analysis of the Sacco-Vanzetti Evidence* (New York, 1996).

2. An important step toward the internationalization of the history of the case is Lisa McGirr, "The Passion of Sacco and Vanzetti: A Global History," *Journal of American History* 93:4 (Mar. 2007): 1085–1115.

3. Henri Guernut, *Une affaire Dreyfus aux Etats-Unis: L'affaire Sacco et Vanzetti* (Paris, 1927). The literature on the Dreyfus affair is extensive; see for example Michel Winock, *L'affaire Dreyfus* (Paris, 1998), Eric Cahm, *The Dreyfus Affair in French Society and Politics* (London, 1996), and Christophe Charle, *Naissance des "intellectuels," 1880–1900* (Paris, 1990). For narrative accounts, see Jean-Denis Bredin, *The Affair: The Case of Alfred Dreyfus* (New York, 1983), David Levering Lewis, *Prisoners of Honor: The Dreyfus Affair* (New York, 1973), and George R. Whyte, *The Dreyfus Affair: A Chronological History* (Basingstoke, U.K., 2005).

4. Carl Schorske, *Fin-de-Siècle Vienna: Politics and Culture* (New York, 1980), chap. 3 ("Politics in a New Key").

5. " 'J'accuse . . . !' Lettre au président de la République par Emile Zola," *L'aurore,* Jan. 13, 1898, 1. For the *intellectuels* and the Dreyfus affair, see especially Charle, *Naissance des "intellectuels."*

6. Schorske, *Fin-de-Siècle Vienna.*

7. The Dreyfus affair played a crucial role in the construction of what became

known in France as the "Republican history of the Republic"; see Madeleine Re-
bérioux, "Histoire, historiens, et dreyfusisme," *Revue historique* 255 (1976): 407–432.
Robert O. Paxton, "The Lesson of the Dreyfus Case," *New York Review of Books,*
Feb. 27, 1986, used the term "morality tale" to explain the "timelessness" of the
Dreyfus story.

8. My work owes a methodological debt to the suggestive article by Robert
Darnton, "It Happened One Night," *New York Review of Books,* June 24, 2004.
Darnton uses the term "incident analysis" to describe a large body of histories that
"focus on an incident, relate it as a story, and then follow its repercussions through the
social order and even across successive periods of time."

9. In this sense, this book answers the call issued by numerous scholars to study
the modern history of the United States in international perspective. See, for example,
Thomas Bender, ed., *Rethinking American History in a Global Age* (Berkeley, Calif.,
2002), and Bender's own attempt at that "rethinking," *A Nation Among Nations:
America's Place in World History* (New York, 2006). For earlier calls see Ian Tyrrell,
"American Exceptionalism in an Age of International History," *American Historical
Review* 96 (Oct. 1991): 1031–1055, and John Higham, "The Future of American
History," *Journal of American History* 80 (Mar. 1994): 1289–1307. For the state of
transnational history, a field still in conceptual flux, see "AHR Conversation: On
Transnational History," *American Historical Review* 111:5 (Dec. 2005): 1440–1464.
For the links between transnational and American historical research, see the various
essays in the *Journal of American History* 86:3 (Dec. 1999), especially David Thelen,
"The Nation and Beyond: Transnational Perspectives on United States History," 373–
397. Two major works that explore American-European connections are Daniel T.
Rodgers, *Atlantic Crossings: Social Politics in a Progressive Age* (Cambridge, Mass.,
1998), and Victoria de Grazia, *Irresistible Empire: America's Advance Through
Twentieth-Century Europe* (Cambridge, Mass., 2005).

10. Schlesinger at www.courttv.com/archive/greatesttrials/Sacco.Vanzetti/schle
singer.html. (accessed Mar. 25, 2008).

11. Katherine Anne Porter, *The Never-Ending Wrong* (New York, 1977).

Chapter 1: "The Two Most Famous Prisoners in the World"

1. For a thorough and even-handed plumbing of the trial record, see Bruce Watson, *Sacco and Vanzetti: The Men, the Murders, and the Judgment of Mankind* (New
York, 2007).

2. Quoted in Eugene Lyons, *Assignment in Utopia* (New York, 1932), 2.

3. Nicola Sacco, letter of July 19, 1927, in *The Letters of Sacco and Vanzetti,* ed.
Marion Frankfurter and Gardner Jackson (1928; New York, 1997), 68.

4. For Sacco and Vanzetti's politics, see especially Paul Avrich, *Sacco and Vanzetti: The Anarchist Background* (Princeton, N.J., 1991), which suggests that the Galleanisti were involved in the 1919 bombing. For Sacco and Vanzetti's time in Mexico,
see pp. 57–90. For the Galleanisti and their activity in the United States, see Beverly

Gage, *The Day Wall Street Exploded: A Story of America in its First Age of Terror* (New York, 2009), esp. chap. 10 ("The Anarchist Fighters"), and Nunzio Pernicone, "Luigi Galleani and Italian Anarchist Terrorism in the United States," *Studi Emigrazione/Etudes Migration* 30 (Sept. 1993): 469–489.

5. At his first trial, for the 1919 Bridgewater holdup, Vanzetti was represented by attorney John Vahey, but later Moore represented him, along with Sacco, at the Dedham trial, with two assistants of local repute, the brothers McAnarney.

6. Michael M. Topp, *The Sacco and Vanzetti Case: A Brief History with Documents* (New York, 2004), 11.

7. See David M. Kennedy, *Over Here: The First World War and American Society* (New York, 1980); Robert K. Murray, *Red Scare: A Study in National Hysteria, 1919–1920* (Minneapolis, 1955); William Preston, *Aliens and Dissenters: Federal Suppression of Radicals, 1903–1933* (Cambridge, Mass., 1963); Julian Jaffe, *Crusade Against Radicalism: New York During the Red Scare, 1914–1924* (Port Washington, N.Y., 1972). For the origins of these policies in an older set of progressive politics, see Gage, *Day Wall Street Exploded.* For connections to the present, see David Cole, *Enemy Aliens: Double Standards and Constitutional Freedoms in the War on Terrorism* (New York, 2005).

8. See Georges Haupt, *Socialism and the Great War: The Collapse of the Second International* (Oxford, 1972); Geoff Eley, *Forging Democracy: The History of the Left in Europe, 1850–2000* (New York, 2002), 123–184. For the Western response to Bolshevism, see, for example, Lloyd Gardner, *Safe for Democracy: The Anglo-American Response to Revolution, 1913–1923* (New York, 1984), N. Gordon Levin, *Woodrow Wilson and World Politics: America's Response to War and Revolution* (New York, 1968), and Arno Mayer, *Wilson vs. Lenin: Political Origins of the New Diplomacy, 1917–1918* (New York, 1967). For background on anarchism, see James Joll, *The Anarchists* (Cambridge, Mass., 1979); George Woodcock, *Anarchism: A History of Libertarian Ideas and Movements* (Cleveland, Ohio, 1962); Daniel Guérin, *Anarchism: From Theory to Practice* (New York, 1970). There has been renewed scholarly interest in internationalist anarchism in its heyday: see, for example, Benedict Anderson, *Under Three Flags: Anarchism and the Anti-Colonial Imagination* (London, 2005), which links the old anarchist cause to the modern antiglobalization movement.

9. See, for example, William M. Tuttle, Jr., *Race Riot: Chicago in the Red Summer of 1919* (New York, 1970), and Jeremy Brecher, *Strike!* (Boston, 1972), chap. 4 ("Nineteen-Nineteen").

10. Gage, *Day Wall Street Exploded;* Avrich, *Sacco and Vanzetti.* See also Mike Davis, *Buda's Wagon: A Brief History of the Car Bomb* (New York, 2007), chap. 1 ("Wall Street 1920"). For a history of the Bureau, see Rhodri Jeffreys-Jones, *The FBI: A History* (New Haven, 2007).

11. See Christopher Lasch, *American Liberals and the Russian Revolution* (New York, 1962). For American intellectual responses to Bolshevism, see David Engerman, *Modernization from the Other Shore: American Intellectuals and the Romance of Russian Development* (Cambridge, Mass., 2003).

12. Eugene Lyons, *The Life and Death of Sacco and Vanzetti* (New York, 1927), 66–70; Lyons, "Italians in American Courts," *Survey,* Nov. 12, 1921, 237–238; Art Shields, *Are They Doomed? The Sacco-Vanzetti Case and the Grim Forces Behind It* (Boston, 1921).

13. This is common to Francis Russell, *Tragedy in Dedham: The Story of the Sacco-Vanzetti Case* (New York, 1962), and, more recently, Topp, *Sacco-Vanzetti Case,* 41, Mary Anne Trasciatti, "The American Campaign to Save Sacco and Vanzetti," in Trasciatti and Jerome Delamater, eds., *Representing Sacco and Vanzetti* (New York, 2005), 27–44, and Michael E. Parrish, *Anxious Decades: America in Prosperity and Depression, 1920–1941* (New York, 1992), 201–202. Parrish, in "Sacco and Vanzetti Revisited: Russell and Young & Kaiser," *American Bar Foundation Research Journal,* 12:2–3 (Spring–Summer 1987): 575–589, a fine review article, argued that Moore was "a genius at public relations. It was he who first turned the South Braintree robbery and murder into a larger social drama that pitted two working-class Italians against the capitalist-dominated legal system of Massachusetts" (577).

14. Trasciatti, "American Campaign," 32.

15. See Jeremy Adelman, "Political Ruptures and Organized Labor: Argentina, Brazil, and Mexico," *International Labor and Working-Class History* 54 (1998): 103–125. For the broader context of Italian working-class activism in Argentina, see also Pietro R. Fanesi, "El anti-fascismo italiano en Argentina (1922–1945)," *EMLA* 4:2 (Aug. 1989): 319–352.

16. FBI SV, pt. 8, pp. 100–107.

17. FBI SV, pt. 1-a, pp. 54, 73; pt. 4-b, pp. 76–79.

18. FBI SV, pt. 8, p. 106.

19. FBI SV, pt. 4-a, p. 44.

20. FBI SV, pt. 8, pp. 49–57.

21. " 'Reds' Plot Revenge on all American Officials in France," *New York Times,* Oct. 21, 1921. As late as November 1921, the Communist International (Comintern) could appeal to the workers of the world to save "the revolutionary strike leaders Sacco and Vangetta [*sic*]." See FBI SV, pt. 6-a, p. 12.

22. See "3-Day Sacco Bomb Plot Is Foiled in Boston," *Boston Telegraph,* Oct. 26, 1921. The Department of Justice denied the existence of such a conspiracy, but the story was carried by both the *New York Tribune* and the *Boston Advertiser* (a Hearst newspaper) on October 27. The editor of the *Advertiser* reportedly admitted to the Bureau agent in Boston that the report was "a figment of [one writer's] imagination." See FBI SV, pt. 2-b, p. 77.

23. Italian leftists were later joined, cautiously, by less radical and even right-wing Italians in the United States and elsewhere, especially after Benito Mussolini became involved in the affair. In the United States, the nationalist Sons of Italy eventually pledged their support for the Sacco-Vanzetti cause. See Philip Cannistraro, "Mussolini, Sacco-Vanzetti, and the Anarchists: The Transatlantic Context," *Journal of Modern History* 68 (1996): 50–51. For the Italian-American press treatment of the case, see Trasciatti, "Framing the Sacco-Vanzetti Executions in the Italian-American

Press," *Critical Studies in Media Communication* 20:4 (Dec. 2003): 407–430, and Evelyn Savidge Sterne, *Ethnic Politics and the Catholic Church in Providence* (Ithaca, N.Y., 2004), 230–231.

24. See, for example, Elizabeth Glendower Evans, "Foreigners," *New Republic*, June 8, 1921, 44–46; Evans, "A New England Mooney Case," *La Follette's Magazine*, Aug. 1921, 121–127. The title referred to the case of Tom Mooney, an IWW labor organizer who was convicted of a 1916 murder by bombing in California on the basis of flimsy evidence. Owing to various pressures, particularly from the new Bolshevik regime in Russia, in 1918 President Wilson intervened with the governor of the state, William Stephens, to have the death sentence commuted to life imprisonment. Mooney was still behind bars in California at the time of the Sacco-Vanzetti affair, and his case never achieved the same degree of either national or international prominence. Although his innocence was widely accepted, he was not released from prison until 1939; he died in 1942. See Richard H. Frost, *The Mooney Case* (Stanford, Calif., 1968). For Sacco and Vanzetti's correspondence with Evans, see *Letters of Sacco and Vanzetti.* For background, see Barbara Miller Solomon, "Brahmins and the Conscience of the Community," in Boston Public Library, *Sacco-Vanzetti: Developments and Reconsiderations—1979* (Boston, 1982), 13–20. The term "Boston Brahmin" has changed over time, but generally it refers to the city's oldest white Anglo-Saxon Protestant families, including the Lowells and the Cabots. The term is credited to an article by Oliver Wendell Holmes, Sr., "The Brahmin Caste of New England," in an 1860 issue of the *Atlantic Monthly,* www.slate.com/id/2096401/sidebar/2096424/ (accessed Mar. 25, 2008).

25. The ACLU focused on the civil liberties aspect of the Sacco-Vanzetti case. The organization and especially its founder, Roger Baldwin, were consistent members of the Sacco-Vanzetti camp but never the most central.

26. See, for example, John N. Beffel, "Eels and the Electric Chair," *New Republic*, Dec. 29, 1920, 129. The title refers to Vanzetti's alibi for the time of the Bridgewater crime: he was selling eels. See G. Louis Joughin and Edmund M. Morgan, *The Legacy of Sacco and Vanzetti* (New York, 1948), 243.

27. See FBI SV, pt. 3-c, pp. 90–91. The agent added that the next speaker "spoke in the Jewish language in violent tone, but his speech could not be understood." For Flynn's devotion to Sacco and Vanzetti, see Helen C. Camp, *Iron in Her Soul: Elizabeth Gurley Flynn and the American Left* (Pullman, Wash., 1995), 105–107. Flynn recounted her involvement in the case up to 1926 in *The Rebel Girl, an Autobiography: My First Life (1906–1926)* (New York, 1955), 298–335.

28. "Anatole France to the People of America," *Nation*, Nov. 23, 1921, 586. Along with the pacifist writers Henri Barbusse, Romain Rolland, and Madame Séverine, France also sent a petition on behalf of Sacco and Vanzetti to President Warren G. Harding. See the pamphlet *World Opinion Says They Shall Not Die* (Boston, 1924).

29. See John Dos Passos, *Facing the Chair: The Story of the Americanization of Two Foreign-Born Workmen* (Boston, 1927). Mencken is the only American writer mentioned in the *World Opinion Says They Shall Not Die* pamphlet of 1924, published

by the Sacco-Vanzetti defense committee. He had written about the case three years earlier: see Mencken, "An Appeal to T.N.T.," *Baltimore Evening Sun,* Oct. 24, 1921. See also Mencken, "Sacco and Vanzetti," *Baltimore Evening Sun,* Apr. 18, 1927.

30. See Trasciatti, "Framing the Sacco-Vanzetti Executions," 415; Elizabeth Glendower Evans, *Outstanding Features of the Sacco-Vanzetti Case, Together with Letters from the Defendants* (New York, 1924), jointly published by the ACLU and the New England Civil Liberties Committee (NECLC).

31. For the National Origins Act (the main component of the Immigration Act, or the Reed-Johnson Act), see Robert W. Gardner and Leon F. Bouvier, "The United States," in William J. Serow et al., eds., *Handbook on International Migration* (New York, 1990), 341–362. For a classic overview, see John Higham, *Strangers in the Land: Patterns of American Nativism, 1860–1925* (New Brunswick, N.J., 1955); see also Desmond King, *Making Americans: Immigration, Race, and the Origins of the Diverse Democracy* (Cambridge, Mass., 2000); Mae M. Ngai, *Impossible Subjects: Illegal Aliens and the Making of Modern America* (Princeton, N.J., 2004), esp. chap. 1 ("The Regime of Quotas and Papers"); Matthew Frye Jacobson, *Barbarian Virtues: The United States Encounters Foreign Peoples at Home and Abroad, 1876–1917* (New York, 2000), esp. chap. 5 ("Accents of Menace: Immigrants in the Republic"); Aristide R. Zolberg, *A Nation by Design: Immigration Policy in the Fashioning of America* (New York, 2006).

32. See Evans, *Outstanding Features of the Sacco-Vanzetti Case.*

33. Allen Raymond, "The Sacco-Vanzetti Trial," *Outlook,* Aug. 20, 1927, 243–244.

34. On February 25, 1927, Dartmouth alumni held a banquet at the Copley Plaza Hotel in Boston. Thayer was cheered, while Professor James P. Richardson, who had testified to Thayer's off-color off-court words on the Dartmouth College football field about Sacco, Vanzetti, and their supporters, was roundly booed. See Joughin and Morgan, *Legacy of Sacco and Vanzetti,* 243, and Chapter 4, below.

35. Sacco and Vanzetti's courtroom speeches, quoted, among other places, in Lyons, *Life and Death of Sacco and Vanzetti,* 136–142.

36. F. Lauriston Bullard, "We Submit," *Boston Herald,* Oct. 26, 1926. Robert Lincoln O'Brien, publisher of the *Boston Herald,* later wrote that he spoke with Ralph Pulitzer, who "declared it a pleasure to give the prize to an editorial so manifestly worthy." Columbia University president Nicholas Murray Butler, O'Brien added, "said that he felt the award would be chiefly useful in its influence upon public sentiment." O'Brien believed that most newspapers in the country shared Bullard's opinion about the case, and he added (as one who believed that Sacco and Vanzetti were guilty) that "the American press has rarely, if ever, been more astray on a great question of public policy, if we accept the ultimate conclusions in this case" (O'Brien, *My Personal Relations to the Sacco Vanzetti Case as a Chapter in Massachusetts History* [1928], 5, Ehrmann Papers, box 2, fold. 13).

37. William Leuchtenberg, *The Perils of Prosperity, 1914–1932* (Chicago, 1958), 80.

38. Historians have frequently used the term "cultural conflicts" to describe these 1920s struggles. But the conflicts of the period were political and social as well as cultural, and the notion of a relatively apolitical decade is largely the product of the 1950s consensus historians' tendency to regard the 1920s, politically, as an era between the decline of progressivism and the new battles that emerged in the 1930s over the Depression, the New Deal, and the developing global crisis. This interpretation was also promoted by radical intellectuals who experienced their primary political awakening in the 1930s: the best example of this is still Malcolm Cowley, *Exile's Return: A Literary Odyssey of the 1920s* (New York, 1951). See the important and balanced essay by Warren I. Susman, "The Culture of the Thirties," in Susman, *Culture as History: The Transformation of American Society in the Twentieth Century* (New York, 1973), 150–183.

39. See Richard Polenberg, *Fighting Faiths: The Abrams Case, the Supreme Court, and Free Speech* (New York, 1987); David M. Rabban, *Free Speech in its Forgotten Years* (New York, 1997); Fred D. Ragan, "Justice Oliver Wendell Holmes, Jr., Zechariah Chafee, Jr., and the Clear and Present Danger Test for Free Speech: The First Year, 1919," *Journal of American History* 58 (June 1971), 24–45.

40. For background, see Stuart Rochester, *American Liberal Disillusionment in the Wake of World War I* (University Park, Pa., 1977).

41. In hindsight, Moore can only be defined as a disaster for the Sacco and Vanzetti cause, including after the two men died. After leaving the case Moore apparently began to spread a rumor that one or both of his clients had been guilty and that he had framed alibis for them. He supposedly told this to the muckraker Upton Sinclair, a Sacco-Vanzetti supporter and the author of *Boston*, a 1928 novel about the case. In 2005 and 2006, Moore returned from beyond the grave to haunt the endless Sacco-Vanzetti "guilty or innocent" controversy when a history buff in California unearthed a 1929 letter from Sinclair to his attorney revealing the author's doubts, based on his conversation with Moore, about Sacco and Vanzetti's innocence. There was nothing new about this story, however: Sinclair's doubts, and Moore's rumors, had already served as the basis for Francis Russell's revisionist writing on the case since the 1960s and had been convincingly refuted by Nunzio Pernicone in "Carlo Tresca and the Sacco-Vanzetti Case" (*Journal of American History* 66:3 [1979]: 535–547). But journalists, writers, and bloggers ignorant of the case and its history eagerly rehashed the story, with renewed attacks on "liberal perfidy"; see for example Jonah Goldberg, "The Clay Feet of Liberal Saints," www.nationalreview.com/goldberg/goldberg200601061019.asp (accessed Mar. 25, 2008). For the news item that reopened the controversy, see Jean Pasco, "Sinclair Letter Turns Out to Be Another Exposé: Note Found by an O.C. Man Says *The Jungle* Author Got the Low-Down on Sacco and Vanzetti," *Los Angeles Times,* Dec. 24, 2005.

42. See Vanzetti's letter to Li Pei Kan ("Little Comrade"), July 23, 1927, in *Letters of Sacco and Vanzetti*, 307–310. Li Pei Kan, also known as Ba Jin (or Pa Chin), from Shanghai, had informed Vanzetti that Chinese leftists had been following the case. He spent the summer of 1927 in Paris protesting the upcoming executions. He later

translated Vanzetti's autobiographical pamphlet and many of his letters into Chinese. Ba Jin (who created his pseudonym by combining the names of the Russian anarchist leaders Bakunin and Kropotkin) was the most prominent anarchist intellectual in twentieth-century China, the author of *Family* (1930–1931) and many other novels and essays. He died in 2005 at the age of one hundred. See Federico Masini, "La vicenda di Sacco e Vanzetti nella formazione del giovane Ba Jin," *Mondo cinese* 18:2 (1990): 27–30; see also John Gittings, "Ba Jin: Chinese Writer Who Made the Journey from Anarchism to Mao and Back Again," *Guardian*, Oct. 18, 2005, 33. For background, see Olga Lang, *Pa Chin and His Writing: Chinese Youth Between the Two Revolutions* (Cambridge, Mass., 1967), esp. 121–124 ("My Teacher Vanzetti").

43. Vanzetti's autobiographical pamphlet was eventually published in France as *Une vie de prolétaire* (Paris, 1985) with a preface by Ba Jin, and in Italy as *Una vita proletaria* (Salerno, 2005).

44. See Vanzetti to Elizabeth Glendower Evans, June 22, 1927, *Letters of Sacco and Vanzetti* on the Beards' book: "I like the style and temper of the authors. Of course, for people of my little education, and not helped by a long past of research and meditations, not enlighten by a Proudhon, a Michelet, Marx, Malatesta and other, these books will make the effect like the effect that a man ignorant in arithmetic would receive in seeing a foreigner-speaking man in an ununderstood language and resolving an algebratic problem on a blackboard. Those lines and letters and number, riductions and operations would explain nothing to the unlearned foreigner. The history . . . would tell plenty of chronicles and of contrasting interests, almost exclusively between a ruling class and another semy-ruling class inspiring to the liberty of a full and sovereign ruling—and thus it would left, at the end of its reading, a bourgeaus worker or little fellow as bourgeaus as at the beginning. Nothing, I found in it until now of the instinctive and intuitive aspirations of the poor, of the hardly articulated but incommensurable souls of the humbles—except if I must believe they are like the master—which, at least now day, it does not seem so to me" (286–287). Vanzetti, combining wit and sadness, added, "The only great trouble [with the book] is that Massachusetts' hanger may not give me time to finish the lecture. All the rest is O.K." See Charles A. Beard and Mary R. Beard, *The Rise of American Civilization* (New York, 1927).

45. Several examples can be found in *America Arraigned!* ed. Lucia Trent and Ralph Cheyney (New York, 1928), including Christ-inspired poetry by Edna St. Vincent Millay, Kathleen Millay, Countee Cullen, John Dos Passos, James Rorty, Louis Ginsberg, and Lola Ridge. Throughout this anthology the execution of Sacco and Vanzetti is referred to as "the crucifixion."

46. See, e.g., Gardner Jackson, "The Reminiscences of Gardner Jackson," Oral History Research Office, Columbia University (1959), 12: "[Vanzetti had] an aura of complete calm and spirituality. He gave you a sense of complete mastery of his own set of circumstances. He had a wonderful rich baritone voice. He was a very dark swarthy guy, with flowing mustache, and deep, liquid brown eyes, with a full head of hair." Roger Baldwin of the ACLU reminisced that the time he spent visiting Vanzetti in prison was "one of the most inspiring experiences of my life" and that the defendant

was "a poetic man" who "could never have murdered anybody" (Robert C. Cottrell, *Roger Nash Baldwin and the American Civil Liberties Union* [New York, 2000], 157–158). Upton Sinclair described Vanzetti as a childlike figure, "of fine, sensitive, gentle nature, a dreamer and an idealist, remote from the possibility of selfish crime" (Sinclair to Fuller, July 1927, Ehrmann Papers, box 1, fold. 11, doc. 60). Joseph Cotillo, a New York State supreme court justice, visited Vanzetti in prison in 1923, and in 1927 wrote to Fuller: "I conversed with him and he opened his soul to me, as he would not to a stranger. His calloused hand and his frank manner did not give me the impression that I was speaking to a criminal or to one who had the consciousness of guilt" (Harvard Law SV news. clip., box 1, fold. 4, doc. 38).

47. See Ralph Colp, Jr., "Sacco's Struggle for Sanity," *Nation*, Dec. 27, 1958.

48. Vanzetti to Defense Committee, Jan. 1, 1927, BPL-Felicani, MS. 2030, fold. 1.

49. *New York World*, May 15, 1927.

50. For the article, see Felix Frankfurter, "The Case of Sacco and Vanzetti," *Atlantic Monthly*, Mar. 1927, 409–432 (the title on the magazine's cover was "The Portentous Case of Sacco and Vanzetti: A Comprehensive Analysis of a Trial of Grave Importance"). For the book, see Frankfurter, *The Case of Sacco and Vanzetti: A Critical Analysis for Lawyers and Laymen* (Boston, 1927). See also Michael E. Parrish, *Felix Frankfurter and His Times: The Reform Years* (New York, 1982), chap. 10 ("The Two Italians"). Frankfurter recalled later in life that he became involved in the case mostly because of personal connections. But his statements on this matter need to be approached with some skepticism, since they contradict his own public record: he had already been involved in the legal struggles against Palmer's policies and had come to Mooney's defense. Along with other legal figures, including Zechariah Chafee, he had testified in the Senate about the wartime and postwar repression of free speech. Frankfurter's recollections also reveal more than a tinge of snobbery, misogyny, and glibness. They give the impression, for instance, that he would not have written about the case had it not become respectable in the elite circles in which he moved. In Harlan B. Phillips's *Felix Frankfurter Reminisces: Recorded in Talks with Dr. Harlan B. Phillips* (New York, 1960), he claimed that until 1926 he knew nothing about the case and refused to comment about it. He finally decided to read the trial transcript because his wife, a friend of Evans's, ceaselessly pestered him to say something about it ("why are you so sticky? Can't you give me some general opinion that I can tell Auntie Bee? She worries me so about it.") His opinion of Evans was that "she was a beautiful young thing when she married Glendower Evans." When her husband died, Frankfurter recounted, she was taken under the wing of Louis Brandeis, who "gradually directed her into ways in which she occupied her time." Frankfurter also claimed that he finally became seriously interested in the case when he read in the newspaper that Thompson, "one of the most prominent lawyers in Boston," had become Sacco and Vanzetti's counsel. "I knew him, greatly respected him, admired him. I knew him somewhat because he was a friend of [Henry] Stimson. They were contemporaries at the Harvard Law School, and he was a great friend of Ezra Thayer, who, as dean, brought me to the law school. That's how I had a kind of feeling of association with him. When I saw this

notice I said, 'Hello!' Up to that time Sacco and Vanzetti had some class conscious lawyers and a blatherskite from the west called Fred Moore, but William Thompson was something else" (210–211). This statement contradicts the recollections of other Sacco-Vanzetti activists. According to Elizabeth Gurley Flynn, Frankfurter had actually recommended Thompson to the defense committee (*Rebel Girl*, 330).

51. Frankfurter, *Case of Sacco and Vanzetti*, 63.

52. The urgency of the Sacco-Vanzetti issue did not prevent Frankfurter from being coy with Sedgwick. Rather than agreeing immediately to write for the *Atlantic*, Frankfurter later recalled, "I thought I'd play with him. . . . [Sedgwick] was very eager to have it published [in the *Atlantic Monthly*]. . . . Oh Lord! He was hot on the trail. No jealous lover ever pursued a beloved object more than he did me" (Phillips, *Frankfurter Reminisces*, 215).

53. "29 Law Professors File Sacco and Vanzetti Plea," *Boston Post*, May 9, 1927. The petition included faculty from Yale, Columbia, Kansas, and Harvard. In June another petition by sixty-one law professors from Columbia, Yale, Cornell, and various other schools arrived at Fuller's office, demanding that he reopen the case (Harvard Law SV news. clip., box 1, fold. 7, doc. 70).

54. Associated Press report, Apr. 14, 1927.

55. Russell Papers, fold. 9, doc. 90.

56. *Harvard Crimson*, quoted in *New Student*, May 4, 1927. During this period and up to the execution, Fuller received a great number of additional petitions and letters from students and faculty in universities across the country. See Harvard SV news. clip., box 1, fold. 7, docs. 72–75.

57. The wiretap of Frankfurter's phone continued until April 1928, about eight months after Sacco and Vanzetti's execution. See Brian Jackson, *Black Flag: A Look Back at the Strange Case of Nicola Sacco and Bartolomeo Vanzetti* (New York, 1981), which reports that the befuddled agents found themselves listening to conversations about laundry bills and the like (116–119).

58. For Felicani, see Boston Public Library, *Sacco-Vanzetti: Developments and Reconsiderations.* Jackson joined the committee at the urging of Arthur Schlesinger, Sr., his professor at Harvard. See Jackson, "Reminiscences of Gardner Jackson," 281. In his *In Retrospect: The History of a Historian* (New York, 1963), Schlesinger Sr. recalled that he persuaded Jackson to go work for the defense committee by telling him, "I only *teach* social history, but you will be helping to *make* it" (128).

59. A number of prominent citizens turned down requests to join the defense committee, some for personal reasons: the president of Williams College, Harry A. Garfield, explained to Jackson that because his father, U.S. president James A. Garfield, had been assassinated in 1881, his participation would be considered "bizarre." See Jackson, "Reminiscences of Gardner Jackson," 202.

60. Sacco, quoted in Max Shachtman, *Sacco and Vanzetti: Labor's Martyrs* (New York, 1927), 50.

61. Trying to explain why Sacco would not sign the petition, the *Boston Post* reported on May 20, 1927, that "according to Dr. Abraham Myerson, the psychiatrist

who examined Sacco when the latter was on a hunger strike . . . Sacco is suffering from an abnormal mental condition which amounts to an obsession, although it is not insanity."

62. Frankfurter, quoted in Joughin and Morgan, *Legacy of Sacco and Vanzetti,* 243.

63. Frankfurter, *Case of Sacco and Vanzetti,* 59. William Thompson, like Fred Moore before him, became convinced that the Bureau of Investigation had framed his clients, and between 1924 and 1927 he exchanged numerous aggressive letters with the Department of Justice, demanding, in vain, that they reveal their investigation files on the case. See FBI SV, passim. See also "The Department of Justice and the Sacco-Vanzetti Case," *New Republic,* Sept. 29, 1926, 150–153. To Sacco-Vanzetti defenders then and since, the "framing" of the two men by the authorities became one of the staples of their cause.

64. See Sanford V. Levinson, "The Democratic Faith of Felix Frankfurter," *Stanford Law Review* 25:3 (Feb. 1973): 441; one example of the liberal attitude is Walter Lippmann, "The Prejudices of Judge Thayer," *New York World,* May 6, 1927.

65. Leuchtenberg, *Perils of Prosperity,* 81.

66. Siegfried's study was translated by H. H. Hemming and Doris Hemming and published the next year as *America Comes of Age: A French Analysis* (New York, 1927). See also "Il y a deux amériques," *Le libertaire,* Aug. 1, 1927.

67. In Argentina, the anarchists and Communists, many of them Italian immigrants, were joined in the Sacco-Vanzetti struggle by the Liga Argentina por los derechos humanos (LADH)—a Latin American version of the French Ligue des droits de l'homme and later a co-founding member at the United Nations of the International Federation for the Rights of Man. The LADH had become increasingly dominant in the Argentinean Sacco-Vanzetti campaign by 1927. See Louis Bickford, "Human Rights Archives and Research on Historical Memory: Argentina, Chile, and Uruguay," *Latin American Research Review* 35:2 (2000): 173.

68. For coverage of these and other British and European reactions, see "Around the World," *Living Age,* Sept. 15, 1927, 471–474.

69. For Loebe see *Monthly Bulletin of the Sacco-Vanzetti Defense Committee,* July 1926, 2; the office of Secretary of State Frank B. Kellogg immediately redirected the message to Fuller's office. For the joint appeal, see *Monthly Bulletin,* Aug. 1926, 3. The cable was sent on July 13, 1926.

70. FBI SV, pt. 9, p. 31.

71. A translation of Frankfurter's article into French appeared as "L'affaire Sacco-Vanzetti" in *Les cahiers des droits de l'homme* (Paris, Apr. 1927).

72. See, for example, Pierre Scize, "Sacco, Vanzetti et le goût du sport," *Le canard enchaîné,* Aug. 10, 1927.

73. H. G. Wells, *The Way Things Are Going: Some Guesses and Forecasts of the Years Ahead* (London, 1927), 249.

74. *Monthly Bulletin,* Apr. 1927. The role and connections of the Filene family in

interwar Europe is shown by Victoria de Grazia, *Irresistible Empire: America's Advance Through Twentieth-Century Europe* (Cambridge, Mass., 2005), chap. 3 ("The Chain Store: How Modern Distribution Dispossessed Commerce").

75. Child, quoted in Joughin and Morgan, *Legacy of Sacco and Vanzetti,* 249–250. Child's primary motivation in speaking out on behalf of Sacco and Vanzetti was probably his close relationship with Benito Mussolini, who tried by diplomatic means to get the two Italian anarchists released.

76. Associated Press report, July 28, 1927.

77. Associated Press report, Aug. 7, 1927; Associated Press report, Aug. 15, 1927. For indirect effects of the Sacco-Vanzetti affair on American foreign relations, see Robert Dallek, "National Mood and American Foreign Policy: A Suggestive Essay," *American Quarterly* 34:4 (Autumn 1982): 359. In the 1920s American officials worried in particular about the possible triumph of communism in Mexico in the long aftermath of that country's agrarian revolution. President Plutarco Elías Calles's new determination to implement the revolutionary programs enshrined in the Mexican Constitution of 1917 (including legislation that threatened the interests of foreign oil companies and landowners) led some in the U.S. State Department, and the comically tactless U.S. ambassador James Rockwell Sheffield, to argue that, in effect, the Soviet Union already controlled the Mexican government from afar. See James J. Horn, "U.S. Diplomacy and 'The Specter of Bolshevism' in Mexico (1924–1927)," *The Americas* 32:1 (July 1975): 31–45.

78. *New York Times,* Aug. 6, 1927.

79. *Boston Herald,* Aug. 6, 1927. Switzerland was the locale of some of the most intense Sacco-Vanzetti protest. An editorial in *Genevois,* in response to the anti-American violence, noted, "America is playing too important a role in the world to compromise all nations in this judicial aberration. She has not the right to strike a fatal blow at the sentiments of justice of the entire world" (quoted in Associated Press report, Aug. 5, 1927). See also Mary Washburn Baldwin, "Swiss Echoes of Sacco and Vanzetti," *Outlook,* Sept. 21, 1927, 80.

80. Associated Press report, Aug. 15, 1927.

81. The literature on Italian fascism and Mussolini's rise to power is vast and beyond the scope of this study. A few examples include Alexander de Grand, *Italian Fascism: Its Origins and Development* (Lincoln, Neb., 2000); Pierre Milza, *Le fascisme italien, 1919–1945* (Paris, 1997); Adrian Lyttleton, *The Seizure of Power: Fascism in Italy, 1919–1929* (2nd ed., Princeton, N.J. 1987); R. J. B. Bosworth, *The Italian Dictatorship: Problems and Perspectives in Interpreting Mussolini and Fascism* (London, 1998).

82. United Press report, Aug. 5, 1927.

83. Quotes in Cannistraro, "Mussolini, Sacco-Vanzetti, and the Anarchists," 34, 57. See also Clay C. Burton, "Italian-American Relations and the Case of Sacco and Vanzetti," in *Italian-American "Radicalism": Old World Origins and New World Developments,* ed. Rudolph J. Vecoli (New York, 1973), 65–80.

84. Cannistraro, "Mussolini, Sacco-Vanzetti, and the Anarchists"; *New York Times,* Aug. 10, 1927. E. H. James to Romain Rolland, Feb. 1, 1928, Fonds RR-BNF. Child translated and wrote the introduction to *My Life,* the English version of Mussolini's autobiography, *La mia vita,* in 1927. Child called Mussolini "the Spartan genius," among other compliments, and maintained his admiration for the fascist dictator well into the late 1930s. For several examples of American liberal infatuation with the duce, see John P. Diggins, *Mussolini and Fascism: The View from America* (Princeton, N.J., 1972).

85. For background, see Philip Cannistraro, *Blackshirts in Little Italy: Italian Americans and Fascism, 1921−1929* (West Lafayette, Ind., 1999); Cannistraro, *Italian Fascist Activities in the United States* (New York, 1977). See also Diggins, *Mussolini and Fascism.*

86. Cannistraro, "Mussolini, Sacco-Vanzetti, and the Anarchists," 32. For two scholarly biographies, see R. J. B. Bosworth, *Mussolini* (New York, 2004), and Pierre Milza, *Mussolini* (Paris, 1999). For the duce's early career and influences, see Gaudens Megaro, *Mussolini in the Making* (Boston, 1938), and A. James Gregor, *Young Mussolini and the Intellectual Origins of Fascism* (Berkeley, Calif., 1979). The Haymarket case, in which seven anarchists were sentenced to death (four were later executed; one committed suicide) after being found guilty by an admittedly prejudiced jury on negligible evidence after an unidentified person threw a bomb into a crowd of protesters and police who were trying to break up a labor meeting at Chicago's West Randolph Street Haymarket on May 4, 1886, can be seen in some ways as a precursor to the Sacco-Vanzetti affair: the protagonists were anarchists (at a time when anarchism was a more important force) condemned to death for their supposed roles in the bombing. Haymarket had a significant political impact, though on a smaller national and global scale than the Sacco-Vanzetti affair. See James Green, *Death in the Haymarket: A Story of Chicago, the First Labor Movement, and the Bombing That Divided Gilded Age America* (New York, 2006); Paul Avrich, *The Haymarket Tragedy* (New York, 1984); Henry David, *The History of the Haymarket Affair: A Study in American Social-Revolutionary and Labor Movements* (New York, 1958); Robert A. Ferguson, *The Trial in American Life* (Chicago, 2007), chap. 6 ("Traitors in Name Only: The Haymarket Defendants").

87. This behavior strengthens the arguments of some scholars that one of Mussolini's principal characteristics was bragging about what he could have done rather than actually doing it. See Bosworth, *Italian Dictatorship,* and Tim Parks, "The Illusionist," *New York Review of Books,* Apr. 7, 2005.

88. Fulvio Sulvich, *Memorie 1932−1936* (Milan, 1980), 24.

89. "Message from Mussolini to the American People," broadcast on December 14, 1926, quoted in Emilio Gentile, "Impending Modernity: Fascism and the Ambivalent Image of the United States," *Journal of Contemporary History* 28 (1993): 17.

90. See Gentile, "Impending Modernity."

91. Associated Press report, Aug. 9, 1927.

92. *Il tribuna,* Aug. 8, 1927; *Il Tevere,* Aug. 23, 1927; *Giornale d'Italia,* Aug. 23,

1927; *Lavore d'Italia,* Aug. 24, 1927; *Il Tevere,* Aug. 24, 1927. Italians' anger over the case did not completely die out, even as the left was increasingly suppressed. For a compilation of radical Italian opinion, see the pamphlet *Tragedia e supplizio di Sacco e Vanzetti* (Naples, 1928). For the ways censorship worked under Mussolini, see Guido Bonsaver, *Censorship and Literature in Fascist Italy* (Toronto, 2007).

93. For a gripping account by a Russian dissident historian favorable to Bukharin, see Roy Medvedev, *Let History Judge: The Origins and Consequences of Stalinism* (New York, 1972); for a scholarly overview, see Sheila Fitzpatrick, *The Russian Revolution, 1917–1932* (New York, 1982), and Orlando Figes, *A People's Tragedy: The Russian Revolution, 1891–1924* (London, 1997); see also Stephen Cohen, *Bukharin and the Bolshevik Revolution: A Political Biography, 1888–1938* (New York, 1973).

94. This policy remained in place until 1935, when Stalin shifted to the "right" in response to the rise of fascism in Europe, leading to the creation of popular fronts throughout the world. For background, see Helen Graham and Paul Preston, eds., *The Popular Front in Europe* (London, 1987); Julian Jackson, *The Popular Front in France: Defending Democracy, 1934–1938* (New York, 1988).

95. J. V. Stalin, *Works,* vol. 10: *August–December 1927* (Moscow, 1952), 221–222; no translator named.

96. Francis Russell, "The 'Second Trial' of Sacco and Vanzetti," *Harvard Magazine* 80 (May–June 1978), 50–54.

97. Stalin, *Works,* 290–291. Ironically, Trotsky would make an attempt to use the cachet of the Sacco-Vanzetti case to promote his own doomed battle against Stalin. When Yakov Blumkin, a Trotsky supporter, was sentenced to death in the Soviet Union in 1930, Trotsky, then in exile in Turkey, wrote to his supporters: "The Blumkin affair should become the Sacco-Vanzetti affair of the Left Opposition [to Stalin]." See Isaac Deutscher, *The Prophet Outcast: Trotsky, 1929–1940* (New York, 1965), 72. Deutscher added that "Trotsky's call found no response."

98. Associated Press report, Aug. 5, 1927.

99. Alexander Berkman, "The Sacco-Vanzetti Case in Russia," *Bulletin of the Relief Fund of the International Working Men's Association for Anarchists and Anarcho-Syndicalists Imprisoned or Exiled in Russia,* Mar. 1928, 2. Berkman, along with his friend, lover, and colleague Emma Goldman, was a leader of the American anarchist movement. Convicted for the attempted murder of the Pennsylvania industrialist Henry Clay Frick, Berkman was deported to Russia in 1919. Berkman and Goldman supported the Bolshevik Revolution in 1917, but after their rapid disillusionment with the Soviet regime, they moved to Germany. Berkman spent his final years in France, where he wrote bleak critiques of the Soviet Union. See Berkman and Goldman, "Sacco and Vanzetti," *Road to Freedom,* Aug. 1929, 1–2. See also Goldman's recollections in her *Living My Life,* 2 vols. (London, 1931), 2:990–991. For background, see Paul Avrich, *The Anarchists in the Russian Revolution* (Ithaca, N.Y., 1973), and Avrich, *The Russian Anarchists* (Princeton, N.J., 1967).

100. Berkman, "Sacco-Vanzetti Case in Russia." In 1941 two Polish Bundists executed by the Soviet authorities were dubbed "the Sacco and Vanzetti of the USSR"

by New York mayor Fiorello La Guardia. See Isabelle Tombs, "Erlich and Alter, 'The Sacco and Vanzetti of the USSR': An Episode in the Wartime History of International Socialism," *Journal of Contemporary History* 23:4 (1988): 531–549.

101. Herriot, quoted in *Boston Herald,* Aug. 3, 1927; MacDonald, quoted in Michael A. Musmanno, *After Twelve Years* (New York, 1939), 315.

102. Kellogg, quoted in Lisa McGirr, "The Passion of Sacco and Vanzetti: A Global History," *Journal of American History* 93:4 (Mar. 2007): 1107.

103. See Lyons, *Life and Death of Sacco and Vanzetti,* 169–180, for several examples.

104. Quoted in Joughin and Morgan, *Legacy of Sacco and Vanzetti,* 273.

105. "Churchmen Sent Plea to Gov. Fuller," *New York Times,* Aug. 23, 1927, 3; "Officers Watch Public Buildings, Churches to Prevent Disorder as Protest to Fuller Decision Grows," *Chicago Daily Tribune,* Aug. 20, 1927; "Sacco-Vanzetti," *Detroit News,* Aug. 21, 1927.

106. The drama and pathos of the deathwatch is perhaps best captured in Jeanne Marks, *Thirteen Days* (New York, 1928). According to Arthur Schlesinger, Sr., Dos Passos, on the day before the executions, planned to dress as Paul Revere, rent a horse, and ride through the countryside shouting "Save Sacco and Vanzetti!" As Schlesinger put it, "Only with difficulty was he persuaded that the tactics of 1775 did not suit the year 1927" (*In Retrospect,* 132).

107. *New York Times,* Aug. 16, 1927; Ruth Crawford, "On the Trial of Sacco-Vanzetti Abroad: The Anger of South America," *Nation,* Oct. 5, 1927, 334; "Rioters Wound Danish Police," *Chicago Daily Tribune,* Aug. 23, 1927, 1; "Geneva Mob Stones League's Offices, Attacks American Shops, Burns Movie Films and Storms Police Station," *New York Times,* Aug. 23, 1927, 5; "Sacco Rioters Wreck Wilson Room at League of Nations," *Chicago Daily Tribune,* Aug. 23, 1927, 1.

108. Letter quoted in Katherine Joslin, *Jane Addams: A Writer's Life* (Urbana, Ill., 2004), 217. For the president's doings at the time of the executions, see "President Catches Eleven Trout," *New York Times,* Aug. 24, 1927, 3. The reporter added that "the fishing was done in Fire Hole Creek and Mr. Coolidge tramped along the stream for two miles."

109. Brandeis explained to Sacco and Vanzetti's lawyers that "if I entertain an appeal, I could be accused, demonstrably, of having prejudice because my home housed the wife of one of the defendants in the case." See Jackson, "Reminiscences of Gardner Jackson," 202–203. Vanzetti, in one of his letters, sarcastically remarked that "it is coming to pass that some justices repel our appeal because they are friendly with us and the other justices repel our appeal because they are hostile to us, and . . . we are led straight to the electric chair" (*Letters of Sacco and Vanzetti,* 324–325).

110. Ehrmann, quoted in Louis Stark, "A Case That Rocked the World," in *We Saw It Happen: The News Behind the News That's Fit to Print,* ed. Hanson Baldwin and Shepard Stone (New York, 1938), 361.

111. Aug. 10, 1927, Harvard Law SV case record, box 2, fold. 20, doc. 6.

112. Stark, "Case That Rocked the World."

113. Ibid.

114. Jane Addams, *The Second Twenty Years at Hull-House* (New York, 1930), 331.

115. Stark, "Case That Rocked the World," 365. There are several vivid accounts of the last-hour appeals to Fuller, in which the Massachusetts governor was described as at best unaware of the momentousness of the event, and at worst as glib and unfeeling. On the sunny warm morning after the execution, he emerged from his office and reportedly greeted reporters with a breezy, "Good day, gentlemen. . . . It's a fine day, isn't it?" The sardonic Communist writer Michael Gold mocked both Fuller ("He is a tall, handsome man, the governor . . . a portly magnifico of the New American Empire, the stern, hard-boiled, genial, ignorant type ruler we are breeding in this country") and the various liberals who begged him for Sacco and Vanzetti's lives: "Two clubwomen arrive from Newport, Rhode Island, women with important husbands. They are pink liberals, and they think the poor Italians should be given another chance, or at least life imprisonment, and they have had tea and dinners with the governor's wife in the past, and they know Mr. Fuller is a good man. . . . Whitefaced liberals with big names troop in all day. . . . They believe in the pure white abstraction they call 'justice.' They are sure one need only present the 'facts' to the governor. They believe in 'reason.' . . . Now they are bumping head first against the stone wall of the capitalist dictatorship and class justice. They are puzzled, alarmed, sickened by the governor's smooth determination. They repeat whole pages of the *Nation* and the *New Republic* at him. Later, they stagger out in to the street, their world shattered. Liberal phrases do not soften a class-conscious governor's heart. They can't understand it at all" (Gold, "It's a Fine Day—Said Governor Fuller," *Daily Worker Magazine,* Aug. 27, 1927). For another example of Gold's writing, see "Lynchers in Frockcoats," *New Masses,* Sept. 1927, 6. For an inside account of a meeting with the governor, see Arthur Garfield Hays, "A Conference with Governor Fuller," *Nation,* Sept. 21, 1927, 285–286

116. Jackson, "Reminiscences of Gardner Jackson," 250.

117. Lyons, *Life and Death of Sacco and Vanzetti.*

118. "Europe Blazes with Sacco Riots," *Chicago Daily Tribune,* Aug. 24, 1927, 1; "Paris Mobs Loot Shops, Battle Police, London Radicals in Night Rioting as Sacco Demonstrations Go On Abroad," *New York Times,* Aug. 24, 1927, 1.

119. Jose Eduardo Igartua, *Arvida au Saguenay: Naissance d'une ville industrielle* (Montreal, 1996), 178; "Stabbed in Sacco Case Discussion," *New York Times,* Aug. 23, 1927, 3.

120. For several immediate examples of Sacco and Vanzetti as artistic inspiration, see Henry Harrison, ed., *The Sacco-Vanzetti Anthology of Verse* (New York, 1927), and *America Arraigned!* In 1928, Upton Sinclair published *Boston,* a novel about the case. One obscure but telling example of the case's international reach in the 1930s was the Yiddish play *Boston,* staged in 1933 by the Yung Teater in Poland; see Stephen J. Whitfield, "The Smart Set: An Assessment of Jewish Culture," in *The Jews of Boston,*

ed. Jonathan Sarna, Ellen Smith, and Scott Martin-Kosofsky (New Haven, 2005), 320. For immediate popular expressions—a tango and a workers' cigarette brand in Argentina, for example—see McGirr, "Passion of Sacco and Vanzetti," 1111–1112.

Chapter 2: Americans Divided

1. Harvard Law SV news. clip., box 1, fold. 5, docs. 50–51.

2. *Boston Herald,* Apr. 27, 1927; "Swedish Appeal for Sacco," *New York Times,* May 10, 1927.

3. *Boston Herald,* May 27, 1927; "Branting Welcomed to Boston By 1,500," *New York Times,* May 30, 1927, 9. For the unique brand of Swedish or Scandinavian social democracy before World War II, see Sheri Berman, *The Social Democratic Moment: Ideas and Politics in the Making of Interwar Europe* (Cambridge, Mass., 1998), and Marquis W. Childs, *Sweden: The Middle Way* (New Haven, 1936).

4. *Boston Herald,* May 20, 1927. Some of Sacco and Vanzetti's intellectual supporters in the United States were more enthusiastic about Branting's trip. From Europe, Henry Longfellow Dana sent an introductory letter on Branting's behalf to Felicani, asking him to arrange for Branting to meet "the high minds," as Dana put it. Dana to Felicani, May 18, 1927, BPL-Felicani, MS. 2030, fold. 7A.

5. *New York World,* June 19, 1927.

6. *Boston Herald,* June 23, 1927; *Boston Herald,* Apr. 27, 1927.

7. F. Lauriston Bullard, "Bay State Is Cleft by Cause Celebre: Old Men Get Apoplectic," *New York Times,* June 26, 1927. See the letter from Sacco to Branting, June 12, 1927, in *The Letters of Sacco and Vanzetti,* ed. Marion Frankfurter and Gardner Jackson (1928; New York, 1997), 62–63. After the formation of the Lowell commission, Branting sent a copy of Sacco's letter to Lowell. "I beg you," he wrote to the Harvard president, "to read these lines which give a picture of the writer" (Branting to Lowell, June 22, 1927, ALLP, box 2, fold. 1).

8. *Boston Herald,* June 23, 1927.

9. Gunnar Myrdal et al., *An American Dilemma: The Negro Problem and Modern Democracy* (New York, 1944). Branting and his American trip have been totally neglected by scholars. His book was published as *Sacco-Vanzetti Dramat* in Sweden in 1928. In 1955 it was translated by Llewellyn Jones (the former literary editor of the *Chicago Evening Post* and president of the Greater Boston American-Scandinavian Forum) and deposited, unpublished, in the O'Connor Papers, fold. 4.5.

10. For a sampling of a vast literature, see John Milton Cooper, *Breaking the Heart of the World: Woodrow Wilson and the Fight for the League of Nations* (New York, 2001), Lloyd E. Ambrosius, *Woodrow Wilson and the American Diplomatic Tradition* (New York, 1990), and Arthur Link, *Woodrow Wilson: Revolution, War, and Peace* (Arlington Heights, Ill., 1979). Thomas J. Knock, *To End All Wars: Woodrow Wilson and the Quest for the New World Order* (Princeton, N.J., 1995), argues that the League of Nations struggle was not between isolationists and internationalists but rather between two kinds of internationalists, conservative and progressive.

11. Roland Boyden was among the "26 prominent citizens," including Richard C. Cabot, A. Lincoln Filene, Mrs. Malcolm J. Forbes, John F. Moors, Samuel Eliot Morison, and Arthur M. Schlesinger, Sr., who posed "16 questions to the Governor," all relating to evidence at the original trial (they had evidently read Frankfurter's book) and joined the call to form a special advisory commission (Harvard Law SV news. clip., box 1, fold. 4, doc. 40).

Bishop Lawrence was one of "five leading Massachusetts citizens" who sent an appeal to Fuller in late April 1927, calling on him to form an advisory commission. His intervention inevitably created some interfaith tension: the Reverend George A. Gordon, for example, pastor of the Old South Church in Boston, criticized the bishop as "impudent." In late April, newspapers in Boston and New York carried Gordon's statement: "The judicial system of Massachusetts is in the hands of experts. This appeal to the governor to try the case by selected citizens means one thing only—a blow at the authority and the superseding of our judicial system." See also the *Springfield* (Mass.) *Union,* Apr. 22, 1927, 69; "Bishop Anderson's Good Advice," FBI SV, pt. 10a, p. 64. The *New York World,* in response, attacked Gordon for his comments. For coverage of the Lawrence-Gordon controversy, see Harvard Law SV news. clip., box 1, fold. 2, doc. 16.

Also in April 1927, the ACLU circulated a petition of support for Sacco and Vanzetti among clergymen and educators and the result was signatures from Harry Emerson Fosdick, Sherwood Eddy, and other Protestant modernist figures. See Harvard Law SV news. clip., box 1, fold. 9, doc. 86. This clerical engagement did not go unchallenged, and the internal controversy forced some of the modernists to justify their stance. See, for example, Edward S. Drown, "Why I Interceded with Governor Fuller," *Churchman,* Oct. 29, 1927, 10–11.

After much public pressure, Cardinal O'Connell—who long considered the Sacco-Vanzetti case a "secular" issue that did not merit his "spiritual" intervention— spoke about Sacco and Vanzetti at a dinner held by alumni of Holy Cross College on April 27, 1927. See Harvard Law SV news. clip., box 1, fold. 8, doc. 80. To the *Boston Herald,* on August 21, 1927, two days before the executions, O'Connell stated that "human judgments and human justice are not infallible, but they represent the only safeguard of order, human civilization and all that is precious in our home life. Only God's judgment and justice are perfect but this perfection . . . is also abounding with clemency and mercy. To God therefore must we all look for the fulfillment of our highest destiny . . . may God's clemency and mercy reach both these men." This was his elliptical way of urging Governor Fuller (his friend) to commute the death sentence. Three days earlier, Cardinal O'Connell had met in his summer home with both Vanzetti's sister Luigia and Sacco's wife, Rosina. For O'Connell's involvement, see Rosario Joseph Tosiello, " 'Requests I Cannot Ignore': A New Perspective on the Role of Cardinal O'Connell in the Sacco-Vanzetti Case," *Catholic Historical Review* 68:1 (1982): 43–56. After the publication of the Lowell report, however, O'Connell quickly expressed his acceptance of the executions. Other religious leaders took up the Sacco-Vanzetti cause in more decisive fashion. Stephen Wise, the Jewish Reform leader, argued for the supremacy of justice over law: "The lawless thing in this hour is to set up a doctrine of judicial infallibility and to maintain that because of it, there shall be no resort to the legal means of review which the law provides. . . . A judicial murder is committed when in a court room the forms of law are observed and the substance of justice or equity is ignored" (*Boston Herald,* May 2, 1927). The role of religion, and religious figures, in the Sacco-Vanzetti affair is worthy of a separate synthetic study.

12. For the Sons of the American Revolution, see Harvard Law SV news. clip., box 1, fold. 9, doc. 86. The resolution was "voted down after a long and spirited debate."

Although Ford's newspaper, the *Dearborn Independent,* attacked the Sacco-Vanzetti cause in December 1926, Ford issued a statement, reported by the Associated Press on August 9, 1927, objecting to the Sacco-Vanzetti executions on the grounds of his principled opposition to the death penalty: "[Sacco and Vanzetti] should not be killed. We cannot approve the state's doing what we would not do ourselves. Killing of human beings is always an act of vengeance. I can't see it any other way. I don't believe in it. Provided the man is guilty imprisonment protects society. If he is not it gives time a chance to turn up new evidence and right a great wrong." On August 22, 1927, one day before the execution, Sacco and Vanzetti's legal defender Michael Musmanno telegraphed to Ford an August 21 letter from Vanzetti, who—without a word of ideology or politics—thanked the industrial magnate for his intervention on his and Sacco's behalf. See Musmanno to Ford, Aug. 22, 1927, Russell Papers, fold. 2. 16. For Ford's anti–death penalty views, see the volume published by the League to Abolish Capital Punishment, *Henry Ford on Capital Punishment* (New York, 1927). For Sacco and Vanzetti's place in the history of the death penalty in the United States, see Chapter 4.

For the Fascist League, see Harvard Law SV news. clip., box 1, fold. 6, doc. 59. On the other hand, the Massachusetts branch of the Ku Klux Klan, "Klan No. 12, Realm of Massachusetts, Invisible Empire, Knights of the Ku Klux Klan," announced that "we are unanimous in favor that the sentence of Judge Thayer be executed." The statement was signed by Charles A. Briggs, "Kligrapp No. 12," from New Bedford, Massachusetts (Harvard law SV news. clip., box 4, fold. 9, doc. 66).

13. Wilson to John Peale Bishop, Oct. 22, 1928, in Edmund Wilson, *Letters on Literature and Politics, 1912–1972* (New York, 1977), 154. See also Wilson, "A Preface to Persius," *New Republic,* Oct. 19, 1927, 237–239; Wilson, "Lobsters for Supper," *New Republic,* Sept. 28, 1927. In a similar vein, the poet William Sloane Kennedy wrote in 1929 that "the legal murder of these poor gentle-souled Italians . . . was like an earthquake leaving a deep zigzag crevice running through society. On which side of the new line do you now belong? That is the important question for every soul in the world" (Kennedy, "Alas for Boston," *Lantern,* July 1929, 15–16).

14. John Dos Passos, *USA* (New York, 1936), part 3 (*The Big Money*), 462–463; Schlesinger's statement can be found at www.courttv.com/archive/greatesttrials/sacco.vanzetti/schlesinger.html (accessed Mar. 25, 2008).

15. "Those Two Men," *Lantern,* Aug. 1929, 5. "Those Two Men" was the general

title given to a project about Sacco and Vanzetti to which many authors contributed. The critic Lewis Mumford concurred. The execution of Sacco and Vanzetti, he wrote, "was an assertion of power against all who believe that our . . . economic institutions are the agents of life, which we have molded for our purposes, not obscure, tyrannous deities, whom we must blindly obey" (ibid., 6–7). During this period, Wilson entered the quasi-Marxist phase of his intellectual trajectory. A few months before the 1929 crash, he estimated that "Americans of today have commenced to think about their life, and about the life of the world at large . . . in the same family with the man who believes that Sacco and Vanzetti ought to have been executed anyway because they were radicals. . . . We find a wife or a daughter, a brother or a son, who holds entirely contrary views. . . . Our worst characteristic today is intellectual and moral cowardice. But who can believe that the new generations will preserve the prejudices and fears of their elders?" (ibid., 5). Edna St. Vincent Millay made similar comments in "Fear": "The tumult is in the mind. . . . The shouting and rioting are in the thinking mind. Nothing has abated; nothing has changed; nothing is forgotten" (*Outlook and Independent,* Nov. 9, 1927). Wilson was later one of several writers to make the connection between the Sacco-Vanzetti execution and the economic crash in the radicalization process of young American intellectuals in the 1930s, and he described the widening generational gulf between the young radicals and their liberal mentors. "The execution of Sacco and Vanzetti," he wrote in 1932, "had made liberals lose their bearings." Croly, Wilson's editor at the *New Republic,* had been in Hawaii on the night of the executions, at a conference of the Institute of Pacific Relations. "When he returned," Wilson wrote, "I was surprised to learn that he did not entirely approve of the way in which we handled the case." The editorials that appeared in the journal in his absence were, in Croly's opinion, "unusually concrete and militant" (Wilson, "The Literary Consequences of the Crash," *New Republic,* May 7, 1932, 19, reprinted in his *The Shores of Light: A Literary Chronicle of the Twenties and Thirties* [New York, 1952], 496). According to Wilson, Croly asked him to write a history of the affair, which Wilson planned to do but never got around to; as he explained in his letter to Bishop of October 22, 1928, "I shall probably never undertake it . . . because I had no first-hand knowledge or participation in it while it was going on, and also because I am so lazy about matters demanding research" (Wilson, *Letters on Literature and Politics,* 154). See also Wilson, "The Men from Rumpelmayer's," in his *The American Earthquake: A Documentary of the Twenties and Thirties* (Garden City, N.Y., 1958), 152–160, and Wilson, *The Twenties: An Intimate Portrait of the Jazz Age by America's Foremost Man of Letters* (New York, 1975), 328–329.

16. William Leuchtenberg, *The Perils of Prosperity, 1914–1932* (Chicago, 1958), 81.

17. Hélène Christol, "The Ethnic Factor in the Sacco-Vanzetti Case," in *Ethnic Cultures in the 1920s in North America,* ed. Wolfgang Binder (Frankfurt, 1993), 175–188; W. E. B. Du Bois, *The Souls of Black Folk* (New York, 1903), 13: "The problem of the twentieth century is the problem of the color-line." Du Bois used the phrase thrice in this collection of essays (1, 13, 35), each time with a somewhat different meaning.

18. See Horace Kallen, "Fear, Freedom, and Massachusetts," *American Mercury,* Nov. 1929, 281–292. A number of scholars have written about the case in the context of Italian-American history, with a focus on radical politics. See Michael M. Topp, *The Sacco and Vanzetti Case: A Brief History with Documents* (New York, 2004), Mary Anne Trasciatti, "Framing the Sacco-Vanzetti Executions in the Italian-American Press," *Critical Studies in Media Communication* 20:4 (Dec. 2003): 407–430, Paul Avrich, *Sacco and Vanzetti: The Anarchist Background* (Princeton, N.J., 1991), and the essays in Rudolph J. Vecoli, *Italian-American "Radicalism": Old World Origins and New World Developments* (Boston, 1973). I avoid using the term *race* in this context, given that it has come to refer exclusively to African Americans, and I agree with scholars who have described it as a euphemistic ideological construct. See Barbara J. Fields, "Slavery, Race, and Ideology in the United States of America," *New Left Review* 181 (May–June 1990): 95–118. The place of Italians (like that of Jews) within the ever-shifting categories of "race" in America is a complex topic that has been dealt with elsewhere; for a local study of Italians and racial politics in this period, see Thomas A. Guglielmo, *White on Arrival: Italians, Race, Color, and Power in Chicago, 1890–1945* (New York, 2004). For two comparable studies, see Eric L. Goldstein, *The Price of Whiteness: Jews, Race, and American Identity* (Princeton, N.J., 2006), and Noel Ignatiev, *How the Irish Became White* (New York, 1995). The controversy over the study of "whiteness" and racial identity is also beyond the scope of this study. Examples of the genre include Matthew Frye Jacobson, *Whiteness of a Different Color: European Immigrants and the Alchemy of Race* (Cambridge, Mass., 1998); David R. Roediger, *Working Toward Whiteness: How America's Immigrants Became White* (New York, 2005); Matthew Pratt Guterl, *The Color of Race in America, 1900–1940* (Cambridge, Mass., 2001). For a sympathetic review essay, see Guterl, "A Word on the Word *White,*" *American Quarterly* 56:2 (2004): 439–447. For critical views, see especially Barbara J. Fields, "Whiteness, Racism, and Identity," *International Labor and Working-Class History* 60 (2001): 48–56, and Peter Kolchin, "Whiteness Studies: The New History of Race in America," *Journal of American History* 89 (2002): 154–173.

19. Sacco and Vanzetti's courtroom speeches, quoted, among other places, in Lyons, *Life and Death of Sacco and Vanzetti,* 136–141.

20. See Tosiello, " 'Requests I Cannot Ignore' "; Trasciatti, "Framing the Sacco-Vanzetti Executions"; Christol, "The Ethnic Factor"; and Chapters 1 and 5. For a brief look at a local Italian-American response, see Anthony V. Riccio, *The Italian-American Experience in New Haven* (Albany, N.Y., 2006), chap. 7 ("Justice Denied: The Execution of Sacco and Vanzetti").

21. W. E. B. Du Bois, *The Autobiography of W. E. B. Du Bois* (New York, 1968), 254. See also David Levering Lewis, *W. E. B. Du Bois: The Fight for Equality and the American Century, 1919–1963* (New York, 1993), 250; Lewis expresses surprise at Du Bois's relative lack of interest in the case. But see Du Bois, "The Terrible Truth," *Crisis,* Oct. 1927, 276, and Du Bois, "As the Crow Flies," *Crisis,* Dec. 1928, 401–402. The unpublished drama, which is four pages long and titled "Sacco-Vanzetti: A Play," is in

the Du Bois papers in the Yale Collection of American Literature, Beinecke Rare Book and Manuscript Library, Yale University, New Haven, Conn. It is not dated and does not have Du Bois's signature, but David Levering Lewis believes that it is an authentic product of Du Bois's pen (correspondence with the author, May 2006). In the second scene, Sacco is working at his machine in the shoe factory in Stoughton. He tells his co-workers that the machine "was invented by a black man." Later, in scene 5, which takes place in the courtroom, the shoemaking machine is behind the judge and its "form . . . is more like a gigantic black man." In the final scene, "the gigantic black man is there with the shadow of the cross behind him and the two electric chairs on either side." Du Bois also spoke at an annual memorial for Sacco and Vanzetti, according to Robert Morss Lovett, "Du Bois," *Phylon* 2:3 (1941): 214. For another example of a black intellectual's response to the case, see the 1927 poem by Countee Cullen, "Not Sacco and Vanzetti," in *On These I Stand: An Anthology of the Best Poems of Countee Cullen* (New York, 1947).

22. Ossian Sweet, a Howard University– and Sorbonne-educated black man, was put on trial (along with his wife and nine other men) in 1925 for murder after defending his Detroit home from a white mob by allegedly shooting at the crowd (his brother was actually the shooter; one white man was killed and another wounded). Sweet, supported by the National Association for the Advancement of Colored People, was defended in court by Clarence Darrow and was probably lucky to have as the presiding judge in his case Frank Murphy—later mayor of Detroit, governor of Michigan, U.S. attorney general, and U.S. Supreme Court justice. Judge Murphy was the opposite, it is fair to say, of Judge Thayer. Sweet's case ended in a hung jury and acquittal at a second trial. See Kevin Boyle, *Arc of Justice: A Saga of Race, Civil Rights, and Murder in the Jazz Age* (New York, 2005).

23. William Patterson, *The Man Who Cried Genocide: An Autobiography* (New York, 1971), 75–91. The ILD adopted the Sacco-Vanzetti cause upon its formation by the fledgling Communist Party of the United States of America (CPUSA) in 1925. Their stated goal was to provide legal and political support to "class war prisoners." For the foundational ILD text, see *Labor Defense Manifesto, Resolutions, and Constitution Adopted by the First National Conference Held in Ashland Auditorium, Chicago, June 28, 1925* (Chicago, 1925). At first the ILD included liberal as well as radical members, and the board included Upton Sinclair and Clarence Darrow, though the Communist leadership increasingly dominated the organization. Robin D. G. Kelley, in his foreword to Andrew H. Lee, ed., *Scottsboro, Alabama: A Story in Linoleum Cuts* (New York, 2003), writes that the ILD "succeeded in turning the Sacco-Vanzetti case into an international cause célèbre." This is wrong: the ILD alone was not capable of this kind of publicity in the mid- to late 1920s, and its role in the Sacco-Vanzetti affair was less significant than it would be in the Scottsboro case of the 1930s, by which time the political context had changed considerably and the Communist movement wielded much more national and international influence.

24. Eugene V. Debs, *Sacco and Vanzetti Must Not Die: An Appeal to American Labor* (Boston, 1927). Part of Debs's "appeal" can be found in the preface to John Dos

Passos, *Facing the Chair: The Story of the Americanization of Two Foreign-Born Workmen* (Boston, 1927), published after Debs's death in 1926. Well aware that American labor in the 1920s never really united around Sacco and Vanzetti's cause, Debs gloomily warned that "to allow these two intrepid proletarian leaders to perish as red-handed criminals would forever disgrace the cause of labor in the United States. The countless children of generations to come would blush for their sires and grand sires and never forgive their cowardice and poltroonery."

25. See Chapter 1. The ILD made a concerted effort to use the popularity of the Sacco-Vanzetti cause to raise awareness of Mooney's plight. See CPUSA, microfilm reel 89. The question of whether the Sacco-Vanzetti case was "unique" in American history divided their intellectual supporters. Especially after the executions, the view that the case was representative rather than aberrational gained the upper hand. To the columnist Heywood Broun, "From a utopian point of view, the trial was far from fair, but it was not more biased than a thousand which take place in this country every year" (Broun, "The Motives of Fuller, Lowell, et al.," *Monthly Bulletin of the Sacco-Vanzetti Defense Committee,* Aug. 1927, 3). To H. L. Mencken the case was "one of a long series of gross perversions of justice in America." All such cases, in his view, "show the same elements." A man suspected of subversive opinions is arrested and accused of some crime, and evidence against him is manufactured: "Then he is convicted by a jury of frightened half-wits . . . with a complaisant judge roaring at him from the bench. . . . Then he is rushed to prison or to death in the name of law and order, with multitudes of respectable people convinced that any show of common justice to him would be a compromise with organized crime. The thing is so familiar in the United States that it ceases to attract much notice. It is only when it happens in a relatively enlightened state, such as Massachusetts, that it seems in any way abnormal. . . . everywhere else it goes on every day, unnoted and unsung." Still, Mencken acknowledged that there was something special about this case: "Two years dead, [Sacco and Vanzetti's] white faces confront the Lowell Committee. Their clammy hands flutter over the bald head of Judge Thayer. They have no more to say in this world, whether wise or foolish, but there is an appalling eloquence in their dead eyes. Perhaps in the long run that eloquence will not go unheeded" ("Those Two Men," 5–6). Mencken had been arrested in 1926 in Boston on an obscenity charge and had a score to settle with that city's authorities. See Carl Bode, ed., *The Editor, the "Bluenose," and the Prostitute: H. L. Mencken's History of the "Hatrack" Censorship Case* (Boulder, Colo., 1988).

26. Norman Thomas, "The Sacco-Vanzetti Case," Aug. 16, 1927. This piece was part of a series of bi-weekly editorials that the League for Industrial Democracy (LID) "furnished without cost to labor papers." For a similar labor view of the Sacco-Vanzetti case, see "Wider Aspects of the Sacco-Vanzetti Case," *Industrial Solidarity,* Sept. 14, 1927.

27. Associated Press report, Aug. 11, 1927; "Girl Red Leader Gets Mind Test in Crime Drive," *Chicago Daily Tribune,* Aug. 24, 1927, 3. The AP report concluded dryly: "Her parents are quiet citizens. Aurora has been reading Third International

propaganda." To the judge at her arraignment D'Angelo explained, "I have heard several professors talk about the case. They would not have said the men were innocent if it was not true. What they said was good enough for me" ("Jail Girl Red Leader," *Chicago Daily Tribune,* Aug. 20, 1927, 1).

28. "Intellectuals Seek to Revive Sacco Aid Here," *Chicago Tribune,* Aug. 21, 1927, 2; "Radicals Fail to Interest Labor in Sacco Strike," *Chicago Tribune,* Aug. 22, 1927, 2. The newspaper did not mention the ruthless union-busting and police brutality that discouraged militant labor activity in Chicago in these years and was probably another significant reason for workers' relative absence from the Sacco-Vanzetti cause. For the control that employers wielded over their workers in the city in the 1920s, see Lizabeth Cohen, *Making a New Deal: Industrial Workers in Chicago, 1919–1939* (New York, 1990), chap. 4 ("Contested Loyalty at the Workplace"). Cohen mentions that on the morning after the executions, August 24, employers in the city took particular care to find out who was absent from work (175). Jane Addams recalled residing among Italian immigrant workers in Chicago in 1927. After the executions, she wrote of a period of "depression and heart searching." The experience made her realize "that fair dealing with the immigrants who come to this country is of primary importance. It requires an understanding of their background and a genuine intellectual effort to obtain the justice which seems just to them as well as that which seems just to us." In that sense, the case "came to seem, in many parts of the world, an acid test of our capacity for this type of justice." It was a test, in her view, that Americans had failed, miserably (Addams, *The Second Twenty Years at Hull-House* [New York, 1930], 333).

29. See Max Shachtman, *Sacco and Vanzetti: Labor's Martyrs* (New York, 1927), 48. Shachtman, then a young ILD member, would soon become an important American Trotskyist leader. After World War II he moved to the right; by the late 1960s he had become an avid supporter of the war in Vietnam. See Peter Drucker, *Max Shachtman and His Left: A Socialist's Odyssey Through the "American Century"* (Atlantic Highlands, N.J., 1994). Some of Shachtman's followers (the "Shachtmanites") would eventually help found the neoconservative movement in America.

30. See Walter Lippmann, *Public Opinion* (New York, 1922) and *The Phantom Public* (New York, 1925). See also Francine Curro Cary, *The Influence of War on Walter Lippmann, 1914–1944* (Madison, Wisc., 1967); Ronald Steel, *Walter Lippmann and the American Century* (Boston, 1980).

31. *New York World,* Aug. 14, 1927. William Thompson, counsel for Sacco and Vanzetti, later explained why the defense worried so much about radical action: "Owing to bomb outrages and similar occurrences, some in other countries and some here, with which neither Sacco-Vanzetti nor their friends . . . had anything to do, the issue was more and more becoming, in the minds of the public, one not between innocence and guilt . . . but between organized society and revolution." Newspapers in Boston, Thompson recalled, "were doing their best to convey the idea that [Sacco and Vanzetti], having no defense at law, were trying to escape in a smokescreen of terrorism and propaganda. Every public demonstration was seized upon to shift the issue and to

increase the prejudice against them. . . . I was only trying to save their lives, not to promote the cause of anarchy. . . . The only hope was to keep the case a 'law case' and prevent it from becoming a 'war case' " (Thompson to Upton Sinclair, July 12, 1928, Ehrmann Papers, box 14, fold. 16). Another Sacco-Vanzetti supporter (and later a loyal Lowell defender), the liberal historian Samuel Eliot Morison, responding to angry Communists who demanded that the Sacco-Vanzetti campaign dissociate itself from the "bourgeoisie," wrote with annoyance: "I don't think Sacco and Vanzetti can be saved in any other way than by enlisting 'bourgeois support'—this being a bourgeois government. Certainly, communist threats here and abroad, simply stiffen the resistance of judges and governor" (quoted in G. Louis Joughin and Edmund M. Morgan, *Legacy of Sacco and Vanzetti* [New York, 1948], 438). The liberals especially despised Upton Sinclair's class-based view of the case and worried about his forthcoming book's effect on public opinion: Frankfurter—who wrote Sinclair a number of letters trying to get the author to change his approach, to "exercise the privilege and the genius of a man of letters to deal with the meaning of things, not with the details out of which meanings arise"—later wrote to William Thompson that "we have an egotistic fanatic on our hands," whose work will be a "poster . . . more or less forgotten before the slower process of accurate education of public opinion in the details of the case will gradually make its way" (Frankfurter to Thompson, Mar. 20, 1928, Ehrmann Papers, box 16, fold. 1).

32. CPUSA, microfilm reel 89.

33. Sacco's letter is quoted in Shachtman, *Sacco and Vanzetti*, 48. Communists did not restrict their attacks to liberals; the socialists, in their view, were perhaps just as bad or worse. Shachtman, in *Sacco and Vanzetti*, singled out for criticism the "bureaucrats in the trade unions," the Socialist Party, and the Yiddish socialist New York daily the *Forward*. See also "Socialist Perfidy in the Sacco-Vanzetti Case," *Daily Worker* Aug. 13, 1927, FBI SV, pt. 11-a, p. 55. For a more moving Communist reaction to the executions, see "We Stand at the Grave of Two Warriors," written by Elizabeth Gurley Flynn and H. M Wicks, the delegate of the CPUSA (Workers' Party faction) to the Sixth World Congress of the Communist International, FBI SV, pt. 13, pp. 50–60. Hicks also wrote a post-execution article, "The Working Class Will Avenge Sacco and Vanzetti," FBI SV, pt. 13, p. 58. Eugene Lyons, less important in the Sacco-Vanzetti campaign in 1927 than in 1921, later remarked that "the aim of many well-intentioned persons was to save our institutions . . . and to do this, saving Sacco and Vanzetti was necessary, but incidental" (quoted in Joughin and Morgan, *Legacy of Sacco and Vanzetti*, 330).

34. Vanzetti declared at the April 5, 1927, sentencing that "the flower of mankind of Europe, the better writers, the greatest thinkers of Europe have pleaded in our favor. The greatest scientists, the greatest statesmen of Europe have pleaded in our favor." Sacco said to Thayer: "You forget all this population that has been with us for seven years, to sympathize and give us all their energy and all their kindness. Among that peoples and the comrades and the working class there is a big legion of intellectual people which have been with us for seven years, to not commit this iniquitous sen-

tence, but still the court goes ahead" ("Sacco and Vanzetti Speak to Judge Thayer," *Monthly Bulletin of the Sacco-Vanzetti Defense Committee,* Aug. 1927, 1–2).

The tension between the defense committee and the Communists worsened in the short term; and in the long run, some of Sacco and Vanzetti's defenders, including Jackson and Musmanno, became actively anti-Communist. After the executions, the defense committee and the ILD accused each other of embezzling funds raised around the world for Sacco and Vanzetti's defense. See Gardner Jackson, "The Reminiscences of Gardner Jackson," Oral History Research Office, Columbia University (1959), 202. James Cannon, Secretary of the ILD, specifically charged Felicani with stealing money from workers' contributions. The ILD was also furious at the defense committee for not attacking William Green, the cautious president of the American Federation of Labor, who did not speak out in Sacco and Vanzetti's defense; for not attacking William Thompson, who resigned from the case in May 1927; and, generally, for "sabotaging mass movements of protest." According to Cannon, the defense committee was "influenced and dominated in its policy by the socialists, the liberals, labor fakers, and predatory lawyers." Earlier, in December 1926, Cannon wrote to the defense committee on behalf of the ILD, accusing them of making money "disappear" and warning that "if the magnificent international protest movement of the masses is in any way weakened or disrupted and Sacco and Vanzetti are thereby deprived of their single real protection, the responsibility will rest upon those who . . . bring demoralization into the class movement" (BPL-Felicani, MS. 2030, fold. 2A). By the late 1930s, however, when the CPUSA was in its patriotic Popular Front stage, ILD veterans had seemingly made their peace with the former defense committee: an August 12, 1937, letter from the ILD to Felicani suggested uniting for the ten-year memorial for Sacco and Vanzetti, in order to "really dramatize" the event (BPL-Felicani, MS. 2030, fold. 7A).

35. There is a rich literature on the transformation of American labor in this period, especially the impact of World War I. One notable statistic: union membership in the United States dropped from five million in 1920 to under three million in 1929. The National Labor Relations Act under the New Deal would change this state of affairs, but in the late 1920s, organized labor, especially in its militant form, was in a dismal state. For a classic overview, see David Montgomery, *The Fall of the House of Labor: The Workplace, the State, and American Labor Activism, 1865–1925* (New York, 1987). For the movement of labor away from the IWW (and other militant groups) and toward the AFL, see Howard Kimeldorf, *Battling for American Labor: Wobblies, Craft Workers, and the Making of the Union Movement* (Berkeley, Calif., 1999). See also David Brody, *Workers in Industrial America: Essays on the Twentieth-Century Struggle* (New York, 1993); James R. Barrett, "Americanization from the Bottom Up: Immigration and the Remaking of the Working Class in the United States, 1890–1930," *Journal of American History* 79:4 (Dec. 1992): 996–1020; Ellis Hawley, *The Great War and the Search for a Modern Order: A History of the American People and Their Institutions* (New York, 1979).

36. *Monthly Bulletin of the Sacco-Vanzetti Defense Committee,* Dec. 1927, 4. See

also James McClurg, "The Colorado Strike of 1927: Tactical Leadership of the IWW," *Labor History* 4:1 (Winter 1963): 68–92, and Charles J. Bayard, "The 1927–1928 Colorado Coal Strike," *Pacific Historical Review* 32 (Aug. 1963): 235–250. In 1914 the same company had reacted even more violently to a miners' strike: company guards shot at workers and their families, killing twenty people in what became known as the Ludlow Massacre. Ironically, Rockefeller's son, John D. Rockefeller, Jr., would help fund the publication of the *Transcript of the Record* of the Sacco-Vanzetti case in 1928, helping to discredit the Sacco-Vanzetti legal process. See Chapter 4.

37. Ed Delaney et al., *The Bloodstained Trail: A History of Militant Labor in the United States* (Seattle, 1927).

38. The IWW pamphlet ended, however, with some words of hope: "The case of Sacco and Vanzetti marks an epoch in the history of the human race. . . . It marks the laying of the foundation for organization and unity of effort. It marks the beginning of the end of ruthless disregard for the rights of the workers" (ibid.). Norman Thomas struck a note of more cautious optimism: "Something of a new spirit of determination is coming into the labor movement." But he also urged his readers to "face squarely the bitter fact that if labor in America had been well-organized industrially and politically, united and alert, Tom Mooney would certainly be out of his cell in California and Sacco and Vanzetti would scarcely be counting the hours until the state . . . leads them to death" ("Sacco-Vanzetti Case").

39. See the quotes in Ralph Easley, "Revolutionary Labor Leadership and the Sacco-Vanzetti Case," ALLP, box 2, fold. 3. On August 8 and again on August 22, Green issued a statement to the press asking Fuller to commute the death sentence to life imprisonment—implying, in the opinion of his many critics, an admission that Sacco and Vanzetti might possibly be guilty. See "Green Appeals to Fuller," *New York Times,* Aug. 23, 1927, 3. To Shachtman, *Sacco and Vanzetti,* this was "a criminal betrayal of the demand of the organized labor movement of which Green is the president. By this request, [he] arrayed himself with the enemies of the labor movement, with the executioners of Sacco and Vanzetti." The AFL Convention in Detroit, in October 1926, had already passed a resolution that the leadership demand "an investigation of the activities of agents of the Department of Justice in the Sacco-Vanzetti case." See Dos Passos, *Facing the Chair.*

40. "Government by Bomb," *Dearborn Independent,* Dec. 11, 1926, 11.

41. The Bureau of Investigation did its best to stir up these fears. To counter what the heads of the Bureau, especially J. Edgar Hoover, saw as the campaign in favor of the defendants, they regularly delivered information to the press on what Sacco and Vanzetti supporters in the country and around the world were doing to hurt or menace Americans. See FBI SV, pt. 8, pp. 20–25; pt. 10-b, p. 64.

42. The development and conceptual formation of "public opinion" are beyond the scope of this book, but scholars of the 1930s have been able to make use of the new polling methods of that period to gauge public opinion; see, for example, John M. Allswang, *The New Deal and American Politics: A Study in Political Change* (New York, 1978). For background, see Sarah E. Igo, *The Averaged American: Surveys,*

Citizens, and the Making of a Mass Public (Cambridge, Mass., 2007), esp. chap. 3 ("Polling the Average Populace").

43. Lionel Trilling, *The Liberal Imagination: Essays on Literature and Society* (New York, 1950), ix; Richard Hofstadter, *The Age of Reform: From Bryan to FDR* (New York, 1955), 12–13.

44. John Henry Wigmore, "J. H. Wigmore Answers Frankfurter Attack on Sacco-Vanzetti Verdict," *Boston Evening Transcript,* Apr. 25, 1927. The headline on page 1 was "Wigmore Attacks Frankfurter."

45. Felix Frankfurter, "Professor Frankfurter Replies to Dean Wigmore," *Boston Evening Transcript,* Apr. 27, 1927, and *Boston Herald,* Apr. 27, 1927; Wigmore, "Wigmore Replies to Frankfurter in Sacco-Vanzetti Controversy," *Boston Evening Transcript,* May 10 and May 11, 1927. For a celebration of Wigmore's career by one of his protégés, see William R. Roalfe, "John Henry Wigmore, Scholar and Reformer," *Journal of Criminal Law, Criminology, and Police Science,* Sept. 1962, 277–300.

46. *Boston Herald,* June 12, 1927. For the NCF's early years, see Christopher J. Cyphers, *The National Civic Federation and the Making of a New Liberalism, 1900–1915* (Westport, Conn., 2002). By the 1920s, under the leadership of Ralph Easley, the NCF had become obsessed with the influence of "reds" in American life.

47. Harvard Law SV news. clip., box 1, fold. 18, docs. 64–68. Others sent Fuller more original and creative suggestions. One citizen wrote, "They do not like our government and we are not taken with them, so send them over to Mussolini and let him convert them." Another, in a letter to the *Boston Evening Transcript,* argued that Sacco and Vanzetti should be deported to Italy, "with enough money to make a fresh start." One woman urged Fuller to release Sacco and Vanzetti into the custody of Bishop Lawrence, "reporting to him from time to time as to their good behavior" (Harvard Law SV news. clip., box 1, fold. 11, doc. 101).

48. Ehrmann Papers, box 11, fold. 2.

49. Letter from Charles Albert of West Somerville, Massachusetts, *Boston Herald,* May 10, 1927.

50. The speech was published as a pamphlet, *Sacco-Vanzetti and the Red Peril, Speech Made By Frank A. Goodwin Before the Lawrence Kiwanis Club, June 30, 1927* (Boston, 1927). Excerpts were also published in the *Boston Traveler,* June 30, 1927, 1, 13. As state motor registrar, Goodwin routinely used the press to attack Massachusetts judges who, in his opinion, were not quick enough to enforce laws that he had pushed for (mainly concerning drunk driving). See Richard W. Hale, "Contempts by Publication," *Virginia Law Review* 27:6 (Apr. 1941): 847–848. One letter to the *Boston Herald,* dated June 4, 1927, pointed out that since 1925, Goodwin had made at least a dozen public attacks on the state courts, with such statements as "the judges who are abusing their power are the ones who are tearing down respect for the law." The writer added: "The violent radical who uttered these statements is Frank A. Goodwin.... It is to laugh." The newspaper published several other letters against Goodwin's "Red Peril" speeches in early July 1927. See Harvard Law SV news. clip., box 4, fold. 10, docs. 75–77.

51. To Goodwin the leader of the cabal was Frankfurter, who had already been involved in the Mooney case: "As a result of the work of Frankfurter and the rest of the gang, [Mooney was] pardoned, notwithstanding the enormity of [his] crime." In reality, Mooney was not pardoned; his death sentence was commuted to life imprisonment. Goodwin remarked that "out of that movement to free Mooney emerged the organization known as the ACLU, around and through which all the unpatriotic and communistic organizations of the country are functioning, and getting their inspiration." The ACLU, in Goodwin's view, was intent on "the destruction of our government by force, the tearing down of religion, the weakening of our army, navy, and other defenses, the destruction of the home, the Boy Scouts, and all the institutions that Americans hold dear." Their ultimate goal was "a Soviet government in the United States."

52. Goodwin may have been thinking of William Allan Neilson, president of Smith College between 1917 and 1939 and an ardent Sacco and Vanzetti supporter. See "The Man with 2,000 Daughters," *Time,* Feb. 25, 1946.

53. The inclusion of the Knights of Columbus on the list meant that, as opposed to the nativist leaders of the Ku Klux Klan, Goodwin was willing to include the "right" type of Catholics in his "100-percent" camp. For background, see Christopher J. Kauffman, *Faith and Fraternalism: The History of the Knights of Columbus, 1882–1982* (New York, 1982).

54. Hofstadter, *Age of Reform,* 76–79, 85–89, demonstrated the centrality of Anglophobia to populist thinking in the United States since the nineteenth century. For a study focusing on H. G. Wells and Harold Laski along with W. T. Stead and G. K. Chesterton, see Robert Frankel, *Observing America: The Commentary of British Visitors to the United States, 1890–1950* (Madison, Wisc., 2007).

55. In *The Future in America: A Search After Realities* (New York, 1906), Wells had already offered a severe critique of American political and social developments. The connections between the Fabianites (including Wells) and American social reformers are described in Daniel T. Rodgers, *Atlantic Crossings: Social Politics in a Progressive Age* (Cambridge, Mass., 1998). We can speculate that Wells shared the disillusionment of many of his American counterparts with American political and social progress—a process that, as they saw it, was contradicted by the Sacco-Vanzetti episode.

56. H. G. Wells, "Wells Assays the Culture of America," *New York Times,* May 15, 1927. Several American critics shared Wells's view of Thayer's "normality." One was the columnist Heywood Broun, who bitterly wrote, "Unfrock [Thayer] and his judicial robes would fall upon a pair of shoulders not different by the thickness of a fingernail. Men like [Oliver Wendell] Holmes and [Louis] Brandeis do not grow on bushes. Popular government, as far as the eye can see, is always going to be administered by the Thayers and the Fullers" (Broun, "The Motives of Fuller, Lowell, et al.," *New York World,* reprinted in *Monthly Bulletin of the Sacco-Vanzetti Defense Committee,* Aug. 1927).

57. Wells published these articles in *The Way the World Is Going: Guesses and*

Forecasts of the Years Ahead (London, 1929), as "The New American People: What Is Wrong With It?" 231–239, "Outrages in Defence of Order: The Proposed Murder of Two American Radicals" (orig. pub. May 29, 1927), 240–251, and "Some Plain Words to Americans: Are the Americans a Sacred People? Is International Criticism Restricted to the Eastward Position?" 252–262.

58. Wells, "Some Plain Words to Americans: Are the Americans a Sacred People? Is International Criticism Restricted to the Eastward Position?" *Way the World Is Going,* 258; Borah, quoted in Jane Addams, *The Second Twenty Years at Hull-House* (New York, 1930), 331. For Borah's response to Wells, see William E. Borah, "Borah Defends Our Democracy," *New York Times,* May 15, 1927. The essay made no mention of Sacco and Vanzetti.

59. Letter from William Stearns David, *Boston Evening Transcript,* Aug. 24, 1927.

60. Wells, "Some Plain Words to Americans," 252–253, 257, 262.

61. The story was reported by the *Kingston* (N.Y.) *Freeman,* July 9, 1929, which asked its readers, "What would we think if every American journalist in Europe who wrote critically of conditions there to his home paper—a very frequent occurrence— were called up by the authorities, deprived of his passport, and threatened with deportation?"

62. "The Electric Chair," *New Statesman and Nation,* Aug. 27, 1927, 612. Some British journals published irate letters from American readers. See "In Reply to America," *Saturday Review,* Sept. 17, 1927, 354–359. For other critical British commentaries on the case, see "Sacco and Vanzetti," *New Statesman and Nation,* Oct. 30, 1926, 70–72; "The Sacco-Vanzetti Case," *Spectator,* Nov. 13, 1926, 849–851; "American Justice," *New Statesman and Nation,* Aug. 13, 1927, 706–707; "Sacco and Vanzetti," *Saturday Review,* Aug. 13, 1927, 212–213; "Sacco and Vanzetti," *Spectator,* Aug. 13, 1927, 245; Leonard Woolf, "The World of Books: From Socrates to Sacco," *Nation and Athenaeum,* Aug. 27, 1927, 695.

63. Wells, "Some Plain Words to Americans," 262.

64. Shaw to John MacKay, Sept. 16, 1927, Ehrmann Papers, box 2, fold. 11. In Shaw's view, Sacco and Vanzetti's supporters had, "by persistent propaganda, succeeded in persuading the whole non-American world from Italy to Japan that the trial was a political trial in disguise." As a result, in European opinion "the execution took the complexion of a martyrdom."

65. Horace Kallen, "Fear, Freedom, and Massachusetts," *American Mercury,* Nov. 1929, 281–292. Kallen was arrested at the memorial for Sacco and Vanzetti in Boston in August 1928 on the charge of blasphemy (according to a revived 1637 law). In his speech, he argued that Sacco and Vanzetti were killed because of their "alien blood" and "ideological non-conformity." Kallen told the audience that there were two forms of anarchism. The first was a "religious sect": "an anarchy envisioned out of the love of man. If Sacco and Vanzetti were anarchists, Jesus Christ was an anarchist." This statement—as he had planned—got him arrested. Kallen added that another kind of anarchy "never is called by its true name. It is not religious but criminal. The practitioner . . . does not recognize himself as an anarchist; he calls himself the champion of

law and order . . . but he champions his law and order that he may use them for the purpose of attaining selfish ends, of expropriating the community, of exploiting his fellowmen, of debauching the government and defeating justice, of making the record which [is] the shame of the United States during the last seven years" (ibid.). For the attempts to repress the memorializing of Sacco and Vanzetti in Boston, see Waldo L. Cook, "Forgetting Sacco and Vanzetti" *Nation,* Aug. 21, 1929, 188–190. See also Jonathan B. Vogels, " 'Put to Patriotic Use': Negotiating Free Speech at Boston's Old South Meeting House, 1925–1933," *New England Quarterly* 72:1 (1999): 3–27.

66. The finest work on the rise of the ideology of immigration restriction among the Massachusetts elite is still Barbara Miller Solomon, *Ancestors and Immigrants: A Changing New England Tradition* (Cambridge, Mass., 1956). There is more work to be done on the topic. In 1928 works by Bertrand Russell, Sherwood Anderson, Theodore Dreiser, H. G. Wells, Upton Sinclair, and Sinclair Lewis, among many others, could not be bought or sold in Boston. See Kallen, "Freedom, Fear, and Massachusetts," and Paul S. Boyer, "Boston Book Censorship in the Twenties," *American Quarterly* 15:1 (Spring, 1963): 3–24. Kallen's insights into Massachusetts and Boston social psychology in the *American Mercury* in 1929 have been largely confirmed by more recent scholarship, including Thomas H. O'Connor, *The Boston Irish: A Political History* (Boston, 1995), and James J. Connolly, *The Triumph of Ethnic Progressivism: Urban Political Culture in Boston, 1900–1925* (Cambridge, Mass., 1998). But for a different view, emphasizing the integration of immigrants and their urban social mobility, see Stephan Thernstrom, *The Other Bostonians: Poverty and Progress in the American Metropolis, 1880–1970* (Cambridge, Mass., 1973), especially chap. 6 ("Yankees and Immigrants"). For a general overview, see John Bodnar, *The Transplanted: A History of Immigrants in Urban America* (Bloomington, Ind., 1985).

67. There is no definitive local social history of the Sacco-Vanzetti case, particularly its relation to the political, economic, and ethnic transformation of Massachusetts from the 1880s to the 1920s. This aspect of the case is made especially interesting by its striking contrast with the popular image of Massachusetts in recent decades as a bastion of weak-kneed liberalism (illustrated, for example, by the failed presidential campaigns of two Massachusetts Democrats, Michael Dukakis in 1988 and John Kerry in 2004). The best starting point for such a study might be Kallen's *American Mercury* essay, which explained the case in the context of a "paranoiac" state of mind in the wake of immigration and growing "crowdedness." For background on the regional economy, see the essays in Peter Temin, ed., *Engines of Enterprise: An Economic History of New England* (Cambridge, Mass., 2000), especially Joshua L. Rosenbloom, "The Challenges of Economic Maturity: New England, 1880–1940," 153–200.

68. *New York World,* May 1, 1927. Broun added that "every theatrical manager knows that there is no money to be made in Massachusetts by any traveling company unless it chances to be a musical comedy. Books Boston still buys with some avidity, but only such as are permitted by the police and the reformers."

69. Kathleen Millay, "Bunker Hill, August 1927," *New York Herald Tribune,* Aug. 14, 1927, sec. 3, p. 7.

70. "Why Boston Wishes to Hang Sacco and Vanzetti," *New Republic,* May 25, 1927, 4–6.

71. See, for example, Michael A. Cohn, "Some Questions and an Appeal," *Haldeman-Julius Weekly,* June 17, 1927: "What do you think would have been the attitude of Emerson of Concord and Thoreau of Walden to the Sacco-Vanzetti outrage were they alive today? Read Thoreau's powerful speech delivered in Boston a few days after the hanging of John Brown in 1859 by the United States government. Where are the John Browns, the Garrisons and the Phillipses to arouse the people of America against the wrongs, evils, and appalling injustices of today? Today it is Sacco and Vanzetti and tomorrow it may be yourself, your son or your brother who may be railroaded to prison or to death." The publisher of the *Weekly,* Emmanuel Haldeman-Julius, was a socialist who moved to Kansas after the ban on his previous newspaper, *An Appeal to Reason,* which was reportedly one of the most widely distributed left-wing weeklies in the world until it was shut down under the 1917 Espionage Act by the postmaster general.

72. *Macon Telegraph,* Apr. 27, 1927. The biblical leader Joshua, the editors explained, "had the right idea. He did not bring Jericho down with any well-considered argument. It was not even enough to send any of his intellectuals out to play persuasive airs upon the flute. All the blare and brass of trumpets was his method. Those walls came down because he dared to make a din. Why should any of us consent now to be polite about Thayer and the dirty work in Dedham?" For Maryland, see John M. Whitmore, "In Memoriam," *Southern Maryland Press,* Aug. 22, 1927. For Kentucky, see James Phelps's letter, *Boston Evening Transcript,* Aug. 8, 1927. Different southern views (and tensions over the case) could be seen in the headline in the Knoxville *News-Sentinel* the day after the executions: "Sacco Sympathizers Deface Baptist Church as Radicals Die in Chair," Aug. 24, 1927, 1. The graffiti written on the local church (captured in large photos) included "God is a fake," "Immortality is a dream," and "Sacco and Vanzetti are martyrs."

73. William Sloane Kennedy, "Alas for Boston!" *Lantern,* July 1929, 15–16. Kennedy, by his own account, had spent the previous two years in Italy, "gathering material and weapons to fight one tyrant there. I came home to find my own country swarming with myriads of tyrants. To find democracy broken down. . . . [In America] there are thousands of Mussolinis to Italy's one. Freedom is dead in America." The *Lantern's* subtitle was "Focusing upon Fascism and Other Dark Disorders of the Day," and its existence is a testament to the link between the Sacco-Vanzetti cause of the 1920s and 1930s antifascism. The journal's two main topics of discussion were the Sacco-Vanzetti case and Mussolini. As the editors saw it, the Sacco-Vanzetti case brought about a "keener realization of the tragedy's importance as a source of illumination for the study of the growing denial of common fairness in America to people whose opinions, race, religion or color are disliked by the authorities." Their stated

goal was to "prevent this country from taking its place beside the Italy of Mussolini in the absolute violation of the instinct of civilized human beings for fair play" ("A Sacco-Vanzetti Memorial," *Lantern,* Aug. 1929, 2).

74. Eliot Paul, "Hands Across the Sea," *Lantern,* Aug. 1929, 26.

75. Bruce Bliven, "Boston's Civil War," *New Republic,* June 29, 1927. Bliven further reported that Frankfurter's *Case of Sacco and Vanzetti* was not displayed in the Boston bookshops; stores stocked it, and would sell it if it was explicitly requested, but otherwise the book could not be seen. Bliven added that in Massachusetts schools, children were not permitted to debate the case, and this was confirmed by the report of a Brockton high school class on "current events" that was asked to vote on a topic to discuss and chose the Sacco-Vanzetti case; the teacher asked the students to vote again, and again they chose Sacco and Vanzetti. The teacher refused to accept the vote, informing the students that they were not old enough to understand the issue. The students refused to choose a new topic; class was dismissed. See Harvard Law SV news. clip., box 4, fold. 10, doc. 70. In another such episode, reported by the *New York Times* of Aug. 22, 1927, a guide at the Massachusetts State Capitol, a fifty-nine-year-old former Boston schoolteacher, was suspended from her job because she was too outspoken in her belief that Sacco and Vanzetti were innocent. The woman, Leonora Jones, had previously written to Governor Fuller and offered to take the place of the two Italians in the electric chair.

76. Robert Lincoln O'Brien, *My Personal Relations to the Sacco Vanzetti Case as a Chapter in Massachusetts History* (1928), 5, Ehrmann Papers, box 2, fold. 13. O'Brien was a prominent figure in Massachusetts public life. The pamphlet was not intended for wide consumption; at the urging of the president of Dartmouth, it was published privately and housed in the college library. William Allen White, "Letter to Governor Fuller," *Boston Herald,* June 7, 1927.

77. White, "Letter to Governor Fuller."

78. Bliven, "Boston's Civil War."

79. *Buck v. Bell,* 274 U.S. 200 (1927).

80. See Louis Stark, "A Case That Rocked the World," in *We Saw It Happen: The News Behind the News That's Fit to Print,* ed. Hanson Baldwin and Shepard Stone (New York, 1938), 361.

81. Their extensive correspondence was eventually published in *Holmes-Laski Letters: The Correspondence of Mr. Justice Holmes and Harold J. Laski, 1916–1935,* ed. Mark A. DeWolfe Howe (Cambridge, Mass., 1953), a 1,650-page volume. See also "The 20-Year Dialogue," *Time,* Mar. 23, 1953.

82. See Michael Newman, *Harold Laski: A Political Biography* (London, 1993); Peter Lamb, *Harold Laski: Problems of Democracy, the Sovereign State, and International Society* (New York, 2004); Rodgers, *Atlantic Crossings;* James T. Kloppenberg, *Uncertain Victory: Social Democracy and Progressivism in European and American Thought, 1870–1920* (New York, 1986); Gary Dean, *Harold Laski and American Liberalism* (New Brunswick, N.J., 2005). For Laski's brief but tumultuous career at Harvard, see Chapter 4.

83. Many scholars still share this admiration. See, for example, Louis Menand, *The Metaphysical Club: A Story of Ideas in America* (New York, 2002), 3–71. For a far less positive view, see Albert W. Altschuler, *Law Without Values: The Life, Work, and Legacy of Justice Holmes* (Chicago, 2000).

84. All letters are in *Holmes-Laski Letters*. See, for example, Laski to Holmes, Nov. 21, 1926: "I hope the incredible [Sacco-Vanzetti case] is settled, for, otherwise, the working-classes will disbelieve in Massachusetts justice" (900); Laski to Holmes, Mar. 20, 1927: "I read Felix's little book . . . and thought it a neat, surgical job" (929). In April, after the Massachusetts supreme court had upheld Thayer's verdict, determining that the executions would take place in August, Laski's tone became more urgent. See Laski to Holmes, Apr. 15, 1927: "I was depressed by the decision of [the court]. . . . Not only has Felix [Frankfurter] made me feel that, at the least, a new trial was essential; but also the feeling here is very deep that the whole thing is an injustice characteristic of the American courts, and it is a thing difficult to combat. . . . It makes me distrust the jury system were it not that Thayer . . . suggests that the average judge is not a whit better" (934). Holmes's first reference to the case was neutral; Holmes to Laski, Apr. 25, 1927: Frankfurter's book "kicked up a commotion. . . . Brandeis says that Beacon street is divided" (938). Holmes also mentioned that Robert Grant, the Boston judge later appointed to serve on the Lowell advisory commission, had called him the day before "and gave me a moderate statement tending [against Sacco and Vanzetti]." Laski's next letter, written just after the formation of the Lowell commission, reflected the sunny optimism of liberals on both sides of the Atlantic when he predicted, "Lowell, I imagine, would be fair." He expected that the members of the commission would read Frankfurter's book and that the result would be "a full pardon." It "would be terrible," he added, "to have an unsatisfactory ending . . . before the attention of Europe" (Laski to Holmes, June 6, 1927, 955).

85. Laski to Holmes, Aug. 9, 1927, ibid., 968.

86. *Moore v. Dempsey,* 261 U.S. 86 (1922). For this episode, which took place in 1919 in Phillips County, Arkansas, where dozens of black defendants were sentenced to death on murder charges after a series of bogus trials run, in essence, by a local lynch mob, see O. A. Rogers, "The Elaine Riots of 1919," *Arkansas Historical Quarterly* 19 (Summer 1960), 142–150, and J. W. Butts and Dorothy James, "The Underlying Causes of the Elaine Riot of 1919," *Arkansas Historical Quarterly* 20 (Spring 1961): 95–104. See also Raymond Pace Alexander, "The Upgrading of the Negro's Status by Supreme Court Decisions," *Journal of Negro History* 30:2 (Apr. 1945): 127–129.

87. Holmes to Laski, Aug. 18, 1927, *Holmes-Laski Letters*, 971.

88. Laski to Holmes, Sept. 2, 1927, ibid., 976–977. See Chapter 1 for events in Geneva.

89. Holmes to Laski, Aug. 18, 1927, ibid., 971.

90. See Michael J. Pfeiffer, *Rough Justice: Lynching and American Society, 1874–1947* (Urbana, Ill, 2004), especially chap. 5 ("Judge Lynch's Demise: Legal and Cultural Change and the Demise of Mobs"). The legal scholar Austin Sarat has been a prominent advocate of the view that modern institutionalized state executions in the

United States evolved from lynch mobs. See Sarat and Charles J. Ogletree, Jr., eds., *From Lynch Mobs to the Killing State: Race and the Death Penalty in America* (New York, 2006).

91. One of the first critical assessments of Holmes's career on the Supreme Court, with a focus on his Sacco-Vanzetti decision, was Martin B. Hickman, "Mr. Justice Holmes: A Reappraisal," *Western Political Quarterly* 5:1 (Mar. 1952): 66–83. Hickman argued that there had been no major legal difference between the Sacco-Vanzetti case and the *Moore v. Dempsey* case, since even the Justice "had said that *habeas corpus* enters from the outside even if all forms have been complied with, to determine whether the forms had been more than an empty shell," and that Holmes ruled differently in the former case primarily because "a victory for Sacco and Vanzetti . . . would have been a symbolic victory for radicalism." Holmes, Hickman concluded, was "a man arrogant beyond the ordinary, a man of narrow and oligarchical sympathies" (82).

92. In subsequent letters, Holmes showed greater concern for the attitudes of intellectual protesters than for the question of whether the executions were just. "The *New Republic* has seemed hysterical to me," he wrote to Laski, "and when . . . it talked of Fuller's Sadic or Sadish thirst for blood I thought it ridiculous" (Holmes to Laski, Nov. 16, 1927, *Holmes-Laski Letters,* 993). Holmes had not carefully read the *New Republic* essay, published a week after the executions, which suggested that Thayer, Fuller, and the Lowell committee seemed to be "filled with an almost sadistic satisfaction, venting their deep-seated grudge by fulfilling the forms of legal procedure against the individuals who have become . . . the symbols of a struggle between classes, between social ideals, between philosophical systems" ("The Ominous Execution," *New Republic,* Aug. 31, 1927). See also Chapter 4. In a subsequent letter to Laski, Holmes expressed hope that Frankfurter and other critics would have no more to say about the Sacco-Vanzetti case, "as I think all those who were interested on that side seem to have got hysterical and to have lost all sense of proportion. . . . [Frankfurter] is so good at his chosen business that I think he helps the world more in that way than he does by becoming a knight errant or a martyr—though I don't undervalue or fail to revere his self sacrifice in his excursions and alarums" (Holmes to Laski, Nov. 23, 1927, *Holmes-Laski Letters,* 999). Three years later, Holmes wrote to Laski—who had still not gotten over the executions—that "you are a good deal more stirred by Sacco-Vanzetti, who were turned into a text by the reds. . . . I doubt if those two suffered anything more from the conduct of the judge than would be a matter of course in England." The only change in Holmes's opinion was his acknowledgment of the possibility that Sacco and Vanzetti had been the victims of prejudice after all: "It was their misfortune to be tried in a community that was stirred up, if not frightened by manifestations the import of which was exaggerated, and, without knowing anything about it, I presume that the jury felt like the community" (Holmes to Laski, July 10, 1930, ibid., 1265–1266). But Holmes was so concerned with "extremists" and "radicals" that he may not have realized that the last sentence of his letter could itself have justified nixing the Sacco-Vanzetti verdict. Laski, for his part, neither dropped the

issue nor was convinced by Holmes's arguments. In 1929 he argued that "the people must be able to have confidence in the fair-minded workings of the courts. No unprejudiced observer can avoid the sense that this atmosphere was absent from the trial of the two men. . . . The world outside Massachusetts will inevitably feel that they were the victims of a political bias before which truth and justice were alike helpless and ashamed" ("Those Two Men," 12).

93. Millay, "Fear," *Outlook,* Nov. 9, 1927. Millay had met with Fuller on the day before the executions, hoping to change his mind, then sent him a moving last-minute letter: "Does no faintest shadow of question gnaw at your mind? For, indeed, your spirit, however strong, is but the frail spirit of a man. Have you no need, in this hour, of a spirit greater than your own? Think back. Think back a long time. Which way would He have turned, this Jesus of your faith? . . . There is need in Massachusetts of a great man tonight. It is not yet too late for you to be that man" (Russell Papers, fold. 2, doc. 13). That same day, August 22, Millay published her poem "Justice Denied in Massachusetts" in the *New York World,* in which she referred to Sacco and Vanzetti (who were still alive) as "the splendid dead."

94. Broun wrote extensively on the case, and his writings can be found in his *Collected Edition of Heywood Broun* (New York, 1941). His column in the *New York World* was eventually terminated by publisher Ralph Pulitzer, who considered Broun's attacks on Lowell and Fuller excessive. According to Gardner Jackson three months after the executions he hosted a dinner party to which he invited Walter Lippmann, Broun, and Dorothy Parker, among others. "The discussion that night," Jackson recalled, "was aimed at what were the lessons to be learned from the Sacco-Vanzetti case. . . . Broun gave Lippmann unshirted hell about his open mind, that was so open the wind whistled through and nothing stuck. It was a devastating attack to which Walter had no answer at all" ("Reminiscences of Gardner Jackson," 281).

95. Addams, *Second Twenty Years at Hull-House,* 338; O'Brien, *My Personal Relations,* 6.

96. See "As Others See Us: Governor Fuller in Berlin," *Living Age,* Nov. 1930, 320.

97. Stark, "Case That Rocked the World," 350–351; *New York Times,* Mar. 21–22, 1929.

98. Stark, "The Grounds for Doubt," *Survey,* Oct. 1, 1927, 38–41; Stark, "Case That Rocked the World," 351. For a similar assessment of Fuller's motives, and his political downfall, see Creighton Hill, "Alvan T. Fuller—Failure," *Lantern,* July–Aug. 1928, 3–6.

99. O'Brien, *My Personal Relations.* Evidence suggests that this sentiment was by no means restricted to white Anglo-Saxon Protestants. A resident of Montana later reported to the defense committee that interest in the Sacco-Vanzetti case was even "bigger in the west," and added that "Americanized Jews, Italians, and Irish were no less voluble in the their condemnation of Sacco and Vanzetti than many of the 100 percenters whose daughters bubble with the spirit of the Revolution" (letter of Hollace Ransdell, Sept 30, 1928, Frank Papers, fold. 1.52).

100. Branting, *Sacco-Vanzetti Dramat,* 9–10. See also Birgitta Steene, "The Swedish Image of America," in *Images of America in Scandinavia,* ed. Paul Houe and Sven Hakon Rossel (Amsterdam, 1998), 145–192.

101. Branting, *Sacco-Vanzetti Dramat,* 19.

102. According to Gardner Jackson, Sacco and Vanzetti's lawyer at the time of their execution, Arthur Hill, insisted after the execution that "[Sacco and Vanzetti] could have been saved if it hadn't been for the agitation on their behalf, the public demonstrations around the world" ("Reminiscences of Gardner Jackson," 282).

Chapter 3: "This Frightful America Whose Heart Is Made of Stone"

1. "Those Two Men," *Lantern,* Aug. 1929, 8–9. "Those Two Men" was the general title given to a project about Sacco and Vanzetti to which many authors contributed.

2. For the Italians' reactions to the case, particularly Mussolini's role, see Chapter 1.

3. Louis Lecoin, *De prison en prison* (Paris, 1946), 137. Unless otherwise indicated, all translations from the French are mine.

4. Ronald Creagh, *Sacco et Vanzetti* (Paris, 1984), 242. For an important discussion of this literature in context see Tony Judt, *Past Imperfect: French Intellectuals, 1944–1956* (Berkeley, Calif., 1992), chap. 10 ("'America Has Gone Mad': Anti-Americanism in Historical Perspective"). One direct product of the Sacco-Vanzetti affair was Fernand Corcos, *L'Amérique . . . Un paradis?* (Paris, 1929); other examples, mostly focusing on the horrors of the impersonal American "machine" culture, include Robert Aron and Arnaud Dandieu, *Le cancer américain* (Paris, 1931); Georges Duhamel, *Scènes de la vie future* (Paris, 1930), published in English as *America the Menace: Scenes from a Future Life,* trans. Charles Miner Thompson (Boston, 1931); Kadmi-Cohen, *L'abomination américaine: Essai politique* (Paris, 1930). For a contemporary (and indignant) survey with many other examples, see Albert Wilder Thompson, "Menace or Mirage? The United States Seen Through French Eyes, 1929–1931," *Modern Language Journal* 17:1 (Oct. 1932): 1–13.

5. For general discussions of anti-Americanism, see the "Roundtable on Contemporary Anti-Americanism," *Journal of American History* 93:2 (Sept. 2006): 414–451, and "Historical Perspectives on Anti-Americanism," *American Historical Review* 111:4 (Oct. 2006): 1041–1129. Roughly, historians can discern a general debate over whether anti-Americanism is "essential" in that it merely takes new forms but is always more or less the same ideology, or an ever-changing phenomenon dependant on cultural and political circumstances. In discussions of European anti-Americanism, France has had the star role, and the literature on French anti-Americanism is voluminous. See, for example, Philippe Roger, *American Enemy: A Story of French Anti-Americanism* (Chicago, 2005), originally published as *L'ennemi américain: Généalogie de l'anti-américanisme français,* Paris, 2002). Roger considers antipathy in France toward the United States as a form of psychological disorder and the reaction to

the Sacco-Vanzetti case as an example of anti-Americanism (127). See also Philippe Matthy, *Extrême Occident: French Intellectuals and America* (Chicago, 1993), and *The Rise and Fall of Anti-Americanism: A Century of French Perception,* ed. Denis Lacorne, Jacques Rupnik, and Marie-France Toinet (New York, 1990), originally published as *L'Amérique dans les têtes: Un siècle de fascinations et d'aversions* (Paris, 1986). In that otherwise valuable volume, Pascal Ory underestimates and misunderstands the agitation in France over Sacco and Vanzetti. Ory is wrong to say that "the U.S. burst on the scene as a political power" only in World War II, that "the violence of Anarchist, Communist, and Socialist organizations [during the affair] was so much part and parcel of the left's combat with the Right in France that a specifically 'American' component scarcely emerged," and that "these [protests] should be viewed more in terms of proletarian 'emotions' than as anything to do with a particular country . . . [since] it is a well-known fact that F. D. Roosevelt's social experiments . . . evoked a very positive overall response among various currents of the French left" ("From Baudelaire to Duhamel: An Unlikely Antipathy," 51–52). The first argument ignores the global power of the United States after World War I and its heightened involvement in European affairs. The second argument does not explain why the Sacco-Vanzetti affair would raise anger specifically toward the French right, and omits the central place of the United States in the French reactions to the case. The third argument transforms the protest into a mere series of riots and conflates two distinct periods, the late 1920s and the early and mid-1930s.

6. Kellogg, quoted in Frank Costigliola, *Awkward Dominion: American Political, Economic, and Cultural Relations with Europe, 1919–1933* (Ithaca, N.Y., 1984), 180.

7. André Siegfried, *Les Etats-Unis d'aujourd'hui* (1926), published in English as *America Comes of Age: A French Analysis,* trans. H. H. Hemming and Doris Hemming (New York, 1927). This was one of many studies of the United States to appear in France in these years; see also Marcel Braunschvicq, *La vie américaine et ses leçons* (Paris, 1929). Braunschvicq was a teacher of Jean-Paul Sartre, Paul Nizan, and Simone de Beauvoir at the Ecole Normale Supérieure.

8. Picqueray's "confession" appeared in her memoir *May la réfractaire* (Paris, 1992), 60–61. See also "Anarchists and the Ambassador," *Literary Digest,* Nov. 5, 1921, 9.

9. Anatole France, "To the People of America," *Nation,* Nov. 23, 1921, 586: "People of the United States of America, hearken to the words of an old man of the Old World, who is not alien to you, for he is a fellow-citizen of all men. In one of your States, two men, Sacco and Vanzetti, have been condemned for a crime of opinion. It is horrible to think that human beings should pay with their lives for the exercise of that most sacred right, the right which we ought all to defend, to whatever party we may belong. Do not let this most iniquitous of sentences be carried out. The death of Sacco and Vanzetti would make martyrs of them, and would cover all of you with shame. You are a great people; you ought to be a just people. There are among you plenty of men of intelligence, men who think. It is to them that I prefer to appeal. I say to them: Fear to make martyrs. It is the unpardonable crime, which nothing can obliterate and

which weighs upon generation after generation. Save Sacco and Vanzetti. Save them for your honor, for the honor of your children and of all the generations yet unborn." The piece was preceded by the original French text.

10. For the petition, see the pamphlet published by the Sacco-Vanzetti defense committee, *World Opinion Says They Shall Not Die* (Boston, 1924): "The president will consider that innumerable hearts of the entire world are with anguish waiting for the freedom of Sacco and Vanzetti and they appeal to the great America to accomplish this great human justice."

11. For a useful survey of French intellectuals' political engagement, see David Drake, *French Intellectuals and Politics from the Dreyfus Affair to the Occupation* (Basingstoke, U.K., 2005); see also Jeremy Jennings, ed., *Intellectuals in Twentieth-Century France: Mandarins and Samurais* (New York, 1993).

12. See the cable sent to Coolidge by Albert Einstein, Romain Rolland, and Henri Barbusse on behalf of "Le comité de défense des victims des fascists et de la terreur blanche," *L'humanité*, Apr. 11, 1927.

13. For a theoretical discussion of the makings of an affair in the context of white-collar crime, see Luc Boltanski, "La dénonciation publique," in his *L'amour et la justice comme compétences: Trois essais de sociologie de l'action* (Paris, 1990), 255–350.

14. A typical LDH pamphlet on the case was Henri Guernut, *Une affaire Dreyfus aux Etats-Unis: L'affaire Sacco et Vanzetti* (Paris, 1927). Guernut became minister of education in 1936 in the Popular Front government. For the early history of the LDH (which exists to this day), see Wendy Ellen Perry, "Remembering Dreyfus: The *Ligue des droits de l'homme* and the Making of the Modern French Human Rights Movement" (Ph.D. diss., University of North Carolina, 1999). For a more critical view, see William D. Irvine, *Between Justice and Politics: The Ligue des Droits de l'Homme, 1898–1945* (Stanford, Calif., 2007). For a contemporary history by an LDH member, later a minister in the Popular Front government, see Henri Eugène Sée, *Histoire de la Ligue des droits de l'homme, 1898–1926* (Paris, 1927).

15. Lecoin, *De prison*, 68–69, 136, and passim. See also Sylvain Garel, *Louis Lecoin: An Anarchist Life* (London, 2000), originally published as *Louis Lecoin et le mouvement anarchiste* (Paris, 1982). The comité's office was located in the working-class 20th arrondisement, in northeastern Paris. For the numbers of signatories, see Anne Rebeyrol and Jean-Paul Roux-Fouillet, "L'affaire Sacco-Vanzetti vue par *Le libertaire* et *L'humanité*" (Mémoire de maîtrise, Paris-I, 1971), 69. One important right-wing intellectual who refused to sign the petition was the symbolist poet and philosopher Paul Valéry, who, as Lecoin remembered it, forced him to endure a "long philosophy lesson" before giving his negative answer.

16. Lecoin, *De prison*, 138–139.

17. Ibid. Costigliola explains that U.S. diplomats, Herrick included, were fearful of Lindbergh's reception in France, given that Nungesser and Coli were still missing, and warned Washington not to let him make the trip. A number of French newspapers had claimed that the missing French aviators were sabotaged by the U.S. Weather Bureau, which had supposedly withheld potentially life-saving meteorological re-

ports. Some French newspapers also reported prematurely that Nungesser and Coli had safely landed in New York; the ensuing disappointment led to angry demonstrations against the newspapers and at the U.S. consulate. But the diplomats were taken aback by the enthusiasm with which Parisians greeted Lindbergh. After landing at the Le Bourget airstrip, Lindbergh was rescued from an overeager mob and taken in secret to the embassy, where he stayed as Herrick's guest in order to "lend the flight an 'official character.'" Lindbergh insisted that his first venture out of the embassy should be to the home of Nungesser's mother. An American diplomat soon gushed in a letter to Washington that "thanks to Captain Lindbergh, America has come into its own here." He also believed that Europeans were now "compelled to admit the genius of the American race" (*Awkward Dominion*, 180–181). See also Robert Wohl, *The Spectacle of Flight: Aviation and the Western Imagination, 1920–1950* (New Haven, 2005), chap. 1 ("The Ambassador of the Skies"); A. Scott Berg, *Lindbergh* (New York, 1998), chap. 7 ("Only a Man"); Raymond H Fredette, "The Making of a Hero: What Really Happened Seventy-Five Years Ago, After Lindbergh Landed at Le Bourget," *Air Power History* 49:2 (Summer 2002): 4–21.

18. This anecdote appears in Lecoin, *De Prison*, 139, but the details should be treated with some skepticism. To my knowledge there is no supporting evidence, although both Rebeyrol and Roux-Fouillet, "L'affaire Sacco-Vanzetti," and Creagh, *Sacco and Vanzetti,* recount the incident as fact. It is arguable, given Lindbergh's later history, which included a highly publicized flirtation with Nazism, whether he would have been inclined to sign a petition in favor of two anarchists. The fact that Lindbergh was constantly surrounded by an army of diplomats (and did not speak or read a word of French) also does not lend much credence to the story. *Le libertaire* of August 21, 1927, reported that two other people tried to enlist Lindbergh's support for Sacco and Vanzetti: the French explorer Charles Soller, and Henry Ford. The newspaper added that Soller also tried to contact the reactionary inventor Thomas Edison. It did not report the result. Two weeks before the executions, Lindbergh was again approached by the Sacco-Vanzetti defense committee, who asked him—apparently in vain—to appeal to President Coolidge on Sacco and Vanzetti's behalf. See *Boston Herald*, Aug. 9, 1927.

Herrick's anger at the Sacco-Vanzetti French camp was reported by his biographer Thomas Bentley Mott: "For years the Red elements of Paris continued to assail Mr. Herrick because Sacco and Vanzetti had not been released from prison. It was in vain that he caused it to be explained that the federal authorities possessed no power to intervene in the case, even had they wished to do so, and that it would be useless for him to make any representations to our government on such a matter, supposing he were thus disposed. Demonstrations in front of the embassy were stopped by the police, but delegations headed by important members of Parliament insisted upon being received by the ambassador and arguing the case. I have never in my life seen him as furious as on one of these occasions. 'Your friends begin by trying to murder me,' he exclaimed, 'and then you come here and ask my help to free two assassins whose sympathizers have made this attempt on my life. And you don't even begin by offering excuses for this dastardly act. Sacco and Vanzetti at least had a trial, but you don't even give me that chance'" (*Myron T. Herrick, Friend of France: An Autobiographical Biography* [Garden City, N.Y., 1929], 290–291).

19. The literature on early French communism is vast; an important study of its beginnings (by a former member of the movement turned bitter foe) is Annie Kriegel's *Aux origines du communisme français* (Paris, 1964); see also Robert Wohl, *French Communism in the Making, 1914–1924* (Stanford, Calif., 1966); Stéphane Courtois and Marc Lazar, *Histoire du Parti communiste français* (Paris, 1995); J. Fauvet, *Histoire du Parti communiste français: 1920–1976* (Paris, 1977); Edward Mortimer, *The Rise of the French Communist Movement, 1920–1947* (London, 1984); David Caute, *Communism and the French Intellectuals, 1914–1960* (New York, 1964). For French anarchism, see David Berry, *A History of the French Anarchist Movement, 1917–1945* (Westport, Conn., 2002); Jean Maitron, *Le mouvement anarchiste en France* (Paris, 1975); Richard Sonn, *Anarchism and Cultural Politics in Fin-de-Siècle France* (Lincoln, Neb., 1989); John Merriman, *The Dynamite Club: How a Bombing in Fin-de-Siècle Paris Ignited the Age of Modern Terror* (Boston, forthcoming). For a panoramic introduction to the French left in the twentieth century, see Jean-Jacques Becker and Gilles Candar, eds., *Histoire des gauches en France,* vol. 2 (Paris, 2004).

20. Letter from Vanzetti, *Le libertaire,* July 10, 1927; Creagh, *Sacco et Vanzetti,* 217. For a pamphlet written by a prominent anarchist figure, see Sébastien Faure, *Deux martyrs, Sacco et Vanzetti* (Paris, 1927). For an example of this tension at the local level, see Yves Cuq, "L'affaire Sacco et Vanzetti à Bordeaux, 1926–1927," *Bulletin de l'I.A.E.S.* 7–8 (1971): 3–4, in Bibliothèque de Documentation Internationale Contemporaine, Nanterre, France.

21. Daniel Manouilsky, "L'affaire Sacco-Vanzetti et ses enseignements pour la lutte révolutionnaire," *L'humanité,* Aug. 10, Sept. 10, and Sept. 11, 1927.

22. For Stalin's involvement and statements regarding Sacco and Vanzetti, and the politics that prompted them, see Chapter 1. Revisionist-conservative writers have made much of Stalin's statements on the Sacco-Vanzetti case (while quoting them briefly and selectively) in an attempt to argue that the international protest over the case was engineered and driven by wily Communist operatives. These writers, some of them deeply influenced by the late ex-Communist historian François Furet, have taken the now-clichéd notion of well-intentioned liberals duped by Communist propaganda a step too far. In reality, European Communists of the 1920s, even talented propagandists like the German Willi Münzenberg, did not have the power to make the Sacco-Vanzetti case an issue of importance for mainstream public or political opinion. Münzenberg did not and could not have "orchestrated the worldwide campaign" for Sacco and Vanzetti, as one writer has bombastically argued. This misconception has slipped into the work of respectable French historians: see, for example, Michel Winock, *Le siècle des intellectuels* (Paris, 2001), 281. Münzenberg, once admired by much of the European left for his fiery anti-fascist activity, has since been the subject of two harsh biographies. For a potboiler account of his supposed superpowers, glamorous lifestyle, and melodramatic downfall at the hands of his treacherous Soviet

puppet masters, see Stephen Koch, *Double Lives: Spies and Writers in the Secret Soviet War of Ideas* (New York, 1994; rep. 2005, with an introduction by Sam Tanenhaus). In "Lying for the Truth: Münzenberg and the Comintern," *New Criterion,* Nov. 1993, Koch described the Sacco-Vanzetti affair as "Münzenberg's idea," a way for the Comintern to shame the United States through "orchestrated multinational mass hysteria." He also described the Communist-despising Gardner Jackson as "one of the witting Münzenberg men on the scene in Boston," as suggested by "best evidence" (which is uncited). For a less fanciful and conspiratorial, better-researched, and equally negative study, see Sean McMeekin, *The Red Millionaire: A Political Biography of Willi Münzenberg, Moscow's Secret Propaganda Tsar in the West* (New Haven, 2003), which confirms that Münzenberg never managed to achieve a propaganda coup via the Sacco-Vanzetti case (202). The definitive product of the post-Communist, or ex-Communist, cynical view of twentieth-century causes célèbres is Furet's *The Passing of an Illusion: The Idea of Communism in the Twentieth Century* (Chicago, 1999), originally published as *Le passé d'une illusion* (Paris, 1995), which, based on the memoirs of the former Communist writer Arthur Koestler, also describes Münzenberg as an all-powerful manipulator of well-meaning Western European minds (213–214).

23. *Le carnet de la semaine,* June 13, 1927. See LDH-BDIC, fold. 798, doc. 44. Léon Blum, the future socialist prime minister, also spoke at this event. The precise number of participants is hard to determine: the Boston writer Henry Longfellow Dana reported to the Sacco-Vanzetti defense committee from Paris that forty thousand persons were in attendance; Dana to Felicani, July 24, 1927, BPL-Felicani, MS. 2030, fold. 7A. French newspapers more plausibly put the number at about ten thousand.

Caillaux was involved in a romantic and legal cause célèbre in 1914, when his wife shot and killed Gaston Calmette, the conservative editor of *Le Figaro* who had unrelentingly attacked and embarrassed her husband in print. After years of controversy and unpopularity, Caillaux returned from the political dead in the mid-1920s when the Radical Party (representing the center-left) came to power and Caillaux was appointed minister of finance. For an interesting study of "l'affaire Caillaux" and its aftermath, including Caillaux's later career, see Edward Berenson, *The Trial of Madame Caillaux* (Berkeley, Calif., 1992), esp. 244–247.

24. Alexander Berkman, "Sacco-Vanzetti Case in Russia," *Bulletin of the Relief Fund of the International Working Men's Association for Anarchists and Anarcho-Syndicalists Imprisoned or Exiled in Russia,* Mar. 1928. For background, see Paul Avrich, *Anarchists in the Russian Revolution* (Ithaca, N.Y., 1973).

25. See E. Armand in *L'en-dehors,* Sept. 1927, 2–3.

26. One of these was Marie Curie, who reportedly signed only one political petition in her life, in favor of Sacco-Vanzetti. See Lecoin, *De prison.*

27. *New York World,* Aug. 21, 1927.

28. Borah and other Americans may have resented the European protests over the Sacco-Vanzetti case, but turn-of-the-century American commentators had not hesitated to criticize the injustices done in France to Dreyfus, while also denigrating the

French national character and exalting Anglo-American legal and political traditions. Egal Feldman, in *The Dreyfus Affair and the American Conscience, 1895–1906* (Detroit, 1981), offers several examples. One of the more ironic, in view of later attitudes, came from a *New York Times* editorialist, who proclaimed: "It is incredible that the [French Supreme Court of Appeal] will do injustice . . . with all the world looking on, with the evidence all displayed, and with the public judging the judges. . . . If Dreyfus is crushed his country will be crushed with him and France will be the scorn of the civilized world" ("Let in the Light," *New York Times,* Mar. 2, 1899).

29. Fernand Collin, "Le procès Sacco et Vanzetti," *Revue de droit pénal et de criminologie* (Aug.–Dec. 1927). For versions of Frankfurter's article, see, for example, "L'affaire Sacco-Vanzetti," a loose translation, in *Les cahiers des droits de l'homme* (Apr. 1927).

30. Collin, "Procès Sacco et Vanzetti."

31. For some useful comparisons, see Rob Kroes, "The Intellectual in America: Introductory Remarks," in his edited volume *The Intellectual in America* (Amsterdam, 1979), 1–10. See also Steven Biel, *Independent Intellectuals in the United States, 1910–1945* (New York, 1992), and Vincent Tompkins, "Twilight of Idols: American Social Criticism, 1918–1930" (Ph.D. diss., Harvard University, 1991). The debate over the role and classification of intellectuals, especially vis-à-vis political power, is beyond the scope of this study. One starting point is the classic essay by Antonio Gramsci, "The Intellectuals," in *Selections from the Prison Notebooks of Antonio Gramsci,* ed. Q. Hoare and G. Nowell-Smith (New York, 1971), 12–13.

32. Associated Press report, July 28, 1927.

33. See, for example, "In Reply to America," *Saturday Review,* Sept. 17, 1927, 354–359.

34. Addams to Rolland, Fonds RR-BNF. For Rolland's life and politics, see R. A. Francis, *Romain Rolland* (Oxford, 1999), David James Fisher, *Romain Rolland and the Politics of Intellectual Engagement* (New Brunswick, N.J., 2004), and Bernard Duchatelet, *Romain Rolland tel qu'en lui même* (Paris, 2002).

35. Between 1919 and 1932, Frank maintained a correspondence with Rolland that is revealing of the latter's profound emotional effect on a generation of young American critics. Frank was particularly enamored of Rolland's project of establishing an international community of letters that would embrace morality, peace, and justice on a universal level, thus countering (he hoped) nationalism, militarism, and other "negative passions" of the times. For the Young America intellectuals, see Casey Blake, *Beloved Community: The Cultural Criticism of Randolph Bourne, Van Wyck Brooks, Waldo Frank, and Lewis Mumford* (Chapel Hill, N.C., 1990). See also Anne Ollivier-Méllios, "L'art, la pensée, la politique: Un débat entre intellectuels français et américains, 1919–1922," *Revue française d'études américaines* 104:76 (Mar. 1998): 104–115. Given this degree of admiration, it should not be surprising that the direct appeal by Rolland on the issue pushed certain American intellectuals toward the Sacco-Vanzetti case. Mumford, for example, would go on to write passionately about it in 1928–1929. American progressive intellectuals admired Rolland as well; Horace

Kallen, for example, implored Rolland in 1930 to deliver a keynote lecture at the New School for Social Research in New York: "I know of no one in the whole world of letters whom I would more dearly have to welcome here" (Kallen to Rolland, Oct. 1, 1930, Fonds RR-BNF).

36. Price to Rolland, May 15, 1927: "The Sacco-Vanzetti case is convulsing the whole public [here.] . . . The liberals have made a strong stand, but for which the pair would have been electrocuted long ago. This has become a very hot poker which our ruling class would like to drop and cannot" (Fonds RR-BNF).

37. Romain Rolland, "Romain Rolland Testifies: A Message to America on the Massachusetts Tragedy," *Nation*, Sept. 28, 1927, 306–307. Rolland later published a French version of this article in his own journal, as "Lettre à un ami américain," *L'Europe*, Oct. 15, 1927.

38. Quoted in Drake, *French Intellectuals and Politics*, 61. See also A. Blum, "Romain Rolland faceà l'affaire Dreyfus," *Relations internationales* 14 (1978): 127–141.

39. Rolland, "Romain Rolland Testifies," 306.

40. *Sacco et Vanzetti, les martyrs du prolétariat* (Paris, 1927).

41. Jean Calas, an eighteenth-century Protestant merchant from Toulouse, was accused by the Catholic authorities of murdering his son, who was apparently planning to convert to Catholicism. Voltaire campaigned to clear Calas of the charges and succeeded in 1765—three years after Calas had been tortured to death. See Janine Garrison, *L'affaire Calas: Miroir des passions françaises* (Paris, 2002); Sarah Maza, *Private Lives and Public Affairs: The Causes Célèbres of Pre-Revolutionary France* (Berkeley, Calif., 1993), chap. 1 ("The Social Imagery of Political Crisis"). Some American Sacco-Vanzetti supporters shared this Dreyfusard sensibility. David Wallerstein, an attorney in Philadelphia, wrote to the socialist leader Norman Thomas: "What the case needed is something I am afraid we do not have in America—a Voltaire" (Wallerstein to Thomas, Oct. 8, 1927, Frank Papers, fold. 1.69).

42. Marie and François Mayoux to Rolland, Dec. 8, 1927, Fonds RR-BNF.

43. See Francis, *Romain Rolland;* Fisher, *Romain Rolland;* Duchatelet, *Romain Rolland;* Drake, *French Intellectuals and Politics.* Immediately after the article appeared, Lucien Price optimistically wrote to Rolland that "I consider it the happiest impulse in an evil hour that you wrote [the piece.] . . . How wide an auditory your letter will reach of course I do not know; but I believe it will be reprinted by other journals and find a broad circulation" (Price to Rolland, Sept. 15, 1927, Fonds RR-BNF). Rolland's warning of an eternal "state of moral warfare" between Europeans and Americans was echoed by a number of American writers who identified with the criticism and grew increasingly alienated from what they saw as the mindlessness and conformism of postwar American society. See Harold Stearns, *Civilization in the United States* (New York, 1922); Sinclair Lewis, "Can an Artist Live in America?" *Nation*, Dec. 9, 1925, 662–663.

44. See Drake, *Romain Rolland*, 61. For another example, this one from a French intellectual on the right, see Paul Valéry, *La crise de l'esprit* (Paris, 1924). The literature

on European identity and the unification vision is beyond the scope of this study. For starting overviews, see Peter M. R. Stirk, ed., *European Unity in Context: The Interwar Years* (New York, 1989), and Carl H. Pegg, *Evolution of the European Idea, 1914–1932* (Chapel Hill, N.C., 1983). See also Arthur Salter, *The United States of Europe* (London, 1931).

45. For two studies of the intrusion of American business and politics into European bourgeois life, see Mary Nolan, *Visions of Modernity: American Business and the Modernization of Germany* (New York, 1994), and Victoria de Grazia, *Irresistible Empire: America's Advance Through Twentieth Century Europe* (Cambridge, Mass., 2005).

46. Costigliola, *Awkward Dominion.* For this financial and diplomatic relationship, especially the role of France, see Stephen A. Schuker, *The End of French Predominance in Europe: The Financial Crisis of 1924 and the Adoption of the Dawes Plan* (Chapel Hill, N.C., 1976); Melvyn Leffler, *The Elusive Quest: America's Pursuit of European Stability and French Security* (Chapel Hill, N.C., 1974); Marc Trachtenberg, *Reparations in World Politics: France and European Economic Diplomacy, 1916–1923* (New York, 1980).

47. See, for example, Lucien Romier, *Qui sera le Maître, Europe ou Amérique?* (1927), published in English as *Who Will Be Master, Europe or America?* trans. Matthew Josephson (New York, 1928). Romier, in evocative and almost prophetic language that can still be heard in European (and American) intellectual circles today, accused Americans of having only one sense to their conception of "liberty"—the God-given right of Americans to unfettered commerce throughout the world. The great Dutch medieval historian Johan Huizinga joined this wave, producing *America: A Dutch Historian's Vision, from Afar and Near,* trans. Herbert H. Rowen (New York, 1972).

48. For an egregious recent example, see Bernard-Henri Lévy, *American Vertigo: Traveling America in the Footsteps of Tocqueville* (New York, 2006). For a cranky but amusing review, reminiscent of the Franco-American debates of 1927, see Garrison Keillor, "On the Road *avec* M. Lévy," *New York Times Book Review,* Jan. 29, 2006, 17. See also Jean Baudrillard, *America,* trans. Chris Turner (London, 1988).

49. Siegfried, *America Comes of Age.* The reactions to the book are worth a separate study. Siegfried sent his manuscript to an array of Americans, including Waldo Frank, Oswald Garrison Villard, Countee Cullen, Louis Brandeis, A. Lawrence Lowell, Walter Lippmann, Myron Herrick, and Douglas Fairbanks. If the responses are any indication, Siegfried's book was *the* book to read among the American intelligentsia in early 1927. Lowell sent Siegfried a typically odd response on March 21, 1927: "The United States is at present a good deal like a Newfoundland puppy, which has not yet got the seriousness of maturity, and gambols about in a thoughtless way without realizing that in doing so it may knock other creatures down."

Perhaps Siegfried's biggest American admirer was H. L. Mencken, who wrote to Siegfried on June 9, 1927, "It has been agreeable . . . to see the great success of your book in the U.S." In the *Nation,* Mencken was not so restrained: "This book seems so good that it seems almost incredible. . . . [this is] the most accurate, penetrating, and comprehensive treatise on the U.S. ever written." The *Christian Register,* on the other hand, criticized Siegfried's reliance on Mencken's *American Mercury* and called him "A French Mencken." See Robert C. Dexter's letter of October 7, 1927: "There is . . . a 'Menckenesque' point of view and even phraseology which often annoys, and is sometimes palpably inaccurate." The author quotes Siegfried: "In intellectual circles . . . the American is decidedly not at his best. In the universities he prefers to go in for sport and flirtations, and in the libraries all he wants is light reading." Dexter responded: "It appears that the author has been fed on a fairly stiff and regular diet of the *American Mercury* and the writings of the *cognoscenti* who gather around its editor. He has overlooked the fact, as does his American colleague, that America and native-born Anglo-Saxon Protestant Americans produce not only the National Security League, but the ACLU; not only [William Jennings Bryan], but Charles W. Eliot; not only Henry Ford, but Jane Addams" (all correspondence and reviews are in the André Siegfried Papers at the Archives d'histoire contemporaine, Fondation Nationale des Sciences Politiques, Paris, S2-19).

50. Edward Timms, *Karl Kraus, Apocalyptic Satirist,* vol. 2: *The Post-War Crisis and the Rise of the Swastika* (New Haven, 2005), 300.

51. See the 1931 essay by Antonio Gramsci, "Americanism and Fordism," in *An Antonio Gramsci Reader, 1916–1935,* ed. David Forgacs (New York, 1988). See also Victoria de Grazia, "The Exception Proves the Rule: The American Example in the Recasting of Socialist Strategies in Interwar Europe," in *Pourquoi n'y a-t-il pas de socialisme aux Etats-Unis?/Why Is There No Socialism in the United States?* ed. Jean Heffer and Jeanine Rovet (Paris, 1987), 167–192. For Laurin's and other Swedish reactions to the case, see Birgitta Steene, "The Swedish Image of America," in *Images of America in Scandinavia,* ed. Paul Houe and Sven Hakon Rossel (Amsterdam, 1998), 173–175.

52. See C. Vann Woodward, *The Old World's New World* (New York, 1991): "The future . . . also appeared [in Europe] at lower social levels in strange attitudes and ideas, new ways of thinking, new styles of living, and alien values. Europeans began to hear these innovations from the mouths of their own children and with increasing apprehension and dismay" (80).

53. *Paris soir,* Aug. 11, 1927, translation in Associated Press report.

54. *Liberté,* Aug. 11, 1927.

55. *L'intransigeant,* Aug. 11, 1927. A similar defense of the United States came from Spain, in the leading right-wing newspaper, *ABC:* "A great democracy, a civilization of the first magnitude, a free, progressive country with modern legislation, is suffering such calumnies. Such agitations always come up whenever there is a pretense at revolutionary attempts and to create a system and impunity on behalf of crime" (translation in Associated Press report). At the time Spain was under the right-wing dictatorship of José Antonio Primo de Rivera. Similar opinions could be found in the right-wing press in Germany, such as *Deutsche Zeitung,* which argued that "surrender to the worldwide protests in favor of the two men would have meant surrender before

the terrorism of the street," and happily concluded after the executions that "the cultured world was spared this."

56. For background, see Rosario Joseph Tosiello, " 'Requests I Cannot Ignore': A New Perspective on the Role of Cardinal O'Connell in the Sacco-Vanzetti Case," *Catholic Historical Review* 68:1 (1982): 51–52. According to the Associated Press report of August 10, 1927, a group calling itself "the European Sacco-Vanzetti Liberation Committee" wrote to the pope that "the Pharisees of Massachusetts will kill them over the protests of the people."

57. Associated Press report, Aug. 3, 1927; *Liberté,* Aug. 11, 1927; *Paris soir,* Aug. 18, 1927. Just four years earlier, after a tour of American industrial plants, Herriot had extolled American industrialization and the country's postwar economic way of life in his *Impressions d'Amérique* (Lyon, 1923).

58. *L'humanité,* Aug. 20, 1927.

59. Herrick to Secretary of State Frank Kellogg, Oct. 12, 1921, FBI SV, pt. 1-a, pp. 12–18.

60. "Le côté politique de l'affaire Sacco," *L'Action française,* Aug. 8 and Aug. 13, 1927. Action française, and Maurras specifically, were going through a tough time. The movement was still popular and influential on the right, but Maurras was excommunicated by the Vatican in 1926 (reportedly because of his agnosticism), a severe blow to a movement based on a Catholic conception of the French nation. For a classic study of Maurras and his movement, see Eugen Weber, *Action Française: Royalism and Reaction in Twentieth-Century France* (Stanford, Calif., 1962). For Maurras's limited but vocal interwar following in the United States, see C. Stewart Doty, " 'Monsieur Maurras est ici': French Fascism in Franco-American New England," *Journal of Contemporary History* 32:4 (1997): 527–538.

61. "Le côté politique de l'affaire Sacco," *L'Action française,* Aug. 5, 1927.

62. The connection between the far right in Europe and the Sacco-Vanzetti case does not end here. The future leader of the British Union of Fascists, Oswald Mosley, a Labour MP in the 1920s, attended the Sacco-Vanzetti rally at Trafalgar Square in London on August 5, 1927. See United Press report, Aug. 6, 1927.

63. For the concentrated power of Communists and other radicals in such working-class suburbs as Bobigny beginning in the 1920s, see Tyler Stovall, *The Rise of the Paris Red Belt* (Berkeley, Calif., 1990).

64. Samuel Putnam, *Paris Was Our Mistress: Memoirs of a Lost and Found Generation* (New York, 1947), 116–117. Carrefour Vavin, now place Pablo Picasso, is where boulevard Montparnasse meets boulevard Raspail in the 6th arrondissement. For another account of an encounter between a romantic American writer in France and working-class Parisians on the day of the executions—this one, however, ending in a mutual raising of glasses—see Matthew Josephson, *Life Among the Surrealists* (New York, 1962), 346–348.

65. For the official police report of the events, see "Le Commissaire Divisionnaire à la Police Judiciaire Barthélemy, à Monsieur le Préfet de Police: Rapport sur

l'ensemble des manifestations du 23 août 1927," in Archives de la Préfecture de Police de Paris, BA-1637. Some details on the Paris riots can be found in André Maury, "L'affaire Sacco-Vanzetti," *Miroir de l'histoire* 117 (1959): 1175–1182. For Montpellier, see United Press report, Aug. 23, 1927. For a recent study of the Paris police and their response to immigrants and radicalism in this period, see Clifford Rosenberg, *Policing Paris: The Origins of Modern Immigration Control Between the Wars* (Ithaca, N.Y., 2006).

66. Italian migration to France grew exponentially after Mussolini's rise to power in Italy. In 1921 there were approximately 45,000 Italian émigré workers in France; by 1926, there were an estimated 450,000. On Italians in 1920s France, particularly their radical politics, see the essays in Pierre Milza, ed., *Les Italiens en France de 1914 à 1940* (Paris, 1986), especially Ralph Schor, "L'image de l'Italien dans la France de l'entre-deux-guerres," 89–109; Loris Castellani, "Un aspect de l'émigration communiste italienne en France: les Groupes de langues italiennes au sein du PCF (1921–1928)," 195–221. For interwar emigration, see Mary Lewis, *The Boundaries of the Republic: Migrant Rights and the Limits of Universalism in France, 1918–1940* (Stanford, Calif., 2007). Italian left-wing writing was more likely to be found in France than in Italy in this period: see, for example, R. Schiavana, *Sacco e Vanzetti: cause e fini di un delitto di stato* (Paris, 1927).

67. *Le temps,* Aug. 24, 1927; *Le temps,* Aug. 25, 1927; *Paris midi,* Aug. 24, 1927. Those who followed the reactions in France to the outbreak of riots in Paris and its surrounding suburbs (as well as in other cities in France) in the fall of 2005 will be reminded by this rich language of certain French politicians and journalists who accused the "émigrés" (most of them actually French citizens, of African and North African descent) of ingratitude for the hospitality of the French republic. Eighty years later, however, the word *godless* has become irrelevant in the discussion of the so-called émigrés, and criticism is now directed at the demonstrators' supposed over-religiosity.

68. These charges were exaggerated. *L'humanité,* while calling for the demonstration on August 23, 1927, also asked activists not to carry any arms and to "make an effort to make the demonstration a peaceful one."

69. All records are in the Archives de la Préfecture de Police de Paris, BA-1637. For one example, see Alfred Oulman, "Ça ne peut pas durer," *Petit bleu,* Sept. 27, 1927.

70. An up-to-date, comprehensive scholarly history of the American Legion is overdue. Particularly welcome would be a study of the Legion in international perspective, given the importance of comparable veterans' movements in interwar Europe —which tended to be pacifist rather than right wing (perhaps because of the enormous difference between the ways Americans and Europeans experienced the war). The relative scholarly neglect of the American Legion is particularly striking in light of the attention paid by historians over the past few decades to the Legion's main competitor for popularity among "100-percenters" in 1920s America, the "second" Ku Klux Klan.

For a relatively sympathetic study, exonerating the Legion of fascist tendencies and placing it in the progressive tradition, see William Pencak, *For God and Country: The American Legion, 1919–1941* (Boston, 1989).

71. The Catholic *Croix de la Charente Angoulême* reported on September 18, 1927, that the French government, at the suggestion of foreign minister Aristide Briand, briefly planned to change the route of the parade because of the threat of violence, but under pressure from veteran groups eventually kept the plan intact. See LDH-BDIC, fold. 798, doc. 53-bis. According to Cuq, "L'affaire Sacco et Vanzetti à Bordeaux," the U.S. consul in Bordeaux, James D. Cheld, asked the police for twenty-four-hour protection of his home. Bordeaux experienced a number of violent events before the Sacco-Vanzetti executions: on August 8, for example, a demonstration ended with casualties and arrests when marchers attempted to break into the U.S. consulate. For Dos Passos's warning, see "John Dos Passos, Boston 7 août," *L'humanité,* Aug. 8, 1927, 1. See also the sarcastic piece by Paul Eluard and Benjamin Péret, "Revue de la presse," *La révolution surréaliste,* Oct. 1, 1927, 63–64. According to Pencak, Massachusetts Legionnaires had received Fuller's decision to push ahead with the execution with a "wild uproar": the legionnaires "clapped, yelled in one big chorus. . . . They stood, then they pounded the chairs. Then the band played 'America' " (*For God and Country,* 166–167). Despite the angered rhetoric of *L'humanité,* the PCF, following the new Stalinist line of noncooperation with the rest of the left, refused to participate in the anti-Legion rally in Paris organized principally by the Comité Sacco-Vanzetti and the LDH. See Rebeyrol and Roux-Fouillet, "L'affaire Sacco-Vanzetti"; Creagh, *Sacco et Vanzetti.*

72. Letter from the Comité Sacco-Vanzetti to Romain Rolland: "Do you not feel that the projected celebration of September 19 in honor of America would be a spit in the face of the justice that we have been defending, an unbearably cruel insult? Do you not think that the French government would be assassinating the two unfortunates over again?" (Fonds RR-BNF). See also *Le libertaire,* Aug. 29, 1927. The objection to the Legion's visit, as Lecoin remembered it, was also based on the idea that the members of the Legion "came to France to drink before returning to the land of prohibition" (*De prison,* 139).

73. Oulman, "Ça ne peut pas durer."

74. See the essay in *Croix de la Charente Angoulême,* Nov. 8, 1927, LDH-BDIC, fold. 798, doc. 53-bis.

75. Lecoin, *De prison,* 141; *Paris soir,* Sept. 21, 1927.

76. Among the attendants at the LDH gathering at place de Clichy was ACLU founder Roger Baldwin, a committed Sacco-Vanzetti activist in the United States, who arrived in Paris to protest the American Legion convention. See David Kennedy, *Over Here: The First World War and American Society* (New York, 1980), 366. In the working-class suburb of Clichy, on the day of the principal Legion celebration, the Communist-led municipality inaugurated a place Sacco-Vanzetti, with about 15,000 (including Baldwin) in attendance. See *Le temps,* Sept. 21, 1927.

77. In 1931, when an Indochinese anticolonial activist was arrested and put on

trial for murder in France, the leading surrealists André Breton, Paul Eluard, Louis Aragon, and Maxime Alexandre, recalling the failure of "world opinion" to stop the executions of Sacco and Vanzetti, called for a boycott of the "Colonial Exhibition" held that year in Paris. See Breton, Eluard, Aragon and Alexandre, "Ne visitez pas l'Exposition coloniale," in *Le livre des expositions universelles 1851–1989*, ed. R. Bordaz et al. (Paris, 1983), 137. The surrealists, if one takes at face value Breton's 1928 novel *Nadja*, had enjoyed "magnificent days of riot called 'Sacco and Vanzetti.'" See also the 1929 essay by Walter Benjamin, "Surrealism: The Last Snapshot of the European Intelligentsia," *New Left Review* 108 (Mar.–Apr. 1978): 2. Another young surrealist artist deeply affected by the Sacco-Vanzetti executions was Luis Buñuel, then in Paris; see Ernesto R. Acevedo-Muñoz, *Buñuel and Mexico: The Crisis of National Cinema* (Berkeley, Calif., 2003), 36.

78. Addams, *Second Twenty Years at Hull-House*, 334. Addams formulated her thoughts on the case in "Efforts to Humanize Justice," *Survey,* Dec. 1929, 275–278.

79. The most evocative description of this phenomenon is perhaps Malcolm Cowley, *Exile's Return: A Literary Odyssey of the 1920s* (New York, 1951); see also Cowley, "The Escape from America," *New York Herald Tribune Books,* Nov. 10, 1929, 1–6. For a European view, see Guglielmo Ferrero, "Ce que les américains cherchent en Europe," *L'illustration,* June 20, 1925, 610–611. For background, see Warren Susman, "Pilgrimage to Paris: The Backgrounds of American Expatriation, 1920–1934" (Ph.D. diss., University of Wisconsin, 1957). See also Susman, "Culture and Civilization: The Nineteen Twenties," in his *Culture and History: The Transformation of American Society in the Twentieth Century* (New York, 1984), 105–121; Patrice Higonnet and Arthur Goldhammer, *Paris: Capital of the World* (Cambridge, Mass., 2005), chap. 13 ("The American Imagination").

80. Higonnet and Goldhammer, *Paris,* 338. The poet Ezra Pound, in one of his amusing anti-bureaucratic rants (written before he fully adopted Italian fascist ideology and went insane while living in European self-exile), divided the American "postwar annual exodus to Europe" into four categories: "the studious, I mean the young, actively acquisitive explorers"; "the cultural, I mean the patient old ladies who have been saving up for some time"; "the drunks"; and "the shoppers" (Pound, "The Passport Nuisance," *Nation,* Nov. 30, 1927). According to Wohl, *Spectacle of Flight,* 10, the behavior of American tourists was sometimes so bad that Parisians stoned American tourist buses in protest.

81. Frank Costigliola, *Awkward Dominion,* 173. See also Harvey Levenstein, *Seductive Journey: American Tourists in France from Jefferson to the Jazz Age* (Chicago, 1998); for a rambunctious American newspaper in interwar Paris, see *The Left Bank Revisited: Selections from the "Paris Tribune," 1917–1934,* ed. Hugh Ford (University Park, Pa., 1972). A registry of American individuals, businesses, and organizations in late 1920s Paris can be found in Alfred M. Brace, ed., *Americans in France: A Directory* (Paris, 1929).

82. "'Vive Sacco-Vanzetti,' Cries Isadora Duncan; 'Bunk,' Says Judge," *Paris Tribune,* Aug. 10, 1927. See also United Press report, Aug. 10, 1927. One can assume

that the actual language used in this conversation was less theatrical and more informal than that described in these sources. Somewhat ironically, Duncan's funeral procession was held in Paris on September 19, the same day as the American Legion parade and the Sacco-Vanzetti rally at Clichy.

83. Elliot Paul, "Hands Across the Sea," *Lantern,* Aug. 1929, 26.

84. *Boston Evening Transcript,* July 29, 1927.

85. Costigliola, *Awkward Dominion.*

86. Ibid.

87. "Those Two Men," 8–9.

88. Raymond Mortimer, "A Formidable Shadow," *Nation and Athenaeum,* Apr. 6, 1929, 18; see also Leonard Woolf, "The World of Books: From Socrates to Sacco," *Nation and Athenaeum,* Aug. 27, 1927, 695. Russell to Gardner Jackson, May 28, 1929. I thank the staff of the Bertrand Russell Research Center in the McMasters University Library, Hamilton, Ontario, for providing me with this document.

89. Peter Berg, *Deutschland und Amerika, 1918–1929* (Lübeck, 1963), 148, 157. For another view stressing the inextricability of anti-Americanism from "philo-Americanism," see the comments by Jessica C. E. Gienow-Hecht: "Anti-Americanism is unthinkable without its flip side, philo-Americanism, and the tension between the two constitutes the very condition necessary to support the existence of both: high expectations and bitter disillusion are always joined at the hip" ("Always Blame the Americans: Anti-Americanism in Europe in the Twentieth Century," *American Historical Review* 3:4 [Oct. 2006]: 9).

90. Like Maurras and the royalists in France, German nationalists also often wrote about the case in European terms. The nationalist *Boersen Zeitung* put it simply on August 24, 1927: "The manner in which the Italians were treated [in the United States] would be impossible in Europe and Germany." Other scholars have shown that the late 1920s marked a period of rapprochement between French and German intellectuals on both the left and the conservative right; one example was the creation of the European Cultural Union, an elitist writers' organization. See Guido Müller, "France and Germany After the Great War: Businessmen, Intellectuals, and Artists in Non-Governmental European Networks," in *Culture and International History,* ed. Jessica C. E. Gienow-Hecht and Frank Shümacher (New York, 2003), chap. 5. For the growing idea of a pan-European "republic of letters" a decade after the war, see Charles S. Maier, *Recasting Bourgeois Europe: Stabilization in France, Germany, and Italy in the Decade After World War I* (Princeton, N.J., 1988), 579–581.

Chapter 4: The "Mob of Broadcloth-Coated, Heavy-Jowled Gentlemen"

1. La Guardia, quoted in the *New York World,* May 26, 1927; *Nation* editorial in Harvard Law SV news. clip., box 1, fold. 4, doc. 41; editorial in *New York World,* July 8, 1927; Bartolomeo Vanzetti to Katherine Codman, July 23, 1927, Ehrmann Papers, box 6, fold. 16. Branting, quoted in *Boston Herald,* June 23, 1927.

2. According to G. Louis Joughin and Edmund M. Morgan, Stratton, who was

NOTES TO PAGE 143

nominated by Lowell, "had no reputation for public affairs, and in the sittings of the committee remained almost completely silent. His colleagues seemed to have been indifferent to his presence and all indications point to a purely formal participation on his part" (*The Legacy of Sacco and Vanzetti* [New York, 1948], 302).

3. In 1923, Lowell commissioned a report on the Jews at Harvard from Charles H. Grandgent, a professor of philology and Romance languages. The report, delivered to Lowell on April 7, contained striking language. It acknowledged the efforts of university professors who "undertook the difficult mission of interviewing representative Hebrews on the subject of our Jewish problem." It concluded that "with regard to the Jew as a Harvard student, he is, on the average, a better scholar [than the gentile]. . . . In morals, he seems to be more prone to dishonesty and sexual offenses, but much less addicted to intemperance" (Grandgent to Lowell, Apr. 7, 1923, BPL-Joughin, fold. 14.3-15.1). For background on Lowell's attitudes toward Jewish faculty and students, see Michael Parrish, *Felix Frankfurter and His Times* (New York, 1982); Stephen Steinberg, "How Jewish Quotas Began," *Commentary*, Sept. 1971, 67–76; Jerome Karabel, *The Chosen: The Hidden History of Admission and Exclusion at Harvard, Yale, and Princeton* (Boston, 2005), chap. 3 ("Harvard and the Battle Over Restriction"). For the segregation of the freshmen dorms, see Nell Irvin Painter, "Jim Crow at Harvard: 1923," *New England Quarterly* (Dec. 1971): 627–634. According to a more recent study, Lowell was also responsible for the expulsion of a dozen homosexual Harvard students and faculty in 1920. See William Wright, *Harvard's Secret Court: The Savage 1920 Purge of Campus Homosexuals* (New York, 2005). There is no scholarly biography of Lowell or definitive study of Harvard's role in the public and political affairs of the period. For a critical sociological study, see Seymour Martin Lipset and David Riesman, *Education and Politics at Harvard* (New York, 1975), a work commissioned by the Carnegie Commission on Higher Education. Joel T. Isaac, "Trials of Belief: The Harvard Renaissance and the Making of Modern Knowledge" (Ph.D. diss., University of Cambridge, 2005), deals elegantly with interwar thought at the university. For a contemporary institutional account see Samuel Eliot Morison, *Three Centuries of Harvard, 1636–1936* (Cambridge, Mass., 1936), 439–484. Oddly, Morison, a Sacco-Vanzetti sympathizer, makes no mention of their case. Ferris Greenslet, *The Lowells and Their Seven Worlds* (Boston, 1946), an anecdotal family portrait, deals somewhat more critically with Lowell (400–404).

4. For the Immigration Restriction League, see Dale T. Knobel, *"America for the Americans": The Nativist Movement in the United States* (New York, 1996), chap. 6 ("Forks in the Road: The American Protective Association and the Immigration Restriction League").

5. See Richard Polenberg, *Fighting Faiths: The Abrams Case, the Supreme Court, and Free Speech* (New York, 1987); David M. Rabban, *Free Speech in Its Forgotten Years* (New York, 1997); Fred D. Ragan, "Justice Oliver Wendell Holmes, Jr., Zechariah Chafee, Jr., and the Clear and Present Danger Test for Free Speech: The First Year, 1919," *Journal of American History* 58 (June 1971): 24–45. Lowell and Lodge debated the League of Nations issue publicly in Boston on March 19, 1919,

with Governor Calvin Coolidge presiding. See Henry A. Yeomans, *Abbott Lawrence Lowell* (1948; New York, 1977), 444–460. In 1920, Lowell signed the appeal of thirty-one Republican Party notables in support of the candidacy of Warren Harding, believing that he would ensure the entry of the United States into the League of Nations. See Arthur Schlesinger, Sr., *In Retrospect: The History of a Historian* (New York, 1963), 128–134. For Lowell's pro-League activism, see Warren F. Kuehl and Lynne K. Dunn, *Keeping the Covenant: American Internationalists and the League of Nations, 1920–1939* (Kent, Ohio, 1997).

6. Yeomans, *Lowell*, 315–316; Morrison, 465–466. Lowell himself encouraged Harvard students to break the strike: "The university desires in a time of crisis to help in any way that it can to maintain order and support the laws of the Commonwealth. I therefore urge all students . . . to prepare themselves for such service as the Governor . . . may call upon them to render. . . . You will, of course, disregard for the present, all your obligations to Harvard, except the supreme obligation of representing her worthily in this crisis." Laski had made his comments at a rally held by the wives of the striking policemen. Conveniently for Harvard, Laski soon thereafter accepted a permanent position at the University of London.

7. See Zechariah Chafee, *Freedom of Speech* (New York, 1920). See also Morison, *Three Centuries of Harvard*, 465. For the Abrams case, see Polenberg, *Fighting Faiths.*

8. Felix Frankfurter to Mark DeWolfe Howe, Sept. 25, 1957, BPL-Joughin, fold. 17.2-18.1. For a contrast with other universities, see Carol S. Gruber, *Mars and Minerva: World War I and the Uses of Higher Learning in America* (Baton Rouge, La., 1975). Especially illuminating is the example of Columbia University president Nicholas Murray Butler, an open foe of academic freedom during the war. Butler was later approached by the modernist Reverend Harry Ward to sign a petition on behalf of Sacco and Vanzetti and refused, explaining that he had "not made a sufficient study of the case in question to warrant his signing any document concerning it" (quoted in Joughin and Morgan, *Legacy of Sacco and Vanzetti*, 258). Lowell had no sympathy for Münsterberg, who died in his Harvard classroom in December 1916, five months before the United States declared war on Germany. And there were limits to his own conception of academic freedom. According to Arthur Schlesinger, Sr., Lowell demanded that the history department rescind its appointment of visiting professor Gaetano Salvemini, a centrist political opponent of Mussolini from the University of Florence who had fled Italy, for diplomatic considerations. The department refused (*In Retrospect*, 92).

9. Upton Sinclair, *The Goose-Step: A Study of American Education* (Pasadena, Calif., 1924). Though published after the war, Sinclair's work was written in prewar muckraking progressive mode, depicting American universities as the lackeys of reactionaries, exploiters, and the capitalist machine. Lowell, in Sinclair's view, was different from other university presidents only in that he showed unlikely courage in his defense of free speech. Sinclair himself had been an ardent prowar spokesman. See his weekly *Upton Sinclair's*, which began publication in April 1918, for examples.

10. Harold Laski to Oliver Wendell Holmes, June 6, 1927, in *Holmes-Laski Letters: The Correspondence of Mr. Justice Holmes and Harold Laski, 1916–1935,* ed. Mark A. DeWolfe Howe (Cambridge, Mass., 1953), 955; Gardner Jackson, "The Reminiscences of Gardner Jackson," Oral History Research Office, Butler Library, Columbia University (1959), 241; Tom O'Connor, "New Light on the Sacco-Vanzetti Case," paper presented at the Dec. 4, 1953, meeting of the Humanist Fellowship of Boston, in BPL-Joughin, fold. 1.2.

11. For the Lowell report, see *The Sacco-Vanzetti Case: Transcript of the Record of the Trial of Nicola Sacco and Bartolomeo Vanzetti in the Courts of Massachusetts and Subsequent Proceedings, 1920–1927* (Mamaroneck, N.Y., 1969), book 5, 5378w–5378z. Key excerpts are in Michael M. Topp, *The Sacco and Vanzetti Case: A Brief History with Documents* (New York, 2005), 161–165. The defense team was not as surprised as other supporters by the report. Although they had greeted the formation of the commission with optimism, they were troubled to learn that Lowell, Grant, and Stratton essentially retried the case behind closed doors, interviewing the jurors, witnesses, and main individuals involved but without the presence of the lawyers, who were questioned separately. Sacco and Vanzetti's attorneys were not allowed to question or cross-examine the judge, the prosecutors, or the jurors. Nor was it understood what the role of this commission was to be; this was never made clear to the public. There was no official record or minutes of its proceedings and no explanation of its reasoning or methodology. The defense committee also objected specifically to Grant, who had reportedly made derogatory comments about Italians in the past, specifically about Sacco and Vanzetti. They also feared the consequences of the well-known animus between Lowell and Frankfurter.

12. Yeomans, *Lowell,* 491, where he also observed, "The minority continued to protest. . . . Happily, minorities are always vocal and often vociferous. Not, infrequently too, they are unrestrained." Yeomans ought to have known better, since he had seen the letters sent to Lowell in response to the report, which contained severe criticism from people as far from socialism as Lowell himself.

13. Thayer, quoted in Joughin and Morgan, *Legacy of Sacco and Vanzetti,* 243; Phil Stong, "The Last Days of Sacco and Vanzetti," in *The Aspirin Age, 1919–1941,* ed. Isabel Leighton (New York, 1949), 179.

14. See *Sacco-Vanzetti Case: Transcript of the Record,* 5368z.

15. Max Shachtman, *Sacco and Vanzetti: Labor's Martyrs* (New York, 1927), 48. For a similar response in German, see Augustin Souchy, *Sacco und Vanzetti: Zwei Opfer amerikanischer Dollarjustiz* (Berlin, 1927).

16. For the reaction in France, see Chapter 3.

17. Massachusetts State Motor Registrar Frank Goodwin, author of the pamphlet *Sacco-Vanzetti and the Red Peril,* claimed in the *Boston Herald* on June 2, 1927, that forming the committee "would be a direct attack on the judiciary of this great old Commonwealth." As Joughin and Morgan point out, Goodwin had made a career of attacking the courts for their "liberal tendencies," and only a year earlier had urged that "it is necessary to limit the discretionary power of the courts. It is a well known fact in

Massachusetts that practically nobody with money is put in jail" (*Legacy of Sacco-Vanzetti*, 301). For Goodwin's speeches against Sacco and Vanzetti, see Chapter 2.

18. *Boston Herald,* Aug. 16, 1927.

19. *Boston Herald,* Aug. 23, 1927. The *Nation* angrily charged that the *Herald*'s about-face was the result of "pressure from Big Business and Back Bay": "When the history of public sentiment in regard to Sacco and Vanzetti is written much will have to be attributed to the poltroonery of the Boston newspapers, with the booby prize going to the *Herald*" (Sept. 7, 1927, 219). The *Herald*'s editorial, to the *Nation,* represented "the depth of pusillanimity." The *New York Times* also reached rather rosy conclusions the day after the executions: "From the whole tragic affair one compensating fact emerges. . . . A love of justice is still a powerful motive in this country. . . . A body of intelligent and disinterested opinion . . . became stirred by the Sacco-Vanzetti case purely out of an unselfish fear that a wrong might have been done . . . and that there was danger lest American criminal procedure should have a stain affixed to it in the eyes of the whole world" (Aug. 24, 1927). From this point of view, the result of the case was, in a sense, perfect: American elites had shown that justice was important, but they had not gone so far as to give in to the pressures of foreigners and radicals. On August 14, however, the *Times* had already begun calling for legal change in the wake of the case: "The long delay in determining the fate of the two men is a reproach to American justice. It is something which is almost impossible to explain satisfactorily to foreigners. . . . Americans abroad this summer have often been called upon to explain this matter to Europeans, but have not been able to do so." The editorial added that "some of the violent rebukes to the United States by the press of countries which have known their own famous miscarriages of justice we might retort upon with the advice to study their own judicial records." But the editorial called on American leaders and lawyers to "set about more energetically the work of reducing that historic grievance, the law's delays, in this country."

20. See *Monthly Bulletin of the Sacco-Vanzetti Defense Committee,* Aug. 1927, 1–2.

21. Croly, quoted in "Press Comment on the Sacco-Vanzetti Execution," *Nation,* Sept. 14, 1927, 252.

22. See, for example, "In Charlestown," *Time,* Aug. 29, 1927, 10: "After seven years of premeditation, blood was shed beside a so-called cradle of American liberty, Boston. The shedding of blood causes restlessness. The restlessness caused by this particular bloodshed was exceptionally widespread, gloomy and violent because, in seven years, a seed of doubt can grow into a harvest of sincere conviction." *Time* summed up in its inimitable style: "Prisoners Sacco and Vanzetti died in the order that their names had been coupled, seven minutes apart." See also "Cut-Off," *Life,* Sept. 1, 1927, 16.

23. "Justice Underfoot," *Nation,* Aug. 17, 1927, 146–147.

24. Ibid. Kirchwey (like many other Sacco-Vanzetti supporters) adopted much more radical political views by the 1930s. See Sara Alpern, *Freda Kirchwey: A Woman of the Nation* (Cambridge, Mass., 1987).

25. *New York World,* July 25, 1927.

26. See for example Walter Lippmann, "Doubt That Will Not Die Down," *New York World,* Aug. 19, 1927. For accounts of the Frankfurter-Lippmann meeting, see Jackson, "Reminiscences of Gardner Jackson"; Parrish, *Frankfurter;* Ronald Steel, *Walter Lippmann and the American Century* (Boston, 1980).

27. "The Ominous Execution" and "Penalties of the Sacco-Vanzetti Execution," *New Republic,* Aug. 31, 1927. The *New Republic's* reaction to the execution can be seen as a generational changing of the guard: Croly was away that week at a conference in Hawaii, and the editorial line was dictated by his younger replacements, including the increasingly radicalized critic Edmund Wilson. See Chapter 2.

28. "Massachusetts the Murderer," *Nation,* Aug. 27, 1927.

29. See Will Soper, "The Sacco-Vanzetti Package in Harvard's Vault," *The Real Paper,* Aug. 2, 1977.

30. There were a few exceptions to historians' neglect of the papers. Louis Joughin, who had published *The Legacy of Sacco-Vanzetti* with Edmund M. Morgan in 1948, examined many of the Lowell papers in the late 1970s while preparing a book on the Lowell commission. He completed a manuscript in 1982 but did not find a publisher. Francis Russell, author of the 1962 *Tragedy in Dedham,* quoted a few of the letters selectively in "The 'Second Trial' of Sacco and Vanzetti," *Harvard Magazine* (May–June 1978): 50–54, giving the false impression that Lowell had received only tepid criticism and replied to it with a conviction that made his correspondents seem ignorant of the case. The magazine's two previous issues had included two articles on Sacco and Vanzetti: Russell, "The Case of the Century, Fifty Years Later," *Harvard Magazine* (July–Aug. 1977): 44–45, and Lewis H. Weinstein, "Sacco and Vanzetti Defended," *Harvard Magazine* (Nov.–Dec. 1977): 6–9.

31. Much of this perception is due to the curiously broad influence and numerous reprintings of Frederick Lewis Allen's *Only Yesterday: An Informal History of the 1920s* (New York, 1931), though Allen's own correspondence with Lowell during the affair contradicts his book's view of the late 1920s as a period of political indifference, seen from the perspective of the early 1930s. Young radical intellectuals who achieved a degree of prominence in the 1930s were also responsible for much of this image; see for example Malcolm Cowley's *Exile's Return.* This view of 1920s intellectuals as escapist was later entrenched in scholarly thinking by, among others, Richard Hofstadter: "Among intellectuals [in the 1920s] . . . there was a marked retreat from politics and public values toward the private and personal sphere, and even in those with a strong impulse toward dissent, bohemianism triumphed over radicalism" (*The Age of Reform: From Bryan to FDR* [New York, 1955], 284). In *The Perils of Prosperity, 1914–1932* (Chicago, 1958), William Leuchtenberg branded intellectuals of the 1920s as either radical or apolitical: "Though writers like Dos Passos and [Millay] were deeply involved in the case, intellectuals were too non-political for radicalism to make a great impact" (81). More recently, Ann Douglas argued in *Terrible Honesty: Mongrel Manhattan in the 1920s* (New York, 1995) that in the 1920s there was a lot going on politically—racial violence, poverty, and worsening economic inequality at home, civil wars and nationalist frenzies in Europe—but that American intellectuals and artists,

for the most part, were depoliticized or indifferent to these events. "The trial of a Queens housewife named Ruth Snyder and her lover . . . for the murder of Ruth's husband," she noted by way of example, "received more coverage than the historic and controversial execution of the accused Boston anarchists" (18). Douglas may be right about the total press coverage (though she does not provide evidence), but in the summer of 1927 no one, aside from possibly Charles Lindbergh, received bigger headlines in Boston and New York newspapers, or more attention from intellectuals in the United States, than Sacco and Vanzetti. In recent years, historians have increasingly challenged this apolitical image of the period; see, for examples, David J. Goldberg, *Discontented America: The United States in the 1920s* (Baltimore, 1999), and Casey Blake, *Beloved Community: The Cultural Criticism of Randolph Bourne, Van Wyck Brooks, Waldo Frank, and Lewis Mumford* (Chapel Hill, N.C., 1990).

32. Letter of Aug. 7, 1927, ALLP, box 2, fold. 2. In one of his columns on Sacco and Vanzetti in the *New York World,* Broun had written, "Will the institution of learning in Cambridge which once we called Harvard be known as Hangman's House?" For Broun's involvement in the case see Chapter 2.

33. Letter of Aug. 1, 1927, ALLP, box 2, fold. 2.

34. Max Glass to Lowell, Aug. 8, 1927, ALLP, box 2, fold. 2.

35. Constant Southworth to Lowell, Aug. 6, 1927, ALLP, box 2, fold. 2.

36. Albert Sprague Coolidge to Lowell, Aug. 20, 1927, ALLP, box 2, fold. 3.

37. Letter of July 19, 1927, ALLP, box 2, fold. 3.

38. Demarest Lloyd to Lowell, ALLP, box 2, fold. 4. In the same spirit, another businessman in New York wrote to Lowell to ask "why you [do] not get rid of such men as Felix Frankfutter [*sic*] and Dean [Roscoe] Pound and several more men connected with your college, who are doing nothing but stirring up trouble in the United States. If I had my way I would deport the entire lot. . . . Your college seems to be honeycombed with communists, anarchists, and every other kind of ists going. Cannot understand why you allow these conditions to prevail in an educational institution. They are dangerous to the growing youth of the community" (C.R. Hurd to Lowell, Aug. 6, 1927, ALLP, box 2, fold. 2).

39. John F. Moors, quoted in Harlan B. Phillips, *Felix Frankfurter Reminisces: Recorded in Talks with Dr. Harlan B. Phillips* (New York, 1960), 132. Similarly, Arthur Schlesinger, Sr., argued that Lowell was almost invariably "fair minded, sagacious, and farsighted. It was these qualities that made him one of Harvard's great presidents." When it came to Sacco and Vanzetti, however, "one can only suppose that a Massachusetts patrician of inherited wealth could not, even while striving to do so, weigh dispassionately the innocence or guilt of 'a good shoemaker and a poor fish peddler,' both of lowly foreign birth" (*In Retrospect,* 134).

40. A definitive scholarly biography of Ickes is due. For an environmentalist focus, see Tom Watkins, *Righteous Pilgrim: The Life and Times of Harold L. Ickes* (New York, 1992). For his New Deal career, see Jeanne Clarke, *Roosevelt's Warrior: Harold L. Ickes and the New Deal* (Baltimore, 1996); Leuchtenberg, *Franklin D. Roosevelt and the New Deal, 1932–1940* (New York, 1963), passim; Alan Brinkley,

The End of Reform: New Deal Liberalism in Recession and War (New York, 1995), passim. Graham White and John Maze, *Harold Ickes of the New Deal: His Private Life and Public Career* (Cambridge, Mass., 1985) is primarily a psychohistorical study of the connection between Ickes's unusual sex life and his political career. Ickes plays an admirable role in Philip Roth's counter-factual fantasy *The Plot Against America* (New York, 2004). Ickes's own *Autobiography of a Curmudgeon* (New York, 1943) covers his pre–New Deal years, while *The Secret Diary of Harold L. Ickes,* vols. 1–3 (New York, 1953), covers the years 1933–1941.

41. Harold Ickes to Lowell, Oct. 14, 1927, ALLP, box 2, fold. 5.

42. Lowell to Constant Southworth, Sept. 22, 1927, ALLP, box 2, fold. 2.

43. Lowell to James Mickel Williams, Aug. 15, 1927, and Lowell to Frederick Lewis Allen, Aug. 15, 1927, ALLP, box 2, fold. 2; Lowell to Sir Horace Plunkett, Apr. 23, 1929, ALLP, box 2, fold. 5.

44. Albert Sprague Coolidge to Lowell, Aug. 29, 1927, ALLP, box 2, fold. 3.

45. Robert L. Hale to Lowell, Aug. 4, 1927, ALLP, box 2, fold. 2. On Hale, see Barbara H. Fried, *The Progressive Assault on Laissez Faire: Robert Hale and the First Law and Economics Movement* (Cambridge, Mass., 1998), and Neil Duxbury, "Robert Hale and the Economy of Legal Force," *Modern Law Review* 53:4 (July 1990): 421–444.

46. Lowell to Hale, Aug. 29, 1927; Hale to Lowell, ALLP, box 2, fold. 2.

47. Lowell to unnamed recipient, Aug. 27, 1927, ALLP, box 2, fold. 3.

48. Michael Musmanno to Robert Alan Aurthur, Apr. 23, 1960, BPL-Felicani, MS. 2030, fold. 7A. See also Chapter 5.

49. Lowell to Plunkett, Aug. 20, 1927, ALLP, box 2, fold. 3; Lowell to Plunkett, Aug. 21, 1927, BPL-Joughin, fold. 15.1.

50. Williams to Lowell, Aug. 8, 1927, ALLP, box 2, fold. 3. See James Mickel Williams, *The Foundations of Social Science: An Analysis of Their Psychological Aspect* (New York, 1920). The book that established Lowell's scholarly reputation was *Governments and Parties in Continental Europe* (Boston, 1896), which was the first study on the topic by an American and the work that led to his invitation to teach at Harvard. Other works by Lowell include *Government of England* (New York, 1908); *Public Opinion and Popular Government* (New York, 1913); *Governments of France, Germany, and Italy* (Cambridge, Mass., 1914); *Public Opinion in War and Peace* (Cambridge, Mass., 1923).

51. Lowell to Williams, Aug. 15, 1927; Williams to Lowell, Sept. 16, 1927, ALLP, box 2, fold. 3.

52. Brandeis, Frankfurter, and Mack all considered Lowell an anti-Semite, and their opinion did not soften over the years: in a 1933 letter to Walter Lippmann, Frankfurter recalled Lowell's objections to Brandeis's appointment to the U.S. Supreme Court and referred to Lowell as "a refined Adolf Hitler" (Frankfurter to Lippmann, Apr. 28, 1933, BPL-Joughin, fold. 17.2-18.1). Gardner Jackson of the defense committee remained convinced to the end that Lowell's decision was influenced by his hatred for Frankfurter. See Jackson, "Reminiscences of Gardner Jackson": "Nobody

but me has seen the exchange [between Lowell and Frankfurter] and it really was vitriolic. I am satisfied that the intensity of Lowell's animosity to Felix was a very large factor in what happened to his mind in the face of the evidence" (280). Michael Musmanno of Sacco and Vanzetti's defense team later wrote: "It is my belief, and I say it with regret, that Fuller, Thayer, and Lowell were men so constituted that in the early days of Hitler's regime they could have found little difficulty in supporting him" (Musmanno to Joughin, Oct. 13, 1948, BPL-Joughin, fold. 1.2).

53. Julian Mack to Lowell, Aug. 16, 1927, ALLP, box 2, fold. 3; Frankfurter, quoted in Harry Barnard, *The Forging of an American Jew: The Life and Times of Julian W. Mack* (New York, 1974), 113. For Mack and the Garvey trial, see Tony Martin, *Race First: The Ideological and Organizational Struggles of Marcus Garvey and the Universal Negro Improvement Association* (New York, 1986), 192. Ironically, Garvey demanded that Mack—a contributing member of the NAACP, an organization that had vehemently attacked Garvey—disqualify himself from the case. Mack admitted his connection to the NAACP but refused to recuse himself. For Mack and the Mencken case, see Marion Elizabeth Rodgers, *H. L. Mencken, The American Iconoclast: The Life and Times of the Bad Boy of Baltimore* (New York, 2005), 304. For Mack and the Daugherty case, see James N. Giglio, *H. M. Daugherty and the Politics of Expediency* (Kent, Ohio, 1978), 188.

54. Lowell to Mack, Aug. 29, 1927; Mack to Lowell, Aug. 31, 1927, ALLP, box 2, fold. 3.

55. Even Columbia University president Nicholas Murray Butler, who had previously refused requests to appeal on behalf on Sacco and Vanzetti, sent a last-minute telegram to Fuller on Aug. 20, 1927, asking the governor to commute the death sentence to life imprisonment: "On behalf of a large body of sober American opinion which, while wholly unmoved by the unreasonable and violent demonstrations, is nevertheless gravely disturbed by the published record of the Sacco-Vanzetti case" (Butler to Fuller, Aug. 20, 1927, BPL-Joughin, fold. 1.2).

56. James Ernest King to Lowell, Aug. 21, 1927, ALLP, box 2, fold. 4.

57. Lowell to Graham Wallas, ALLP, box 2, fold. 3; Lowell to Albert Shaw, Oct. 7, 1927, ALLP, box 2, fold. 5. *American Review of Reviews,* an offshoot of the British journal *Review of Reviews,* had been consistently hostile to the Sacco-Vanzetti cause: see "The Progress of the World" (Sept 1927): 227–236, in which the Lowell report is described as "a notably interesting document . . . one that would be likely to satisfy almost any open-minded reader possessed of normal mentality." Shaw, an erstwhile progressive and activist in the National Civic Federation, was also a government informant: in 1921 he had offered his services to the Department of Justice in providing information on any pro–Sacco and Vanzetti activity that he knew of. See Shaw's letter to Bureau of Investigation director W. J. Burns, Nov. 1, 1921, FBI SV, pt. 3-c.

58. As a pacifist, Villard held a lifelong noninterventionist position, leading him to oppose both U.S. participation in the League of Nations in 1919 and America's entry into World War II in 1941. In 1909 he co-founded the NAACP, and built a center of strength in the New York *Evening Post.* Until 1917 he was close to Woodrow Wilson

but fell out with the president over American intervention in World War I. See Michael Wreszin, *Oswald Garrison Villard: Pacifist at War* (Bloomington, Ind., 1965). For Villard's stewardship of the *Nation* and his subsequent falling out with Kirchwey, his successor, over World War II, see the afterword by Victor Navasky to Katrina Vanden Heuvel, ed., *The "Nation," 1865–1990: Selections from the Independent Magazine of Politics and Culture* (New York, 1990), 513–530.

59. See, for example, Freda Kirchwey, "Some Mass Demonstrations," *Nation* Oct. 5, 1927, 337–338.

60. Oswald Garrison Villard to Lowell, Aug. 9, 1927, ALLP box 2, fold. 2.

61. In his memoir *Fighting Years: Memoirs of a Liberal Editor* (New York, 1939), Villard made clear that he was not a mere "witness" to this meeting; rather, he had tried to save Sacco and Vanzetti by using his connections to have Fuller invite MacDonald to dinner. Despite the British leader's "convincing" argument for clemency, Villard recollected that "I got the impression at the time that the case was beyond the governor's grasp." The memoir contains an interesting anecdote: MacDonald's wife was making the case for Sacco and Vanzetti forcefully, according to Villard, when Fuller excused himself to receive a phone call. When he got back to the room, MacDonald picked up where his wife had left off but much less effectively. Writing in 1939, Villard was still unable to shake off his frustration: "I shall never be able to understand. These men *guilty*? Never" (507–510). He made no mention in the memoir of his correspondence with Lowell, nor is there any mention of the Sacco-Vanzetti case in Wreszin's biography. Daniel T. Rodgers points out that MacDonald had been Villard's "political 'ideal' " since the end of World War I (*Atlantic Crossings: Social Politics in a Progressive Age* [Cambridge, Mass., 1998], 308).

62. Villard to Lowell, Aug. 9, 1927; see also Oswald Garrison Villard, " 'A Decent Respect to the Opinions of Mankind,' " *Nation*, Aug. 24, 1927, 172–173.

63. Lowell to Villard, Sept. 23, 1927, ALLP, box 2, fold. 2.

64. Dewey's name appears on numerous petitions by organizations formed *after* the executions. To the best of my knowledge, his name appeared once before the executions, in a petition published in the *New York Tribune* on Aug. 22, 1927. For background on Dewey and politics, see Alan Ryan, *John Dewey and the High Tide of American Liberalism* (New York, 1997), and Robert Westbrook, *John Dewey and American Democracy* (Ithaca, N.Y., 1993). According to some scholars, the 1920s was when Dewey was closest to socialism, and his outlook ebbed and flowed largely on the basis of his intellectual relationship with the "Soviet experiment." See David Engerman, "John Dewey and the Soviet Union: Pragmatism Meets Revolution," *Modern Intellectual History* 2:2 (Apr. 2006): 33–63. Sidney Hook, in *John Dewey: An Intellectual Portrait* (New York, 1995), observed that during his career Dewey championed two public causes: Sacco and Vanzetti in 1927 and Leon Trotsky in 1937, in the debate over whether to grant asylum to the exiled Bolshevik leader (24–25).

65. John Dewey, "Psychology and Justice," *New Republic*, Nov. 23, 1927, 9–12, repr. in *Characters and Event: Popular Essays in Social and Political Philosophy by John Dewey*, ed. Joseph Ratner (New York, 1929).

66. Horace Kallen, "Fear, Freedom, and Massachusetts," *American Mercury,* Nov. 1929, 281–292; Edna St. Vincent Millay, "Fear," *Outlook and Independent,* Nov. 9, 1927.

67. See for example Harvey O'Higgins, "The Nervous American," *American Mercury,* Sept. 7, 1929, 61–63; Joseph Jastrow, "Our Prejudices: Psychological Analysis of Replies to Edna St. Vincent Millay," the *Outlook,* Nov. 23, 1927, 364–365, 373, 384; Edwin B. Wilson, "The Scientist and the Psychiatrist," *American Journal of Psychiatry* 84 (July 1927), 23–26.

68. For Dewey's growing interest in psychology and psychiatry, see Gary Gerstle, "The Protean Character of American Liberalism," *American Historical Review* 99:4 (Oct. 1994): 1057–1058.

69. For Du Bois's and Mencken's views see Chapter 2.

70. Dewey's sense of personal responsibility for the Lowell report was shared by Felix Frankfurter: one day before the execution the law professor wrote to Roscoe Pound, "To have seven years of systematic perversion of the machinery of justice validated by the authority of the president of Harvard University, when in fact he himself unwittingly is part and parcel of the social forces which help to explain the conviction and forthcoming execution of two innocent men, does too far-reaching violence to my notions of law and justice to enable me to rid myself of a sense of personal responsibility for such a wrong" (Frankfurter to Pound, Aug. 22, 1927, BPL-Joughin, fold. 17.2–18.1).

71. Dewey's support of the war in 1917, which led to some of his most unconvincing writings and his break with his young and brilliant protégé Randolph Bourne, were expressed in such essays as "In Time of National Hesitation," *Seven Arts,* May 1917, 3–7; "Conscience and Compulsion," *New Republic,* July 14, 1917; "Force, Violence, and Law," *New Republic,* Jan. 22, 1916, 295–296; and especially "What Are We Fighting For?" *Independent,* June 22, 1918, reprinted as "The Social Possibilities of War" in *Characters and Events,* 551–560.

72. Robert Grant, *Fourscore: An Autobiography* (Boston, 1934), 374. Grant was not the most impressive figure who could have been appointed to the commission. After retiring from the bench, he spent most of the 1920s writing breezy novels and pushing for a uniform national divorce law; the most critical problem facing the country as he saw it was "the hypocritical use of temporary residence in an easy-going state for the purposes of divorce," which, he explained, "offended my decency." He wrote articles like "A Call to a New Crusade" in *Good Housekeeping,* which asked, "What are the women of the United States doing to cure the abuse of the divorce remedy in this country?" and "Better Marriage Is Within Reach" in *Pictorial Review.* In his memoir he described the worldwide protest over the Sacco-Vanzetti case as "hysteria. . . . A group of young intelligentsia from New York paraded like dancing dervishes before the State House." This "point of view," he explained, "is explicable only by hysteria" (368–373).

73. According to Henry F. Pringle, *The Life and Times of William Howard Taft* (New York, 1939), 1047–1048, Taft openly disapproved of the agitation on behalf of

Sacco and Vanzetti and veered between pleading ignorance ("I don't know anything about this criminal prosecution of two Italians, as I think they are") and attacking their supporters ("[Frankfurter] seems to be closely in touch with every Bolshevist, Communist movement in this country"). He could not understand how Sacco and Vanzetti had been able to escape punishment for so long and "to rouse in their behalf a great deal of money . . . and the active manipulation of bomb throwers throughout the world." Taft also urged the president of Yale University to punish those on the faculty who were involved in the case, especially the dean of the law school, Robert M. Hutchins. To Elihu Root—who would later help fund the publication of the transcript of the record of the Sacco-Vanzetti case—Taft wrote in May 1927 that Frankfurter was "an expert in attempting to save murderous anarchists from the gallows or the electric chair" (quoted in Michael Parrish, "Sacco and Vanzetti Revisited: Russell and Young & Kaiser," *American Bar Foundation Research Journal,* 12:2–3 [Spring–Summer 1987]: 579).

74. In 1932, Fuller briefly returned to the headlines when he publicly opposed Governor Joseph Ely's nomination of Felix Frankfurter to the Massachusetts supreme court on the grounds that Frankfurter was "an open sympathizer with murderers." The former governor warned that if Frankfurter's appointment went through there would be "no reason why murder should not flourish in Massachusetts" ("Name Frankfurter to Bay State Bench," *New York Times,* June 23, 1932, 23). Eventually helping to discredit Fuller was his successor, Ely, who wrote to Herbert Ehrmann (after the publication of the latter's 1933 book on the case) that "before I read your new book . . . I had some doubt as to the guilt of Sacco and Vanzetti. When I had finished, I had no doubt of their innocence. . . . The result was quite likely a grave miscarriage of justice" (Sept. 27, 1933, Ehrmann Papers, box 3, fold. 8).

75. Joughin and Morgan, *Legacy of Sacco and Vanzetti;* F. Lauriston Bullard, "Bay State Bar Head Criticizes Lawyers," *New York Times,* Dec. 9, 1928. President Nutter added that "the Sacco-Vanzetti case showed serious imperfections in our methods of administering justice."

76. See the introduction by William Douglas to the 1969 reprint of *Sacco-Vanzetti Case: Transcript of the Record.* In 1939 the Massachusetts state legislature, in chapter 341 of the *Laws of 1939,* stated: "In a capital case the entry in the supreme judicial court shall transfer to that court the whole case for its consideration of the law and the evidence, and the court may order a new trial if satisfied that the verdict was against the law or the weight of the evidence, or because of newly discovered evidence, or for any other reason that justice may require." See Robert P. Weeks, ed., *Commonwealth vs. Sacco and Vanzetti* (Englewood Cliffs, N.J., 1958), 263.

77. See examples in BPL-Joughin, fold. 1.2.

78. For some examples, see "Vanzetti Was Innocent," *New Republic,* Nov. 7, 1928, and the thirty-page "Vanzetti Was Innocent: Frank Silva Confesses Bridgewater Crime," *Outlook and Independent,* Oct. 31, 1928, 1053–1083; see also Waldo Cook, "Celebrated Trial," *Survey,* Aug. 1, 1929, 490–491. Silas Bent, the veteran *New York Times* reporter who first broke the Frank Silva story, accused the mainstream press of

not helping Sacco and Vanzetti even though they had leads and tips on the gangs that had committed the Bridgewater and South Braintree crimes—information that would have exonerated the two men. See "Those Two Men," *Lantern,* Aug. 1929, 8–10. To Bent this was part of the sad pattern of American journalism: "Why did the newspapers, with the single exception of the *Denver Post,* ignore the Teapot Dome scandal? The answer . . . is that the press of the United States is now so callous, lazy, and incompetent that it no longer goes out of its way in the cause of justice or to expose official graft." On the Massachusetts gangs, "the hordes of sensation-mongers made no move. These facts are a black stain upon American journalism. . . . This phase of the significance of the Sacco-Vanzetti case might well be taken to heart by every newspaperman in this country who still accounts himself honest." Bent published *Ballyhoo: The Voice of the Press* (New York, 1927), which excoriated the press for its sensationalism and laziness, for exploiting stories about sex while being puritanical about them, and for ignoring the world outside the United States. For Bent's criticism of yellow journalism, see his "Hearst—A Yellow Among Yellows," *Lantern,* Feb. 1929, 6–8.

79. At Canter's trial, which ended with his conviction and sentencing to one year in prison, Sacco and Vanzetti's conservative attorney William Thompson gave shattering testimony about Fuller and Lowell's conceptions of due legal process. As Thompson recalled, he had tried to persuade the two to allow him to cross-examine witnesses if they were going to retry the case. But Fuller refused; "He found," Thompson stated, "that if people came to him privately and quietly, he as a businessman was able to get the truth out of them a great deal more effectively than it could be got publicly or in court. I said: 'that is an illusion characteristic of a certain type of businessman, but it is a dangerous illusion.' " Thompson further accused Fuller of condemning Sacco and Vanzetti simply because of public opinion. Quoted in Waldo Cook, "Forgetting Sacco and Vanzetti," *Nation,* Aug. 21, 1929, 188–190. For the legal significance of the Canter case, see Frederick F. Schauer, "Language, Truth, and the First Amendment: An Essay in Memory of Harry Canter," *Virginia Law Review* 64:2 (Mar. 1978): 263–302.

80. See Philip Littell's review of *The Letters of Sacco and Vanzetti* in the *New Republic,* Jan. 2, 1929, 191: "I remember how I felt when Governor Fuller appointed the Lowell commission. . . . I felt certain that President Lowell would think it dishonorable to judge any cause without mastering it. . . . Well, the Lowell report showed me how thoroughly I had misunderstood President Lowell. Yet even now, even with that report in mind, I still do not imagine him reading these letters through without becoming so nearly certain of Sacco and Vanzetti's innocence as to wish that he had thought, in the summer of 1927, their guilt a little doubtful." For a discussion of the impact and origins of this publication, see Richard Polenberg's introduction to the 1997 edition of *The Letters of Sacco and Vanzetti.* The collection was presented to Fuller on the inauguration of his successor, Joseph Ely, in 1928, in front of the state house; Fuller responded by throwing the book to the ground. See "Fuller Spurns Book of Sacco Letters," *New York Times,* Jan. 4, 1929, 8; "The Decline of Massachusetts," *Nation,* Aug. 21, 1929, 184.

81. Rockefeller made two successive contributions of five thousand dollars to the project through Raymond B. Fosdick, later the president of the Rockefeller Foundation. See Rockefeller to Fosdick, Nov. 15, 1927, BPL-Joughin, fold. 15.2-16.1. Rockefeller requested that his contribution be made anonymously but later agreed to attach his name to the project. Joughin, working on his and Morgan's *Legacy of Sacco-Vanzetti* in 1947, asked Rockefeller to confirm his participation. At first Rockefeller's lawyers denied it, but after seeing a draft of the work Rockefeller confirmed the details. T. J. Ross to Joughin, Aug. 12, 1947, BPL-Joughin, fold. 1.2.

82. Ralph Hanlow to Lowell, Feb. 1929, ALLP, box 2, fold. 2.

83. The Sacco-Vanzetti National League published a pamphlet, *Ten Questions That Have Never Been Answered!* (New York, 1928), documenting the omissions of the Lowell Commission, and addressing Fuller and Lowell, "who have so many times expressed high sentiments and lofty ideals."

84. Kirchwey quoted in Stuart Banner, *The Death Penalty: An American History* (Cambridge, Mass., 2002), 226, 358n40. The connection between the Sacco-Vanzetti affair and the history of the death penalty in the United States deserves further investigation; for a local study, see Alan Rogers, *Murder and the Death Penalty in Massachusetts* (Amherst, Mass., 2008), chap. 6.

85. Lowell to Mr. Cohen, Apr. 10, 1929, quoted in Joughin and Morgan, *Legacy of Sacco and Vanzetti*, 319.

86. "Lessons for Liberals," *New Republic*, Sept. 28, 1927, 136–138; for another example, see Shaemas O'Sheel, "The Thing: Reactions of a Realist," *New Republic* Sept. 7, 1927, 61–63.

87. Beard, quoted in Joughin and Morgan, *Legacy of Sacco and Vanzetti*, 331.

88. Gardner Jackson, "Was President Lowell Conscious," *Lantern*, Aug. 1929.

89. Paul Kellogg in *Survey Graphic*, Oct. 10, 1927. The *Survey Graphic* provided some of the most insightful coverage of the case: see, for example, Jane Addams, "Efforts to Humanize Justice," *Survey Graphic*, Dec. 1929, 275–278, 309–311, 313. For a description of Kellogg's and Addams's involvement in the Sacco-Vanzetti affair from the perspective of progressive social workers, see Patrick Selmi, "Social Work and the Campaign to Save Sacco and Vanzetti," *Social Service Review* 75:2 (Mar. 2001): 115–134.

90. Paul Kellogg, "A Sacco-Vanzetti Memorial," *Lantern*, Aug. 1929, 7.

91. Bertrand Russell, *Autobiography* (New York, 1998), 219.

92. Bertrand Russell, "The Danger of Creed Wars," *Sceptical Essays* (London, 1928), 228–229. Russell added that "the real crime of Sacco and Vanzetti was that they were anarchists." But he did not think that this kind of behavior was unique to the United States: "Persecution for opinion is . . . tolerated in all countries," including some in which the Sacco-Vanzetti case was protested mightily. In Switzerland, for example, "it is not only legal to murder a communist, but the man who has done so is exonerated for his next crime on the ground that he is a first offender." Russell's writings on the affair, however, could often be glib and uninformed: "Very few Americans . . . know the truth about Sacco and Vanzetti; condemned to death for a

murder for which another man has confessed, and the evidence for which has been acknowledged by policemen engaged in collecting it to have been a 'frame-up.' A new trial was refused to these men partly on the ground that the man who confessed to the murder was a bad character. Apparently, in the opinion of American judges, only persons of good character commit murders." Wit aside, no authority figure had ever openly confessed to a "frame-up."

93. Lowell to Gardner Jackson, Aug. 5, 1929, ALLP, box 2, fold. 5: "I do not care to speak at the meeting . . . for I have nothing to add to what I have stated in our report. In my opinion the men were undoubtedly guilty, and the evidence would have been deemed by everyone conclusive had it not been for the sympathy excited by the claim that they were 'reds.' " Lowell to Robert Sanborn, Sept. 2, 1929, ALLP, box 2, fold. 6. According to Lowell's biographer, every year until the end of his life, the anniversary of Sacco and Vanzetti's death brought him "letters and telegrams, usually anonymous, of bitter, personal abuse" (Yeoman, *Abbott Lawrence Lowell,* 483).

94. Lowell to Plunkett, Apr. 23, 1929, ALLP box 2, fold. 3.

95. *Walled in This Tomb: Questions Left Unanswered by the Lowell Committee in the Sacco-Vanzetti Case, and Their Pertinence in Understanding the Conflicts Sweeping the World at This Hour* (Boston, 1936). Other liberals later also saw a link between the Sacco-Vanzetti case and the dangerous political phenomena of the 1930s. In Frankfurter's opinion, offered two decades later, the execution of Sacco and Vanzetti showed that "those who have no scruples, who are ruthless, who don't give a damn, influence gradually wider and wider circles, and you get the Hitler movement in Germany, the Huey Long ascendancy in Louisiana, McCarthyism cowing most of the Senators of the U.S." (Phillips, *Frankfurter Reminisces,* 206).

96. See BPL-Joughin, fold. 1.2. According to some of the local reporters, the copies were burned.

97. Ibid. See also Roger Baldwin and Corliss Lamont, "Harvard Heretics and Rebels," *Nation,* June 10, 1936, 733. The alumni made no mention of Harvard's extensive ties to Nazified universities in Germany, its continuing discrimination against Jews and African Americans, and Conant's anti-Semitism and deep reluctance to welcome Jewish academic refugees. In 1936, the same year that Conant invited Roosevelt to the tercentenary to speak about freedom and democracy, he sent an official representative to the 500-year celebration of the University of Heidelberg, by then under official Nazi administration. See S. H. Norwood, "Legitimating Nazism: Harvard University and the Hitler Regime, 1933–1937," *American Jewish History* 92:2 (June 2004): 189–223.

98. Lowell to Bruce Bliven, Mar. 27, 1936, ALLP, box 2, fold. 7. Lowell's papers from the period show that he was also an avid collector of material attacking the Sacco-Vanzetti defense committee, especially Frankfurter. Several examples can be found in ALLP, box 2, folds. 2–7.

99. Richard Norton Smith, *The Harvard Century: The Making of a University to a Nation* (Cambridge, Mass., 1998), 99.

100. "Judge Musmanno's Account of Conversation with President A. Lawrence

Lowell, at Cotuit, Mass., on Thursday Morning, August 11, 1938," ALLP, box 2, fold. 7. Lowell refused even to acknowledge that Sacco and Vanzetti were radicals or, as he put it, "Reds" (his word for radicals of any sort). As far as he was concerned, they were ordinary criminals, and the claim that they were Reds was used to shield them from the criminal prosecution. There is no external corroboration that Lowell made these statements to Musmanno, but Musmanno sent the text to Lowell twice so that the latter could confirm or deny what he had written. Lowell wrote back, "I had no intimation that what I took to be a long friendly conversation was intended for publication. Doubtless, much of my language was informal; but your report seems to me to give an impression of something like flippancy, which I was, and always have been, very far from feeling" (BPL-Joughin, fold. 15.1). From this exchange I conclude that Musmanno conveyed Lowell's words accurately, though Lowell was not aware that they would be published. For the book, see Michael Musmanno, *After Twelve Years* (New York, 1939). The year before, Lowell published a self-celebratory volume, *What a University President Has Learned* (New York, 1938), which made no mention of the case.

101. Frederick Lewis Allen to Lowell, Aug. 8, 1927, ALLP, box 2, fold. 7.

102. Allen, *Only Yesterday,* 75.

103. Allen was not the only prominent journalist to change his mind about the case. William Allen White was another. On the day of the execution in 1927, he wrote, "Sacco and Vanzetti probably were guilty." In 1941, he publicly switched sides: "I am now satisfied that Sacco and Vanzetti were innocent of the crime for which they were executed. Their execution was a crime for which America lost prestige in the eyes of millions all over the world." See White, *Forty Years on Main Street* (New York, 1941), 183–184.

104. Federal Writers' Project of the Works Progress Administration for the State of Massachusetts, *Massachusetts: A Guide to Its Places and Its People* (Boston, 1937), 144, 76, 144.

105. For an account of this episode, which showed that the public divisions over Sacco and Vanzetti in Massachusetts were nearly as acute in 1937 as they were in 1927, see Christine Bold, " 'Staring the World in the Face': Sacco and Vanzetti in the WPA Guide to Massachusetts," *Massachusetts Historical Review* 5 (2003): 94–124. One ironic difference, however, was that in 1937 Sacco-Vanzetti supporters appeared to be the ones wielding the power, while the opponents found themselves in the role of protesters.

Chapter 5: "A Kind of Madness"

1. Murray Kempton, *Part of Our Time: Some Ruins and Monuments of the Thirties* (New York, 1955), 56.

2. The 1950s liberal historiography of interwar political culture in the United States includes Arthur Schlesinger, Jr., *The Age of Roosevelt,* vol. 1: *The Crisis of the Old Order* (Boston, 1957); Richard Hofstadter, *The Age of Reform: From Bryan to*

FDR (New York, 1955); Robert K. Murray, *The Red Scare: A Study in National Hysteria, 1919–1920* (Minneapolis, 1955); and Frederick Hoffman, *The Twenties: American Writing in the Postwar Decade* (New York, 1955). For later scholarship focusing on the role of literary figures, see Daniel Aaron, *Writers on the Left: Episodes in Literary American Communism* (New York, 1961), and James Gilbert, *Writers and Partisans: A History of Literary Radicalism in America* (New York, 1968).

3. Malcolm Cowley, "Echoes of a Crime," *New Republic,* Aug. 28, 1935, 79. For the consensus historians, see John Higham, *History: Professional Scholarship in America* (Baltimore, 1965), 212–232.

4. Hofstadter, *Age of Reform,* 20.

5. Roosevelt, quoted in Gardner Jackson, to Herbert Ehrmann, July 3, 1952, Ehrmann Papers, box 2, fold. 7A. Jackson added that "Mrs. Roosevelt's response troubles me deeply because I think it is symbolic of the extent of the political terror in this period." For the 1958 hearings, see Tom O'Connor, ed., *Record of Public Hearing Before Joint Committee on the Judiciary of the Massachusetts Legislature on the Resolution of Representative Alexander J. Cella Recommending a Posthumous Pardon for Nicola Sacco and Bartolomeo Vanzetti, Massachusetts State House, Boston, April 2, 1959* (Boston, 1959). For (sympathetic) coverage of this process, see Norman Thomas Di Giovanni, "Progress of Sacco and Vanzetti," *Nation,* Apr. 18, 1959, 331–332. See also "Sacco, Vanzetti Haunt State House in Boston," Associated Press report, Jan. 3, 1959; Joseph M. Harvey, "Trial of Sacco and Vanzetti Still Debated," *Boston Globe* Apr. 1, 1959. In 1960 more ground was made on behalf of the Sacco-Vanzetti cause when the Massachusetts Joint House and Senate Judiciary Committee, in response to the 1960 resolution on the issue, refused to "condone or criticize the action taken by the [Massachusetts] courts." Veteran Sacco and Vanzetti defenders, naturally, focused on the significance of the first verb.

6. H. W. Freeman to CBS, May 11, 1958, BPL-Joughin, fold. 16.2-17.1. Louis Joughin, co-author of *The Legacy of Sacco and Vanzetti,* was the "historical consultant" for CBS. A teleplay of the program, along with letters to the network, is in BPL-Joughin, fold. 16.2-17.1.

7. "The Sacco-Vanzetti Story," teleplay by Reginald Rose, in Beinecke Rare Book and Manuscript Library, Yale University. In 1972 Rose presented a play in two parts, *This Agony, This Triumph,* based on the original television show.

8. Westbrook Pegler, "Drama Rules over Truth on Airwaves," *Boston Globe,* Aug. 2, 1960.

9. Michael Musmanno to Aldo Felicani, June 4, 1960, BPL-Felicani, MS 2030, fold. 7A.

10. Ibid.

11. See materials in Ehrmann Papers, box 11, fold. 7.

12. The French version of the Baez-Morricone theme song, performed by folk singer Georges Moustaki, was "La marche de Sacco et Vanzetti," later covered by such French stars as Mireille Mathieu. Montaldo had been an assistant director in the

production of *The Battle of Algiers,* a seminal film in left-wing European culture in the 1960s.

13. The interest in Sacco's origins specifically can be tied to a more general trend: the fascination among Italian intellectuals and social scientists with the so-called southern question.

14. Also in 2001 another composer, Anton Coppola, finished a three-and-a-half-hour opera entitled *Sacco and Vanzetti.*

15. Mino Roli and Luciano Vincenzoni, *Sacco e Vanzetti* (Rome, 1960).

16. Robert Clements, "Letter from Rome: The Triumph of Sacco and Vanzetti," *Columbia University Forum* (Fall 1961): 32–37, available in O'Connor Papers, fold. 1a.23.

17. *L'unità,* quoted ibid.

18. Clements, "Letter from Rome." Caryl Chessman was convicted by the state of California as a sex offender in 1948 and executed in 1960 in spite of widespread opinion that his trial had been unfair and that he was innocent. Like Sacco and Vanzetti, Chessman was an attractive figure, who seemed, to many, completely incapable of committing the crimes of which he had been accused. See Theodore Hamm, *Rebel and a Cause: Caryl Chessman and the Politics of the Death Penalty in Postwar California, 1948–1974* (Berkeley, Calif., 2001). Hamm makes a distinction between the mobilization around Sacco and Vanzetti, which did not consist of a sustained principled opposition to the death penalty, and the later (more minor) mobilization around Chessman's cause, which did. At the time of Clements's trip to Europe, a play based on Chessman's story was staged at Barcelona's Guimera Theater.

19. Clements, "Letter from Rome." In his lecture, Clements announced that he was "prejudiced in favor of Italians," and as proof, pointed to the fact that at the time he was president of the American Association of Teachers of Italian.

20. Robert Clements, "Knight-Errants in Error?" *New York Times Book Review,* Jan. 30, 1966. For De Gaulle's complex relationship with the United States, and vice versa, especially toward the end of his life, see Richard Kuisel, *Seducing the French: The Dilemmas of Americanization* (Berkeley, Calif., 1993), chap. 6 ("The Gaullist Exorcism: Anti-Americanism Encore"), and Robert O. Paxton and Nicholas Wahl, eds., *De Gaulle and the United States: A Centennial Reappraisal* (Providence, R.I., 1994).

21. Einstein, quoted in Armand Gatti, *Chant public devant deux chaises électriques* (Paris, 1966), 8.

22. See Alvise Passigli, "Sacco e Vanzetti: Un caso di storia sociale americana," *Ponte* 17:2 (1961): 208–215. One notable exception to the view of the case in an American context is Armand Gatti's play *Chant public devant deux chaises électriques,* which narrates the Sacco-Vanzetti drama from six sites around the globe. See also the review by Jean-Jacques Gautier in *Le Figaro,* Jan. 28, 1966. On sporadic revivals of interest, see "Sacco et Vanzetti: Le procès qui bouleversa le monde rouvert 36 ans après," *Paris soir,* Oct. 29, 1963; "Coupables ou non, Sacco et Vanzetti n'ont pas

eu leur chance," *Paris soir,* Oct. 30, 1963. There is little European scholarship on the Sacco-Vanzetti affair, and even less that does not deal exclusively with its American (or anarchist) component. American scholars over the years narrowed the significance of the Sacco-Vanzetti case by focusing almost exclusively on the question of Sacco and Vanzetti's guilt or innocence; European historians, to the degree that they dealt with the affair at all, narrowed the story further by ignoring its crucial European and international components. One exception is Ronald Creagh's *Sacco et Vanzetti* (Paris, 1984), an insightful overview written from an anarchist perspective. French scholars have contributed somewhat to the study of the ramifications of the case in the United States. See Creagh, "La classe ouvrière américaine et l'affaire Sacco et Vanzetti," in *Les Etats-Unis à l'épreuve de la modernité: Mirages, crises et mutations de 1918 à 1928,* ed. Daniel Royot (Paris, 1993), 109–122; Hélène Christol, "The Ethnic Factor in the Sacco-Vanzetti Case," in *Ethnic Cultures in the 1920s in North America,* ed. Wolfgang Binder (Frankfurt, 1993), 175–188; Christol, "L'affaire Sacco-Vanzetti et les écrivains américains" (thèse de lettres, Paris IV, 1980). Louis Joughin was commissioned to write about the case by French journals in the 1960s. See Joughin, "Quelques problèmes posés par un procès célèbre: L'affaire Sacco-Vanzetti," *Bulletin de la Société d'histoire moderne* 4 (1965): 8–11, supplement to *La revue d'histoire moderne et contemporaine,* and Joughin, "Problèmes historiques posés par un procès célèbre," *Revue d'histoire économique et sociale* 1 (1969): 92–105.

23. Robert Noah, *The Advocate* (New York, 1963).

24. Milton Esterow, "'Advocate' a Hit—On TV, That Is: Viewers Praise TV's 'Advocate,'" *New York Times,* Oct. 16, 1963.

25. Alfred Kazin, "The World as a Novel: From Capote to Mailer," *New York Review of Books,* Apr. 8, 1971.

26. Guy Paschal, "The Failure of the Lowell Commission in the Sacco-Vanzetti Case," in O'Connor Papers, fold. 4.43. Another Harvard senior thesis on the Lowell commission followed in 1958, and there were two more by the 1980s.

27. Donald E. Graham, "President Lowell and the Sacco-Vanzetti Case," *Harvard Crimson,* Apr. 17, 1963.

28. John Beffel to Tom O'Connor, Jan. 11, 1965, O'Connor Papers, fold. 1a.12.

29. See materials in BPL-Joughin, fold. 1.2.

30. Michael Musmanno, "The Armchair Theorists Begin to Comment on the Sacco-Vanzetti case" (unpublished), BPL-Felicani, MS. 2030, fold. 7A.

31. Kempton, *Part of Our Time,* 46, 56. See also the comment by Edward Shils: "The case of Sacco and Vanzetti drew the sympathy of many American intellectuals who otherwise had very little interest in politics. . . . It brought them into a circle of ideas with which they had had no connection before. It also made them familiar with the idiom of the Communist party" ("Intellectuals and Their Discontent," *American Scholar* [Spring 1976]: 192).

32. Arthur Schlesinger, Sr., *In Retrospect: The History of a Historian* (New York, 1963), 133–134.

33. "Those Two Men," *Lantern,* Aug. 1929, 8.

34. Einstein, quoted in Gatti, *Chant publique*, 8.

35. William F. Buckley, Jr., and L. Brent Bozell, *McCarthy and His Enemies: The Record and Its Meaning* (Chicago, 1954), 245. See also William F. Buckley, Jr., *God and Man at Yale: The Superstitions of Academic Freedom* (Chicago, 1951). For a sympathetic biography, see John Judis, *William F. Buckley, Jr.: Patron Saint of the Conservatives* (New York, 1988).

36. George H. Nash, *The Conservative Intellectual Movement in America Since 1945* (New York, 1979), 106; see also Jeffrey Hart, *The Making of the American Conservative Mind: The "National Review" and Its Times* (Wilmington, Del., 2005); for the religious aspect of Buckley and Bozell's activism and of the new conservatism, see Patrick Allitt, *Catholic Intellectuals and Conservative Politics in America, 1950–1985* (Ithaca, N.Y., 1995). See also Michael Paul Rogin, *The Intellectuals and McCarthy: The Radical Specter* (Cambridge, Mass., 1967).

37. See John Andrews, *The Other Side of the Sixties: Young Americans for Freedom and the Rise of Conservative Politics* (New Brunswick, N.J., 1997); Gregory L. Schneider, *Cadres for Conservatism: Young Americans for Freedom and the Rise of the Contemporary Right* (New York, 1999).

38. Robert H. Montgomery, *Sacco-Vanzetti: The Murder and the Myth* (New York, 1960), 71, 81, 289, 323–324, 370–371.

39. William F. Buckley, Jr., "Sacco and Vanzetti, Again," *American Legion Magazine,* Oct. 1960, 14–15, 47–50. For the Scottsboro case, see Chapter 2.

40. In a forum hosted by the *American Historical Review* in 1994, Alan Brinkley argued that partly because of the lingering influence of the consensus historians of the 1950s, scholars had underestimated conservatism's prominent place in American life and had not done enough to bring into the mainstream the scholarship on American conservatism that *was* available. See Brinkley, "The Problem of American Conservatism," *American Historical Review* 99:2 (Apr. 1994): 409–429. For a different view of the field, published two years earlier in the same journal, see Michael Kazin, "The Grass-Roots Right: New Histories of U.S. Conservatism in the Twentieth Century," *American Historical Review* 97:1 (Feb. 1992): 136–155. Scholars have since paid enormous attention to modern conservatism, especially its 1960s rebirth: some examples include Jonathan Schoenwald, *A Time for Choosing: The Rise of Modern American Conservatism* (New York, 2001), Lisa McGirr, *Suburban Warriors: Grassroots Conservatism in the 1960s* (Princeton, N.J., 2001), Rick Perlstein, *Before the Storm: Barry Goldwater and the Unmaking of the American Consensus* (New York, 2001), Kevin M. Kruse, *White Flight: Atlanta and the Making of Modern Conservatism* (Princeton, N.J., 2005), and Kim Phillips-Fein, *Invisible Hands: The Making of the Conservative Movement from the New Deal to Reagan* (New York, 2009).

41. Alger Hiss was formerly the head of the Carnegie Endowment for International Peace. Accused of spying for the Soviet Union by Whittaker Chambers (a senior editor at *Time* and a self-proclaimed former Communist sympathizer), Hiss was convicted of perjury (but not espionage) and sentenced to two concurrent five-year sentences, of which he ultimately served forty-four months in prison. For

an unsympathetic account of Hiss's ordeal, see Allen Weinstein, *Perjury: The Hiss-Chambers Case* (New York, 1978). Chambers's autobiography, *Witness* (Chicago, 1952), was a national best seller, and Chambers became a mentor and father-figure to Buckley, Bozell, and many other young conservatives.

42. See Chapter 2.

43. See Chapter 1.

44. Tom O'Connor to William F. Buckley, Jr., Oct. 6, 1960, O'Connor Papers, fold. 1.35. O'Connor more systematically set forth his ideas in "The Origin of the Sacco-Vanzetti Case," *Vanderbilt Law Review* 5 (June 1961): 2–9, a negative review of Montgomery's book.

45. William F. Buckley, Jr., "The Testament of Vanzetti," *National Review*, Jan. 14, 1961, 15–16. There was nothing new about Buckley's suspicions. The controversy over the Sacco and Vanzetti letters, and the supposed alterations (or inventions) made by editors Marion Frankfurter, Aldo Felicani, and Gardner Jackson, began immediately after their publication and continued on and off for decades. It was first raised, and dismissed, in a review by Edward Shanks, "An American Tragedy," *Saturday Review*, Mar. 30, 1929, 435. The Paris edition of the *Herald Tribune* also suggested in 1929 that Jackson and Marion Frankfurter had fabricated the letters, or most of them. See Gardner Jackson, "The Reminiscences of Gardner Jackson," Oral History Research Office, Columbia University (1959), 297. For background, see the introduction by Richard Polenberg to the reissued *Letters of Sacco and Vanzetti*, ed. Marion Denman Frankfurter and Gardner Jackson (New York, 1997). Bruce Watson has shown that many of Sacco and Vanzetti's letters that never made it into the collected volume were far more violent and radical than those that Frankfurter and Jackson chose to make public (*Sacco and Vanzetti: The Men, the Murders, and the Judgment of Mankind* [New York, 2007)]. There were even more suspicions about Vanzetti's highly eloquent last words to reporter Phil Stong in prison: "If it had not been for these thing . . . I might have live out of my life, talking at street corners to scorning men. I might have die, unmarked, unknown, a failure. Now we are not a failure. This is our career and our triumph. Never in our full life can we hope to do such work for tolerance, for joostice, for man's onderstanding of man, as now we do by an accident. . . . Our words—our lives—our pains—nothing! The taking of our lives—lives of a good shoemaker and a poor fish-peddler—all! That last moment belongs to us—that agony is our triumph!" These doubts culminated in an article by James Grossman, "Vanzetti and Hawthorne," *American Quarterly* 22:4 (Winter 1970), 902–907, which—if I read it correctly—argued that Vanzetti was unconsciously parroting the style of the nineteenth-century master. The original quote from Vanzetti appeared in the *New York World*, May 13–15, 1927, and was reprinted in Stong, "The Last Days of Sacco and Vanzetti," in *The Aspirin Age, 1919–1941,* ed. Isabel Leighton (New York, 1949), 169–189. For a survey of the debates over Vanzetti's eloquence, see Fred Somkin, "How Vanzetti Said Goodbye," *Journal of American History* 68:2 (Sept. 1981): 298–312.

46. As Eastman remembered, before Tresca had a chance to elaborate on his

revelation, the two were interrupted by other people entering the room; two years later, in 1943, before Eastman was able to talk with him again about the case, Tresca was assassinated by contract hit men. See Max Eastman, "Is This the Truth About Sacco and Vanzetti (That Sacco Was Guilty but Vanzetti Was Not)?" *National Review,* Oct 21, 1961, 261–264. In the course of the 1920s, Tresca and his lover and fellow activist Elizabeth Gurley Flynn had helped recruit Fred Moore as Sacco and Vanzetti's first attorney, but he had fallen out with several of the leading Sacco and Vanzetti defenders, especially Felicani and the other Galleanisti. For a convincing analysis of the Eastman-Tresca controversy, its significance for scholars, and the limitations of Tresca's supposed revelations, see Nunzio Pernicone, "Carlo Tresca and the Sacco-Vanzetti Case," *Journal of American History* 66:3 (1979): 535–547.

47. Max Eastman to F. Russell, Mar. 1961, Russell Papers, fold. 1.8.

48. *National Review,* Oct. 21, 1961, 261.

49. Eastman, "Is This the Truth About Sacco and Vanzetti?"

50. O'Connor to Eastman, undated letter, O'Connor Papers, fold. 1a.32.

51. James Grossman, "The Sacco-Vanzetti Case Reconsidered," *Commentary* 33:1 (Jan. 1962): 31–44.

52. The most important study in this regard is Paul Avrich, *Sacco-Vanzetti: The Anarchist Background* (Princeton, N. J., 1991), which is not part of the revisionist scholarship.

53. For a brief but highly suggestive discussion of Sacco and Vanzetti in the context of the American radical tradition, see Eric Foner, "Sacco and Vanzetti, the Men and the Symbols," *Nation,* Aug. 20, 1977, 135–141. See also Foner's comments in "Sacco-Vanzetti Reconsiderations, 1979: A Symposium," in Boston Public Library, *Sacco-Vanzetti: Developments and Reconsiderations—1979* (Boston, 1982), 93–96. That conference, which marked the deposit of the Felicani papers in the Boston Public Library, with contributions from Eric Foner, Barbara Miller Solomon, Daniel Aaron, and Louis Joughin, called for a thorough social history of the case, which has yet to be written.

54. Grossman, "Sacco-Vanzetti Case Reconsidered."

55. More than two decades after the appearance of *Tragedy in Dedham,* Russell published *Sacco and Vanzetti: The Case Resolved* (New York, 1986), which argued that Sacco was guilty of the murder and that Vanzetti was an accessory after the fact. Russell's new and supposedly clinching evidence was a dubious bit of triple hearsay from the son of a dead former immigrant who once reportedly claimed to have been in the Italian anarchist inner circle and thus knew the "truth" about Sacco and Vanzetti—which he supposedly shared with his son, dramatically enough, while breathing his last. The book also showed how personal, ugly, and lacking in substance the debate over guilt or innocence had become over the years. Russell took the opportunity to hit back at Sacco and Vanzetti supporters—all dead by then—who had criticized him over the years, including one who had aided him in his early research and who had once, Russell informs us, mistakenly sent him a "dozen pornographic photographs." Russell also claimed that Musmanno, later a judge at the Nuremberg trials, enjoyed wearing

military uniforms under his robes at the Nuremberg hearings and had "liaisons" with several women who had been on Hitler's staff. For an even-handed review of this strange book, see Rosario J. Tosiello in the *New England Quarterly* 61:2 (June 1988): 313–316.

56. Francis Russell, "The Tragedy in Dedham: A Retrospect of the Sacco-Vanzetti Trial," *Antioch Review* 15 (Winter 1955–56): 387–398, reprinted in abridged form in *American Heritage* 9 (Oct. 1958): 52–57.

57. After the publication of Russell's book O'Connor wrote increasingly emotional letters. To James Cannon, on June 20, 1963, he wrote that Russell had turned out to be "contemptible." He had a "female mind." Upton Sinclair was "naïve." Fred Moore was "hapless." Russell was a "social snob" with "plenty of money," so he "got hold of something that appealed to his basic nature." See the various letters in O'Connor Papers, folds. 1a and 3b. In his article "Why I Changed My Mind About the Sacco-Vanzetti Case," *American Heritage,* June–July 1986, 107–108, Russell recalled that "while writing my book [in 1962], I let . . . O'Connor read my manuscript chapter by chapter, even the last one in which I stated that Sacco was guilty. He said nothing at the time, though later, when he passed me on the street, he refused to speak to me. After his death, when his papers were given to Brandeis University, I discovered that he and Judge Musmanno had launched what they called 'Operation Assault' to persuade book editors not to review my 'meretricious' book." (Russell erred in his description, since the term O'Connor used was actually "Operation Ambush.") Perhaps Russell's most enraged correspondent was Musmanno, who informed Russell that he was "one of the most sorrowful disappointments I have [had] in my whole life. For a couple of years now I have been looking forward eagerly to your book. I felt that this indeed would be the answer to the Fullers, the Lowells, the Thayers, and their benighted apologists. When Montgomery's book was published, it disturbed me for a moment but then as I thought of your book, I experienced a sensation close to joy because I felt you would pulverize Montgomery. And to think that you are now teaming up with that man who has revealed the most stupid kind of ignorance on the case is quite shocking. . . . Do me the favor of sending me a copy of your book . . . so I can see with my own eyes just how much you have disappointed the faith of Felicani, Jackson, O'Connor, Justice Frankfurter and all the noble sincere hearts who have worked to clear the names of those so grossly wronged men, Sacco and Vanzetti" (Michael Musmanno to Francis Russell, Dec. 28, 1961, BPL-Joughin, fold. 15.2-16.1).

58. John Dos Passos, *Facing the Chair: The Story of the Americanization of Two Foreign-Born Workmen* (Boston, 1927); Dos Passos, *USA* (New York, 1936), part 3 (*The Big Money*), 462–463.

59. The Spanish Civil War is often considered—especially by anti-Communist writers—to be the final defeat of the anarchist movement at the hands of ruthless Stalinism. See Burnett Bulloten, *The Grand Camouflage: The Communist Conspiracy in the Spanish Civil War* (London, 1961), which appeared around the same time that Dos Passos corresponded with Russell; Vernon Richards, *Lessons of the Spanish Revolution, 1936–1939* (London, 1953); and most recently, Stanley Payne, *The Spanish*

Civil War, the Soviet Union, and Communism (New Haven, 2004). For a completely different view, stressing the logic of the pro-Stalinist position (and, more important, reiterating the essential anti-Franco position), see Paul Preston, *The Spanish Civil War: Reaction, Revolution, and Revenge* (New York, 2007).

60. See Townsend Ludington, *John Dos Passos: A Twentieth Century Odyssey* (New York, 1980), and Virginia Spencer Carr, *Dos Passos: A Life* (Garden City, N.Y., 1984). See also John P. Diggins, *Up From Communism: Conservative Odysseys in American Intellectual History* (New York, 1975).

61. John Dos Passos to Francis Russell, Aug. 30, 1960, Russell papers, fold. 1.3.

62. Ibid.

63. Dos Passos to Russell, Apr. 19, 1961, Russell Papers, fold. 1.8.

64. Dos Passos to Russell, Oct. 21, 1961, BPL-Felicani, MS 2030, fold. 7A.

65. Louis F. Post, *The Deportations Delirium of Nineteen-Twenty: A Personal Narrative of an Official Experience* (New York, 1923). Post, once considered a champion of free speech and protector of radicals' rights, signed the deportation orders for many radicals, including Emma Goldman.

66. Dos Passos to Russell, Oct. 21, 1961.

67. Dos Passos expressed similar ideas in his *The Best Times: An Informal Memoir* (New York, 1966), 208–209. He had also written the introduction to Buckley's polemic *Up From Liberalism* (New York, 1959).

68. James Rorty, " 'This Is Our Agony . . . ,' " *New Leader,* Sept. 26, 1960, 12–13: "I, who 35 years ago marched in a protest parade before the Massachusetts State house and subsequently denounced Massachusetts justice in an extremely bad poem . . . believed those denials [of guilt made by Sacco and Vanzetti]. . . . What one concludes from [Montgomery's] book is that Sacco and Vanzetti were in all probability guilty, and that certainly, in view of the numerous appeals and hearings by the Governor and the Lowell Committee, the full resources of Massachusetts justice were expended in their behalf. But there remains that inextinguishable doubt." Rorty was one of the editors, along with Eastman, of the *New Masses* in the early 1920s.

69. James Rorty to Russell, Jan. 15, 1961, Frank Papers, fold. 4.107.

70. The film, *Der Fall Sacco und Vanzetti,* directed by Peter von Zahn, was aired on West German television on August 23, 1963, the thirty-sixth anniversary of the executions. A transcript of Dos Passos's comments on the program is in BPL-Felicani, MS. 2030, fold. 7A. In 1968, speaking to college students at the height of the New Left activism, Dos Passos refused to make a link between the protest against the Vietnam War—*the* left-wing cause of the late 1960s—and the agitation over Sacco and Vanzetti in the 1920s. With age, he explained at a talk at Union College, he had come to understand "the way the human race works: in simple terms, top dog always gets to the top, no matter what the system is. . . . No change in ideology changes that basic fact" (Frank Gado, ed., "An Interview with John Dos Passos," *Idol: Literary Quarterly of Union College* 45 [1969]: 22–23).

71. Katherine Anne Porter, *The Never-Ending Wrong* (New York, 1977), 17–19. The most notable part of this unfocused, passionate volume, written shortly before the

author's death at eighty-four, is Porter's recollection of a conversation with a Communist activist who was arrested with her during the Boston "deathwatch." Porter expressed her hope that Sacco and Vanzetti might yet be saved, but the woman supposedly scoffed: " 'Saved,' she said . . . 'who wants them saved? What earthly good would they do us alive?' " For a discussion of Porter's (and other liberals') relation to the case, see Terry Cooney, "Trials Without End: Some Comments and Reviews on the Sacco-Vanzetti, Rosenberg, and Hiss Cases," *Michigan Law Review* 77:3 (Jan.–Mar. 1979): 839–840.

72. Michael E. Stewart, "Two Murders, a Robbery, and the Eternal Myth," unpublished MS, Harvard Law SV case record, box 42, fold. 16.

73. Roland D. Sawyer to Herbert Ehrmann, undated, Ehrmann Papers, box 11, fold. 10.

74. Roscoe Pound to Ehrmann, May 31, 1962, Ehrmann Papers, box 11, fold. 11. For Pound's earlier activism, see Richard Polenberg, *Fighting Faiths: The Abrams Case, the Supreme Court, and Free Speech* (New York, 1987), and David M. Rabban, *Free Speech in Its Forgotten Years* (New York, 1997). Pound believed in Sacco and Vanzetti's innocence earlier than he claimed here. In a January 1927 letter to Richard W. Child, former U.S. ambassador to Italy, he argued (four months before Frankfurter's article appeared): "I have serious misgivings that what the public and most of the profession assume to be a mere cause of two aliens convicted by a jury after a technically fair trial, may yet be recognized as one of the most unfortunate miscarriages of the machinery of criminal justice in our history. Such miscarriages are serious intrinsically. My fear is that this particular one will prove much more serious in its effects. . . . The profession ought to be concerned with the right and justice of the cause, reflecting that the ultimate effect on confidence in our criminal courts will be the more serious should a factitious, temporarily-built-up confidence fail us" (Pound to Child, Jan. 3, 1927, BPL-Joughin, fold. 17.2-18.1).

75. See H. N. Hirsch, *The Enigma of Felix Frankfurter* (New York, 1981), 97. For another perspective on Pound's legal career, see also John Fabian Witt, *Patriots and Cosmopolitans: Hidden Histories of American Law* (Cambridge, Mass., 2007), 211–278.

76. See Louis Joughin, "Reviews of Books," *American Historical Review* 3 (Jan. 1963): 488–489.

77. See, for example, "The Case Reversed," *Economist*, Aug. 3, 1963, 445. Robert Corham Davis, who had been editor of the *Harvard Crimson* in 1927, remembered seeing Sacco and Vanzetti's corpses after the executions: "Looking down on their faces, I naively, impressionistically, came to the conclusion (one to which some of their dedicated supporters later also came) that Vanzetti was innocent but Sacco appeared capable of the crimes with which he was charged" ("The Mail," *Harvard Crimson*, Sept. 29, 1983).

78. "Operation Ambush": O'Connor to Louis Joughin, July 9, 1962, BPL-Joughin, fold. 14.3-15.1; James Cannon to Michael Musmanno, May 23, 1963, O'Connor Papers, fold. 1a.21; Musmanno, "Armchair Theorists."

79. Kennedy's secretary Myer Feldman acknowledged receipt of the book and promised, "I will see that the senator gets it" (Feldman to Ehrmann, Oct. 28, 1960, Ehrmann Papers, box 3, fold. 12). See Herbert B. Ehrmann, *The Case That Will Not Die: Commonwealth vs. Sacco-Vanzetti* (Boston, 1969).

80. Aldo Felicani to Rose Pesotta, Jan. 24, 1962, and Musmanno to Felicani, June 6, 1962, BPL-Felicani, MS 2030, fold. 7A; Herbert Ehrmann to Norman Podhoretz, June 7, 1963, Ehrmann Papers, box 4, fold. 6. Podhoretz had explained to Ehrmann in a letter of June 6, 1963, that Grossman's article had appeared nearly eighteen months earlier, rendering the response moot (Ehrmann Papers, box 4, fold. 6). A *Washington Post* review by the liberal Supreme Court justice Abe Fortas nicely captured the book's main problem: Russell, the reviewer granted, was a copious researcher and a gifted writer, but the entire book was misdirected (and as Joughin would later point out in the *American Historical Review*, without documentation): "[The book] asks a question that cannot be answered, namely, did Sacco and Vanzetti commit the crime they were charged with? Instead, he should have asked the far more important question, 'should Sacco-Vanzetti have been executed?'" (Fortas, "Sacco, Vanzetti—and Justice," *Washington Post*, Aug. 12, 1962). For a more typically enthusiastic response to Russell's work, see Naomi Bliven, "Accessories After the Fact," *New Yorker*, Dec. 8, 1962, 235–243.

81. Letters of rejection from Knopf and other publishers in Ehrmann Papers, box 4, fold. 6; Michael A. Musmanno, "Was Sacco Guilty?" *New Republic* Mar. 2, 1963, 25–30; Musmanno, "The Sacco-Vanzetti Case: A Miscarriage of Justice," *American Bar Association Journal* 47:1 (Jan. 1961): 28–34; Musmanno, "The Sacco-Vanzetti Case," *Kansas Law Review* 2:4 (May 1963): 481–525; James Cannon, letter to the editor, *New Republic*, Mar. 23, 1963.

82. Lindsay Rogers to Felix Frankfurter, Dec. 19, 1960, Ehrmann Papers, box 3, fold. 13; Rogers to Edmund M. Morgan, Mar. 31, 1953, BPL-Joughin, fold. 23; Fred J. Cook, "New Light on Sacco-Vanzetti," *Nation* Dec. 22, 1962, 442–451.

83. Eastman to Russell, Apr. 6, 1961, Frank Papers, fold. 4.107; David Felix, *Protest: Sacco-Vanzetti and the Intellectuals* (Bloomington, Ind., 1965), 170. This dated work is of little value to historians. It is also misleadingly titled. Only the second part actually deals with intellectuals, in a superficial sense.

84. I can testify that after describing the content and purpose of this study, the first question I am almost always asked is, "So did they do it?"

85. In the 1980s, Russell wrote a series of articles on the case in the *New York Review of Books*, positing Sacco's guilt and Vanzetti's complicity, most notably "Clinching the Case," Mar. 13, 1986, available at www.nybooks.com/articles/5182.

86. Erwin Griswold to Ehrmann, July 7, 1969, Ehrmann Papers, box 7, fold. 18.

87. Sacco-Vanzetti Files, Tamiment Library, New York University.

88. Dukakis based his decision on Commonwealth of Massachusetts, *Report to the Governor in the Matter of Sacco and Vanzetti,* July 13, 1977 (written by his chief legal counsel, Daniel A. Taylor), and on the advice of the Massachusetts attorney and Harvard law professor Alan Dershowitz. The declaration was accompanied by a

rancorous debate that recalled the Sacco-Vanzetti wars of the past. The indefatigable Buckley wrote that "At the rate we are going, the only man left who will be universally acknowledged to have been guilty of anything is Adolf Hitler" (*Boston Globe,* Aug. 10, 1977). The then-editor of the *National Review,* George F. Will, in "The Trial That Scarred a Generation," echoed Buckley: "Prevailing prejudices, and abuses of power, made the moment ripe for a counterattack from 'progressives.' And many 'progressives,' who in the best of times have their fair share of prejudices, used the Sacco-Vanzetti case as an excuse to fall upon Massachusetts with angry glee. In the 1920s, Massachusetts was what Arkansas was in the 1950s and Mississippi was in the 1960s. It was the state that people, especially intellectuals, loved to hate" (*Washington Post,* Aug. 18, 1977). A Republican in the Massachusetts Senate attacked Dukakis for "using the Senate chambers for a Cecil B. De Mille production. . . . From his proclamation, you would have thought these men were victims of a lynch mob" (*Boston Globe,* Aug. 2, 1977, 2). See also "Senate Condemns Dukakis' Sacco-Vanzetti Proclamation," *Boston Herald American,* Aug. 9, 1977, 1.

89. See "Sacco and Vanzetti Reconsidered," *Economist,* July 30, 1977, 33. Berlinguer's appeal should be seen in context: the Italian Communist Party (PCI) hoped to forge good relations with the Carter administration by affirming its acceptance of NATO and the European Community as part of its "historic compromise" and commitment to a democratic and nonviolent road to power. But by a year later it had become clear that even the PCI's most American-friendly Eurocommunism would not be enough to persuade the Carter administration to accept the PCI's sharing in power in Italy. For background, see Adrian Lyttleton, "Italia Nostra," *New York Review of Books,* Mar. 9, 2006; Paul Ginsborg, *History of Contemporary Italy: Society and Politics, 1943–1988* (London, 1990), chap. 10 ("Crisis, Compromise, and the 'Anni di Piombo,' 1973–1980").

90. See W. J. Rorabaugh, *Kennedy and the Promise of the Sixties* (New York, 2002). One tangible connection to Sacco and Vanzetti was the appointment of Schlesinger (along with other liberal scholars) as an adviser to the Kennedy administration. For the inside view, see Arthur Schlesinger, Jr., *A Thousand Days: John F. Kennedy in the White House* (New York, 2002).

91. In the tantalizingly brief words of David Riesman and Nathan Glazer, "The Sacco-Vanzetti case united the liberals, the Rosenberg case divided them" ("The Intellectuals and the Discontented Classes," *Partisan Review* 22:1 [Winter 1955]: 64). Intuitively, it is tempting to link the two cases (and that of Alger Hiss) as major left-wing causes célèbres with vibrant afterlives. Both cases emerged out of "Red Scares," and both ended in executions. In both cases, the accused were members of minority groups. Both cases aroused much European anger. Both cases were highly controversial from legal standpoints. Both cases have been the subject of much scholarship concerned with the question of guilt or innocence. Both cases have come to symbolize, for many, the persecution of political nonconformism in the United States in times of a perceived external menace. And the two cases had in common the involvement of J. Edgar Hoover and the FBI. But these specific similarities are somewhat outweighed

by the differences. The Sacco-Vanzetti affair began as a provincial trial for robbery and murder; the Rosenbergs were tried by the federal government for espionage, a political crime. Sacco and Vanzetti were anarchists and profoundly opposed to communism; the Rosenbergs were Stalinists and would have been deeply opposed to anarchism had it still been politically relevant in their day. Sacco and Vanzetti were immigrants and aliens in the United States; the Rosenbergs were citizens. Once convicted, Sacco and Vanzetti were charismatic prisoners, open and outspoken about their political affiliation and beliefs; the Rosenbergs hid their loyalties and evoked much less public sympathy. More crucial, Sacco and Vanzetti were supported by an eclectic public, including liberals and other groups well outside the anarchist movement, and became a truly divisive issue in the American mainstream and around the world; the Rosenbergs were championed by few, abandoned by most liberals, and were a cause principally of and for the Communist movement at home and abroad. (They also spent less time than Sacco and Vanzetti in prison between their convictions and executions.) In the 1950s and 1960s, the link between the two cases was probably more evident for European left-wing observers than for Americans, and in the United States it was probably more suggestive for the conservative right than the liberal left. In any case, Sacco and Vanzetti's most prominent American supporters were not to be found in the Rosenbergs' camp once the couple faced execution. The Rosenbergs barely appear in the American sources discussed in this chapter. For a synthetic study of the context of the Rosenbergs' trial, see Ellen Schrecker, *Many Are the Crimes: McCarthyism in America* (Princeton, N.J., 1998). See also Terry Cooney, "Trials Without End: Some Comments and Reviews on the Sacco-Vanzetti, Rosenberg, and Hiss Cases," *Michigan Law Review* 77:3 (Jan.–Mar. 1979): 834–859, which focuses on the role and attitudes of liberals in these controversies but does not make specific comparisons; Michael Parrish, "Cold War Justice: The Supreme Court and the Rosenbergs," *American Historical Review* 82:4 (Oct. 1977): 805–842; and Robert A. Ferguson, *The Trial in American Life* (Chicago, 2007), chap. 7 ("Killing the Rosenbergs").

92. Musmanno to Robert Alan Aurthur, Apr. 23, 1960, BPL-Felicani, MS 2030, fold. 7A.

Postscript

1. "The Legend of Tennessee Moltisanti," *The Sopranos,* season 1, episode 8, 1999; Matthew Waxman, "Tough Crowd: NBA Has Trouble Pleasing Fans, Including Me," http://sportsillustrated.cnn.com/2005/writers/matthew_waxman/06/14/nba.blues/index.html, June 14, 2005 (accessed Mar. 28, 2008).

2. See "U.S. Developer to Build a City Within a City," *Moscow Times,* Nov. 30, 2004.

3. A recent absurdist novel, Mark Binelli's *Sacco and Vanzetti Must Die!* (New York, 2006), recasts the two men as Italian anarchist equivalents of Laurel and Hardy, a vaudevillian slapstick duo who finally make it to the big screen by specializing in knife-throwing (*Never a Dull Moment, A Couple of Cut-Ups*), kangaroo boxing

(*Sacco and Vanzetti Meet the Heavyweight Champion, Primo Carnera*), and pie-fighting (*Sacco and Vanzetti Dessert the Cause, A Couple of Wops in a Jam*). Sacco and Vanzetti also played key roles in Kurt Vonnegut's 1979 novel *Jailbird,* and have appeared, as it were, in many other prominent works of American fiction, including Philip Roth's *The Human Stain* (2000).

4. "Those Two Men," *Lantern,* Aug. 1929, 17.

Index